LEARN HOW TO
DRAW&PAINT

DRAWING • WATERCOLOUR • OIL & ACRYLIC • PASTEL

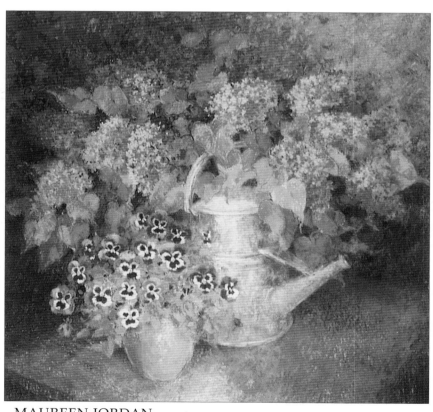

MAUREEN JORDAN
LILAC TIME

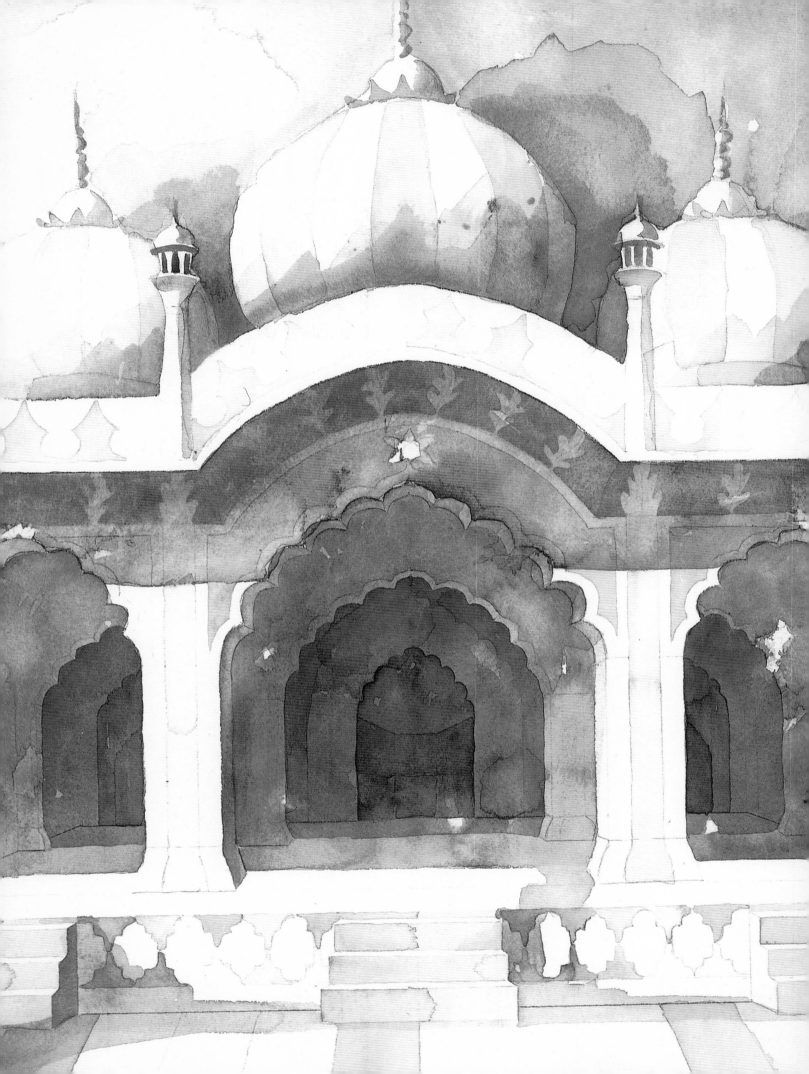

LEARN HOW TO
DRAW & PAINT
DRAWING • WATERCOLOUR • OIL & ACRYLIC • PASTEL

Hazel Harrison

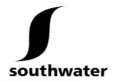

southwater

OLIVIA FRASER
SAFDARJUNG'S TOMB

This edition is published by Southwater,
an imprint of Anness Publishing Ltd, Blaby Road, Wigston,
Leicestershire LE18 4SE; info@anness.com

www.southwaterbooks.com; www.annesspublishing.com

If you like the images in this book and would like to investigate using them
for publishing, promotions or advertising, please visit our website
www.practicalpictures.com for more information.

Publisher: Joanna Lorenz
Project Editor: Samantha Gray
Designer: Michael Morey
Production Manager: Stephen Lang
Photographers: Paul Forrester and John Freeman
Typeset by MC Typeset Limited

A CIP catalogue record for this book is available from the British Library.

Previously published as *How to Paint & Draw*

PUBLISHER'S NOTE
Although the advice and information in this book are believed to be accurate and
true at the time of going to press, neither the authors nor the publisher can accept
any legal responsibility or liability for any errors or omissions that may have been
made nor for any inaccuracies nor for any loss, harm or injury that comes about
from following instructions or advice in this book.

CONTENTS

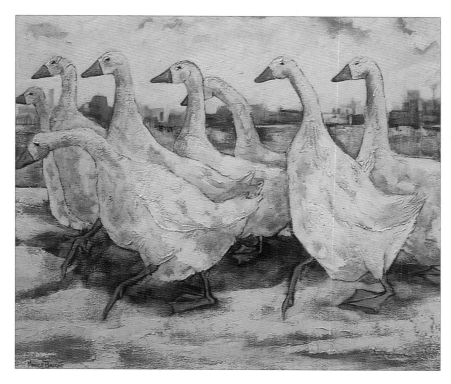

MADGE BRIGHT
STEPPING OUT

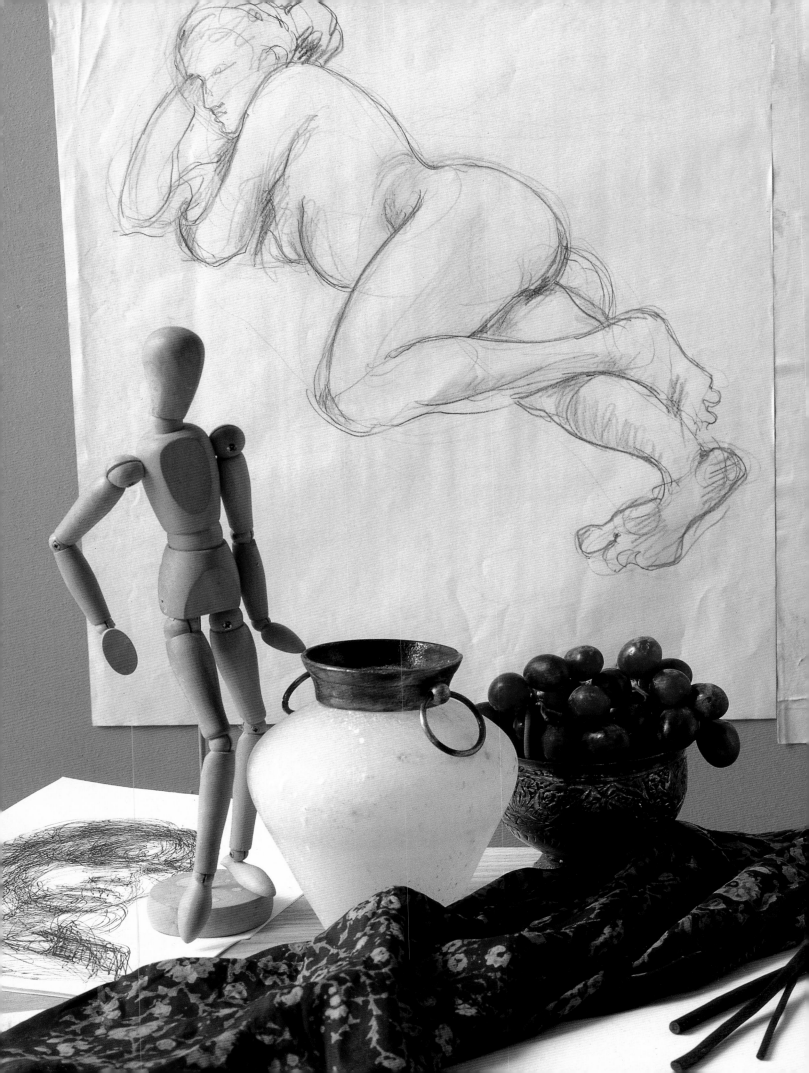

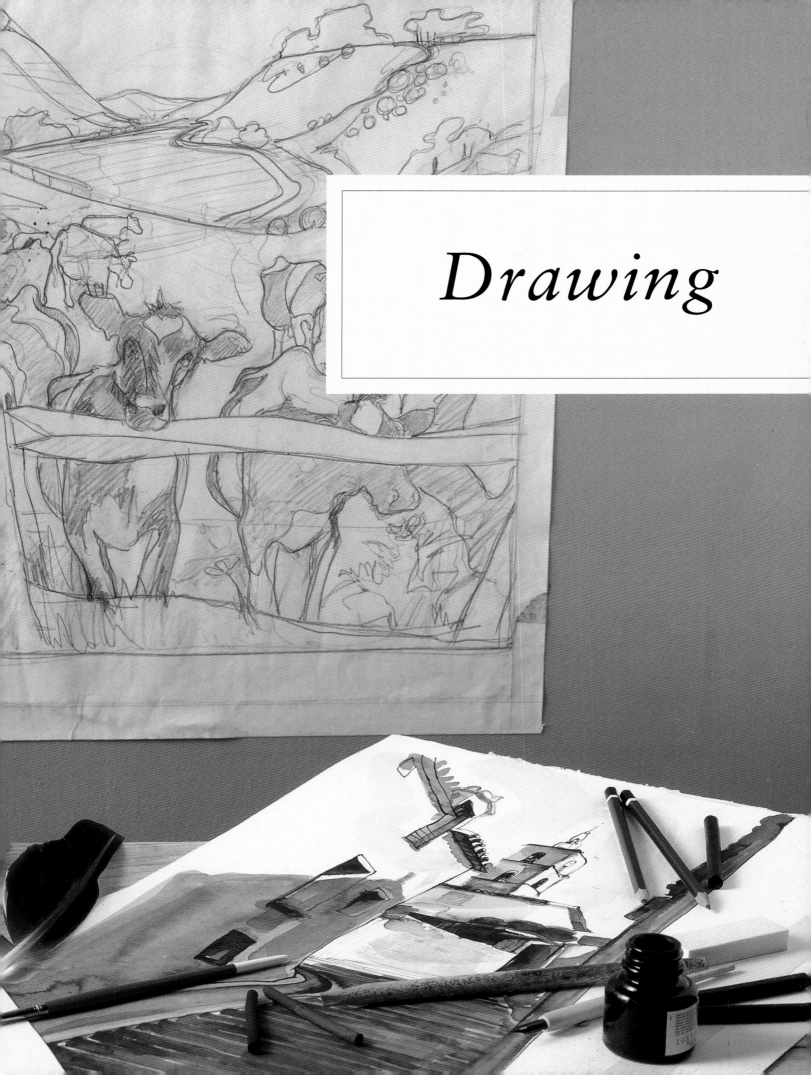

Drawing

Introduction
DRAWING

It is not easy to define the word "drawing" because it embraces a wide range of related but different activities. At its simplest it can be described as marks made on a sheet of paper, and in this sense it is one of the most basic of all human activities. Young children enjoy scribbling with a pencil or crayon as soon as they have developed sufficient manual dexterity to grip the implement, and long before they consider relating what they are doing to the world they see around them.

This enjoyment of the lines and marks made by various drawing implements is an important factor in all drawing, and para-mount in the work of some artists – the modern Swiss painter and draughtsman, Paul Klee, described his drawing as "taking a line for a walk". For most artists, however, drawing also performs a descriptive function: it is a direct response to the visual stimuli of our surroundings.

LEARNING TO DRAW
Drawing is often regarded as a special gift, and it is true that there are people who seem

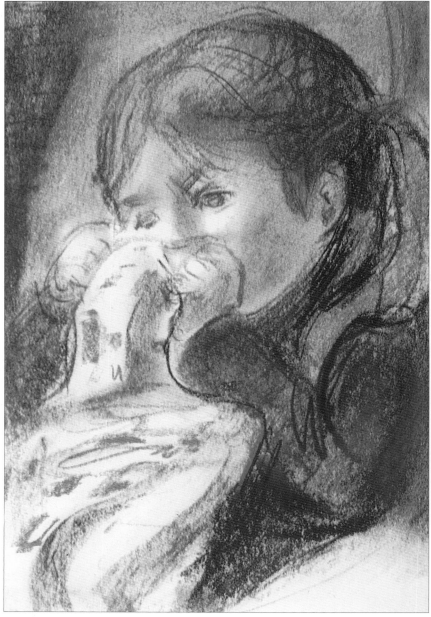

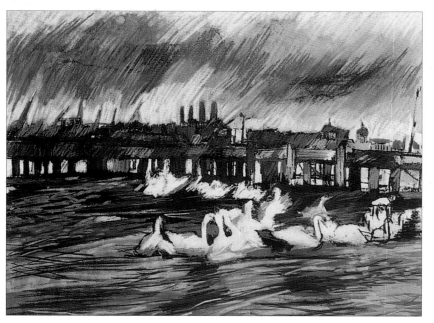

TED GOULD
CLAIRE
(Above) *Pastel is a lovely medium for portraiture and is particularly well-suited to studies of children, as it creates gentle effects in keeping with the subject. On the face and clothing the artist has applied the colours lightly, rubbing them slightly into the paper to create soft blends, reinforced with crisp linear drawing.*

PIP CARPENTER
SWANS ON THE THAMES
(Left) *Pastel need not be a soft and delicate medium; it is extremely versatile and responsive to the artist's visual interests and ways of working. Here the artist has created energetic and exciting effects in the picture by laying heavy strokes of unblended colour, using the tip of the pastel stick.*

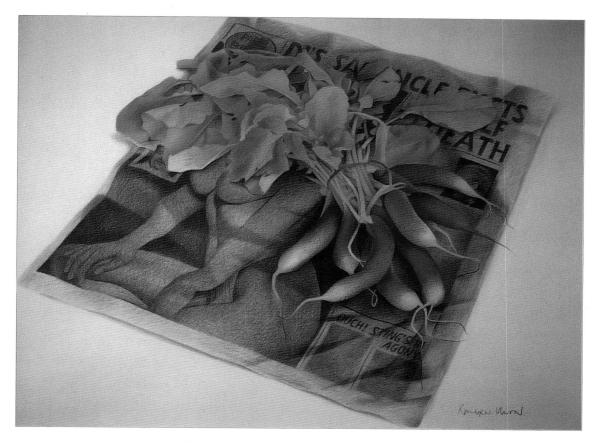

ROBERT
MAXWELL WOOD
YESTERDAY'S
NUDES, RADISHES
(Left) *In his picture, this
artist uses coloured
pencil in a completely
different way to John
Townend (below). He
achieves meticulous
detail and considerable
depth of colour with
successive layers of
coloured pencil, using
a delicate shading
technique so that almost
no lines are visible.*

to be able to draw quite effortlessly. Yet
drawing, like writing, is a skill which can be
acquired; if the motivation is there, most
people can learn to draw accurately. In the
past, students were taught to draw in a
certain way, with the emphasis on
mastering a specific set of techniques, but
this ignored the essential fact that drawing
is first and foremost about seeing.

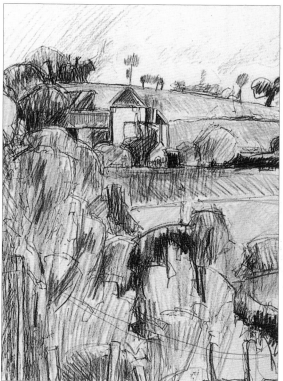

TED GOULD
GIRL SKETCHING
(Right) *Wax crayon is a
less subtle drawing
medium than pastel, but
it has the advantage of
not smudging and is thus
useful for sketchbook
drawings and quick
impressions. In this
lively drawing, the artist
has built up the forms
and colours with a
network of loose
hatching and cross-
hatching lines.*

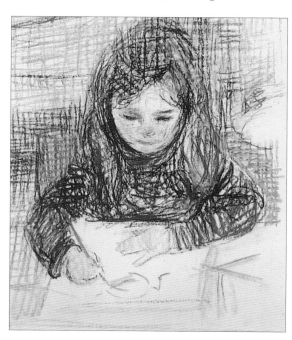

JOHN TOWNEND
SUMMER VIEW BEYOND THE POOL
(Above) *This artist works out of doors directly from
his subject, and finds coloured pencil ideal for his
particular approach. He uses the medium in a free and
instinctive manner, with bold hatching lines varying
in direction according to the forms he is describing.*

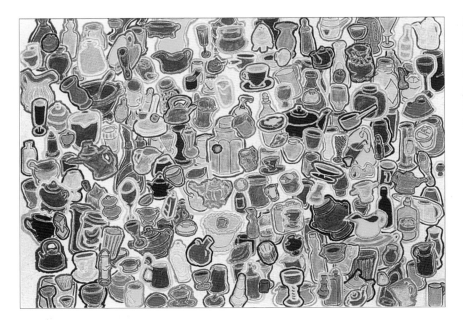

DAVID CUTHBERT
POLLY WANTS A POT
(Left) *In this delightful and inventive drawing, coloured pencil has been pressed heavily into the paper to achieve areas of heavy, almost flat colour. The two-dimensional pattern element is stressed by the use of coloured outlines.*

Although technical skill is important, it is not the first stage in learning how to draw, as it is pointless to develop techniques in a void. You may produce beautifully even lines of hatching and cross-hatching but still find that you have failed in the primary task of drawing, which is to describe the subject to your own satisfaction. Such failures are nearly always the direct result of poor observation, not of inadequate technique.

It sounds easy enough to say that if you want to learn how to draw all you need to do is to look at things, but it is not that simple, because you have to learn to look in a certain way, analytically and objectively. This can be a surprisingly hard skill to master, as it involves looking at a subject with a fresh eye every time, abandoning preconceptions. Our brains are cluttered with information which can be actively unhelpful in the context of drawing, leading us to quite the wrong conclusions – we tend to draw what we know from experience rather than what we see with our own eyes.

PAUL BARTLETT
STILL LIFE WITH MAN-MADE AND NATURAL OBJECTS
A combination of pastel and pastel pencil has been used for this exploration of shapes and forms. The light brown paper chosen by the artist has allowed him to build up both highlights and shadows with light overlays of white and brown pastel. It has also given a subtle touch of colour to what is essentially a monochrome drawing.

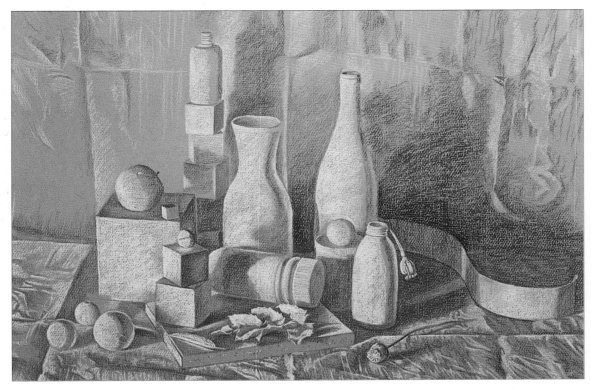

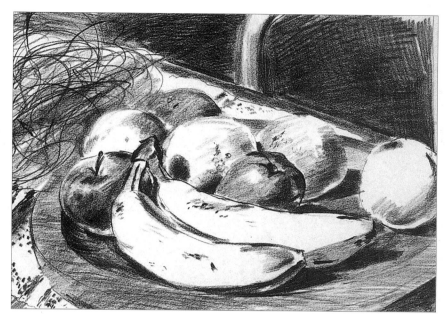

GERRY BAPTIST
BANANAS AND OTHER FRUIT
(Left) *This lovely drawing is also a study of form, done in very soft pencil, which blunts easily and thus provides broader, bolder effects than hard or medium pencil. Both this and Bartlett's still life are carefully composed, showing that a drawing in monochrome can make as complete a statement as a coloured drawing or painting.*

PAUL BARTLETT
SELF PORTRAIT
(Below) *A comparison between this drawing and Gerry Baptist's demonstrates the versatility of the pencil. Here the effect is almost photographic in its minute attention to detail and texture and its subtle gradations of tone.*

A classic example is relative size, which can be hard to get right, particularly when you are drawing familiar objects. If you place one large object on a table with a much smaller one in front of it, the chances are that you will make the larger one too large because of your prior knowledge of it. But in fact the effects of perspective will have caused it to "shrink", so that it may be smaller than the object nearer to you. The only way to approach drawing a known subject, whether it be a portrait, an apple on

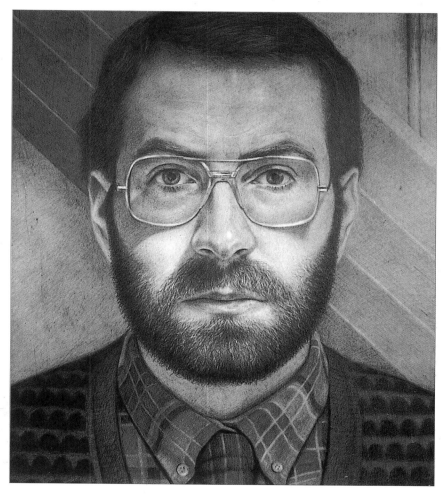

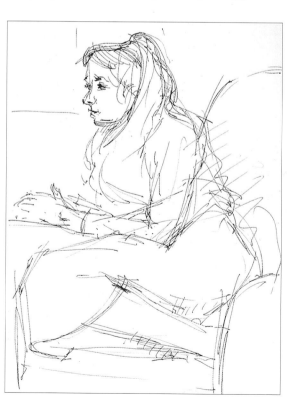

TED GOULD
GIRL IN AN ARMCHAIR
(Left) *Pen and ink can achieve intricate and elaborate effects, but it is also a lovely medium for rapid line drawings. In this figure study the artist has caught the essentials of the pose in a few pen strokes, sometimes superimposing lines where the first drawing was incorrect or needed clarifying.*

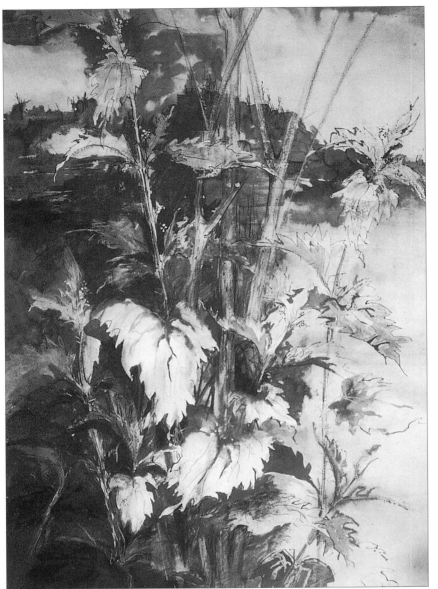

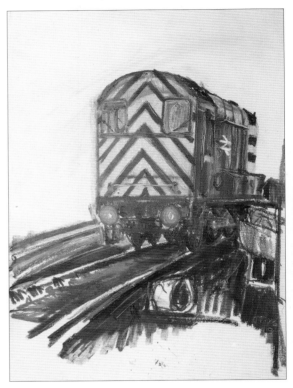

SHUNTING LOCOMOTIVE AT BOW
(Below) *For this sketch, made on location, the artist has used oil pastel, an ideal medium for bold effects and quick impressions, as colours can be built up rapidly. Also, unlike soft pastel, oil pastel does not smudge and does not require fixing. The sgraffito technique has been used to add touches of linear detail to the side of the coach.*

ELISABETH HARDEN
NETTLES
(Above) *The attractive combination of pen lines and washes of diluted ink (watercolour can also be used) allows tones to be built up with greater speed than is possible with line alone. Pen and wash is ideal both for broad treatments and the kind of delicate effect seen in this drawing.*

a plate or a tree, is to force yourself to abandon preconceptions by pretending to yourself that you have never seen it before. Only in this way will you be able to assess it thoroughly and draw it accurately.

DIFFERENT KINDS OF DRAWING

A drawing can be many things: it can be a few lines of "visual shorthand" in a sketchbook, made to remind the artist of some salient point in a subject; it can be a first step in painting, subsequently hidden by layers of paint and thus having no independent existence; it can be a finished work of art in its own right, planned, composed and executed with as much thought as a painting.

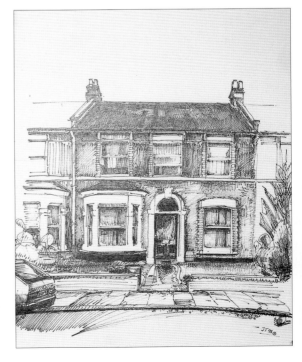

PIP CARPENTER
THREE FISHES
(Right) *This is also a mixed-media work, but a more unusual combination has been used: oil paint, used thinly on paper, and coloured pencils. There are no set rules about mixed-media drawing; only by experimenting will you discover which work well together and which do not.*

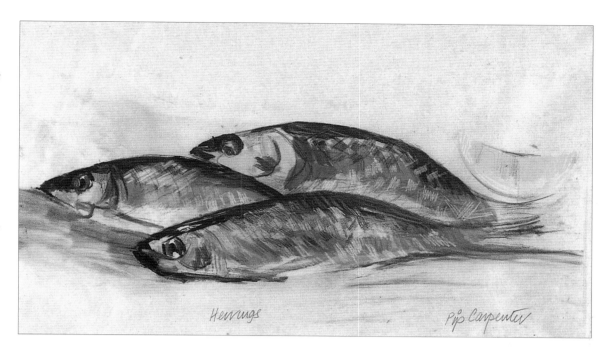

The kind of drawing you make depends on how you view the purpose of the activity – why are you drawing? You may draw simply because you love to do so, in which case, once you have mastered the "alphabet" of drawing you will find it a satisfying means of self-expression. You may have aspirations to become an illustrator, or you may simply want to improve your observational skills because you enjoy painting.

If you view drawing as a necessary foundation skill for painting, accuracy will be the main aim, and it does not matter very much which medium you use, but for those who enjoy drawing for its own sake, it is rewarding to experiment with different media. There is now a wider choice of drawing materials than ever before, from the traditional graphite pencil to a whole range of colourful and versatile pastels, coloured pencils, inks and felt-tipped pens. The word "drawing" no longer conjures up an image of timid grey pencil marks on white paper – much more exciting effects than this are achievable.

JOAN ELLIOTT BATES
WHITE VILLAGE, SOUTH SPAIN
(Right) *In this delightful drawing – which could be described equally well as a painting – the artist has used pen and ink with light washes of watercolour. These have spread the ink in places so that there is no obvious boundary between line and colour. When using a mixture of media it is important that the two work together, or the drawing will lack unity.*

JOHN TOWNEND
EAST END FAMILY HOUSE
(Opposite) *In this pen-and-ink drawing, tones have been built up by hatching and cross-hatching, a method which can create a somewhat mechanical impression, but which has been used loosely here, with the lines almost scribbled over one another in varying directions. Pen and ink is a good medium for rapid location sketches like this, as the impossibility of erasing encourages a decisive approach.*

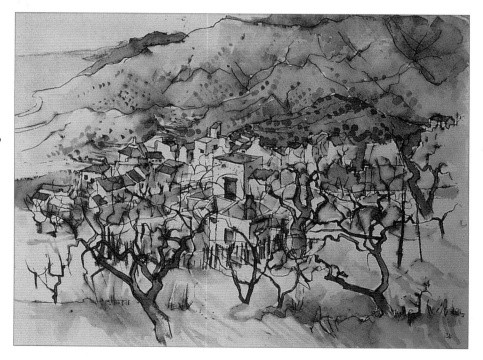

MONOCHROME DRAWING MATERIALS

Many people picture a drawing as a work in monochrome – pencil, pen and ink or charcoal. In the past most drawings were indeed in one colour or perhaps two, largely because colour drawing materials, with the exception of pastels, did not arrive on the art scene until relatively recently. Now there are a great many, which are discussed later. However, because most people begin drawing with monochrome materials we will look at these first.

PENCILS

These are the most basic of all drawing tools, as well as being one of the most sensitive and versatile. Few artists would be without a selection of pencils. Although they are sometimes incorrectly described as "lead", pencils are in fact made of graphite, a form of carbon, and began to be manufactured in the 18th century after the discovery of a deposit in the north of England. They are made in different grades, from 8B, which is very soft, to about 4H, which is much too hard for ordinary

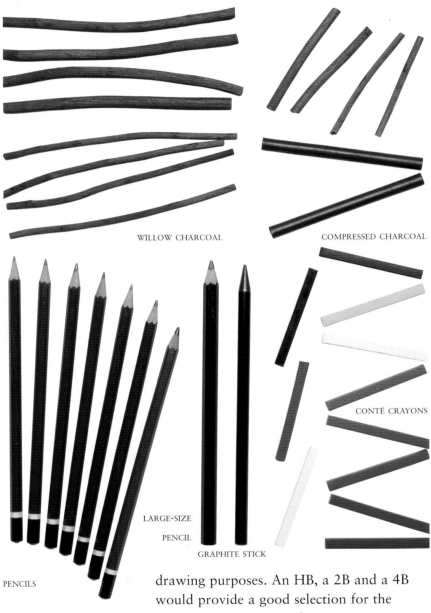

WILLOW CHARCOAL

COMPRESSED CHARCOAL

CONTÉ CRAYONS

LARGE-SIZE
PENCIL

GRAPHITE STICK

PENCILS

SHARPENERS

CARTRIDGE PAPER FIXED
TO DRAWING BOARD
WITH MASKING TAPE

ERASER

SCALPEL

drawing purposes. An HB, a 2B and a 4B would provide a good selection for the beginner to practise with.

CONTÉ CRAYONS

These are square-sectioned sticks, similar to hard pastels in consistency. They are made in black, white, and a selection of "earth" colours – browns and red-browns. They are capable of much bolder effects than pencil, and are excellent both for crisp, decisive lines and for areas of solid dark tone, as they can be sharpened to a point or broken into short lengths and used sideways. The

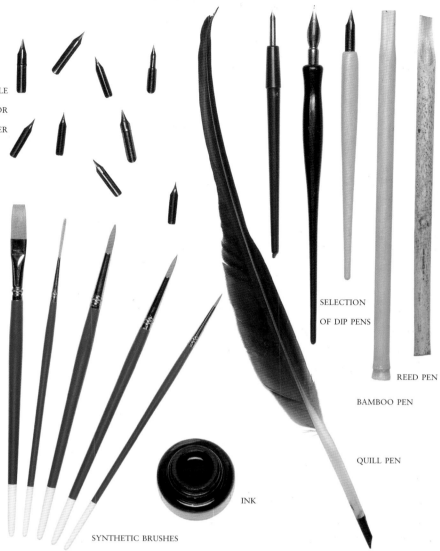

only drawback is that Conté cannot be erased easily.

CHARCOAL

This is one of the most popular of all the monochrome media. Because it encourages a bold, uninhibited form of drawing, art teachers often recommend it to novices. Charcoal is made from fired twigs of wood, such as willow, and is sold in different thicknesses. It smudges easily, and corrections can be made simply by wiping it off; however, this makes it less suitable than pencil for small-scale sketchbook work.

Compressed charcoal is also available, in both stick and pencil form. This produces deeper, richer blacks than ordinary charcoal, but is less easy to erase.

PENS, INKS AND BRUSHES

There are a great many different kinds of pen, ranging from modern felt- and fibre-tips to "old-fashioned" implements such as quills and reed pens. Perhaps it is best to start with one of the inexpensive wooden or plastic handles sold with a set of various interchangeable nibs which will enable you to practise your "handwriting" in pen and ink; this type of pen may well remain a favourite item of equipment, as it does for many professional artists.

There is a variety of drawing inks on the market, but they can be divided into two basic types: water-soluble and waterproof, the latter being shellac- or acrylic-based. Water-soluble ink can be diluted with water and is therefore useful for wash drawings, where you want a range of greys as well as black. Waterproof ink should never be used in reservoir-type pens, as it clogs them up. Felt- and fibre-tipped pens are also made in waterproof and water-soluble versions – check in your art shop, as they are not

always clearly labelled. Brushes are not a necessity, but they are sensitive drawing implements, producing an expressive line.

PAPERS

The most common surface for drawing is plain white cartridge (drawing) paper. For wash drawings, make sure that you buy good-quality cartridge (drawing) paper.

Some artists prefer to use a paper with a texture for charcoal drawings. Textured paper can also be used for Conté drawings. If you want solid blacks (or browns), however, stick to smooth cartridge (drawing) paper.

ADDITIONAL EQUIPMENT

A rigid board of some kind is required to support the paper. You will also need erasers, a craft knife and a can of spray fixative if you intend to use charcoal.

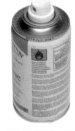

SPRAY FIXATIVE

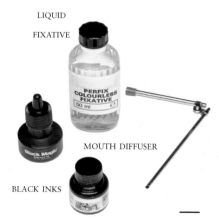

LIQUID
FIXATIVE

MOUTH DIFFUSER

BLACK INKS

Monochrome Techniques
PENCIL

As the pencil is such a versatile drawing implement, it allows each artist to develop his or her own "handwriting" in drawing. There are so many different ways of using pencil that no one technique or set of techniques can really be singled out as belonging particularly to this medium.

LINE AND TONE

The grade of pencil and the subject you choose to draw are both major influences on the way you use the pencil. An HB pencil, for example, gives light, fine lines, so it is not suitable for broad effects involving heavy shading and smudging methods. This relatively hard pencil would be a good choice for a subject such as flowers, where fine lines and delicate areas of tone could be built up by light shading or hatching and

cross-hatching. The latter technique, which is used in all the line media, is dealt with in more detail under pen and ink.

Soft pencils, such as 6B and 8B, can create thick dark areas; indeed a drawing in soft pencil can look very similar to one in Conté crayon. These pencils are most suitable for drawings in which line plays a subsidiary role. They are ideal for rendering tonal effects, such as light and shade in a landscape or the modelling on forms – perhaps a face or figure seen in strong side-lighting. If you are drawing or sketching out of doors, rather than working from a subject that you have set up specially at home, take a good selection of pencils with you, as your initial direct response to the subject will often dictate the kind of drawing that you make.

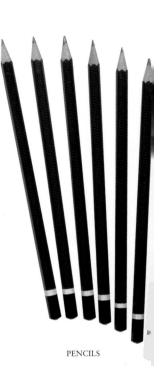

PENCILS

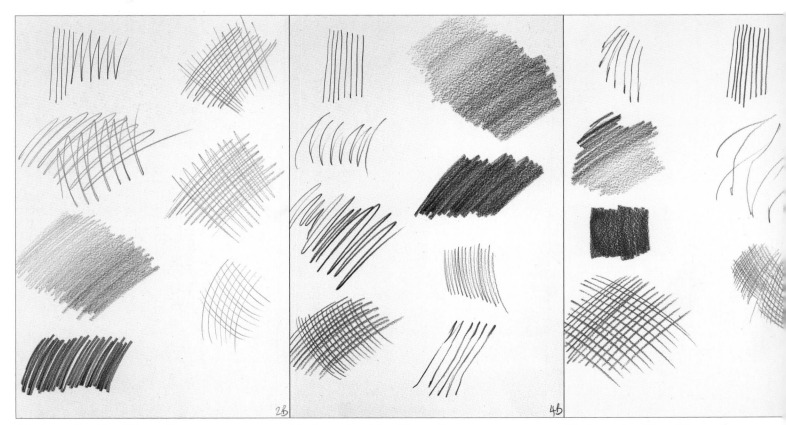

Marks made with a 2B pencil

Marks made with a 4B pencil

Marks made with an 8B pencil

FROTTAGE

This is a specialist technique which is worth knowing about. It is not restricted to pencil drawing – charcoal, Conté crayon or pastel can also be used. The term "frottage" comes from the French verb *frotter*, to rub, and the method will be familiar to anyone who has made or seen brass rubbings. A piece of paper is placed over a textured surface, or one with an incised pattern, and soft pencil is rubbed over the paper. The method is often used to create areas of pattern or texture in a drawing – for example, patterns of wood grain taken from a rough piece of timber could be incorporated into a still life. The effects which can be achieved vary according to the paper used. Brass rubbings are done on thin paper because this yields the crispest and clearest impressions; on ordinary drawing paper, pencil frottage produces a more blurred result which may suggest a texture without being specific as to its nature.

Frottage method

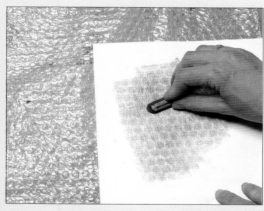

You need a soft pencil and fairly thin paper for a clear impression. Here a graphite stick (a pencil without the wooden casing) is used to take a rubbing from a piece of bubble wrap.

6 (Right) The finished collage shows an interesting use of frottage, which can be difficult to use in a "normal" drawing.

Collage of frottage textures

1 A variety of frottage textures has been obtained from surfaces in the artist's home. These have been made on thin cartridge (drawing) paper, which has given good impressions; it is also easier to stick down than thick paper.

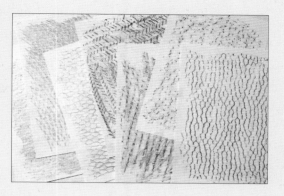

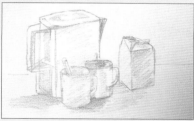

2 A working drawing is made first to plan the composition, with light shading indicating where the dark and light tones are to be placed.

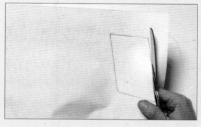

3 A tracing has been made from the drawing, and lines are transferred to the back of each piece of paper. The first piece is cut out.

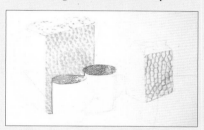

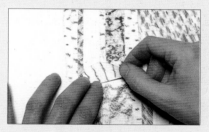

4 The artist moves the collage pieces around for the best placing before gluing them down in their final positions.

5 At a certain point, she begins to depart from the shapes in the master drawing, letting the collage develop independently.

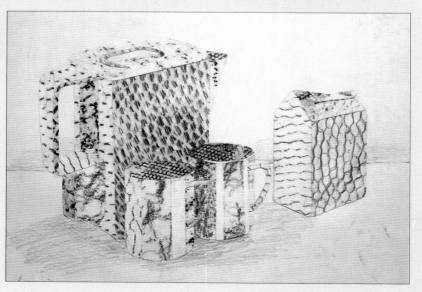

CHARCOAL

Charcoal is a wonderfully versatile medium, responsive to the slightest change in the amount of pressure applied, depending on how the stick is held. Fine sticks of willow charcoal can produce either delicate effects or tough, crisp lines resembling those in certain pencil drawings, while at the other extreme, a thick stick of charcoal or compressed charcoal used on its side allows you to build up deep, rich areas of tone.

Ordinary cartridge (drawing) paper has a smooth surface, which does not hold the charcoal well, so for drawings where tone is more important than line, you may need either to spray the work with fixative at intervals or to use a paper with more texture, such as Ingres paper, watercolour paper or recycled paper. These will grip the charcoal dust more firmly and allow you to achieve a denser coverage. For line drawings or fine, light effects, however, cartridge (drawing) paper is ideal.

ERASING TECHNIQUES

Charcoal can be erased completely, but this is somewhat laborious and not in keeping with the boldness and immediacy of the medium; it is more usual to rub down any incorrect lines, producing an area of grey with "ghost lines" which can be drawn over. These, which are often an exciting feature of drawings in charcoal, are helpful from a practical point of view too, as it is easier to correct or amend a drawing when the wrong lines are still visible.

The ease with which charcoal can be rubbed down has given rise to an interesting technique known as "lifting out". This

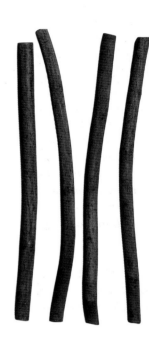

WILLOW CHARCOAL

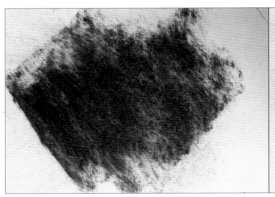

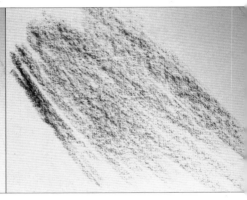

Charcoal on Ingres paper

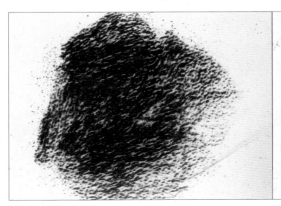
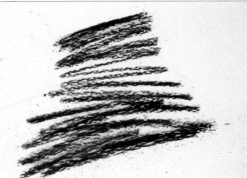
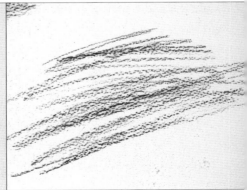

Charcoal on watercolour paper

Lifting out charcoal

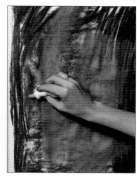

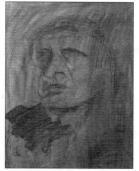

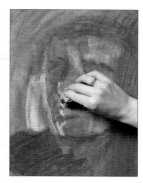

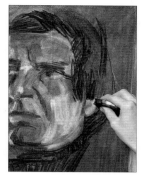

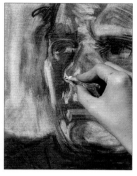

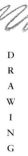

1 *Having covered a sheet of cartridge (drawing) paper with charcoal, the artist wipes it down with cotton wool (a cotton ball) to produce grey.*

2 *A rough drawing over the grey background establishes the darker tones of the picture and provides a guide for the highlights to be lifted out.*

3 *Using a putty eraser, the artist works on the main light areas of the subject, using the side of the eraser for broad strokes and the corner for finer detail.*

4 *The darker areas have been defined with further bold applications of charcoal, and the corner of the eraser is now used to create a new highlight.*

5 *For the finer details, the putty eraser is pulled into a point and used as one might use a pastel stick or pencil.*

6 *(Right) The method encourages bold drawing and dramatic, painterly effects – the lifted-out highlights look similar to brushstrokes.*

reverses the usual drawing procedure, in which the darkest tones are built up gradually; here you work from dark to light, picking out the highlights with a putty eraser. This method is often applied to figure drawing – art teachers find it encourages an unfussy approach – but any subject which has strong contrasts of tone can be drawn in this way.

The usual method is to start by covering the whole of the paper with charcoal, rub it down to produce an overall mid-grey and then make a line drawing over this. The drawing is in turn rubbed down to produce a ghost image which provides a guide for the next stage – that of lifting out the highlights. Once the main highlights are in place, the mid-tones are established by working more lightly with the eraser, after which the darks can be strengthened if necessary with further applications of charcoal. It is not as difficult as it sounds, and you can achieve quite precise effects with the putty eraser, which can be pulled into a point for fine lines and used on the flat for large areas.

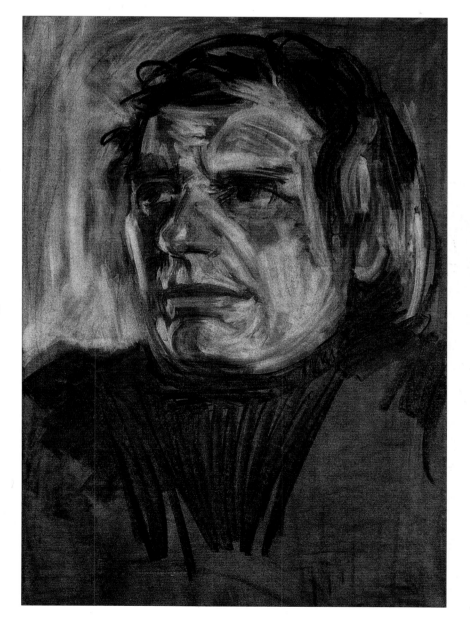

CONTÉ CRAYON

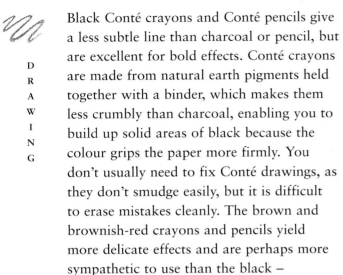

Black Conté crayons and Conté pencils give a less subtle line than charcoal or pencil, but are excellent for bold effects. Conté crayons are made from natural earth pigments held together with a binder, which makes them less crumbly than charcoal, enabling you to build up solid areas of black because the colour grips the paper more firmly. You don't usually need to fix Conté drawings, as they don't smudge easily, but it is difficult to erase mistakes cleanly. The brown and brownish-red crayons and pencils yield more delicate effects and are perhaps more sympathetic to use than the black – throughout the history of art the so-called "sanguine" (red-brown) chalks or crayons have been much favoured for portrait and figure drawings.

PAPER TEXTURE

As with charcoal drawings, the texture of the paper plays a part in the final appearance of the work, but here the smoother the paper, the darker the drawing will be. A textured surface, such as pastel paper or medium-surface watercolour paper, breaks up the strokes, allowing tiny specks of white to show through to create a slight speckling which can be highly effective in a light- or mid-toned drawing.

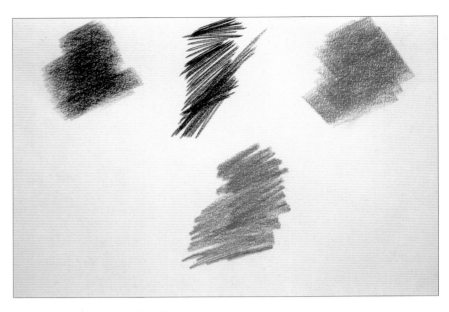

Conté crayon on cartridge (drawing) paper

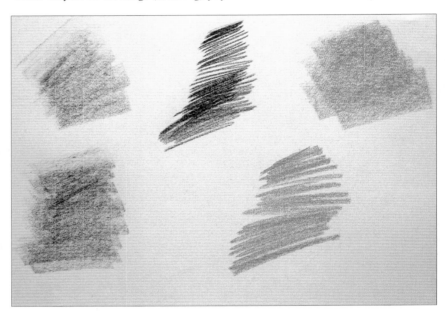

Conté crayon on Ingres paper

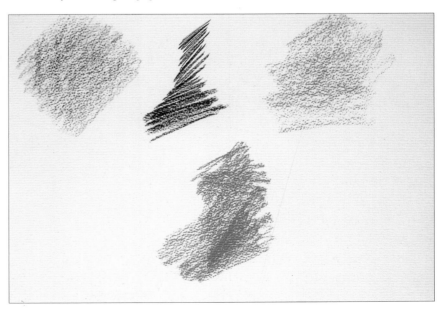

Conté crayon on watercolour paper

WORKING À TROIS COULEURS

Drawings in sanguine Conté crayons are often done on a lightly coloured paper, usually a warm cream or light brown, which enhances the rich colours. For a low-key effect, black Conté can be used on a grey or blue paper, which provides a middle tone. Such drawings can be left as they are, with only dark and mid-tones, but a traditional technique is to pick out the highlights in white Conté, using, in effect, three colours – hence *trois couleurs*. This is an excellent way to model form, and the method was extensively used by the old masters for nude studies. Areas of the paper are left uncovered, while the light and dark tones are achieved by shading with white and black (or sanguine and brown) Conté respectively. Very subtle and beautiful effects can be achieved in this way.

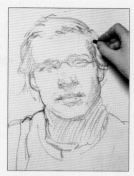

1 *The artist is working on off-white Ingres paper, and has begun the drawing in dark brown Conté crayon. She uses black to strengthen some lines slightly.*

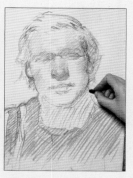

2 *A middle tone has been established with loose diagonal hatching lines of sanguine crayon; black is again used lightly on the shadowed side of the face and neck.*

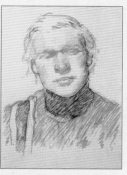

3 *The face is now beginning to take on solid, three-dimensional form, although the crayon work is still light and delicate.*

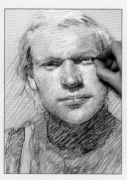

4 *Highlights have been added in white crayon, and the whole face comes alive with the definition of the eyes.*

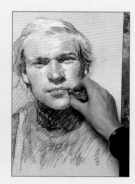

5 *A putty eraser is used to soften the patch of dark shading at the corner of the mouth. Conté cannot be erased completely, but it can be softened and smudged.*

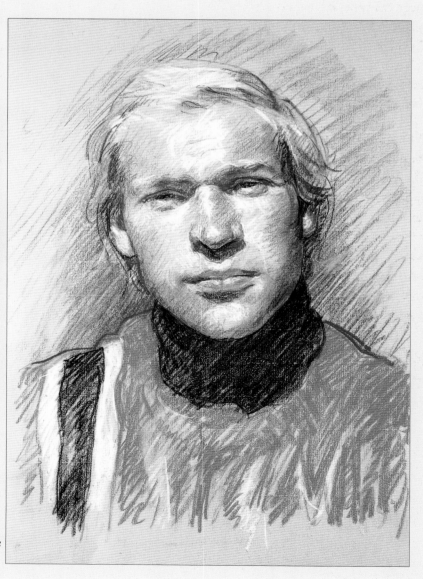

6 *(Right) The finished drawing has the look of a painting, although only three colours have been used, plus white and the colour of the paper.*

PEN & INK

The pencil was a relatively recent arrival on the art scene, but pen and ink have been with us for many centuries; in China, inks were being made as early as 2,550 BC, and in Ancient Egypt reed pens were used for both writing and drawing. Reed pens, bamboo pens and quill pens – the latter being the standard writing implement in Europe until the 19th century – are now enjoying a major artistic revival, and are well worth experimenting with. They can be bought from specialist suppliers or you can make your own, as many artists do.

However, there are also many different types of ready-made pen on the market today, all of which create different effects.

SCRIBBLE DRAWING

You can also build up tones and forms in a looser, less-organized way, by scribbling with the pen. This is a harder technique to handle than hatching and cross-hatching as it has a random quality – you must learn to let the pen do the work, moving around freely until the correct density is built up. It was a technique much used by Picasso when in revolt against traditional methods, and can give a dynamic quality to a drawing.

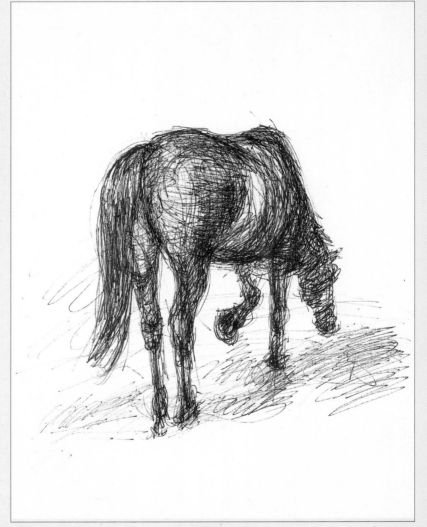

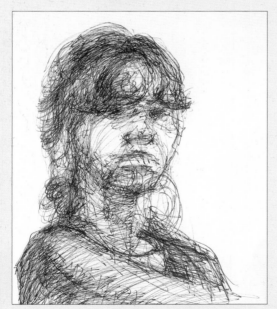

1 *A fine fibre-tipped pen has been used for this self-portrait, and the forms have been constructed in a free and spontaneous way, with the pen moving almost randomly over the paper.*

2 *Here the same technique has been used for an animal drawing. In this case the artist worked from a photograph because scribble drawing takes longer than a line sketch in pencil or charcoal, and is thus not ideal for a live, moving subject.*

HATCHING AND CROSS-HATCHING

As pen and ink is uncompromising in its linearity – you can't shade and smudge as you can with pencil and charcoal – tones must be described with a network of lines. Hatching lines are those which go in one direction, while in cross-hatching a further set of lines is made on top of those in the opposite direction. Obviously the closer together the lines are, the darker the tone will be.

These methods offer numerous possibilities, because, although the lines should be roughly parallel, they need not be straight and even. The traditional method of hatching was to use a series of slanting lines, and this is still the commonest technique, but the lines can curve slightly to follow the shape of certain objects. This can give a less-mechanical look to the finished drawing, and also helps to build up a three-dimensional impression.

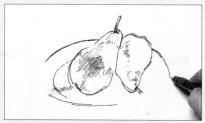

1 *The artist is using a fine, metal-pointed pen of the kind used by graphic designers, and is working on a sheet of good-quality cartridge (drawing) paper.*

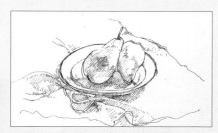

2 *She will introduce more of the drapery at a later stage, but she begins with the pears on the plate. Notice how she has varied the hatching lines, from long diagonals to small dots and dashes.*

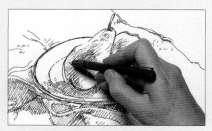

3 *The forms of the pears are built up more solidly with further hatching lines, which are denser and closer together at the centre of the pear, where there is an area of dark shadow.*

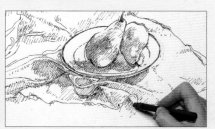

4 *With pears and plate complete, further work is then carried out on the drapery, with lightly scribbled lines deepening the shadow in the foreground.*

5 (Right) *The drawing is a convincing rendering of three-dimensional form, and the variety of different lines creates a lively effect. Although all roughly diagonal, they are only parallel and evenly spaced where the artist wanted to describe the flat plane of the table top.*

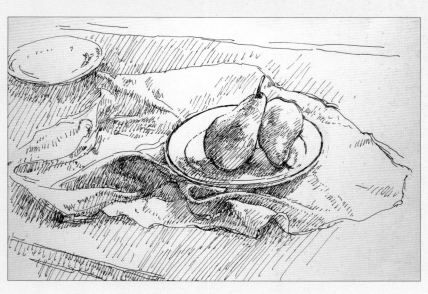

You really need to try them out to discover which ones you prefer, but fortunately most good art shops will let you do this, and provide pads of paper for scribbling on.

To some extent your choice will depend on the kind of drawing you intend to do and where you are working. For example, a fibre- or felt-tipped pen would be unlikely to provide the delicacy of line needed for a flower study, but might be ideal for quick outdoor sketches in the town or countryside, as a bottle of ink is not required. Don't neglect the possibilities of the humble ballpoint pen either – this can be a useful drawing tool, with the added advantage of being familiar to handle.

LINE & WASH

Another way to build up areas of tone in a pen-and-ink drawing is to combine the line element with washes made from diluted water-soluble ink or black watercolour. This method is used in watercolour painting, when the washes are in colour, but it is equally effective for introducing tone to monochrome drawings.

It is an attractive and enjoyable technique, allowing you to work more freely and rapidly than you can with pen alone, because you don't have to rely on the line to provide the tone. Both Rembrandt and Nicolas Poussin in the 17th century exploited line and wash with consummate skill, producing beautifully expressive drawings. The technique is closely associated with figure drawing, but it is equally suitable for other subjects, such as landscapes, urban scenes and flowers.

PENS AND PAPERS

A varied line gives the best effect, so this might be the time to try out quill, bamboo or reed pens. You can use drawing pens or felt-tips, but these tend to create a slightly rigid impression because the line is always the same thickness. Interesting effects can be created by working with a bamboo pen on a slightly textured watercolour paper, rather than cartridge (drawing) paper, as this produces a "dry", broken line.

If you intend to use a good deal of wash you may need to stretch the paper first, otherwise it could buckle under the water and spoil your work. Soak the paper in a bath for a few minutes, lift it out carefully and shake off the excess water, then place it on a drawing board and stick gumstrip (gummed brown paper tape) all around the edges, smoothing the paper with a damp sponge as you work. Leave it to dry naturally if possible; if you put it in front of

Using brush and reed pens

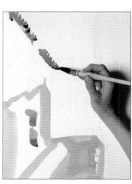

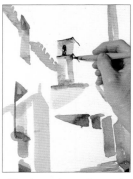

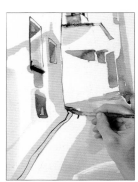

1 *This subject has contrasting areas of light and shadow, so the artist begins by working in tone, using a large soft brush and water-soluble ink.*

2 *A reed pen is used, with undiluted ink, to draw into the washes. These pens give a bolder but more sensitive line than mechanically produced drawing pens.*

3 *Line is not intended to play a dominant role, so pen and brush-work are developed at the same time, with darker washes now painted over the pen lines.*

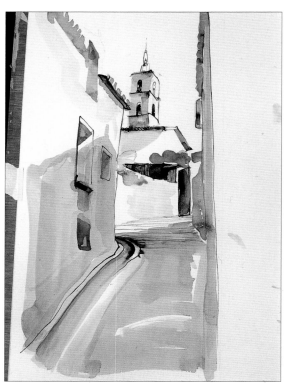

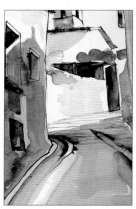

4 *The drawing is at a halfway stage, and the artist assesses it to see which areas require further definition. Notice that, because water-soluble ink has been used, the washes of diluted ink have spread and softened the pen lines.*

5 *The shadow on the left-hand building has been deepened with further washes, and the reed pen is used again, this time with well-watered ink, to make light lines at the top of the steps.*

the fire or use a hairdryer, the tape will dry before the paper and may tear off.

WORKING METHODS

In order to produce a well-integrated drawing, try to develop the line and wash together, rather than "filling in" a line drawing. One way to do this is to use water-soluble ink in the pen, as you can spread this with a brush and clean water in places to soften the line and then apply more washes as required. However, some artists prefer the line to remain crisp; they use waterproof ink in the pen and water-soluble ink for the washes. You can also reverse the normal procedure (which is to begin with the drawing) and lay some washes first in order to establish the tonal structure of the subject, using pen later to add details and touches of definition. This could be a particularly suitable approach for a landscape subject.

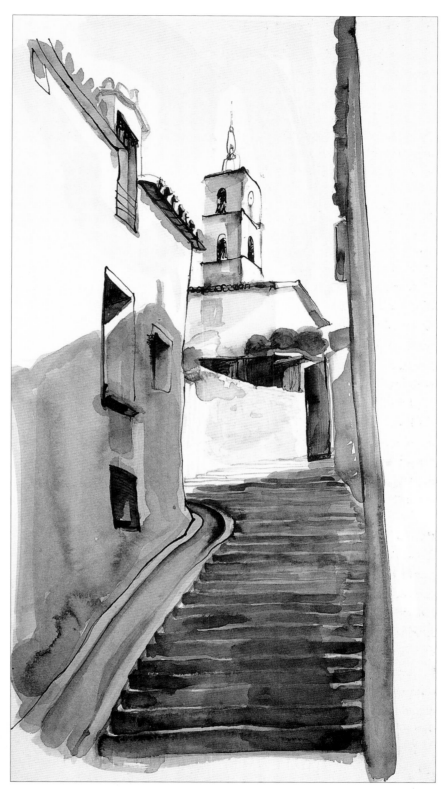

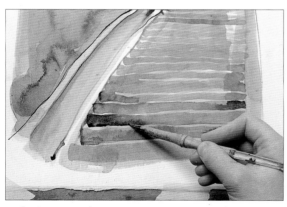

6 The steps play an important part in the composition, as they lead the eye in towards the focal point, which is the church tower, so they are defined carefully with a combination of washes and decisive pen work.

7 The bold, broad lines of the reed pen complement the loose washes to create a well-integrated drawing. At the bottom of the wall on the left, the artist has exploited one of the semi-accidental effects known as backruns, which quite often occur in wash and watercolour work, to suggest the texture of old plasterwork.

BRUSH DRAWING

In a pen-and-wash drawing, the pen provides the linear element; you can, however, dispense with the pen altogether and make drawings entirely with a brush, a method which takes you into the area of painting. The tip of a good brush can provide quite fine definition and, if this is combined with washes, the effect is similar to that of a pen-and-wash drawing but softer, and the line and tone are automatically well-integrated because the same implement has been used for both. Rembrandt made some wonderful brush-and-wash figure drawings, and the great 19th-century English landscape painter, John Constable, used the method for landscape sketches – it is particularly well suited to quick on-the-spot tonal studies.

A variant on the method is to work on dampened paper, which spreads and diffuses the washes to create soft effects, ideal for subjects such as misty landscapes and certain weather conditions. The paper must be stretched first, as explained on the preceding pages. Until you have practised the method it can be tricky to control the flow and spread of the ink, so begin with the larger areas of light washes and save the more detailed work done with the point of the brush until the later stages, when the paper has begun to dry or dried completely.

Ink and wash

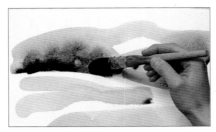

1 *Having laid some light washes of watered ink, the artist works into them before they have dried so that the darker ink spreads and diffuses softly.*

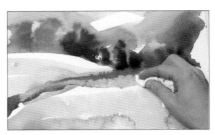

2 *Still working wet into wet, she uses a piece of kitchen paper to control the flow of the ink. In the foreground, the washes have formed blobs with irregular edges, an effect she likes and therefore makes no attempt to correct.*

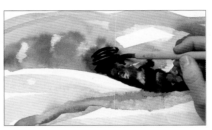

3 *The original ink washes on the trees have dried out to some extent, and the undiluted black ink now introduced hardly spreads at all. The artist is using a Chinese brush, which is ideal for this kind of drawing.*

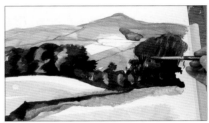

4 *For the final stages a crisp effect was needed, so the paper was left to dry before further work was done on the background, the foreground wall and now the trees.*

5 *(Right) The brush-and-wash method allows you to build up an impression of the landscape more rapidly than is possible with a pencil or pen. The finished picture also provides a good example of the way accidental effects can enhance a drawing or painting; the backruns in the foreground provide a touch of interest and echo the shapes of the trees.*

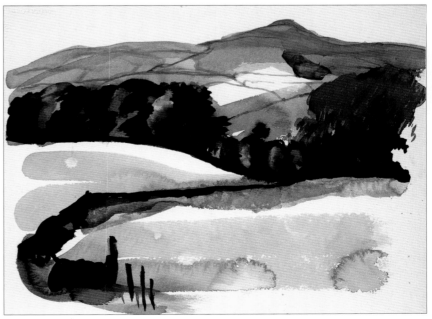

Brush and paint

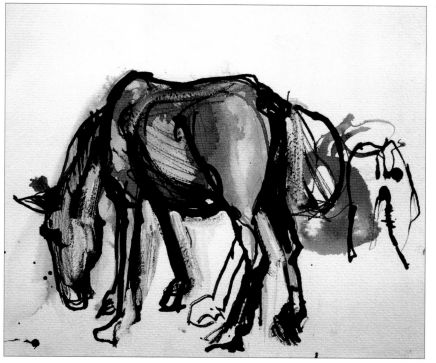

(Above and right) *In these studies, brush drawing has been taken a step further towards painting, with a combination of ink and watercolour used.*

Brush and ink

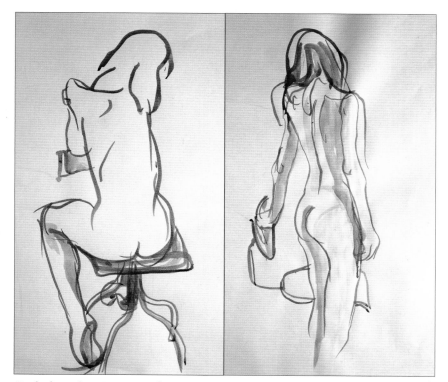

Both these drawings were done in no more than ten minutes, with slightly diluted brown ink and a Chinese brush. The method is excellent for quick figure drawings and studies of movement.

THE BRUSH AS LINE

Another kind of brush drawing is that done with line alone, using the brush purely as a drawing tool. This also takes practice, and is slightly unnerving initially because you cannot correct errors; nevertheless it is an exciting method to try, and you may find that it releases some inhibitions and makes your drawing freer and less fussy. You can do almost anything with a brush, depending on the type you use, how you hold it and the amount of pressure you apply, so it is worth making some "doodles" to explore the possibilities. The Oriental artists and calligraphers, who have exploited the potential of brush drawing for centuries, have evolved many different hand positions; sometimes they work with the brush vertical and held loosely near the top of the handle rather than gripped firmly at the ferrule.

COLOUR DRAWING MATERIALS

Drawing with pencils, charcoal and pens provides valuable practice and can be highly satisfying too, but with the coloured drawing media you can really experiment and produce works which are as expressive and as polished as any painting. Today's artists are in the fortunate position of having a wide range of high-quality materials to choose from – the only problem being where to start.

COLOURED PENCILS

These make a good starting point for anyone launching into colour; they are easy to use, handling in the same way as the familiar graphite pencil, and you can start with a few colours and built up a more extensive collection gradually.

Like all colour media they are made from pigment held together with a binder. The quantity of binder used varies from one manufacturer to another, so you will find

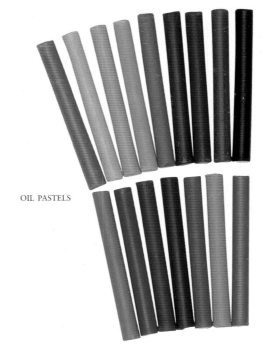

OIL PASTELS

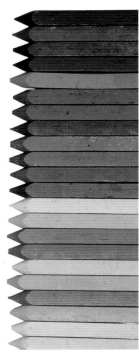

HARD PASTELS

differences in consistency between brands. Some pencils are soft, chalky and opaque, resembling pastels; some are slightly greasy, and others are hard and fairly transparent. You will only discover which ones you like by trying them out, which is one very good reason for starting with a small range.

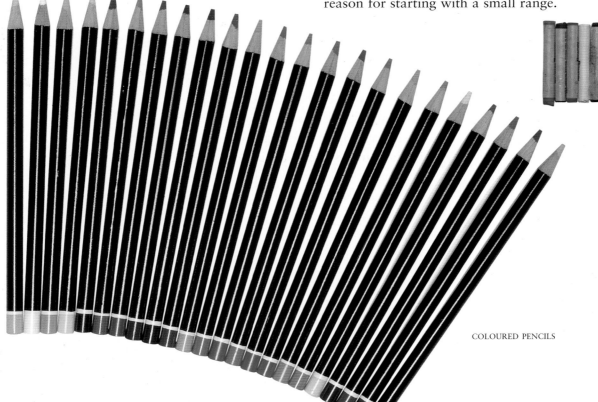

COLOURED PENCILS

SOFT PASTELS

DRAWING

Some manufacturers make water-soluble pencils as well, which are particularly useful because you can use them both wet and dry, spreading the colour in some parts of a drawing and using lines in others.

PASTELS

Pastels are made in soft and hard versions, with the former, sold in the form of cylindrical sticks, being favoured by "pastel painters". These are almost pure pigment, bound with a tiny amount of gum, and are consequently very crumbly. Hard pastels, made with a higher proportion of binder, come in square-sectioned sticks. They produce much crisper, clearer lines and do not smudge as easily. Pastel pencils are also good for linear effects – they are somewhere in between hard and soft pastels in their consistency. Spray fixative is necessary for any drawings in pastel.

Oil pastel have the great advantage of not requiring fixative, as the pigment is bound with waxes and oils. The variation in consistency from range to range is enormous, with some pastels being quite hard and others almost melting in your hand, but there are two basic categories: wax-oil pastels and non-wax ones, simply called oil pastels. The former have their devotees, but in general they are less malleable than standard oil pastels, which are a versatile and fluent drawing medium.

INKS AND MARKERS

Coloured drawing inks, like black inks, can be divided into two broad types: waterproof and water-soluble. They are made in a wide range of brilliant colours and can be mixed together to increase the range further. Some waterproof inks are bound with shellac, which means they can't be mixed successfully with water-based inks, but others are acrylic-based – they are known as liquid acrylics and they behave in use very much like water-soluble inks, except that they are impermeable when dry.

If you want your work to last, guard against the type of ink called "brilliant watercolour"; this is made not from pigment but from dyes, which can fade and discolour. The colours are temptingly vivid, but they are made for graphic reproduction work, where the discoloration of the original may not matter.

Some coloured felt-tipped pens are also prone to fading and should be checked carefully before buying. These pens are made either with broad wedge-shaped tips (these are sometimes called markers) or with fine tips, and the ink used in them can be water-or spirit-based. They are ideal for those who like a bold approach to drawing.

PAPERS

For coloured-pencil and oil-pastel work, and ink drawing, good-quality cartridge (drawing) paper can be used, though some artists who specialize in coloured pencil or oil pastel like to use a rougher texture and sometimes a pre-coloured paper. For chalk-pastel work, smooth paper is not usually suitable, as the pigment tends to fall off, so it is best to use either one of the papers made specially for pastel work – Ingres or Mi-Teintes paper – or watercolour paper. If you like the texture of the latter but prefer to work on coloured paper, you can tint it with a light wash of water-colour first.

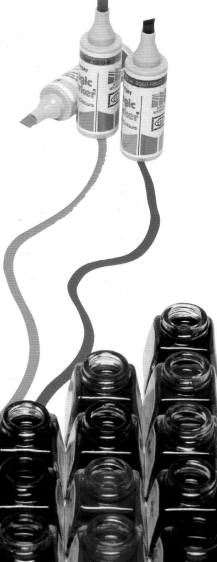

MARKERS

COLOURED INKS

COLOURED PENCIL

Although coloured pencils are becoming increasingly popular with fine artists, both for sketching and for finished works, at one time they were mainly associated with illustration work, and are still widely used for this purpose. In order to accommodate commercial demands, manufacturers produce coloured pencils in a wide range of hues and shades – some offer as many as two hundred. However, as colours can be mixed on the picture surface, it is not necessary to buy a complete range and, even if you did, you would still have to rely on mixing to some extent, particularly for dark colours, which can only be achieved by building up in layers.

COLOUR MIXING

Colours can be mixed in a number of different ways, the classic method being hatching and crosshatching, explained under pen and ink drawing. This method allows you to achieve subtle colour mixing effects as well as considerable depth of colour. Blues lightly hatched over yellow and then crosshatched in places with deeper blues will produce beautifully varied areas of green, while colour could be introduced into shadow areas by hatching and crosshatching over black with dark blues and purples.

While this is a good method for highly finished, detailed work, it is not a rapid process, added to which too many tight layers of hatching and crosshatching can make a drawing appear overworked and lacking in spontaneity. For a looser effect, tones can be built up simply by shading, the method you would naturally use with an ordinary graphite pencil. Colours can also be mixed in this way, with yellow shaded over red producing orange, and yellow over blue making green, for example.

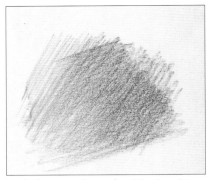

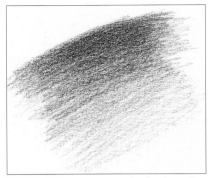

Colours and tones can be built up by careful shading.

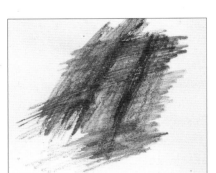

Colours are often mixed by hatching and cross-hatching.

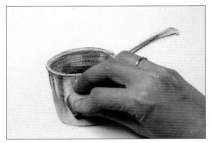

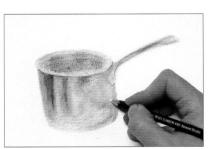

The tip of a water-soluble pencil has been dipped in water before laying the colour over the blue.

Both pencils have been dipped in water, and a wet brush taken over the whole area to produce this effect.

Burnishing

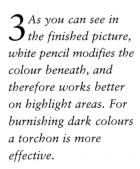

1 *The colours must be built up solidly in the part of the drawing to be burnished. Here a white pencil is used to burnish highlights.*

2 *An eraser removes a little of the pigment, but also pushes the remaining particles into one another, creating soft blends.*

3 *As you can see in the finished picture, white pencil modifies the colour beneath, and therefore works better on highlight areas. For burnishing dark colours a torchon is more effective.*

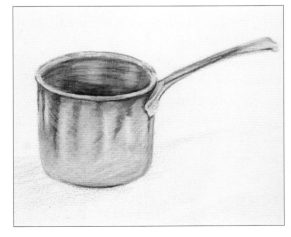

With water-soluble pencils the colour-mixing possibilities are increased; you can spread colour into a wash with water and a clean brush, overlay this with another colour, mix the second colour into the first with more water, and so on. However, don't overdo mixing wet washes of colours, as some of the coloured pencil pigments have a chalky quality and leave a muddy, colourless mess when mixed wet.

BURNISHING

This method can be used to increase the brilliance of colours in certain areas of a drawing, but it is not suitable for water-soluble pencils used wet. Having been built up thickly, the colours are then rubbed with a plastic eraser or torchon (a rolled paper stump sold for blending pastels). This action pushes the particles of pigment into one another so that no separate lines or marks are visible; the grain of the paper is flattened to produce a sheen.

IMPRESSING

If you draw with coloured pencil on a heavily textured paper, most of the pigment will be deposited on the top of the weave; impressing follows the same principle. "Blind" lines are pressed into the paper with a knitting needle or paintbrush handle and, when coloured pencil is applied on top, the lines show as white. The method is also known as white line drawing.

You can use impressed lines simply for variety in a drawing, but quite intricate pattern effects are possible too. If the white line is to play a major role in the drawing it is helpful to use tracing paper to place the lines accurately. Draw up your design, trace it – or draw it directly onto tracing paper – then lay the tracing on your drawing paper and go over the lines with a hard pencil.

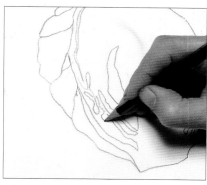

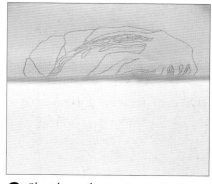

1 *If you are uncertain of the design you can work it out first on ordinary paper and then trace it, but in this case the artist draws directly onto the tracing paper.*

2 *She places the tracing paper over the working surface and, before starting the impressing, fixes it at the top with a piece of masking tape to prevent slippage.*

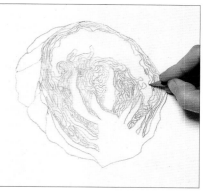

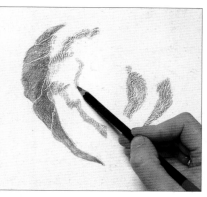

3 *She goes over all the lines with a hard pencil. You can use any pointed implement for this, but a pencil is the best choice for a complex design, as you can keep track of which lines you have drawn over.*

4 *The lines show up clearly through the coloured pencil, which is applied quite heavily. The working surface is smooth watercolour paper which, being thicker than cartridge (drawing) paper, produces more positive indentations.*

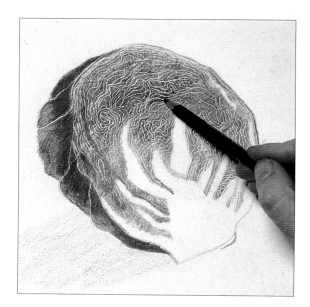

5 *With several reds and orange-reds shaded over one another, black is now used lightly to give greater depth of colour, contrasting with the white lines.*

PASTEL TECHNIQUES

There is always argument about whether a work in pastel should be classified as a drawing or a painting, but this merely underlines the fact that there is no real boundary between the two. In general, a pastel with an obvious linear emphasis is considered to be a drawing while those in which colours are built up thickly in layering techniques and line plays a minor role, are clearly paintings, although not done with a brush.

PASTEL MARKS

In the context of drawing, it is the mark-making capacity of pastels rather than their ability to build up colours that is most important, and in this field they are supreme among the media. A coloured pencil can only produce lines and, although these can be thick, thin, heavy or light, there are few other possible permutations. Pastels, whether you use the hard or soft variety, have a far greater inherent range: they can be sharpened to a point to produce crisp, incisive marks, used blunt for softer lines, or broken into short lengths and used sideways to make strokes of colour.

Pastel pencils are less versatile in mark-making terms, handling very much like coloured pencils except that they are considerably softer. They are also softer than hard pastels and cannot produce the same fine lines that are possible with the edge of a square-sectioned hard pastel stick. However, they are pleasant to use, and excellent for relatively small-scale work. The colour can be partially spread with water and a clean brush to produce a wash effect and to soften lines where necessary.

OIL PASTELS

Oil pastels don't make very crisp lines either, but they are ideal for bold drawings

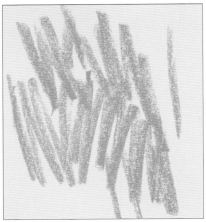

SOFT PASTEL

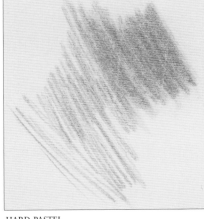

HARD PASTEL

OIL PASTEL

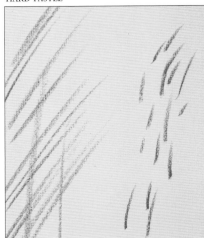

PASTEL PENCILS

and vivid, solid areas of colour. Some artists prefer them to soft pastels, as they are less crumbly, less fragile and do not require fixing. Furthermore, they allow you to make use of a technique called sgraffito, in which one layer of colour is scratched back to reveal another. A variety of effects can be achieved in this way, from fine lines made with a sharp implement to more subtle broken-colour effects, achieved by scraping back successive layers of colour with the edge of a knife.

PAPERS

The quality of the lines and marks you make with pastels, whichever kind you use,

Oil-pastel sgraffito

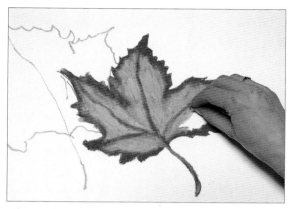

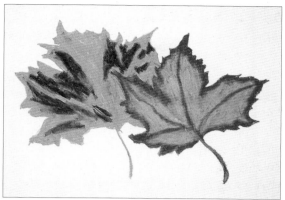

1 *Working on a smooth-surfaced watercolour paper, the artist lays the colours thickly, making sure that the oily pastel is pushed well into the paper.*

2 *Some areas of these first colours will be overlaid with darker ones, but selected parts will be either left uncovered or revealed by scratching, so the artist has chosen them with the finished effect in mind.*

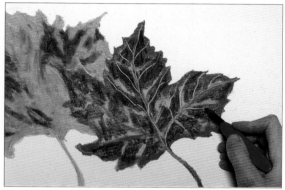

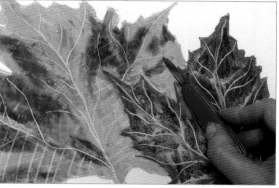

3 *With dark green now laid thickly on top of the yellow, the point of a knife is used to scratch fine lines. This has also removed a little of the original colour, but the lines are not white because the pigment has stained the paper.*

4 *The sgraffito effect has been built up all over the leaves, with varying pressure of the knife. Here it is used quite lightly.*

is considerably affected by the paper you work on. For a pastel painting, where you intend to build up colours thickly, it is usual to work on textured paper, as smooth paper does not grip the pigment sufficiently firmly. This reduces the solidity of the line, breaking up the stroke slightly so that some of the paper shows through. For purely line work, where you don't intend to lay one colour over another, you can use smoother paper, which gives a solid, unbroken line without the paper showing through. You might also try one of the special papers sold for pastel work – velour paper. This provides a line which is both solid and soft, with slightly fuzzy edges.

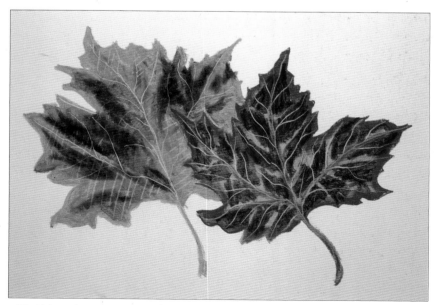

5 *Although you can scratch into light colours to reveal dark ones in exactly the same way, the technique is most effective when worked dark to light, as in this drawing.*

INKS & MARKERS

The idea of drawing with a brush can be taken a step further by using several different colours of drawing inks. These can be painted on straight from the bottle, mixed to produce a wide range of colours, or diluted with water (if you use water-based or acrylic-based inks) to form light washes of colour. In this way you can produce anything from a drawing made with several bold brushstrokes to something which closely resembles a painting in watercolour.

Coloured inks can be combined with black inks, applied either with a brush or a pen, or used in mixed-media techniques with other painting or drawing media such as acrylic paints, charcoal or oil pastels.

DRAWING WITH MARKERS

Markers and coloured felt-tipped pens are exciting to draw with, but because they are not capable of subtle effects, they are more suitable for sketches and quick impressions. Both markers (the chunky implements with broad wedge-shaped "nibs") and felt-tips are basically reservoir pens containing ink, which may be either spirit- or water-based. Water-based inks are better for sketching than spirit-based ones which tend to "bleed" into the paper so that some of the colour comes through onto the other side. The inks are transparent, so colours can be mixed on the paper surface by laying one over another; they can also be used in conjunction with drawing inks.

Markers on textured paper

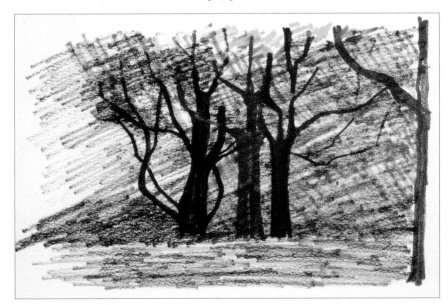

Used on smooth paper, markers create a solid, uncompromising line, but here the texture of the watercolour paper has broken up the strokes to produce a lighter effect.

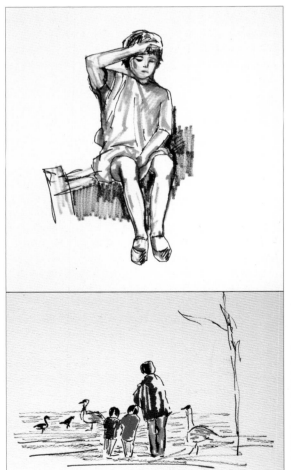

(Right, above and below) *Markers appeal to those who enjoy a bold approach, as they are not capable of subtle effects. They are, however, well suited to quick sketches such as these.*

Drawing with coloured inks

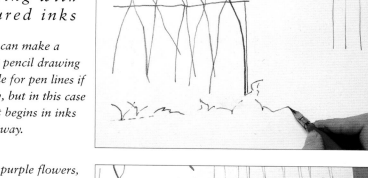

1 You can make a light pencil drawing as a guide for pen lines if you wish, but in this case the artist begins in inks straightaway.

2 The purple flowers, and some lightly drawn red ones behind them, have provided a key for judging the other colours, and the artist now describes the shape of the patch of grass by making dark blue pen marks over green.

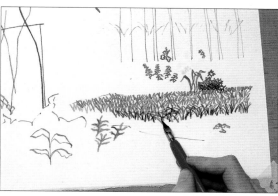

4 The broad-nibbed pen is used again, as this area of the picture needs bold effects. Even with just one pen, the marks can be varied according to how it is held – notice how in the small plant on the left, the line changes from thick to thin.

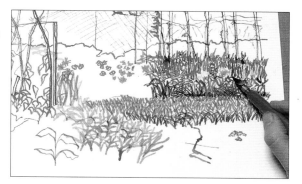

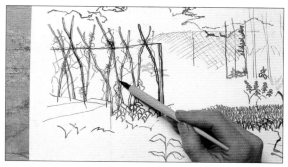

3 She is using a selection of different pens and has swapped the original broad-nibbed pen for a finer one in order to vary the quality of the lines.

WAX RESIST

One of the best-known of the mixed-media drawing methods is wax resist, which is based on the incompatibility of oil and water. A drawing is made with wax crayons, wax oil pastels, an oil bar (oil paint in solid form) or an ordinary household candle, then water-based inks are laid on top; the wax subsequently repels the ink, creating a variety of fascinating effects.

5 The background and right-hand area of foreground have been left until last, as the artist wanted to establish the central area before deciding how to treat the other parts of the picture. The contrast between the fine lines used for the background and the bolder drawing of the foreground and middleground helps to create a sense of space as well as adding interest to the drawing.

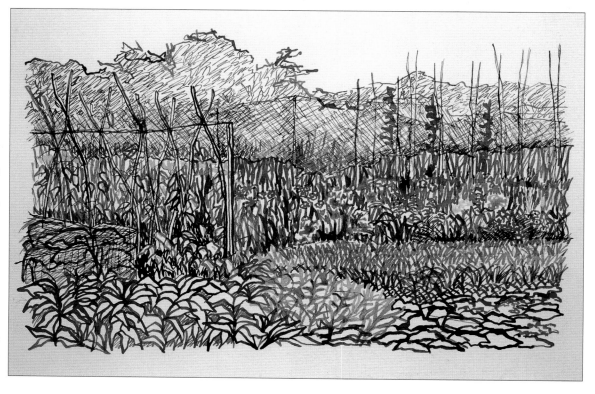

COMPARATIVE DEMONSTRATION

There is a wide range of colour drawing media on the market today, and you may need to experiment with several in order to discover which one suits your own style and pictorial interests which can be expensive. However, you can learn a lot by looking at and responding to other artists' work. For example, you may like the effects you see in coloured pencil drawings better than those achieved by pastel or oil pastel, in which case you would do well to follow this initial response. Here two artists demonstrate two

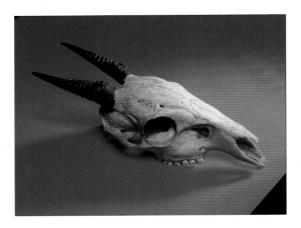

very different media in order to show how the medium affects your way of working. Elizabeth Moore creates subtle effects with coloured pencil, while Judy Martin has chosen oil pastel, a much bolder medium capable of strong, vivid colours.

Coloured pencil on cartridge (drawing) paper

1 *When there is any build-up of coloured pencil it cannot be erased, so the artist begins by working very lightly, making sure that the skull is correctly drawn before she continues.*

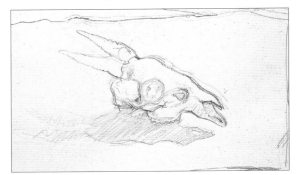

2 *Having established the overall colour of the skull, laying one colour over another in places, she now works on the shadow, which plays an important part in the composition of the drawing.*

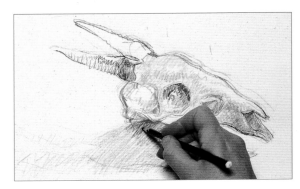

Oil pastel on coloured paper

1 *With a very light pencil drawing as a guide, the artist has begun with patches of white, dark browns and greys. Excited by the reflected colours on the skull, she works on these at an early stage.*

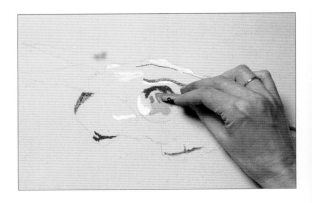

2 *The darkest and brightest areas of the picture have now been established – the vivid red background and one of the animal's horns. The red was particularly important because it would be difficult to assess the colours needed for the skull without some of this colour in place.*

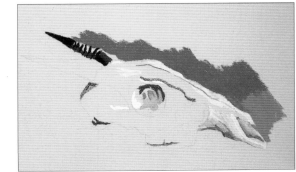

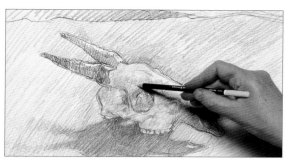

3 *In any line medium, whether pencil, coloured pencil or pastel, it is important to vary the marks you make, and here you can see a wide range, from long hatching lines on the table top to shorter, curving strokes describing the forms of the skull.*

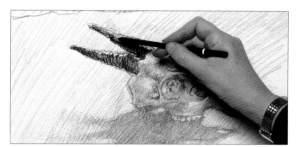

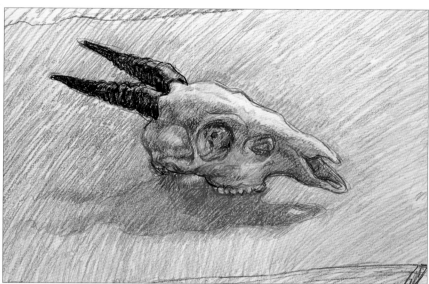

4 *Here again, over earlier light hatching, the artist has applied short jabs, squiggles and curving lines that follow the direction of the forms. Notice also the variety of colours describing the skull, and the subtle mixtures produced by laying one colour over another.*

5 *If you compare the finished drawing with the oil-pastel one, you will see the extent to which the medium dictates the treatment of the subject. Because it is difficult to cover large areas with coloured pencil, the artist has only suggested the red paper, making the skull the most colourful part of the painting.*

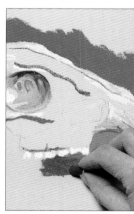 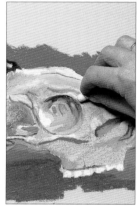

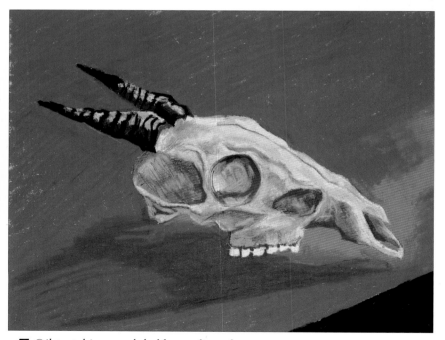

3 *As in the coloured pencil drawing, the shadow plays an important part in the picture. Although the arrangement is the same in both cases, the lighting was altered to produce a longer, more angular shadow.*

4 *The colours of the skull are now intensified. Because she is working on coloured paper, the artist uses white pastel for the highlights rather than "reserving" them as she would on white paper.*

5 *Oil pastel is a much bolder medium than coloured pencil and, being soft, it covers large areas relatively quickly. These qualities have allowed the artist to exploit the dramatic red, black and white colour theme of the subject.*

MAKING ACCURATE DRAWINGS

Having looked at the different drawing media and seen the various effects they can achieve, the next step is to learn how to use them to make a drawing that describes your subject with the required degree of accuracy so that it looks 'real'. Accurate drawing should in no way be confused with detailed drawing – a few lines can provide a better likeness of a subject, whether it be a face, a figure or a landscape, than any amount of careful detail. It is largely a matter of getting the shape, the proportion and the relative scale of an object right, and this requires first and foremost careful observation and constant checking.

Learning to draw is like learning to write – the basic skills must be mastered before you can make them work for you. It is easy to be put off by early failures in drawing and to decide you simply haven't got "the gift", but you can minimize such failures by following some simple strategies, at least when you first start to draw.

DRAWING SIGHT SIZE

Most artists use some system of measuring when they draw, and this is easiest if you draw the size you see. The term "sight size" is self-explanatory, and many people draw in this way naturally. Others don't – they tend to try to draw as near as possible to life size, and have to force themselves to reduce their drawings.

You can check very easily what sight-size is by placing an object such as a mug on a table and holding up a sketchbook in front of it, in the position from which you might draw it. Then close one eye and make two marks on the paper, one for each side of the mug. If you are outdoors drawing a landscape or an urban scene you can make a series of these "placement marks" across the top of your paper. This can be done

Working sight-size

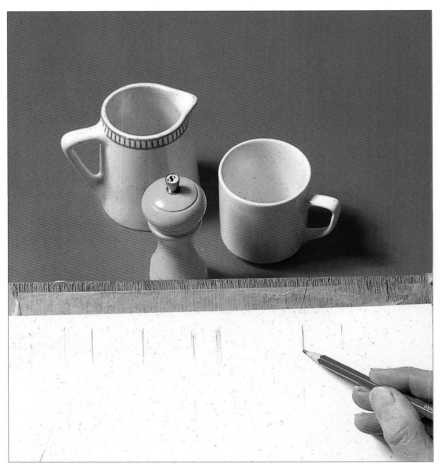

either by holding up a pencil at the same level as your drawing and moving your thumb up and down it, or by using a ruler and reading the measurements.

It may seem a mechanical way of drawing, but when accuracy is required it is very helpful. If you are making an under-drawing for a painting, for example, rather than just drawing for its own sake, accuracy is more important than expressive qualities, and you will avoid having to make corrections when you paint.

MEASURING BY COMPARISON

Drawing sight-size is easier than trying to scale objects up or down in your mind, but it doesn't always work because a sight-size

1 *With one eye closed, the artist begins by making a series of marks across the top of the paper so that he can establish the horizontal measurements. When drawing a small still-life group of this kind, you need to be quite close to the subject.*

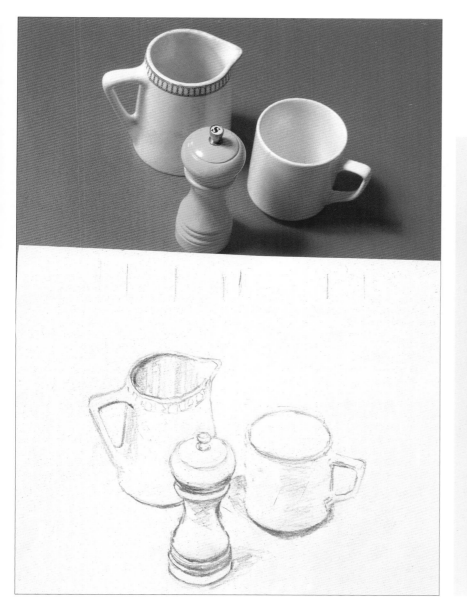

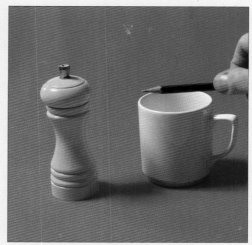

Making relative measurements

If you are not working sight-size, establish a "key" size, such as the width of the mug here, and relate the other objects to it. Make sure to hold the pencil at arm's length each time, as the measurements will not be accurate unless your hand is always exactly the same distance from the objects.

2 *With the first measurements marked in, the artist worked in the normal way, that is, with both eyes open. Only when he saw that something was not quite right in his drawing did he take further measurements, such as the height of the objects and the width of the ellipses.*

drawing can be very small. You can test this out in the same way as before, but this time hold the sketchbook close to the mug first and then about a metre away – the mug will become very small in relation to the paper. Drawing as small as this can be inhibiting – in a life class, for example, the model may be some distance away from you and, if you want to draw boldly in charcoal, sight-size will place unnecessary restrictions on your approach. In such cases you can still use systems of measuring, but you need to establish one "key" size and check everything else against this.

In a figure drawing the head is taken as the unit of measurement – there is more about human proportions later – but in any

drawing some major feature will help you work out relative sizes. In a drawing of an interior, for example, there may be a table or other piece of furniture which plays an important part in the composition. If you draw this in lightly first, you can then work out the scale of other features, such as the height and width of a window behind it, again by holding up a pencil. Try this out with the mug on the table again; first measure the height and then check the relative width. When not drawing sight-size, you must hold the pencil at arm's length and make sure you are always in the same position – the measurements will change as soon as you bend your arm or move forwards or backwards.

DRAWING SHAPES

Drawing involves, among other things, defining a shape by means of its outline, a fact which immediately establishes a kind of falsehood because no object is flat and there are no true outlines in nature. However, we still have to invent this outline because it gives us the shape.

MAKING AN OUTLINE DRAWING

It is not a bad idea to practise drawing shapes by setting up a simple group of still life objects – perhaps a mug, a plate and a bottle – and approaching them as two-dimensional shapes, drawing them in outline alone. This is not normally the way to make a good drawing because, although it may be accurate in terms of shape, there will be no suggestion of form and the objects will not look solid. However, it is a useful exercise as it does force you to look carefully and to analyse the shapes.

MAKING COMPARISONS

Drawing outlines becomes much easier when you begin to compare one shape against another and to check the relative sizes, as explained on the previous pages. Look, for example, at the way the shapes relate to one another. If you have placed them so that they overlap, how and at what point do they do this? Ask yourself how much larger, taller or wider one shape is than another, and in the case of a tall object such as a bottle, what the proportion of width to height is. A common fault is to treat each part of the drawing in isolation; it is no good drawing a perfectly shaped apple if it is too big for the plate on which it sits.

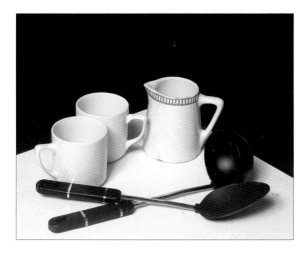

Improve your observational skills by setting up a group of household objects and drawing them first as positive and then as negative shapes.

Drawing outlines

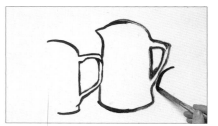

1 *This form of drawing is not easy and you will have to make corrections, so use a medium that allows this. The artist is drawing with a brush and acrylic paint, which she can correct by overpainting in white.*

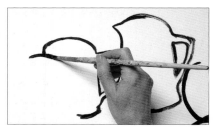

2 *Drawing an ellipse is difficult at the best of times, but even more so when you can only draw the top half. However, by looking carefully at the subject, the artist has managed well.*

3 (Right) *The drawing of the spoon and ladle was not satisfactory, so white paint is now used to paint out the incorrect lines.*

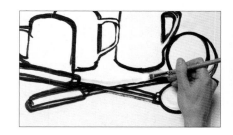

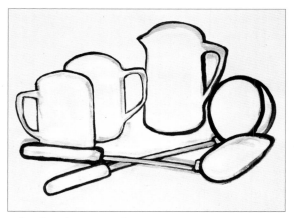

4 *The white paint does not completely cover the black, and a ghost line remains, which can be a helpful guide when correcting the drawing. If you erase completely, as you would in a pencil drawing, you are likely to repeat exactly the same mistake.*

NEGATIVE SHAPES

Drawing negative shapes

Another useful way to check the accuracy of a drawing is to look at the shapes between and behind the objects, known as negative shapes or negative space. If you are drawing a mug with a handle, forget about the handle itself and try to assess the shape of the piece of space between it and the edge of the mug. It can be helpful to draw these shapes before you turn to the positive ones; sometimes you may not have to draw the actual objects at all.

Drawing the negative shapes only is another exercise often set by art teachers and, although it seems slightly perverse, it helps you to sharpen your observational skills. It is also enjoyable, as it forces you to look at things in a completely different way and thus abandon any preconceptions. When your drawings become more ambitious, you can still use these systems of checking and comparing. Negative shapes are very useful in figure drawings, for example, when something has gone wrong but you are not sure what. In a standing pose with arms akimbo, you may have struggled so hard to describe the difficult forms of the limbs that you have failed to relate them properly to the body. You can often discover the mistake by checking the shapes of the spaces between arms and body.

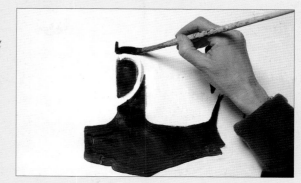

1 *Again using a brush and acrylic paint, the artist is now drawing the still-life group "in negative", that is, she is painting only the shapes between the objects.*

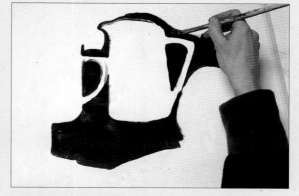

2 *Drawing in this way involves an initial effort of will, but it can simplify matters. Once you have trained yourself to look for the negative shapes, such as those made by the handles here, they can be easier to recognize than the objects themselves.*

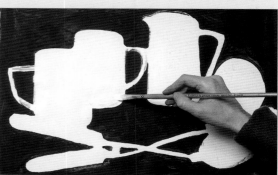

3 *As in the previous drawing, the artist uses white paint to make corrections. It is almost impossible to get everything right the first time in this kind of drawing.*

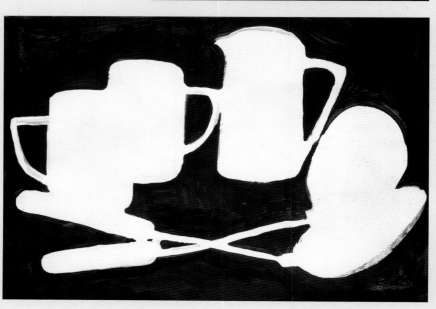

4 *Apart from helping you to observe carefully, drawing negative shapes has another function – it teaches you to consider the relationship of one shape to another, and thus to compose your work. This drawing, although not completely accurate, is lively and full of interest because of the balance between the light and dark shapes.*

DRAWING FORM

So far we have looked at systems of measuring and checking to produce accurate outlines, shapes and proportions, but there is, of course, more to it than this. Drawing is a matter of creating illusions – you are portraying a three-dimensional world in two dimensions, and a good drawing must give a convincing impression of the three-dimensional form of an object as well as its outline.

JUDGING LIGHT AND DARK

Unfortunately no system of measuring can help you to describe the solidity of an object; here you must rely on direct observation, and this is less easy than it sounds. Form is described by the light that falls on an object, which creates light and

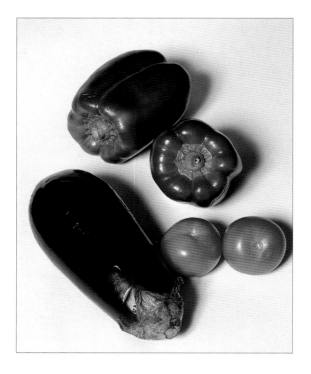

For this exercise you need a selection of rounded objects, preferably lit from the side to create well-defined areas of light and dark.

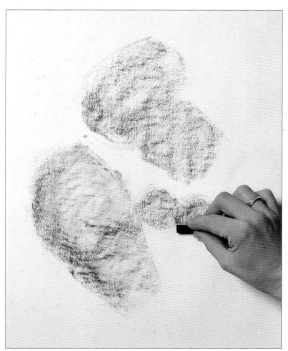

1 *Working entirely with the side of the charcoal stick, and thus avoiding the temptation to use line, the artist begins by blocking in the shapes of the various vegetables.*

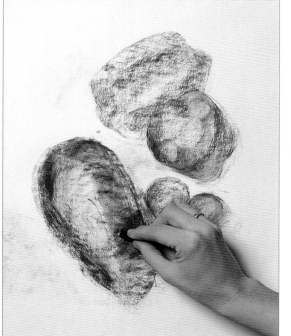

2 *Again using a short length of thick willow charcoal held on its side, she builds up the darker area of the aubergine (eggplant).*

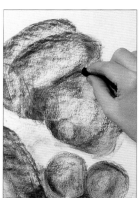

3 *The deep shadow between the two vegetables creates a dark line, so here the tip of the charcoal is used. Because charcoal is soft and smudgy, however, it does not give the impression of an outline.*

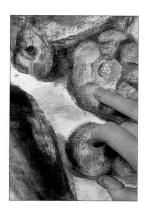
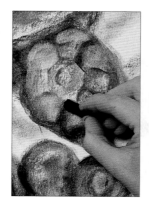
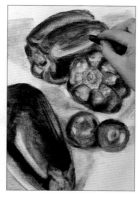
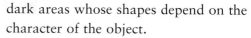

4 *A finger tip is used to rub off some of the charcoal, creating soft highlights.*

5 *The dimples at the top of the green pepper create rapid transitions of light to dark, so the shadows are deepened with the tip of the charcoal.*

6 *Because charcoal does not adhere well to smooth paper – the artist is working on cartridge (drawing) paper – dark areas often need to be re-established and emphasized towards the end of the drawing.*

dark areas whose shapes depend on the character of the object.

If we lived in a black-and-white world it would be relatively easy to assess these differences in tone (the lightness or darkness of a colour), but more or less anything you choose to draw, whether it be a face or an apple on a plate, has colour. This confuses the issue, because our eyes register colour rather than tone, making it difficult to place the light and dark areas. It helps to half-close your eyes, which blurs the colour and cuts out much of the detail, allowing you to see more clearly in terms of tone.

FORM AND OUTLINE

Outline can be distinctly unhelpful when building up the impression of form, because a hard outline around a shape immediately makes it look flat. The outline of a round or cylindrical object, such as an apple or mug, delineates the boundaries of the form, that is, where it begins to turn away from you; if you put more emphasis on this than on the nearest part of the object, then the illusion of solidity is destroyed.

A good way to practise drawing form is to use tone from the beginning, avoiding outline altogether if you can, or drawing just a light outline for guidance. Try working with a broad medium such as charcoal used sideways, or try the lifting-out method. Of course you don't have to use charcoal – form can be described perfectly well in pencil or even pen and ink – but charcoal will help you to avoid a linear approach.

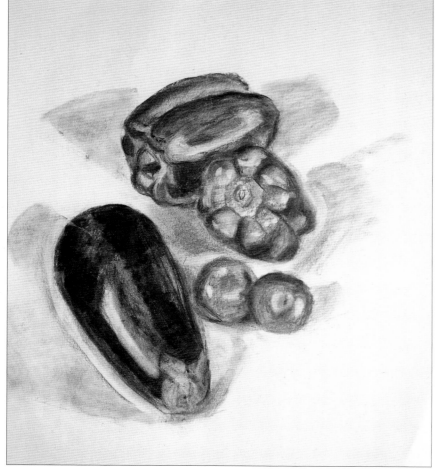
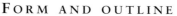

7 *Another danger with charcoal drawings is that the highlights can become lost through smudging, but this is easily remedied by the lifting-out technique. It has been used here for the two main highlights on the aubergine (eggplant) and the smaller ones on the top of the pepper.*

DRAWING WITH LINE

Having just explained how form is built up with tone, it may seem contradictory now to say that you can create an impression of three dimensions with line alone. It all depends on the quality of the line and how you vary it in your picture – whether it is solid and dark, light and delicate or soft and scarcely visible.

LOST AND FOUND EDGES

As we have seen, drawing a hard outline around something destroys its solidity because objects don't have hard outlines. Some of the edges may be relatively well defined because there is a shadow beneath, but others will be very soft and sometimes difficult to distinguish. These "lost-and-found" edges are an important concept in drawing, as they define volume. You can see the effect even on the simplest object, while more complex ones, such as flowers or the human face, are a mass of hard and soft edges caused by the different characters of the forms and the way they turn away from the light. By accurately observing these differences in line quality, you can produce a drawing which describes form without using any kind of shading. Although not easy to do, it is worth practising, as the results can be very expressive.

Observing edge qualities

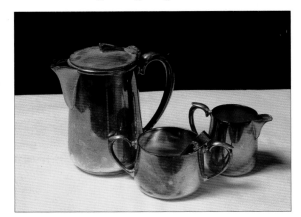

A combination of lost-and-found edges can be discerned in any object, depending on the lighting, the shapes and colour. If you can reproduce them accurately, you will be able to draw with line alone.

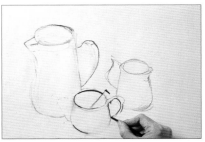

1 *Using medium willow charcoal, the artist begins with a light drawing, and is now strengthening the found edges on the sugar container.*

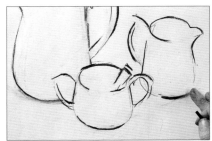

2 *She continues to clarify the edges, smudging the charcoal where softer lines are needed, such as in this shadow area. Edges at the bottoms of objects are often almost lost.*

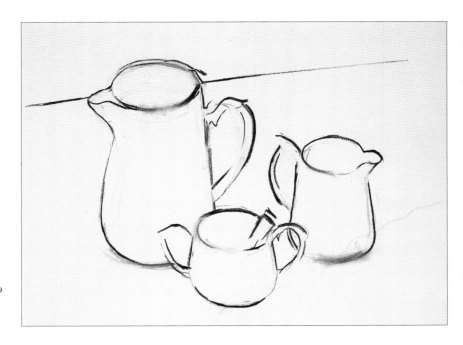

3 (Right) *Although there is no shading on the objects, the drawing gives a convincing impression of three-dimensional form, due partly to the lost-and-found edges and partly to the accurate drawing of the shapes, particularly the ellipses.*

Drawing with contours

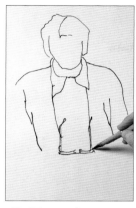

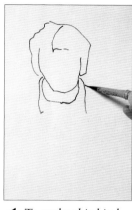

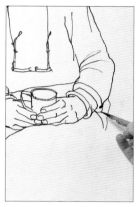

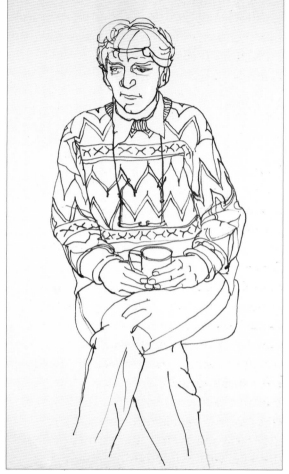

1 *To make this kind of drawing, it is helpful to restrict yourself to a medium which does not lend itself to shading. The artist is using a fine reed pen and black ink.*

2 *Having drawn in the basic outline of the model's head and upper body, she begins to add details such as the shirt collar and dangling spectacles.*

3 *Observing the lines made by the cuffs and the folds at the bent elbows has allowed the artist to describe the arms with no need to use shading.*

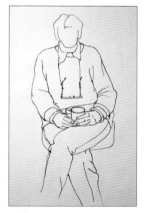

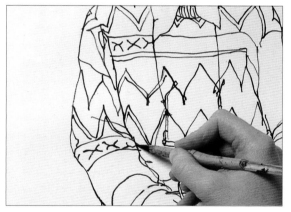

4 *Although not yet finished, the drawing is beginning to give a good impression of shape and form.*

5 *Pattern is a useful aid in the context of form, and here you can see how the behaviour of the pattern helps to explain the curves of the shoulders and the position of the arms.*

6 *The majority of drawings are a combination of line and tone, but it can be instructive to restrict yourself to line on occasion. Like all kinds of drawing exercises, this one gives you valuable practice in analysing your subject.*

CONTOURS

These are another way of using line to describe form. Contours are not the same as outlines; they are lines that follow the shape of the form. An obvious example would be a pattern curving around a piece of china; less obvious contours are provided by clothing – perhaps the sleeve of a shirt forming a series of folds and creases which define the form below, or the criss-cross of laces on a pair of shoes. Indeed, the clothed human figure provides a wealth of contours, from the line of a waistband indicating the curve of the body, to the cuff of a sleeve or a watch strap explaining the structure of the wrist. Not all objects, of course, provide such convenient clues to form – it would be difficult to describe an apple with contour lines – but, if they are there, try to use them in your picture, whether you draw with line alone or with line and tone together.

SKETCHING

There is no real difference between sketching and drawing, but the word sketch implies a quick study made either for pleasure or for reference, while a drawing can be a finished work with its own pictorial aims. There is, or can be, however, a difference between sketching for its own sake and making studies to be used as reference for another work, whether a finished drawing or a painting.

COLLECTING VISUAL MATERIAL

Artists often go through their sketchbooks to get ideas for compositions or simply to refresh their memories on some detail of a scene. The more you sketch, the more reference material you will have, and sketching also helps to polish up your observational skills. In some cases, however, sketches are made not randomly but to gather material for a composition, in which case it is necessary to consider the kind of visual notes required.

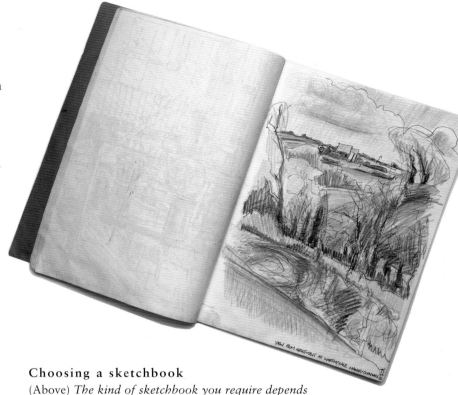

Choosing a sketchbook

(Above) *The kind of sketchbook you require depends on your method of working and the kind of visual notes you wish to make. Some artists have two or three in different sizes and formats. John Townend uses a large book for coloured-pencil drawings like this, and a smaller one for pen-and-ink drawings.*

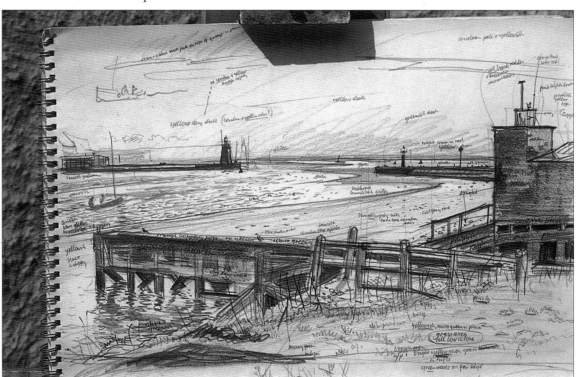

Sketching for painting

(Left) *This sketch by Stephen Crowther was made as the first stage in planning an oil painting, and the artist has made copious written notes to remind him of the colours. Using a large spiral-bound sketchbook enables him to remove the sheet and pin it up near his easel.*

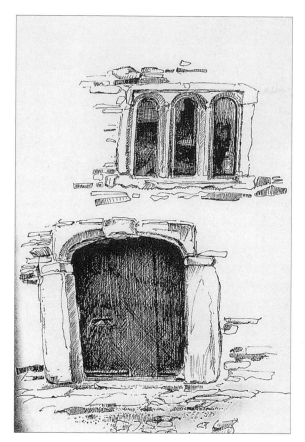

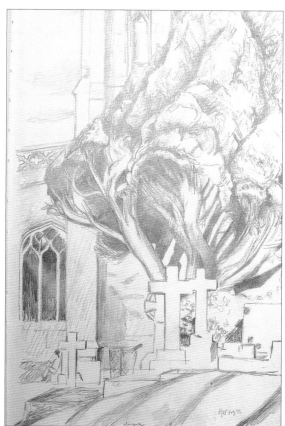

Choosing the medium
(Far left) *When you are out sketching it is wise to take a selection of different drawing media, as you may find that a particular subject is better suited to one than another. John Townend likes coloured pencil for landscapes, but prefers pen and ink for architectural subjects, where colour is less important than line.*

Collecting ideas
(Left) *David Cuthbert does not make sketches with a specific painting in mind, but he has several sketchbooks in which he notes down anything he sees, often taking photographs at the same time so that he has a store of possible ideas to hand.*

Making colour notes
(Below) *Gerry Baptist works mainly in acrylic, using vivid colours, and his watercolour sketches reflect his artistic preoccupations; a monochrome pencil sketch would therefore not provide the information that he needs for his paintings.*

Depending on the kind of work you are planning, you may need sketches in colour and tone as well as in line. Trying to make a painting from a line sketch in pencil or pen and ink is virtually impossible; you will have no idea what colour the sky was or which areas were dark and which ones light. It is wise to make a habit of including all the information possible on your sketches – if you don't have time to sketch in colour, make written notes about the colours. Do not simply write "blue" or "green", but try to analyse the colours; as long as you can understand the notes, this can be more valuable than sketching in colour, particularly if you intend to use one medium for the sketches and another for the painting. A sketch in coloured pencil, for example, would be very difficult to translate into watercolour or oil.

MATERIALS

For sketching you can use any drawing media with which you feel comfortable. Pencil is a good all-rounder, as it allows you to establish tone as well as line. Pen and ink

is useful for small sketches, but less so for tonal studies. Coloured pencils are tailor-made for colour sketches, and so are pastels and oil pastels, although neither of the latter is suitable for small-scale work. You can buy large sketching pads containing different colours of pastel paper, or you can clip pieces of paper to a drawing board.

Sketchbooks, usually containing cartridge (drawing) paper, can be bought in many shapes and sizes. Unless you like to work small, don't be tempted by a tiny address-book size, as you may find that it restricts and frustrates you.

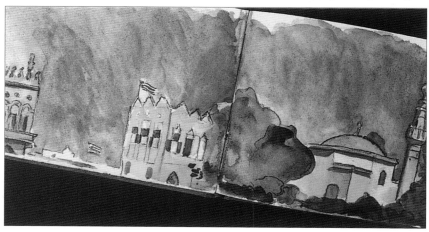

FIGURE DRAWING

The old saying that "If you can paint people you can paint anything" reflects the fact that the human figure is one of the most challenging of all subjects, whether you are drawing or painting. The importance of figure study as a training ground for aspiring artists was recognized in the past, when drawing from life formed an important part of any art student's education. Nowadays there is less emphasis on it, at any rate in art schools, but amateurs flock to life classes, and many professionals return to them at stages during their careers to brush up their skills.

Joining a life class is not essential if you intend to restrict yourself to the clothed figure or to portrait studies; you can usually find someone who is willing to pose for you, or you can draw yourself in a mirror. However, for nude studies you must have a model as well as a decent-sized room in which to draw, so a class is the best answer; alternatively, you could share the cost of a model with friends or colleagues.

THE PROPORTIONS OF THE FIGURE

In the main, drawing is learned by practice, not from books, but books can provide some advice and point out things you may overlook when drawing. Figure drawings often go wrong because the proportions are not properly understood and, although human figures vary greatly, it is helpful to bear in mind some basic rules. These will prevent you from making heads and feet too small – a common error – and help you to analyse what is special about the body you are drawing.

Allowing for individual differences, the human body is approximately seven-and-a-half heads high. The mid-point of the body is slightly above the genital area, with one

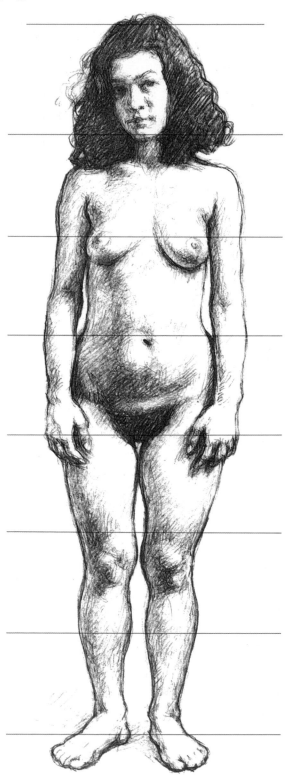

Proportions
Although the general rule is that the body is about seven-and-a-half heads high, it is essential to remember that there are variations; this model's head is relatively large. Observing these individual differences will give authenticity to your drawings.

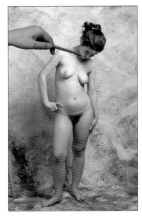

Checking angles
In a pose like this it is important to represent accurately the slope of the shoulders and hips. Establish the precise angle by holding your pencil at arm's length and adjusting it until it coincides, then take it carefully down to the paper and mark in the line.

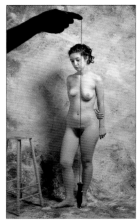

Checking balance
The centre of balance is vital in a standing pose, and you can check this either with a pencil or a plumbline, as shown here. This is a slightly laborious method, but is more accurate than holding up a pencil, where there is a danger of tilting it away from the vertical.

quarter point above the nipples and the other just below the knees. If arms are hanging loose by the side of the body, the wrists will be below the mid-point of the body, with the fingertips reaching to mid-thigh. The hand is about the same length as the face, from chin to forehead – try this out by covering your own face with your hand – and the length of the foot is approximately equal to the whole height of the head.

FORESHORTENING

In figure drawing, the head is always used as the unit of measurement, enabling you to make comparative measurements. Measuring systems become particularly important when the figure, or any parts of it, are foreshortened. Foreshortening is the perspective effect which causes things to appear larger the nearer they are; in a reclining figure, seen from the feet end, the feet will be large and the legs very short. It can be difficult to assess the effects of foreshortening accurately, partly because you know a leg is a certain length and find it hard to believe what you see, and partly because the forms themselves often change. In a seated figure seen from the front the thighs will be wide and short, because the flesh is pushed out by the body's weight.

Some degree of foreshortening is generally present in figure drawing and, because the effects created are often surprising, it is vital to take measurements. As you draw, hold your pencil out at arm's length to check the relative lengths and widths of limbs and body, returning to the head as the basic unit of measurement.

BALANCE AND WEIGHT

You can also use the outstretched pencil method to check angles, another common problem area. The angle of the shoulders or

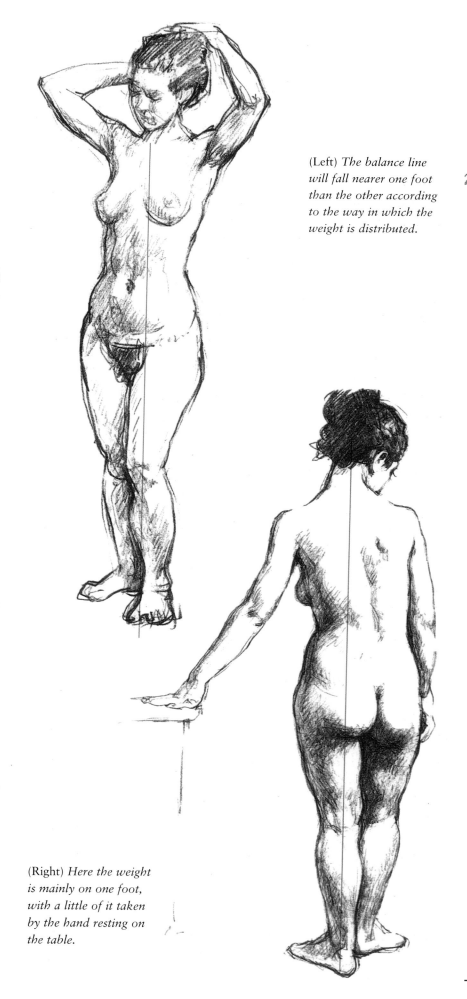

(Left) *The balance line will fall nearer one foot than the other according to the way in which the weight is distributed.*

(Right) *Here the weight is mainly on one foot, with a little of it taken by the hand resting on the table.*

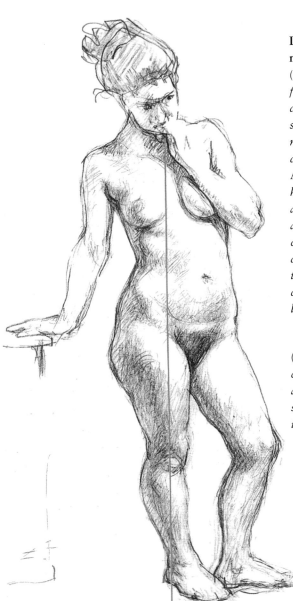

Drawing movement
(Right) *To depict the figure in motion, a difficult but rewarding subject, you need a medium which actively discourages detail. In Arms Swing Hil Scott has drawn with a brush and diluted Chinese ink, adding touches of charcoal line. The definition is minimal, yet the drawing is an elegant description of the fluid lines of body and arms.*

(Left) *Here the weight is divided between the arm and the right leg, and the shoulders and hips slope in opposite directions.*

(Below) *Very little weight is taken by the feet in this stance, so the balance line falls some way outside them.*

tilt of the hips often provides the key to the pose. In a standing figure with the weight on one leg, for example, the shoulders and hips slope in opposite directions; whenever one part of the body moves, another does so in compensation, to maintain the balance. Hold out your pencil and align it with the shoulder or hip line and then, very carefully, take the pencil down to the drawing and mark in the angle as a guide line.

In a standing pose, "balance lines" can be helpful; these give you the position of the feet in relation to the body. It is vital that this is correct, as your drawing will not look convincing unless you convey an impression of the way in which the body's weight is distributed, and the feet, of course, are the bearers of the weight.

Choosing the right medium

(Right) *Children are notoriously restless and usually have to be drawn very fast. It is thus wise to choose a medium which enables you to work quickly and broadly. Ted Gould has used brown Conté crayon for his lovely Mother and Child, suggesting both form and detail with a few deft touches.*

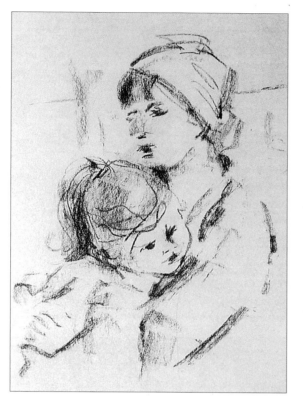

Balance lines are taken from the middle of the neck in a front or back view, and from the ear in a side view, down to the feet. If the model is standing with the weight evenly distributed, the balance line will be between the feet, but if most of the weight is on one leg it will be considerably nearer the weight-bearing foot. The most accurate way to provide yourself with these vertical references is to use a plumbline, which simply consists of a piece of string with a weight at one end.

The way in which the distribution of weight affects the body is less obvious in a seated pose, but it is equally important to identify it, or the drawing will look stiff and unnatural. Here again it is essential to check alignments, either with a pencil or a plumbline. You can either use the same system of balance lines or mark in a central

The standing figure

(Right) *As explained on the previous pages it is vital to analyse the pose and to understand how the weight is distributed and how the whole body is affected by any movement. In his two brush-and-wash drawings James Horton captures beautifully both the swing of the body, and also its three-dimensional quality of mass and weight.*

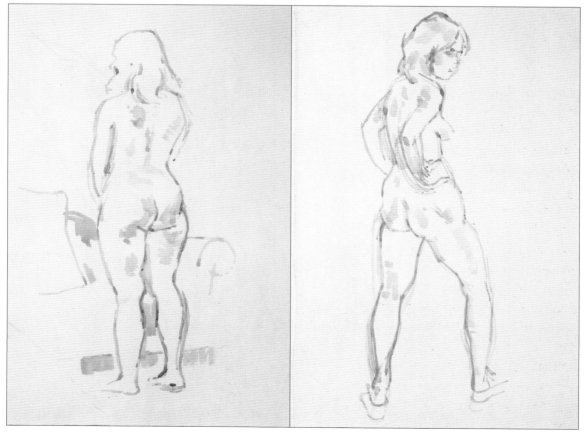

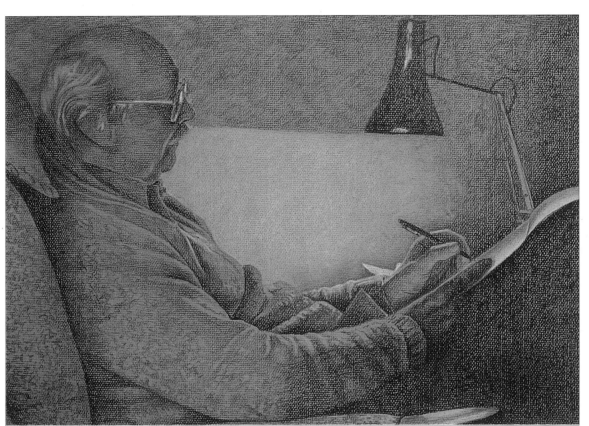

Composing the drawing

(Left) *Drawings can be made for practice, or they can simply be sketches of something which happens to take your fancy. A drawing, however, can also be carried out with the intention of producing a finished work, in which case you must consider composition. Paul Bartlett's* Father with Lamp *is as carefully composed as any painting, with the sweeping curves of the figure, chair and writing pad balanced by the table and the dark upright of the lamp.*

vertical line to which you can relate the position of the feet, head and various parts of the torso.

THE CLOTHED FIGURE

Drawing people with their clothes on is perhaps slightly easier than drawing the nude, if only because there is more opportunity to practise. You don't need a "proper" model because you can draw people anywhere as long as you restrict yourself to quick sketches. For more thorough and detailed studies, friends and family may oblige, indeed many people are flattered to be asked to pose.

Clothing can be helpful in defining the forms beneath it, providing a set of contour lines, but it can also disguise form and confuse the issue in a bewildering way. A thin garment, for example, reveals the body, while a heavy overcoat gives little idea as to the shapes beneath or to the way its wearer is sitting or standing. In such cases you must look for clues, such as the angle of a protruding wrist and hand, the bend of an elbow or the slope of the shoulders.

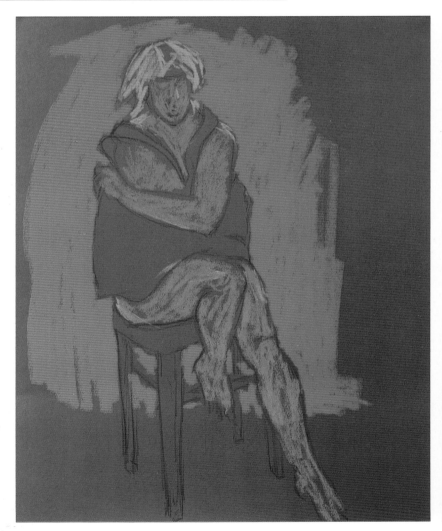

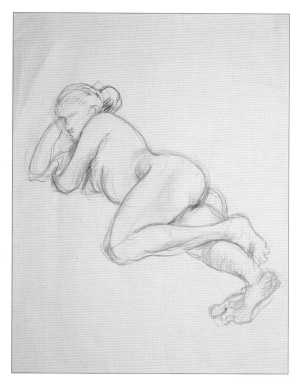

Whatever kind of garments your subject is wearing, try to visualize the body beneath. Analyse the pose just as you would in a nude study, taking measurements and checking alignments of head, shoulders, feet and so on, and perhaps drawing in some light guidelines to indicate key points, even if you can't see them. Clothing can be difficult to draw; it often forms complicated shapes of its own and you can become so involved with drawing folds, or the pattern on a fabric, that you fail to make sense of the figure itself.

Rounded forms

(Above) *This simple pencil drawing by Elisabeth Harden concentrates on the rounded nature of the female form. The relaxed pose of the model and raised left leg are depicted in a flowing outline, with no sharp angles used at all.*

Composing with shapes

(Opposite) *In his pastel drawing, Elly, David Cuthbert has made an exciting composition by reducing detail and concentrating on the interplay of shapes – the curves of the limbs counterpointing the more geometric shapes of the clothing and chair.*

Drawing light

(Right) *Forms are described by the way in which the light falls on them, so in life drawing or portraiture it helps to have a fairly strong source of illumination. In Gerry Baptist's simple but powerful charcoal drawing, the light comes from one side, slightly behind the model, making a lovely pale shape across the shoulders and down the hip and leg.*

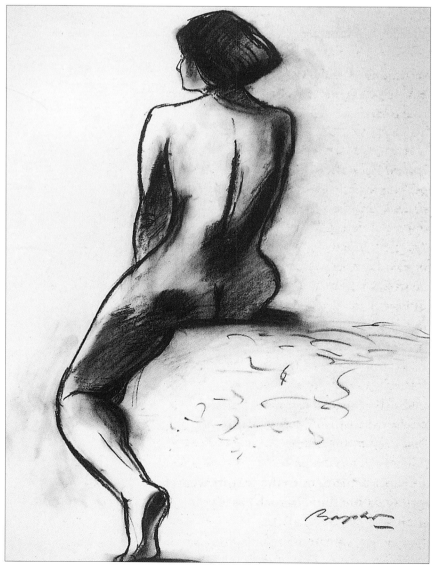

PASTEL DEMONSTRATION

James Horton is primarily a landscape painter, working mainly in oils, but for drawings he frequently uses pastels, which he finds particularly well suited to figure work. Pastel is both a drawing and a painting medium, depending on how it is used, and he exploits its linear qualities, building up colours with light layers of hatching and crosshatching so that each line remains distinct. He avoids the techniques closely associated with pastel painting, such as side strokes, blending and overlaying layers of thick, solid colour.

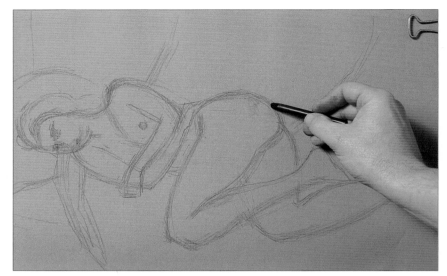

1 *Because pastels cannot easily be erased it is important to begin with an accurate drawing. This is made with a stick of compressed charcoal; pencil should not be used for pastel work, as the slight greasiness of the graphite repels the pastel colour.*

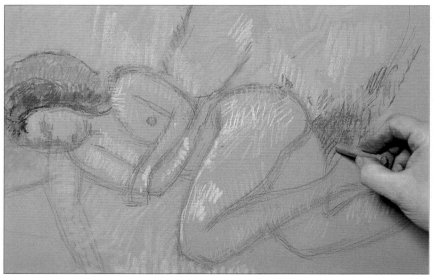

2 *The artist begins by placing small areas of colour all over the picture, relating the rich background colours to the subtler flesh tints. The coloured paper (Ingres) provides a middle tone, making it easier to work up to the highlights and down to the darks.*

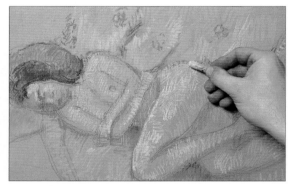

3 *This stage clearly illustrates his method of hatching and cross-hatching. He holds the pastel stick lightly and takes care to vary the lines so that they do not all go in the same direction.*

4 *(Right) The colours are gradually built up, but the first colours are allowed to show through each application, creating a network of lines and marks which gives a livelier effect than smooth blends.*

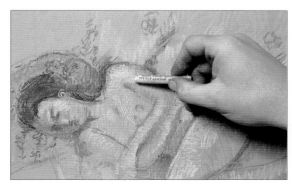

5 *At this stage much of the paper is still uncovered, but it does not need to be covered completely, as the light greenish-brown is very close to the colour of the shadows on the flesh. Choosing the right paper colour is an important aspect of pastel work.*

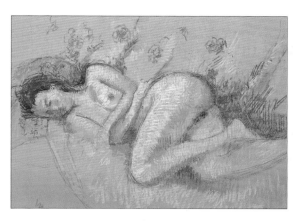

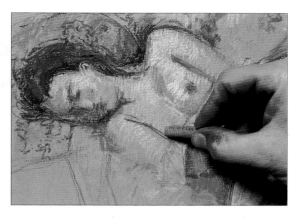

6 *The compressed charcoal is used again to darken and define areas of the hair and to sharpen up the drawing. Charcoal mixes well with pastel, and can be a better choice than black pastel, which makes solid and sometimes over-assertive black lines.*

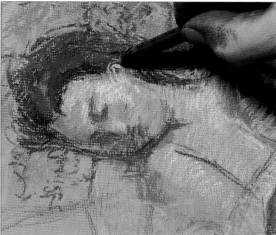

7 *(Above) The process of building up the darker colours and defining details continues, with brown pastel now used lightly to draw the side of the arm. On the shoulder, some of the original charcoal drawing is still visible, and has been strengthened by curving lines of red-brown pastel behind it.*

8 *(Below) The artist has not attempted to treat the background or foreground in detail, concentrating instead on the rich, golden colours of the body. This vignetting method, in which the focal point of the picture is emphasized by allowing the surrounding colours to merge gently into the toned paper, is a traditional pastel-drawing technique.*

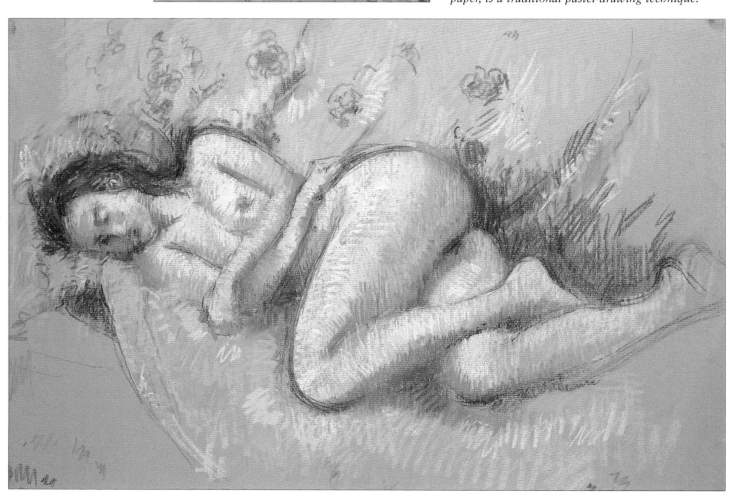

ANIMALS

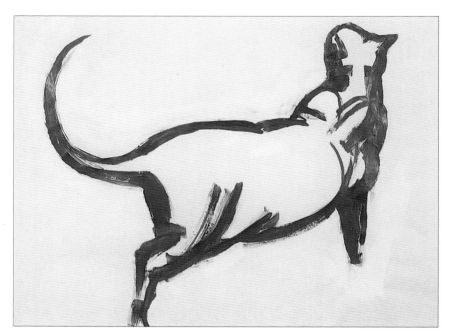

Drawing animals can be rewarding and frustrating in equal measure. Whether they are wild creatures, farm animals or household pets, animals make wonderful subjects – it is enjoyable simply watching them – but unfortunately they are not the most co-operative of models. Even cats, which generally sleep for long periods, have a tendency to wake up and walk away as soon as you reach for your sketchbook. However, many artists have portrayed animals successfully, purely because they were fascinated by them, and this should be your sole criterion in choosing your subject matter.

OBSERVATION AND SKETCHING

As with any branch of drawing, the secret lies in careful observation of detail, the determination not to be put off by failures and, most important of all in this context, the ability to tailor your methods to your subject. You will certainly not be able to produce the kind of finished drawing you might achieve with a figure or an architectural subject, but you can make quick sketches, and a good sketch often says more than any amount of detail and polish.

You may find it difficult at first, because it does require some practice to be able to grasp the essentials of a subject and get them down on paper in a few minutes, or maybe just a few seconds. However, you will find that even your first, perhaps not very successful sketches will have sharpened your observational skills, and the next sketches will be better for this reason. Sketching is a knack, and it really does become easier the more you do it. Use a medium you know you can control well and one that enables you to work quickly in both line and tone – soft pencil, Conté crayon or pastel are all suitable.

Rhythm and movement
(Above) *In an animal drawing, as in a figure study, it is important to convey the living quality of the creature and the way it moves, so choose a medium which allows you to work rapidly and freely. Judy Martin's* Cat Study *is a large-scale drawing: she likes to work "from the elbow", and has drawn directly with a brush and acrylic paint. The diagonal placing of the animal on the paper, together with the sweeping curve of the tail, give a strong sense of movement.*

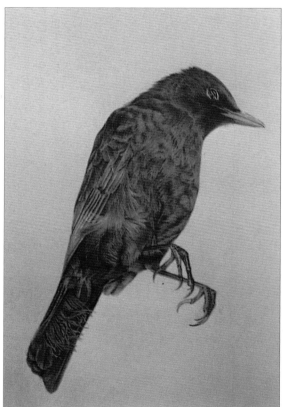

Drawing texture
Texture, whether the rough, shaggy hair of a dog, the soft fur of a cat or the lustrous plumage of a bird, is one of the most attractive features of animal subjects, but you cannot concentrate on these qualities when you are trying to draw animals in motion so you will often have to work from photographs or museum specimens. In his pencil drawing Dead Bird *Robert Maxwell Wood has taken advantage of the mortality of all creatures, to provide himself with an excellent subject for close study.*

Shape and pattern

(Right) *This pencil drawing is a preliminary design for a print, a medium in which three-dimensional form is less important than the arrangement of shapes. What first attracted Elisabeth Harden to the subject was the shapes of the animals' markings, which she has stressed with firm outlines and shading.*

Multiple drawings

(Far right) *Animals tend to repeat their movements, and another approach is to do several drawings on one page and work on them at the same time, as Vicky Lowe has done in her brush-and-wash studies of rabbits. Not only does this help in practical terms, as you can move on to another drawing as soon as the creature moves, but it also creates an impression similar to an animated cartoon.*

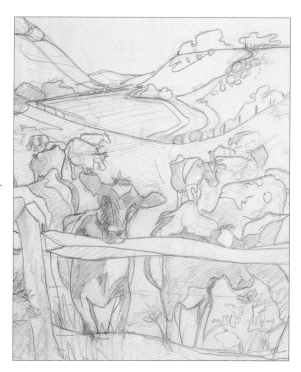

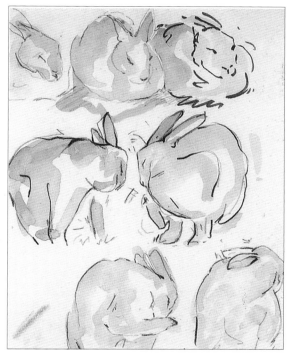

REPEATED MOVEMENTS

There is an element of memory involved in drawing anything in motion, particularly if the movement is rapid, because our eyes simply can't keep up with it. There is no one split second in which you can say "Ah, that's what the legs are doing." It is interesting to note that even the great 18th-century British artist George Stubbs, who specialized in horses, was unable to portray them convincingly in motion. It was not until the era of photography that the sequence of movements made by a

galloping horse was fully understood. Now that we know how a horse moves, it is much easier to appreciate the repetitive nature of most animals' movements. Look for these repeated movements when you are sketching, making several small sketches on the same page so that you have a complete visual record of all the different positions of the legs and body.

PHOTOGRAPHIC REFERENCE

The advent of photographs was invaluable to the 19th-century painters in correcting misconceptions about movement, and they still play an important part in providing reference for drawings and paintings. If you want to draw wild animals – which seldom even appear to order, let alone stay still – photographs are generally the only option available for reference.

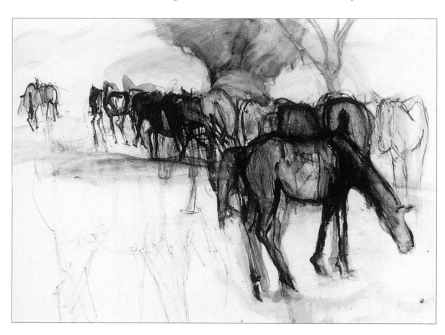

Keeping up with movement

(Left) *Even when quietly grazing, animals will shift their weight from one leg to another and make other small changes in their position. Do not try to change your drawing each time; instead simply draw one line over another, as Karen Raney has done in her coloured-ink drawing of* French Horses. *As can be seen, she has begun with light lines and washes, and has delayed finalizing the positions of limbs and feet with more positive colours until the later stages.*

COLOURED-PENCIL DEMONSTRATION

Judy Martin is not a professional animal artist; indeed she sees herself primarily as an abstract painter. She has, however, always been fascinated by animals, and at one point in her career drew and painted little else. From time to time she returns to such subjects with enjoyment, working mainly from photographs but always interpreting photographic reference in order to create her own compositions and colours. Here a photograph is used as the basis for the cat, but the background and foreground are imaginary.

1 *Here the artist is working with water-soluble pencils on watercolour paper. She begins by laying some light lines and then washes over them. This releases some of the colour and softens the pencil marks without disturbing them.*

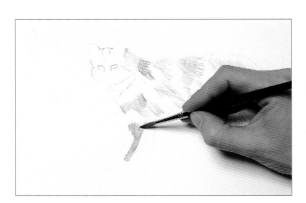

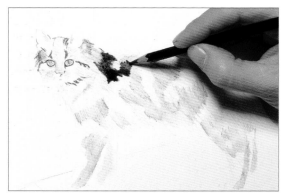

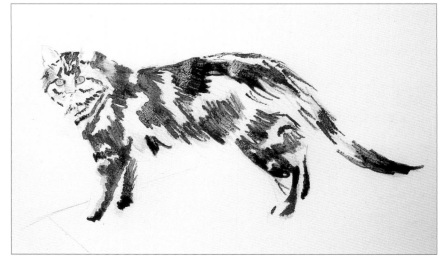

2 *A different effect is created by dipping the pencil into water before applying it. As you can see, this produces a more solid area of colour.*

3 *With dry coloured pencils, dark colours have to be deepened gradually, but water-soluble pencils make it easier to establish the dark tones at an early stage.*

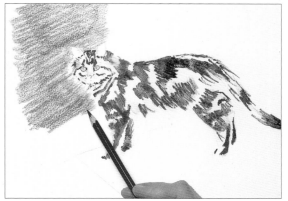

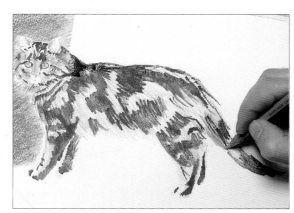

4 *With the dark and light tones of the cat established, the artist can now consider the background. A solid area of colour on the left is needed to provide a balance for the animal, plus a contrast of textures, so here she uses the pencil dry.*

5 *Warm reddish browns have been introduced with a dry pencil to suggest the texture of the fur. A wet grey pencil creates a soft effect on the tail.*

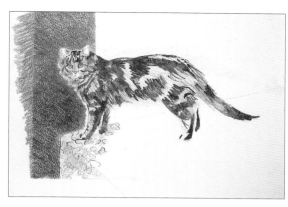

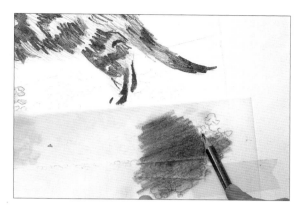

7 (Right) *Building up a complex pattern is a slow process and it is easy to make mistakes; to guard against this, a tracing is made from the completed area and the lines transferred to the working surface.*

6 (Above) *The dark background has been completed, with black cross-hatched over the blue, and a patterned cloth (which was not in the photograph) has been invented to create some interest in the foreground. As it is difficult to work without visual reference, a piece of fabric from the artist's collection of still-life draperies provided the basis for the pattern.*

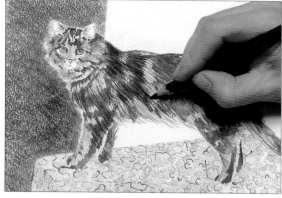

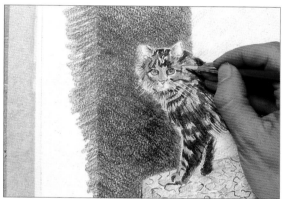

8 *With the background and patterned cloth finished, the artist returns to the focal point of the picture, and builds up detail and texture with a combination of wet-and-dry applications of pencil.*

9 *Finally, she uses white gouache paint and a small brush to touch in the whiskers. Coloured pencils are less opaque than either pastels or gouache paints, so clear whites cannot be produced by drawing over dark colours with white pencil.*

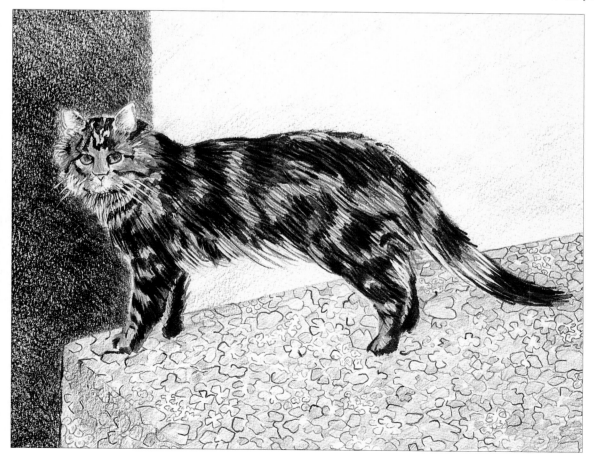

10 *In any finished drawing, the composition is as important as the representation of the subject; here careful planning has balanced the elongated shape of the cat's body with the patterned cloth and the dark rectangle of the background.*

BUILDINGS

The man-made environment of cities, towns and villages provides a wealth of varied and exciting drawing subjects, whether you are interested in architectural styles or simply in atmosphere. It is sometimes thought that drawing buildings is a special skill, but, although detailed "architectural renderings" are specialized and have a particular purpose, buildings and townscapes present no more of a problem than any other subject, and are almost certainly easier than drawing the nude figure. What puts many people off is the word "perspective" – most of us know that linear perspective is based on mathematics and, for those of us who failed to grasp geometry at school, that is quite enough to cause alarm and despondency.

CONVERGING PARALLELS

It is true that the laws of perspective were arrived at originally through mathematics, but it is not true that they cannot be understood by non-mathematical people. The basic rules are really very simple, and they always bear out the evidence of your own eyes. Most people must at some time have walked or driven down a straight road and noticed how the two sides converge in the distance. This apparent meeting of receding parallel lines is one of the many tricks the eye plays with reality – the lines don't really meet, but in visual terms they do, and drawing is concerned with what we see. Without perspective it would be impossible to create the illusion of our three-dimensional surroundings on a flat piece of paper.

As parallel lines appear to come closer and closer together until they meet, it follows that things get smaller the further away they are. Imagine a row of identical buildings along the road. If you were to

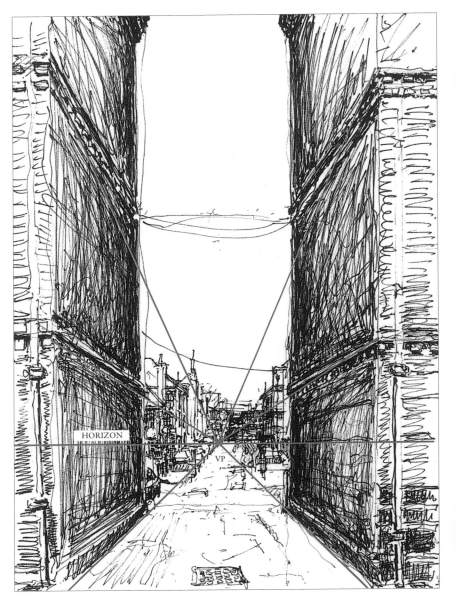

draw one line through the top of the roofs and another below the doors, they would be receding parallel lines too, and would meet at the same place as those for the sides of the road, with the houses becoming smaller and smaller. Again, the effect of this law of diminishing size is something that everyone must have observed.

VANISHING POINTS

The place where the parallel lines meet is called the vanishing point, for obvious reasons, and it is located on an imaginary line called the horizon. This is the most important fact of all because, although the line is imaginary, it isn't arbitrary – it is your own eye level. This is why perspective changes as soon as you move your own

Central vanishing point

(Above) *The drawing has been done from a central position, so the vanishing point is also in the centre, with the receding parallel lines sloping down to the horizon line, which is at the level of the artist's eye. In fact the receding lines at the top of the drawing are not entirely correct – they should slope more steeply – but drawings can often be the better for small inaccuracies in the perspective.*

Moving position

(Right) *The artist has now moved to the left in order to see more of the right-hand wall, and the vanishing point has also changed position. The horizon, however, remains constant, as this drawing has been done from the same level as the first one.*

viewpoint, even from a sitting to a standing position. You have changed the horizon, the vanishing point and the direction of the parallel lines.

There is, of course, one further complication: there are often two or more different vanishing points, depending on your angle of viewing. If you are drawing a house from an angle, both planes will be receding from you, so lines drawn through the tops and bottoms of each would meet at their own separate vanishing points. In an old town or village, houses may be set at odd angles to each other, resulting in many different vanishing points.

PERSPECTIVE BY EYE

In such cases you cannot possibly establish the exact position of each vanishing point, but it is important to mark in the horizon line and, if possible, the vanishing point for one key building of the scene before you. You can work out the other receding lines by holding up a pencil or ruler and tilting it

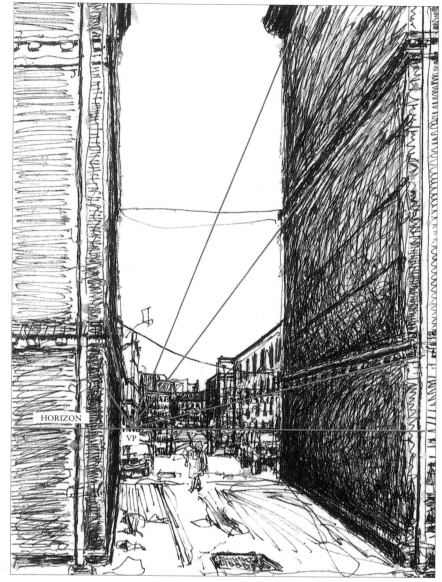

Two vanishing points

(Left) *The majority of architectural subjects have at least two different vanishing points, depending on how many planes there are and the angle from which they are viewed. Here there are two, with the converging parallels sloping more sharply down to the horizon line on the right. All three drawings, by John Townend, are in pen and ink.*

Continued ▷

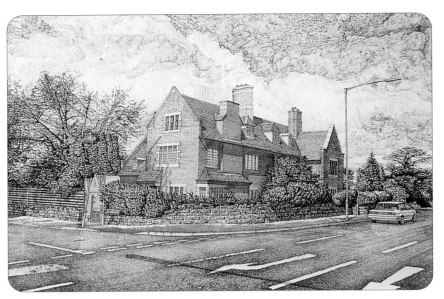

Perspective and proportion

(Left) *In Paul Bartlett's pen-and-ink drawing, a study made for a painting, the perspective is impressively accurate, as is the observation of the building's proportions. Notice the care taken over the number of bars in each window and the exact size of each brick and roof tile.*

Shapes and colours

(Below) *Town scenes, which present a variety of different elements, provide an opportunity to explore contrasts of shape, surface texture and colour. In his sketchbook study in coloured pencil, David Cuthbert's interest has been primarily in the lively patterns made by the buildings, street furniture, flags and shadows.*

Interiors

(Below) *The inside of a building is as interesting and rewarding to draw as the exterior, and you have the additional bonus of being protected both from the weather and inquisitive eyes. In his pen-and-ink drawing* The Church Organ Before Renovation *John Townend has made an exciting composition based mainly on the interplay of curves and diagonal lines.*

until it coincides with the angles of the roof, window tops or other features, as explained under figure drawing.

You do not have to get all the vanishing points exactly right – indeed this will be impossible, as many of them may be outside the picture area – but do make checks from time to time if you see something that doesn't look right. If you misjudge one angle and try to relate all the others to it the drawing will become distorted. And if you are bad at drawing straight lines don't be afraid to use a ruler, at least at the start of a drawing. Vertical lines really do have to be vertical in architectural subjects.

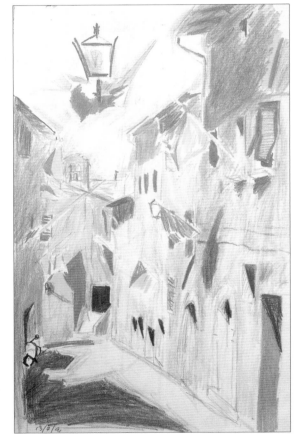

SCALE AND PROPORTION

Proportion is every bit as important as perspective – perhaps even more so. While it is correct (or reasonably correct) perspective which makes a drawing look realistic and the building not about to fall over, it is well-observed proportion which conveys character. You would not expect to draw a portrait without paying attention to the size of your sitter's eyes in relation to his

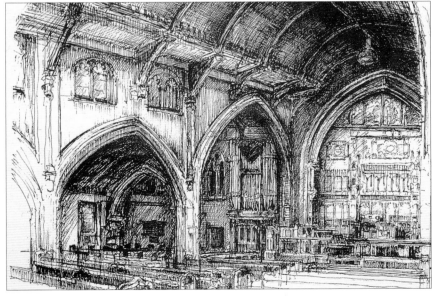

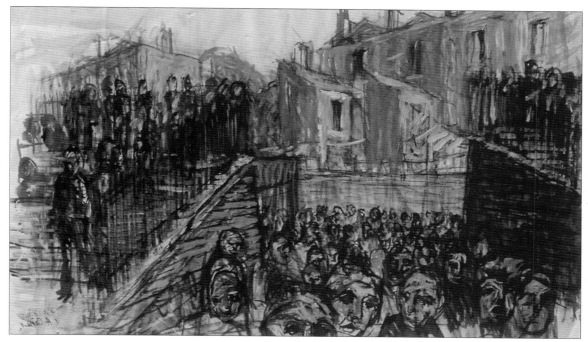

Composition

(Below) *Making a finished drawing from sketches or photographs gives you more chance to adjust reality. Ray Evans sketches continually to amass a store of visual information, and when he makes finished drawings he often combines elements from several sketchbook studies. His* Port Isaac *is in pen and watercolour.*

or her face, but it is surprising how many people ignore the importance of the size of windows and doors, or the heights of roofs in relation to walls.

When drawing a designed building such as a historic cathedral or fine country house, such factors are naturally taken into account, because the grand scale of the building or the carefully planned balance of the architectural features are the principal attractions of the subject. But scale and proportion are always important, even when your subject is an old wooden barn or a higgledy-piggledy collection of cottages or town houses; these are the characteristics which will give your drawing a convincing "sense of place".

Relative sizes can be measured by holding up a pencil at arm's length and moving your thumb up and down it, but if you are drawing sight-size you can be more accurate by using a ruler to read off the actual measurements. Work out the height of the building in relation to its width, the proportion of wall to roof, and the number and size of the windows. Don't forget that the laws of diminishing size make the spaces between windows become smaller as they recede, as well as the windows themselves – this is a trap for the unwary. Be particularly

careful with doors, as they will look structurally impossible if they are too small, and bizarre if they are too large – doors are designed so that the average person can pass comfortably in and out without having to stoop or walk in sideways. People in a townscape give an indication of scale as well as creating a feeling of atmosphere, but make sure that the doors you put in can accommodate them.

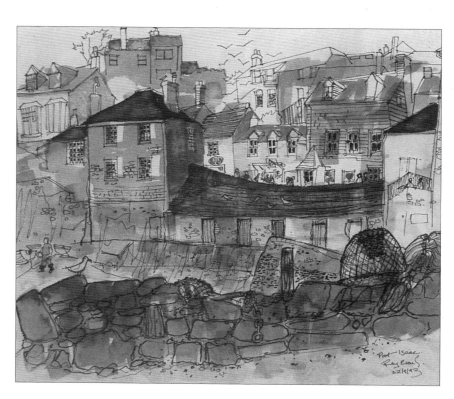

MIXED-MEDIA DEMONSTRATION

Karen Raney is an artist who enjoys experimenting with different media and different techniques, in both her drawings and her paintings. Her subject matter is as varied as her methods, but as a city dweller she is particularly interested in the challenge and stimulation of urban scenes. She uses photographs as a starting point when it is not possible to work direct from the subject – which can be difficult in towns and cities – but does so selectively, rejecting any elements in the photograph which she does not require for her composition.

1 *The artist intends to use a version of the sgraffito technique in combination with pencil and Conté crayon. She has begun by scribbling all over the paper with an oil bar, which is similar to a thick, soft oil pastel. Having drawn over this with Conté crayon, she now applies more in selected areas.*

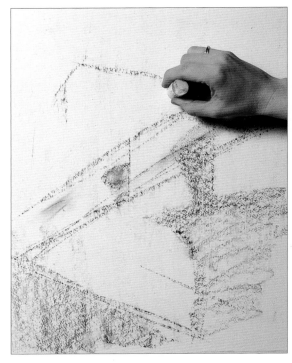

2 *The Conté crayon is smudged with a finger so that it mixes into the layers of oil bar beneath. The oil and the texture of the heavy watercolour paper have broken up the Conté marks, creating a nice soft effect.*

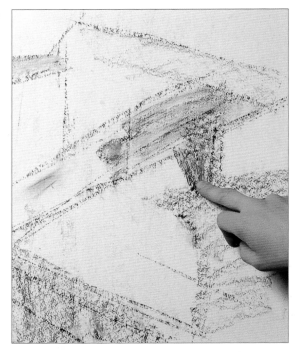

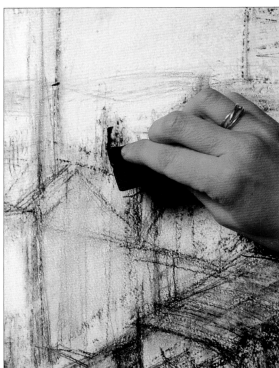

3 *Conté crayon is now inscribed more heavily over the first applications of oil and crayon. The drawing is kept loose and free at this stage, with the shapes evolving very gradually.*

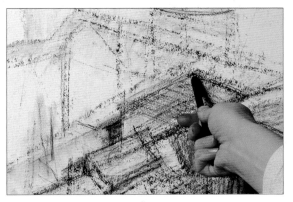

4 *The Conté has been applied quite heavily over the oil crayon, and the corner of a plastic card is employed, firstly to scratch into it and then to re-apply the resulting mixture of oil and Conté, which has become rather like paint.*

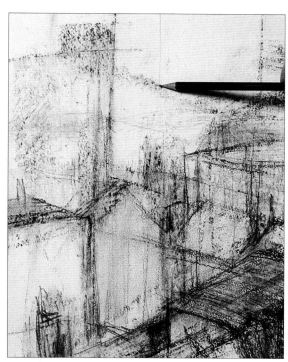

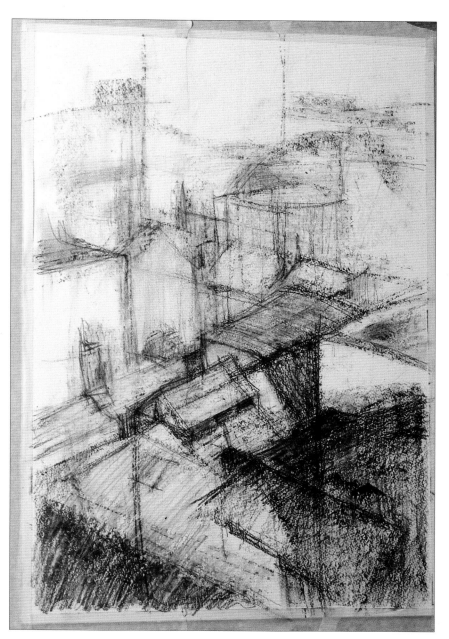

5 *The composition is allowed to emerge gradually, as the artist wished to establish the foreground before deciding on how many of the background buildings to include. She now uses a soft pencil to mark the side of a more distant building.*

6 (Right) *Detailed definition will be left until the final stages; concentration now is on the composition, the main perspective lines and the distribution of lights and darks.*

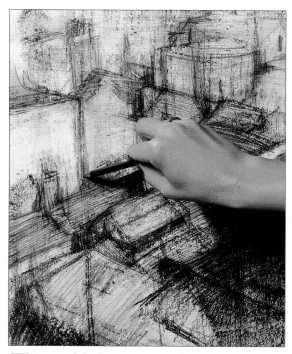

7 *Some of the lines are strengthened with soft pencil. In this photograph you can clearly see the effect of scratching and scraping with the plastic card, particularly in the foreground.*

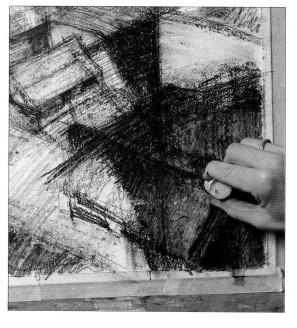

8 *A further application of oil bar again mixes with the Conté crayon beneath to produce a soft paste which can be manipulated and moved around.*

Continued ▷

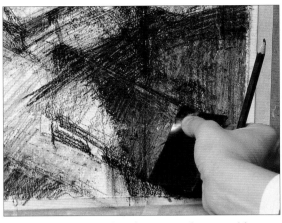

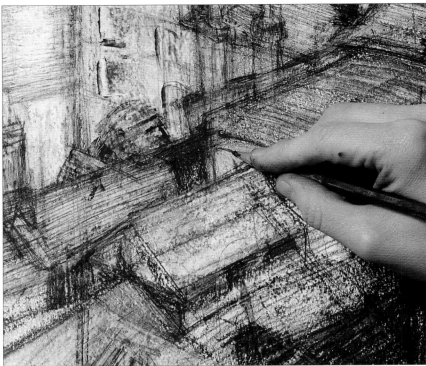

9 *The card is used to draw into the paste-like substance. The effect resembles brushmarks in a painting, with the corner of the card making a positive dark line.*

10 (Right) *The picture is sufficiently advanced for the artist to begin work on the details of the buildings and here she uses a 2B pencil, applying pressure to bite through the thin layer of oil bar.*

11 *To suggest the texture of the building on the left, she has applied a further layer of oil bar and now draws into it, using the pencil lightly so that it only partially dislodges the oily underlayer.*

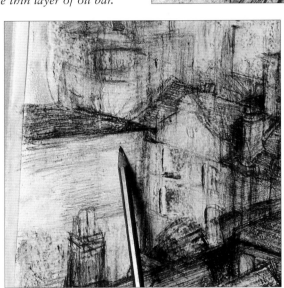

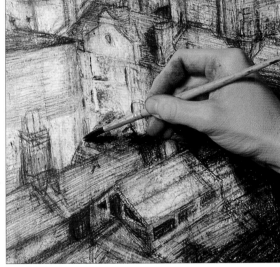

12 (Above) *A further hint of texture is given by painting over the lines of oil and Conté with white gouache. This also lightens an area which was previously rather too dark.*

13 *With all the details of the foreground buildings now completed, the artist turns her attention to the details in the background. Here she needs a soft effect to suggest distance, so she smudges the Conté-and-oil mixture with her fingertip.*

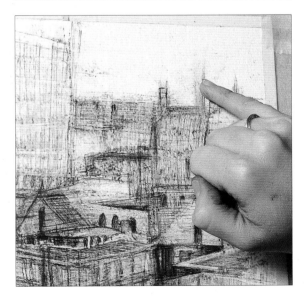

14 (Opposite) *The finished picture is not only an exciting evocation of a cityscape, it is also fascinating in terms of technique. The repeated layering and scraping of the Conté crayon and oil have produced a wonderful surface texture and density of tone which give the drawing something of the richness of an etching.*

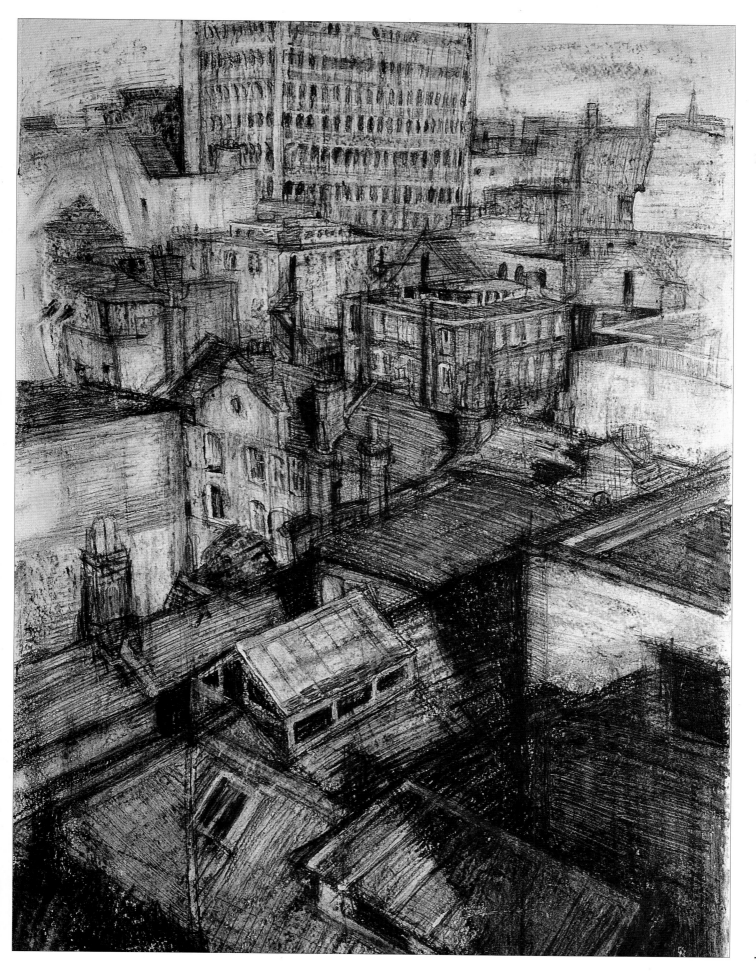

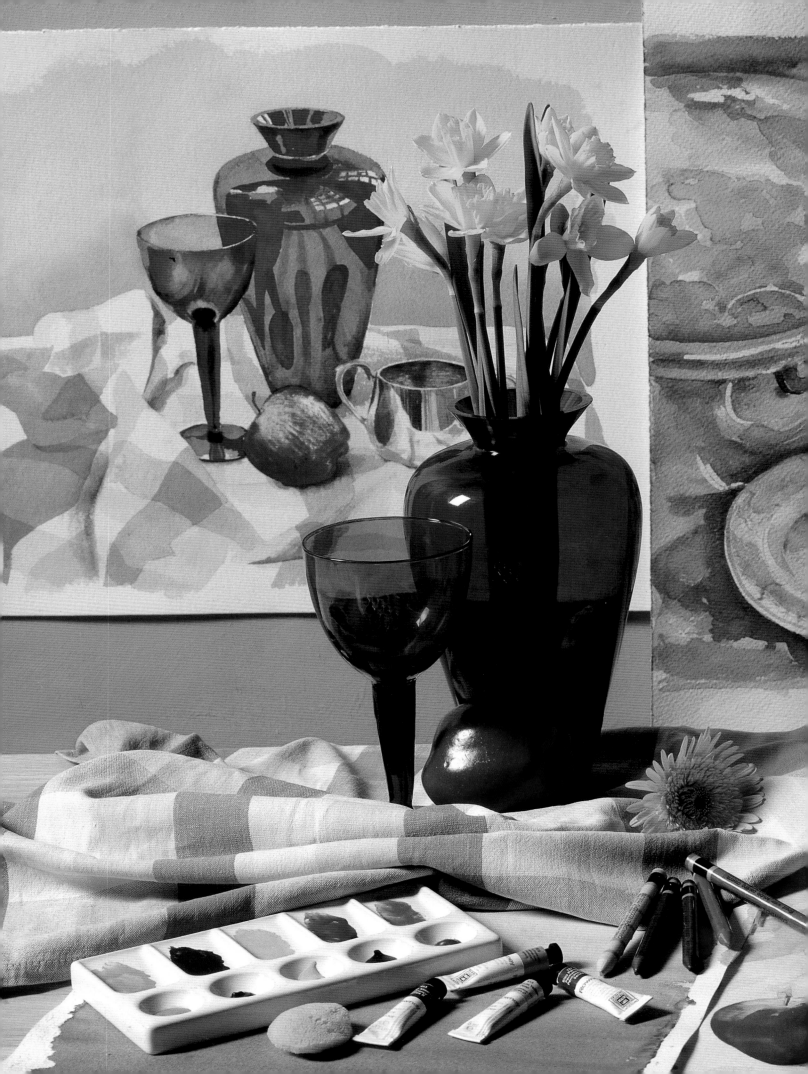

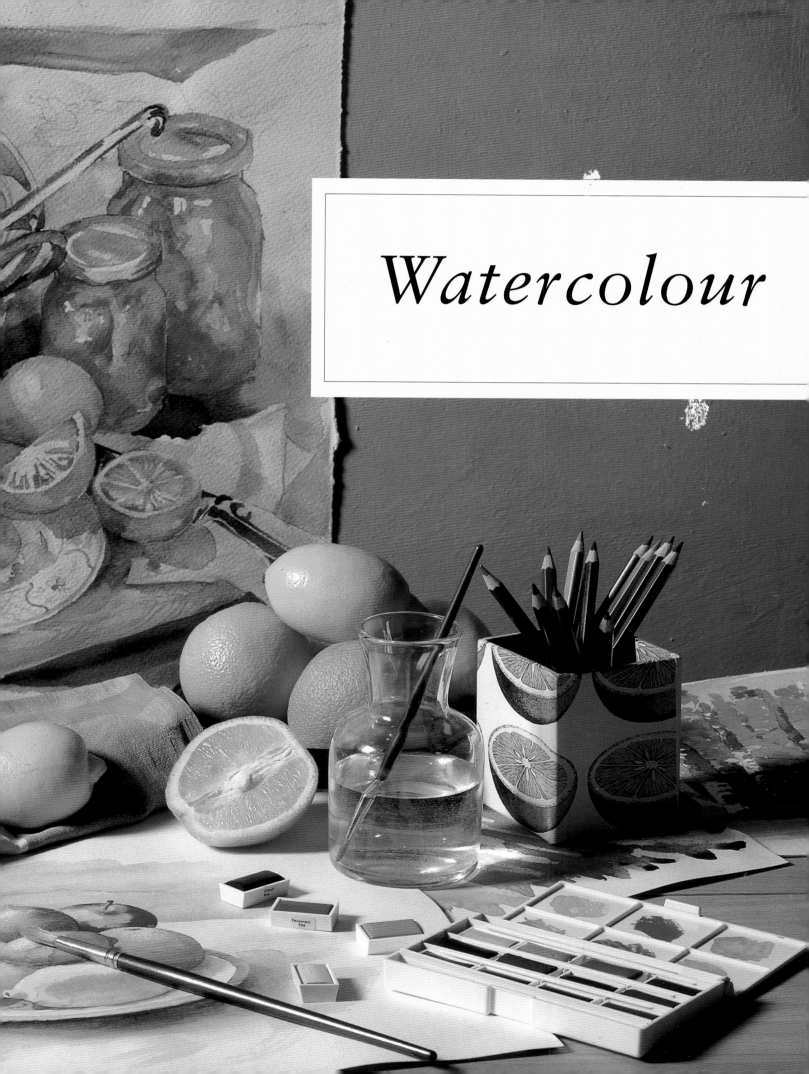

Watercolour

Introduction
ABOUT WATERCOLOUR

W
A
T
E
R
C
O
L
O
U
R

Since the 19th century, watercolour has been without question the most popular medium among amateur painters, and it continues to hold its position of pre-eminence today. It is not hard to find reasons for this. The rise of the medium coincided with the Victorian love of scenery and the natural world. Landscape and flowers were, and still are, the most frequently painted subjects, and water-colour, with its fluidity, freshness and sparkle, is perfect for both.

It is far from being a medium solely for amateurs. More and more professional artists are turning to watercolour, and their subject matter is less limited. The medium is used for portraits and figure studies, for still lifes and cityscapes – indeed anything which can be painted is painted in watercolour.

WATERCOLOUR IN THE PAST
In fact, there is nothing new about the medium's popularity with professionals. Although we see mainly oil paintings when we visit historic collections of paintings, giving the impression that watercolour was regarded as a poor relation, this was dictated more by market forces than by anything else. On the whole, patrons and

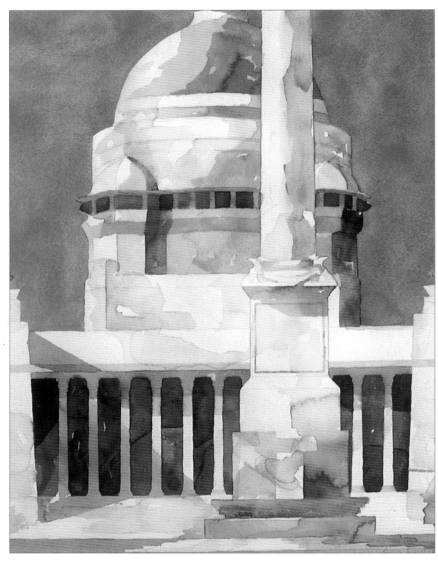

OLIVIA FRASER
VICEROY'S HOUSE, NEW DELHI
(Above) *This striking painting, with its deep, rich colours, quickly dispels one of the common myths about watercolour – that it is a wishy-washy medium. The artist has controlled the paint with great assurance, taking the dark colour of the sky carefully around the edges of the building, and, on the building itself, laying one wash over another to create a patchwork of crisp-edged shapes.*

(Left) *Most watercolour artists own a selection of watercolour tubes and pans.*

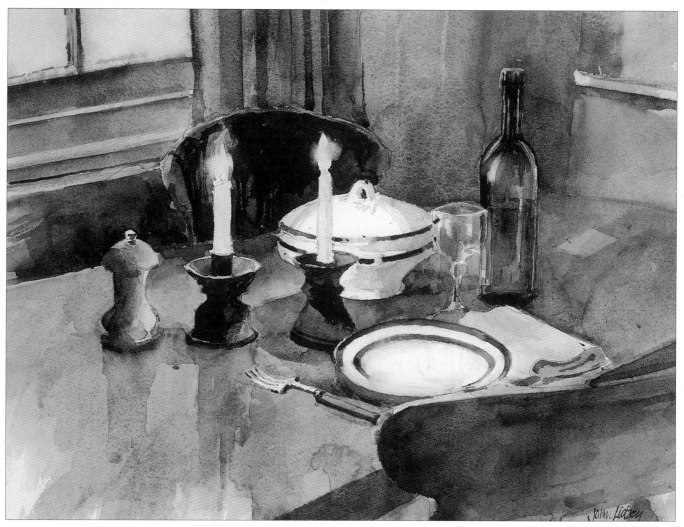

JOHN LIDZEY
STILL LIFE WITH CANDLES

(Above) *This artist enjoys the unpredictability of watercolour; he encourages colours to bleed into one another, forming pools and backruns. However, although this still life appears free and spontaneous both in arrangement and in the manner of execution, the artist has chosen and placed the objects to form a pleasing composition, and he controls the watercolour with equal care, using pieces of cotton wool (cotton balls) to halt the flow of colours and to lift out soft highlights such as those on the candle flames and glass.*

RONALD JESTY
KIPPERS

(Right) *Although this painting and John Lidzey's are both still lifes, they could not be more different in approach and technique. Here there are no pools or runs of paint, and each edge is meticulously clean and clear. Jesty likes to try out unusual viewpoints in his still-life paintings, and here he has chosen to look down on the subject so that he can exploit the pattern made by the fish and the dark triangles.*

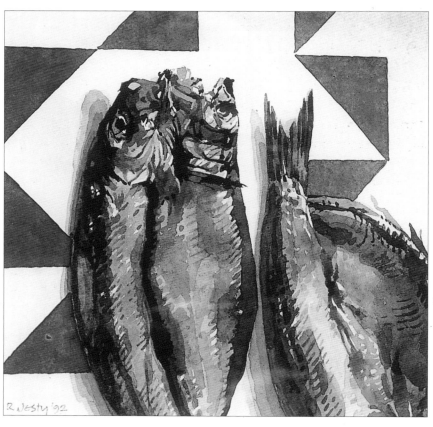

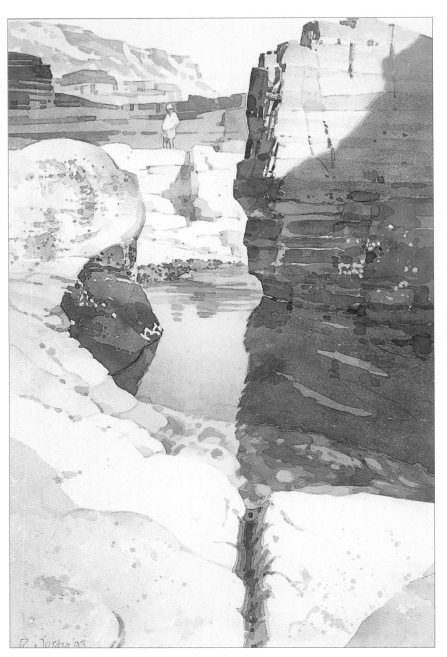

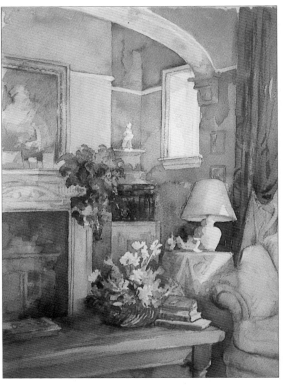

ELISABETH HARDEN
BLUE INTERIOR

(Above) *Painting interiors is a branch of still-life painting, although the subject is wider – you are dealing not just with objects but with their relationship to the surrounding space, so the perspective must be correct and the composition well planned. The artist begins with rough sketches to plan the composition, then makes a careful drawing.*

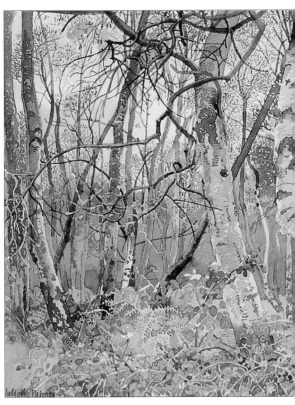

RONALD JESTY
ROCK POOL

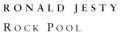

(Above) *This artist achieves his crisp effects and dense, glowing colours by working wet on dry, reserving highlights by painting carefully around them. You can see this effect on the background hills, the dark areas of rock and the water, where small patches of light-coloured paint have been left uncovered by later dark washes of colour.*

buyers wanted large, imposing oil paintings, particularly for commissioned portraits, so artists tended to reserve watercolour for their more private works, or for sketches used as reference for oil paintings.

A notable exception to this general rule was a group of 18th-century English painters who worked entirely in watercolour, painting landscapes and seascapes. Most particularly, the work of John Sell Cotman and Thomas Girtin (a genius who died tragically young) is well worth looking at in books of reproductions, as are the watercolours of J.M.W. Turner, whose unconventional and innovative techniques

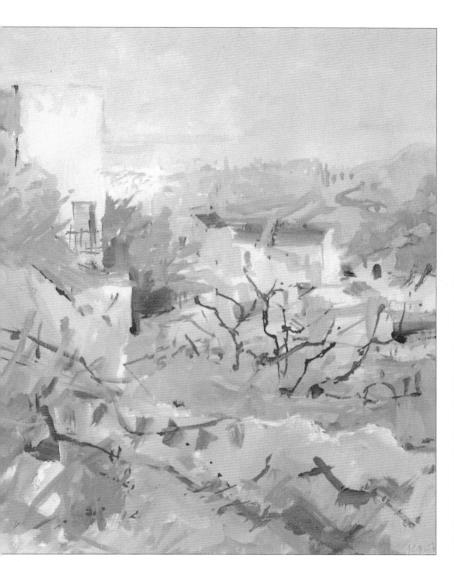

KEN PAINE
AMELIA

(Below) *At first sight, this expressive portrait might well be mistaken for an oil painting, but in fact it is watercolour with the addition of Chinese white. The artist made no initial pencil drawing, but started immediately with a brush and thin paint, gradually increasing the amount of white.*

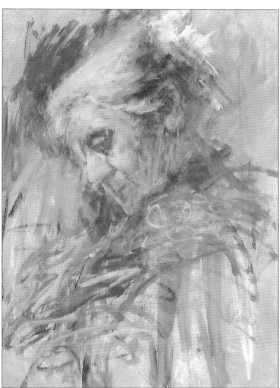

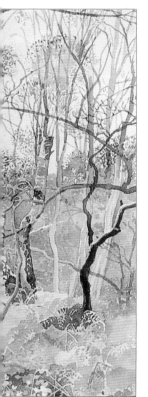

JOAN ELLIOTT BATES
FROM THE MULE PATH, SOUTH SPAIN

(Above) *Opaque paint has also been used for this charming landscape painted on location, but in this case it is gouache rather than watercolour mixed with white. The effect is very similar if the gouache is used fairly thinly, as it has been here, although you can achieve thicker, more solid colour if required.*

JULIETTE PALMER
BIRCH TRUNKS

(Left) *In this evocative and intricately detailed painting there is a strong emphasis on the pattern formed by the intertwining trunks and branches. The textures too have been described with great care, with a succession of small, delicate brushstrokes used for the trunks and distant clumps of twigs. The fine highlights in the foreground, which play an important part in the composition, were reserved by painting darker washes around lighter colours.*

are an endless source of inspiration. The giant of watercolour painting in America, at a slightly later date, was Winslow Homer, whose magical landscapes are now accorded the recognition they deserve (in his own lifetime, his oil paintings were better known).

MYTHS AND PREJUDICES

For some reason, watercolour has attracted a more comprehensive – and often inexplicable – list of dos and don'ts than any other medium. People feel that there is a "correct" way of working and that any departure from this constitutes a kind of unfaithfulness to the medium. For example, we are told that we must never use opaque white because it will spoil the lovely translucence of the colours; while good painting aids such as masking fluid are

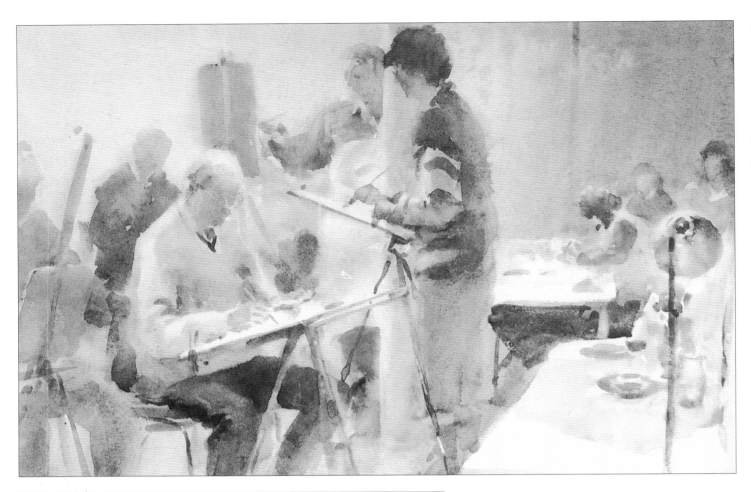

TREVOR CHAMBERLAIN
STILL-LIFE SESSION AT THE SEED WAREHOUSE

(Above) *Figure groups are not the easiest of subjects to tackle in watercolour, as it is not possible to make extensive corrections, but this painting shows that in skilled hands there is nothing the medium cannot do. Each brushstroke has been placed with care and, although the artist has worked largely wet into wet, he has controlled the paint so that it has not spread randomly over the surface.*

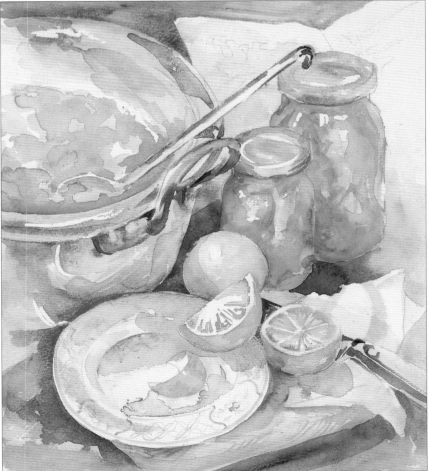

ELISABETH HARDEN
MAKING MARMALADE

Here the contrast between warm and cool colours has been skilfully exploited to highlight the dominant colour – orange. Although the colour scheme is deliberately limited, the artist has introduced a range of greens, blues and warm yellow-browns into the shadows to create variety and form colour links which unify the composition.

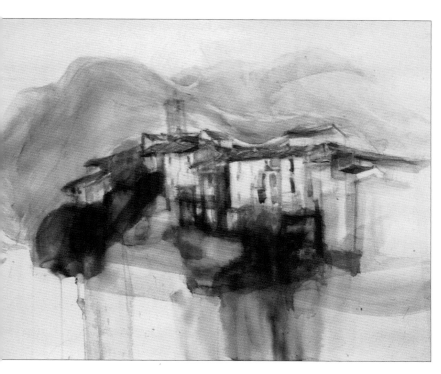

KAREN RANEY
ST-LAURENT-DE-CERDANS
(Left) *Watercolours are usually painted with the board held flat or at a slight angle, but in this on-the-spot painting the artist has worked with the board upright on an easel, causing the paint to run down the paper at the bottom of the picture. She has left the foreground otherwise undefined – the runs of paint hint at reflections in water.*

MIKE BERNARD
COW PARSLEY AND HOUSE
(Below) *Bernard seldom uses one medium on its own; here he has combined watercolour with expressive pen drawing. This has allowed him to introduce touches of detail into the foreground while keeping both the drawing and the watercolour washes unrestrained. The heads of the cow parsley are ink blots dropped from the pen, which have spread in places into the surrounding colours, and the linear highlights were achieved by scratching into dry paint.*

described as "mechanical" and therefore in some way immoral. Eyebrows are raised if you try anything new – it is simply not done. Interestingly, all these theories of correct procedure have only sprung up in this century, while the more rigid rules surrounding oil painting were the product of 18th- and 19th-century academic tradition and have since been largely abandoned. The best 19th-century watercolours, particularly those by Turner, reveal an enormous variety in the methods used, as well as many practices which might be frowned upon today. Turner used opaque paint; he moved the paint around on the picture surface and allowed colours to run; he smudged paint with his fingers and even scratched into it in places. In short, he used the medium as the servant of his ideas rather than the other way around.

The other myth about watercolour is that it is a particularly difficult medium to use. It is true that once you have made a mistake it isn't always possible to put it right, plus, of course, it can be hard to paint in the way that someone else thinks you should. Producing a good painting is never easy, whatever medium you use, but, once you have found your own way of working, the difficulties will be minimized.

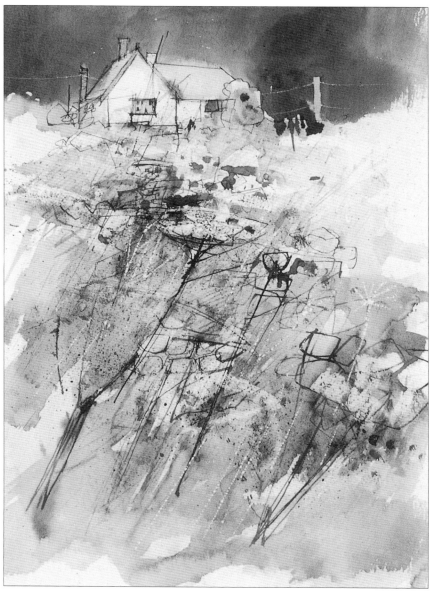

PAINTS & BRUSHES

One of the many delights of watercolour is that initially you don't need a great deal in the way of materials: a small paintbox of colours, a few brushes, some paper and a jar for water, and you can make a start. The materials and equipment listed here are the basics; as you become more experienced and develop your own style and way of working, you may want to try out special brushes or a particular kind of palette, therefore it is best to start simply and build up as you go along.

THE PAINTS

Watercolours are produced in tubes, pans and half-pans; the only rather hard decision to make if you are starting from scratch is which to buy. Both have their advantages and disadvantages. Tube colours enable you to make strong, bright colours and to mix up a lot of paint quickly (ideal for those who work on a large scale). However, they are slightly tiresome for outdoor sketching as, unlike pans, they don't fit neatly into a paintbox. Pans are perhaps the most popular choice. They control the paint neatly so that colours don't run into one another, but it is more difficult to release the paint; indeed, you may have to scrub with your brush for some time to produce enough colour for a large wash.

Whichever type you decide on, do make sure that you buy the best-quality paints, known as "artist's" colours. Most manufacturers produce inexpensive ranges, sometimes called "student's" colours and sometimes given a name coined by the particular manufacturer. These usually contain a smaller proportion of pigment than artist's colours and are bulked out with fillers, sometimes making it impossible to achieve any depth of colour or to avoid patchiness, particularly over large areas.

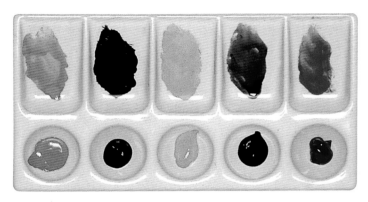

WATERCOLOUR PALETTE

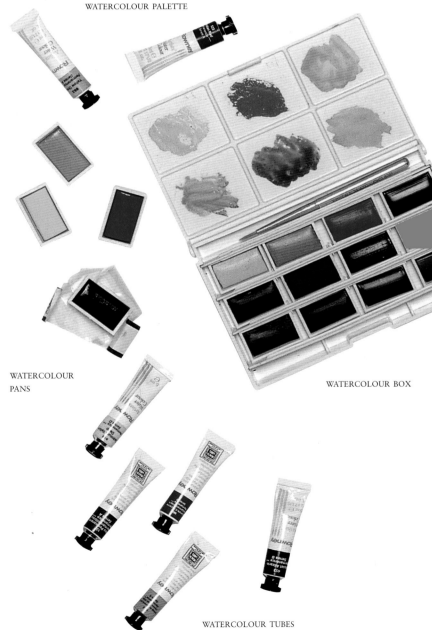

WATERCOLOUR PANS

WATERCOLOUR BOX

WATERCOLOUR TUBES

PAINTBOXES AND PALETTES

The kind of paintbox or palette you choose will depend on whether you are using pans (or half-pans) or tubes. For pans, you need a paintbox specially made for holding them in place, either with divisions for each pan or one long slot in which they all sit side by side. If you opt for tubes you must buy a separate palette or several small ones – or use an improvised palette such as an old plate. At one time you could buy metal paintboxes with small compartments into which the paint was squeezed; these have largely disappeared now, though you might still be lucky enough to find one.

BRUSHES

The best brushes for watercolour work are undoubtedly sables, but they are not recommended as part of a "starter kit" because they are prohibitively expensive, at least in the larger sizes. There are now many synthetic brushes, as well as sable and synthetic mixtures; brushes made from other soft hair such as ox and squirrel are also available. You may find you want to invest in one or two sables later on; if so, take heart from the fact that they are almost literally an investment – they will last a lifetime if you look after them.

Brushes are made in two basic shapes: round and flat. The former are essential, and you will probably require three different sizes: a small one for detail and two larger ones – the size will depend on the scale on which you work. Large flat brushes are useful for laying washes, but you won't need more than one to start with. There are other types of brush, such as mop brushes, which are also good for washes, but like sables these are expensive and should be regarded as a luxury item. You may want to invest in them later on.

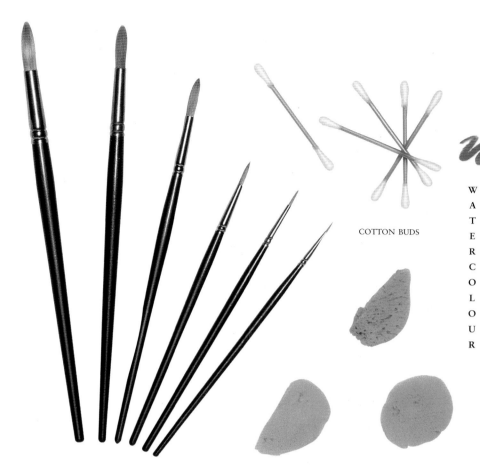

COTTON BUDS

SELECTION OF WATERCOLOUR BRUSHES

WATERCOLOUR SPONGES

OTHER ITEMS

Most watercolour painters have a small natural sponge in their box of equipment, which can be used for "lifting out" paint and for mopping up paint that threatens to run. It is also a good alternative to brushes for laying washes. Of course, you also need a jar to hold water, and paper.

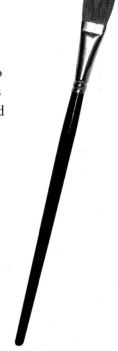

FLAT WATERCOLOUR BRUSH

PAPER

Watercolours are nearly always done on white paper; you can work on coloured paper, but this is the exception rather than the rule. The luminous quality that attracts so many people to watercolour work is the result of the white paper reflecting back through the layers of transparent paint. Colours are made lighter by using the paper as the white – heavily diluted paint allows much of the paper to show through, while thicker paint covers it.

PAPER SURFACES AND WEIGHTS

Basically there are three types of watercolour paper: rough, medium rough and smooth. They are all machine-made and are given names derived from the method of production. Rough paper has no alternative name, but smooth paper is known as "hot-pressed" and medium paper as "Not" (i.e. not hot-pressed), or sometimes as "cold-pressed". There are also handmade papers, which vary widely in texture. These are expensive and not always easy to handle; they are best left until you have gained a considerable degree of skill.

The vast majority of watercolour painters, amateur and professional alike, use Not surface paper. This has a slight texture, which holds the paint in place but does not break up the colour. Rough paper can be hard to manage, as the heavy texture tends to interfere with detail, and smooth paper can produce blotchy effects because the paint slides about on it.

All these papers are made in different weights, expressed as pounds (lb). This refers to the weight of a ream of paper – 500 sheets. Weights vary between 70lb, which is very thin, and 300lb, which is so thick that it resembles board. The thicker the paper the more it costs, but very thin paper must be stretched first.

STRETCHING WATERCOLOUR PAPER

Stretching the paper before use prevents it from buckling when you put on the wet paint. Colours laid over ridges and bumps may take a long time to dry out – and sometimes never do so, thus spoiling the effect of your finished work. Paper which is lighter than about 200lb usually needs to be stretched, particularly if you use a lot of wet washes or work wet into wet. The paper used for most types of watercolour sketching pads is 140lb, which will certainly buckle if you work on a large scale and build up many layers of colour, but it is reasonably safe for small-scale outdoor work.

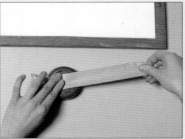

1 ROUGH 2
NO

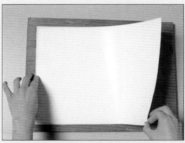

1 *Soak the paper for a few minutes in a bath or sink. When you are sure it has absorbed the water evenly, lift it out by one corner, shake off the excess moisture and place it on the drawing board.*

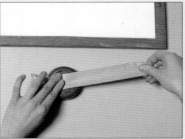

2 *Cut four pieces of gumstrip, one for each side, and dampen well by running them across a wet sponge. The gumstrip should be 2.5 cm (1 in) wide for an average-sized painting and up to 5 cm (2 in) wide for a larger one.*

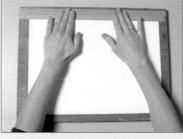

3 *Place a piece of gumstrip along one long edge of the paper and smooth it out firmly from the centre, to ensure that it makes contact with both paper and board at every point.*

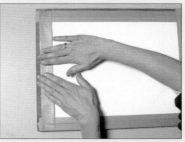

4 *Repeat the process for the second long edge and then each alternate short edge. Don't worry if the paper begins to buckle slightly; it will dry flat.*

HITE
(90LB)

4 HOT-PRESSED

5, 6, 7 AND 8 TINTED NOT

GUMSTRIP

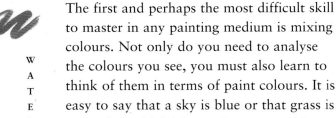

Colour
ADVICE ON MIXING

The first and perhaps the most difficult skill to master in any painting medium is mixing colours. Not only do you need to analyse the colours you see, you must also learn to think of them in terms of paint colours. It is easy to say that a sky is blue or that grass is green, but which blue and green would you choose from your paintbox? Which other colours could you mix in to achieve the effect you can see in your subject?

Most of this comes with experience and, it has to be said, after a certain amount of trial and error. But it is useful to know some facts about the paint colours themselves in order to understand what may or may not happen when you mix them.

PRIMARY AND SECONDARY COLOURS
Red, blue and yellow cannot be produced by mixing other colours, so they are called the primary colours. When mixed in pairs, these make the secondary colours: green

from blue and yellow; purple from blue and red; orange from red and yellow. But there is a slight complication here because the primary colours are not absolute – if you look at the starter palette below you will see that there are three different versions of each blue and yellow and two of red.

So before you begin to mix secondaries, you need to know which are the best primary colours to choose to mix the exact shade you want. All colours have different biases, or leanings towards other colours. Of the two reds in the starter palette, for example, one (cadmium red) is vivid and slightly yellow, while the other (alizarin crimson) leans towards blue. To mix bright secondaries you must choose the two primaries that are biased towards each other. Thus ultramarine (red biased) and alizarin crimson make a good purple, but ultramarine and cadmium red do not. For more muted secondaries, choose primaries which have an opposing bias.

Making bright mixtures
The mixtures shown here have all been made from two primary colours which have a bias towards each other. The resulting colours (secondaries) are all vivid, excepting the olive green.

Making subtle mixtures
Here primaries which have an opposite bias combine to make more muted mixtures.

Mixing browns and greys
Different permutations of the primary colours can produce a wide range of tertiary colours – browns, greys and muted greens. The proportion of each colour will depend on the mixture you are aiming at and on the strength of the individual colours – some pigments are stronger than others.

A STARTER PALETTE

The vast range of colours produced by paint manufacturers can be very bewildering for the beginner. How do you choose from this profusion, and how many colours do you need? In fact you don't need very many because you generally have to mix colours to produce equivalents to those you see in the real world. This suggested palette contains twelve colours, which may be over-generous – some of the great watercolourists of the past used no more than three or four.

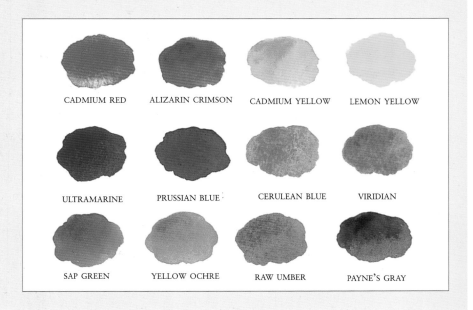

CADMIUM RED   ALIZARIN CRIMSON   CADMIUM YELLOW   LEMON YELLOW

ULTRAMARINE   PRUSSIAN BLUE   CERULEAN BLUE   VIRIDIAN

SAP GREEN   YELLOW OCHRE   RAW UMBER   PAYNE'S GRAY

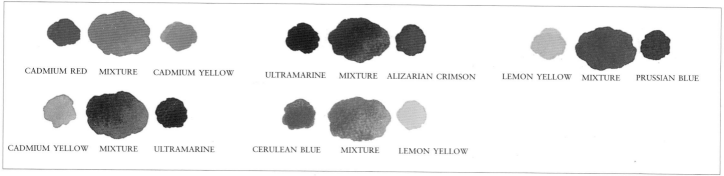

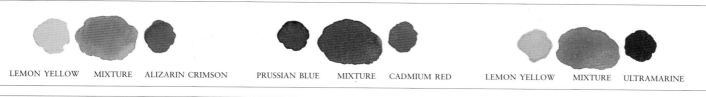

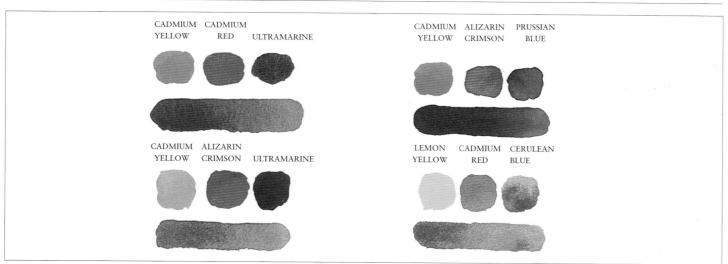

TERTIARY COLOURS

A secondary colour is a mixture of two other colours; when a third colour is added, the result is known as a tertiary colour. These are the so-called neutrals – the browns, beiges and "coloured greys" which play an important part in painting. There is no recipe for mixing these colours because there are so many possible ways of achieving them, but an interesting and varied range can be created simply by mixing three primary colours in different proportions.

WHY MIX?

You may wonder why it is necessary to mix secondary and tertiary colours at all when there are so many ready-made greens, purples and browns. But even if you were to buy a whole manufacturer's range you would seldom have exactly the right colour; furthermore, mixed colours are more subtle and more convincing than bought ones simply because you are making them up yourself, in direct response to a subject.

It is not always necessary to mix completely from scratch. The starter palette contains two secondary colours (the two greens) and two tertiary ones (raw umber and Payne's gray), all of which form good foundations for mixtures and can sometimes even be used as they are in certain areas of a picture. However, you would be well advised to practise colour mixing as much as possible, making charts like the ones shown here, as this will give you the hands-on experience for which there is no substitute.

A Painting in Six Primaries

Making colour charts like those shown on the previous pages will help you to devise useful colour mixtures, giving you valuable experience in handling the medium; but the best way to learn to paint is to do it – that is, to paint an actual subject, choosing and mixing the colours accordingly. The idea behind this exercise is to discover whether you can make all the secondary and tertiary colours that you need for your work by using only the primary colours – two reds, three blues and three yellows.

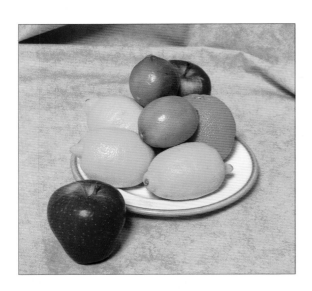

You can choose any subject that appeals to you, but don't make it too complicated. You could set up a simple still life like the one shown here or, if you like to paint landscape, you could work from a photograph. Another alternative would be to copy a painting you like from a book of reproductions. There is nothing wrong with learning by copying. In this case, as you are only using six colours, your copy won't be exact; it will be what is known as a "transcription".

COLOURS USED *cadmium red, alizarin crimson, cadmium yellow, lemon yellow, ultramarine, Prussian blue*

1 *Having begun with a light brush drawing in yellow, the artist now paints in the shadow beneath the plate. This warm colour, mixed from cadmium red with small touches of ultramarine and lemon yellow, will later be modified by other colours laid on top.*

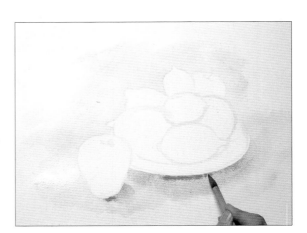

2 *The lemons present no problems, and the colours for these first washes do not require mixing. The lighter areas are pale lemon yellow, and the darker ones a stronger solution of cadmium yellow. Again, shadows will be added at a later stage.*

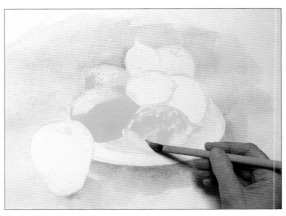

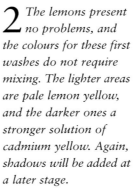

3 *Here the amount of water added to the colours is crucial. The paler pink at the top of the apple is well-watered alizarin crimson; beside this is a slightly stronger wash of the same colour, while for the body of the apple the crimson is more concentrated. Now a little blue is added to darken the red and tone it down slightly.*

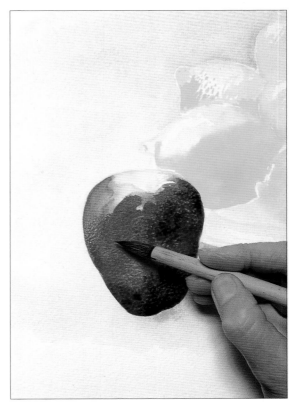

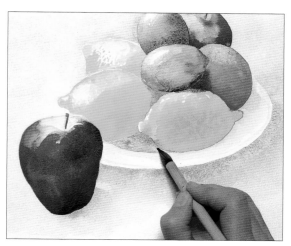

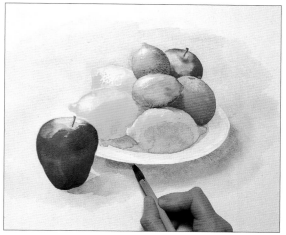

4 *The grey for the plate is mixed from ultramarine with small additions of lemon yellow and alizarin crimson, while the limes are mainly lemon yellow and Prussian blue, with light overlays of ultramarine for the shadows. These have been painted wet into wet so that they merge gently into the greens.*

5 *The same grey as that used for the plate is now washed over the original pinkish colour seen in Step 1. In watercolour work, colours are not only mixed in the paintbox or palette, they can also be modified and altered on the paper by laying one wash over another.*

6 *(Below) Final touches were added to darken the shadowed side of the lemon with a well-diluted mixture of ultramarine, lemon yellow and cadmium red, and to build up the forms of the other fruit with darker shadows. It is usually wise to avoid combining more than three colours, as this can make the mixture muddy; the majority of the mixtures here are of only two colours.*

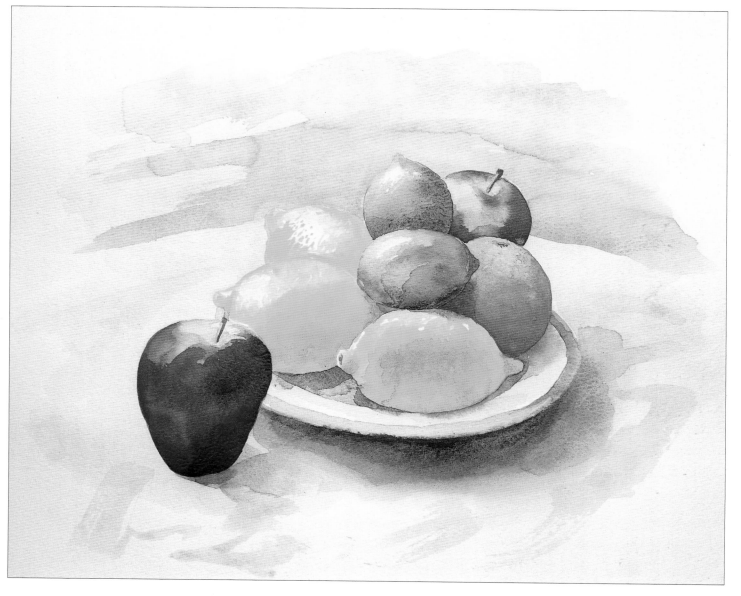

LAYING WASHES

Basically, watercolour painting is the process of building up a picture through a series of washes of paint diluted with water. A wash can cover the whole of the paper, half of it (perhaps for a sky) or just a small part; it can be roughly defined as colour that covers a wider area than an individual brushstroke could. In the later stages of a painting, definition may be added with small brushmarks or fine lines, but the washes come first and, because they are central to painting in watercolour, the first skill you must master is that of laying a completely even wash of colour.

MIXING COLOUR FOR A WASH

Washes must be laid quickly to prevent hard edges from forming. You cannot stop to make up more colour, so you must ensure that you have enough – washes use up a surprising amount of paint. The paint should be added to the water, not vice versa, but don't start with a large amount of water, or you could waste a good deal of paint achieving a strong enough mix. Instead, put a small amount of water into a saucer, palette or paintbox, pick up some colour with a moistened brush and stir it into the water. If it looks too light, add more paint, and if too dark add more water, repeating the process until you have the depth of colour you require. Stir the paint in well with the brush each time so that the particles of pigment are thoroughly dissolved and there are none left on the brush, otherwise you will have unsightly

DAVID CURTIS
SAILING BOATS
(Below) *The clear, pale sky behind the boats is achieved with a flat wash of watercolour.*

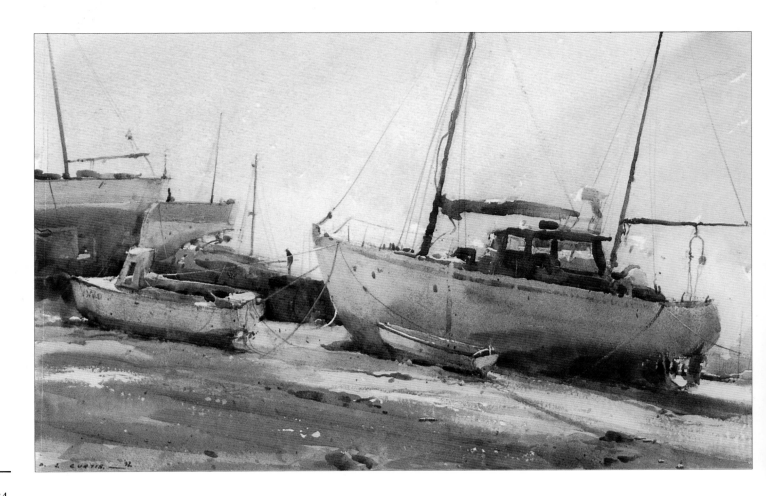

Flat wash on dry paper

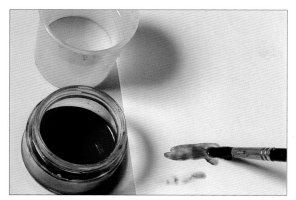

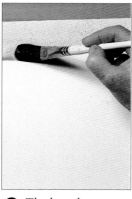

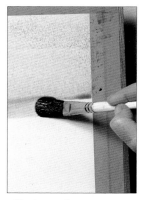

1 *The wash has been mixed in a jar rather than a paintbox because it is intended to cover a large area. Watercolour dries much lighter than it appears when wet, so the colour is tested on a spare piece of paper and allowed to dry before the wash is laid.*

streaks of colour. Before laying the wash, check the colour by painting some on a spare piece of paper and letting it dry. Watercolour becomes much lighter as it dries, and the colour may not be what you originally expected.

LAYING THE WASH

The kind of brush you use is a matter of personal preference. Some artists like a large round brush, others prefer a flat one, and some eschew brushes altogether and lay washes with a sponge. Whichever "tool" you use the method is the same. Unless you are using very heavy paper it should first be stretched on a board and propped at a slight angle. The brush (or sponge) is then swept right across the paper from one side to the other; as soon as this first band of colour is in place, the brush is recharged and another band laid below, slightly overlapping the first. This process is repeated until the whole area is covered.

The tilt of the board encourages the paint to run down the paper so that each new "line" of colour mingles with the one above. Some artists like to dampen the paper with clean water before laying a wash, to encourage the colours to blend and to avoid any lines forming between bands. It is worth trying out both methods in order to discover which you prefer.

2 *The board, on which the paper has been stretched with gumstrip, is propped at a slight angle, and the brush is taken smoothly from one side to the other.*

3 *Several successive bands of colour have now been laid. The angle of the board encourages the paint to flow downwards into each new band, so there are no perceptible boundaries.*

Flat wash on damp paper

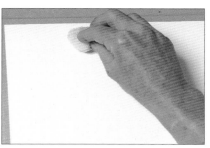

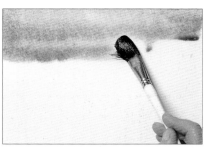

1 *The paper is first dampened all over with a small natural sponge, which is a vital piece of equipment in watercolour work.*

2 *The way the paint runs down the damp paper can be alarming initially, but it will dry perfectly flat. This is a quick, effective method for covering large areas.*

Laying a flat wash with a sponge

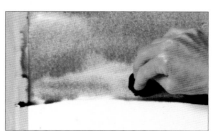

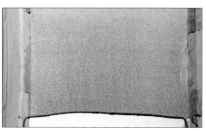

1 *Again working on damp paper, the sponge is taken from one side to the other. At this stage it is hard to believe that it will dry flat.*

2 *But it has. Because the paper was dampened, the darker areas of colour have flowed into the lighter ones, and the earlier irregularities have completely disappeared.*

Laying a gradated wash

1 *A band of full-strength colour is laid across the paper as usual; for each successive band the brush is dipped into the water and then into the paint mixture.*

2 *For artists who are interested in landscape painting this is the most useful type of wash, particularly for skies, which are usually lighter at the bottom.*

Laying a variegated wash

1 *Three colours are to be used and have been mixed up separately. The green touches the blue above so that the two colours blend together with no hard edges.*

2 *On this occasion the board is held flat and the paper is dry. The effect relies on the colours remaining distinct; on damp paper they would flow into one another and mix.*

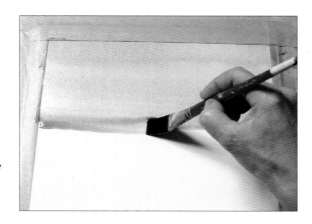

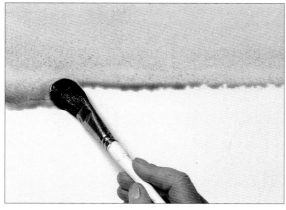

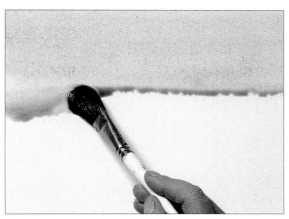

GRADATED WASHES

Skies are darker at the top than the bottom and a colour wash should reflect this. Laying gradated washes, as they are called, is more difficult than laying flat ones; the need to make the colours progressively weaker or stronger can result in a stripy effect if you are not careful. You can work from light to dark, adding more paint for each band, but it is much easier to control the effect if you begin with the full-strength colour and add more water each time. If you want a wash which is darker at the bottom, simply turn the board upside down and work in the same way.

For each new band of colour, dip the brush into the water before dipping it into the paint in order to weaken the wash mixture by exactly the same amount each time. For a more obvious gradation, you can dip the brush twice into the water, or even use water alone for the second band, in which case the colour from the bottom of the first band will flow into the dampened area, thus creating a paler shadow of itself. Gradated washes must always be done on dry paper, otherwise the different strengths of colour will even out.

VARIEGATED WASHES

Washes frequently contain more than one colour. For instance, an area of grass in a landscape might vary from blue-green to yellow-green, or the sea could contain distinct colour fluctuations. In this case you need to mix in advance all the colours you require, washing your brush between each new colour to keep it pure.

Multi-coloured washes can be controlled quite precisely as long as you test all the colours on spare paper before you start. If you are aiming for a perfect blend of colours, with no obvious boundaries, it is best to work on dampened paper; a frequent feature of such washes, however, is that they are not regular and perfect – it all depends on what you want. You can also make exciting random effects by dropping new colours into a still-damp wash, a technique known as wet into wet, which is discussed later.

COMPLICATED EDGES

Laying a wash to cover a piece of paper entirely is easy enough once you have got the hang of it, but how do you lay a wash that starts and stops exactly where you want it to? You may, for example, want to lay a wash for a sky, below which is a complex skyline of buildings or trees which must stay clean, because it is to be painted in different colours.

In fact, this is much easier than it sounds, but it does rely on making a good drawing to establish exactly where to stop the wash. There are two ways of working and the one you choose depends on whether you like to lay washes on damp or dry paper. If you prefer the former, simply dampen the paper in the area of the wash only, taking a wet brush carefully around your drawn outlines. Lay the wash as usual and it will stop obediently at the dry paper. If you want to lighten the colour slightly and ensure a smooth and even texture, then dab it with blotting paper which will absorb some of the excess paint.

The other method is to work upside down, taking the colour around the edges first. If you want a wash which is darker at the top, leave the board to dry upside down and at an angle; the colour will flow down – that is, up in terms of your picture.

Tricky edges: method 1

1 *The wash is to be laid on the sky but not the hills, so the paper has been dampened in the sky area only. The paint stops flowing as soon as it reaches the edge of the dry paper.*

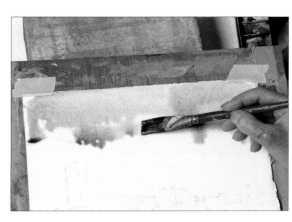

2 *Notice that the sky wash has dried completely flat. The paper is now dampened again, this time between the sky and the buildings, and a loose multi-coloured wash is laid.*

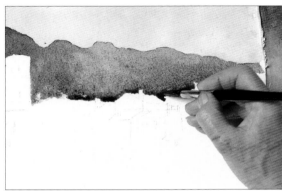

Tricky edges: method 2

1 *The board is turned upside down and a deep blue wash laid around the line of the roofs. A round brush with a good point is best for this method.*

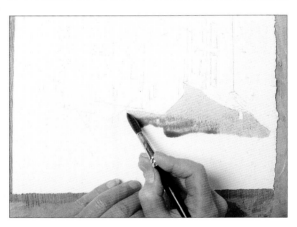

2 *The board has been tilted so that the paint flows downwards, that is, to the top of the sky area. It is left to dry in this position.*

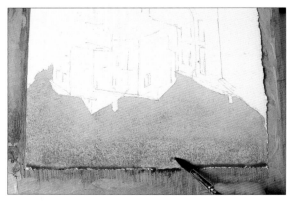

MAKING AN UNDERDRAWING

Unless you are just making quick sketches or coloured "doodles" to try out techniques and colour effects, it is important to start your work with a plan of campaign, which means a drawing. This establishes where to place the first washes and which areas to reserve for highlights. Bear in mind too that it is not easy to make major corrections to watercolours, so an initial drawing will save frustration later on.

You may groan at the idea, because it prevents you from getting down to what most people regard as the fun part of the exercise, which is putting on the colour. Also, of course, it seems a waste of valuable painting time – if you are working out of doors, every second counts. You may find in such cases that it is better to make the drawing on one day and paint on the next. Changing light is less important when you are drawing than when you are painting.

Too elaborate a drawing is unnecessary and you should keep it faint, otherwise the pencil marks may show through the lighter areas of colour. Avoid shading and try to restrict yourself to outlines, while making sure that you know what the outlines mean. If you have to amend the drawing, erase the wrong lines as soon as you are confident that the drawing is correct. Take care over erasing as the surfaces of some papers become scuffed rather easily, causing unpleasant blotches when the paint is applied. Use a soft plastic eraser or a kneaded putty one, keeping the pressure light to avoid spoiling the paper surface.

Making a pencil drawing

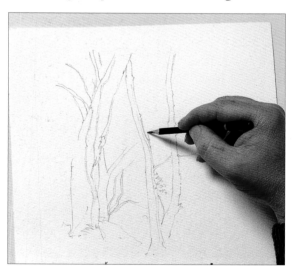

1 *The artist is using a fairly soft pencil (4B). Anything harder than a 2B could indent the surface of the paper, and is less easy to erase if you make a mistake.*

2 *(Right) The drawing has been kept to outlines only, but the lines are strong enough to provide a guide for the applications of paint. If the drawing is too pale it will quickly become obscured by the first washes.*

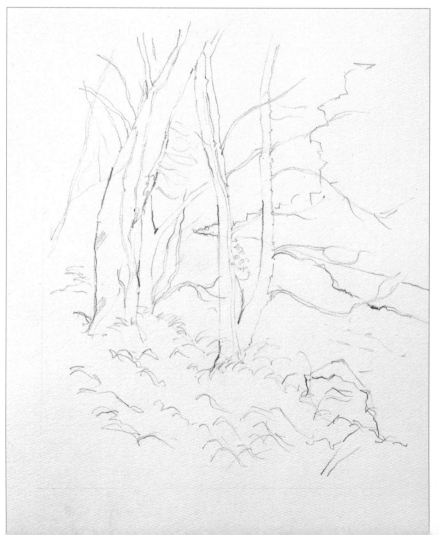

Squaring up

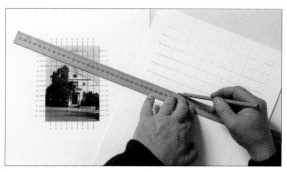

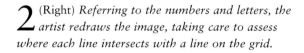

1 A grid of squares has been drawn over the photograph, and a larger grid is now marked out on the paper. Numbering the squares is important, as it is easy to make mistakes when transferring the visual information.

2 (Right) Referring to the numbers and letters, the artist redraws the image, taking care to assess where each line intersects with a line on the grid.

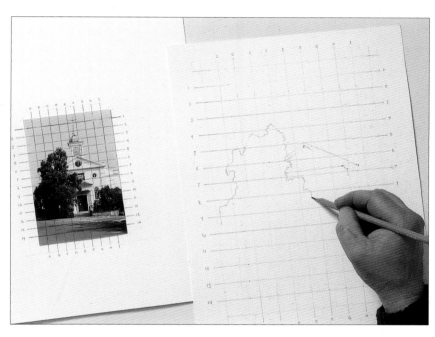

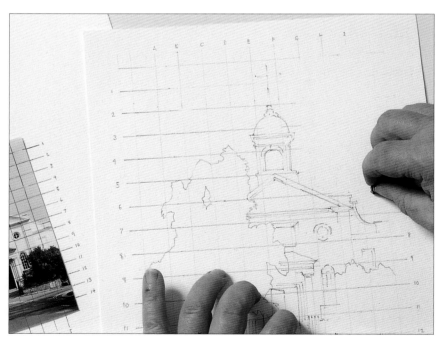

3 The grid lines are erased in the areas which are to be light in the painting because they would show through pale washes. A putty eraser is used to avoid any risk of scuffing the paper.

If you are working from a photograph (and don't be ashamed, because many artists do), you can enlarge the image and transfer it to the painting surface by a tried-and-tested method called squaring up. Using a ruler, draw a measured grid over the photograph and then another one, with larger squares, on the paper. You will have to work out the sizes of the squares mathematically according to the size you want your picture to be. For example, if those on the photograph are 1.3 cm (½ in) and those on the paper are 2.5 cm (1 in), the painting will be twice the size of the photograph. Once you have drawn the grids, simply transfer the information from one to the other, checking carefully to see where each line intersects a grid line. This is well worth the effort for any complicated subject, such as architecture, where one wrong angle can throw everything out. It is actually much easier for the eye to judge the exact angles of a subject by comparison with the straight right-angles of a grid.

WORKING WET ON DRY

Watercolour paints are transparent, and consequently paintings are built up in layers, working from light to dark. It is seldom possible to achieve a really dark colour with just one wash, because the paint must be diluted with water in order to spread, and the white of the paper will always show through to some extent. Thus the darkest colours are achieved by laying one wash over another until the required depth is achieved. This layering method, known as wet on dry because each wash must be fully dry before the next is added, is the "classic" watercolour technique. When each wash dries, it forms hard edges at the boundaries; these edges are a positive feature of wet-on-dry painting, adding crisp energy to the image.

The method relies for its success on careful planning. It is not wise to pile on too much colour; as a general rule you should limit yourself to not more than three overlaid washes, as otherwise the colours will begin to lose their clarity, becoming stirred up and muddy. Thus when you begin a painting you need to have a clear idea of what the finished work is to look like, as only in this way can you estimate the depth of colour you need for the first washes. Overlaid washes should always be restricted to relatively small areas of the picture.

You also need to plan the highlights. As you already know, the white in watercolour comes from the paper. White highlights are achieved by "reserving", which means leaving the shape as white paper and painting around it. Highlights are not always white, but areas of a light-coloured wash can be reserved in the same way, by leaving parts showing through overlaid washes. White highlights can be added in opaque paint, but for purity and sparkle you can't beat unblemished white paper.

Overlaid washes

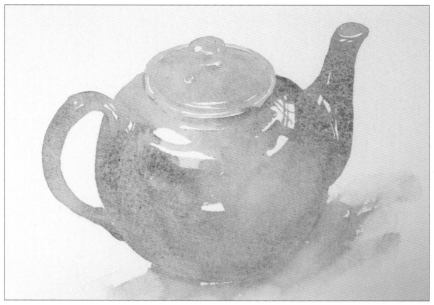

1 *The reflective surface produces blues and whites among the browns, so the artist has begun with a grey-blue wash, slightly darker in the shadow areas, reserving the areas of pure white highlight by painting around them.*

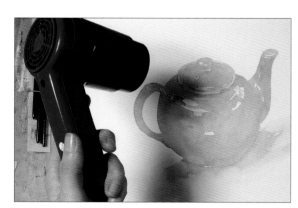

2 *Each wash must be completely dry before the next one is painted on top, so a hairdryer is used to speed up the process. This is a very useful piece of equipment when working indoors.*

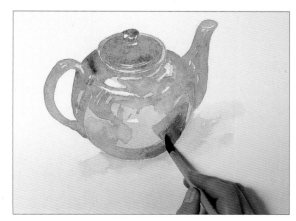

3 *The same light brown used for the top of the teapot is now introduced at the bottom. It is best to work from top to bottom whenever possible, to avoid smudging wet paint.*

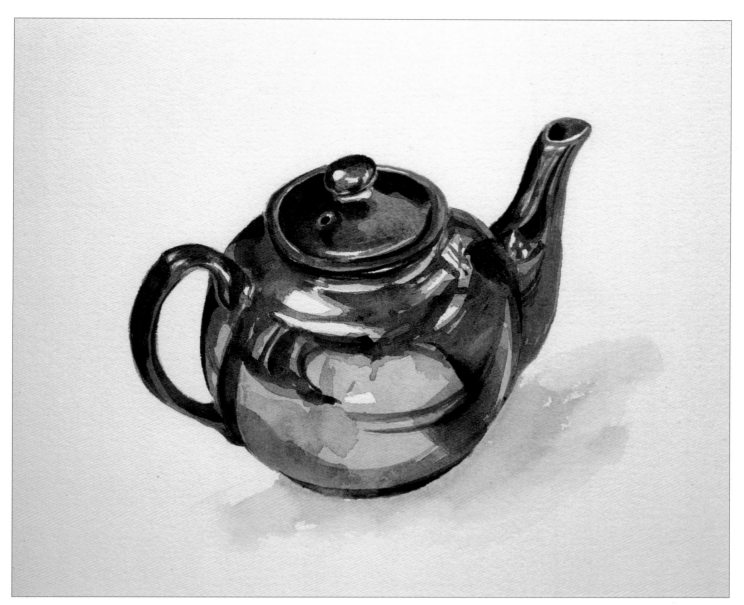

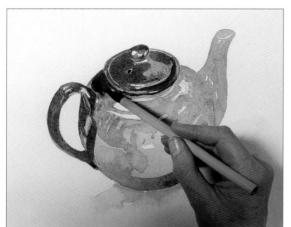

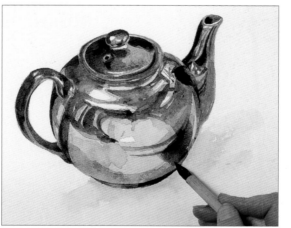

6 (Above) *Shiny surfaces reflect light and shadow from their surroundings, creating very sharp and distinctly shaped areas of light and dark. The crispness produced by using the wet-on-dry technique is ideal for conveying these qualities in a painting.*

4 *A darker mixture of the same brown is used for the shadowed areas. Notice that, on the lid of the pot, an area of blue-grey formed by the brown painted over the blue in Step 3 has been carefully reserved as a highlight.*

5 *The darkest colours are left until the final stages and placed very carefully. These shadows, like the highlights, define the form of the object.*

WORKING WET INTO WET

This method, which involves applying new colours before the first ones have been allowed to dry, is often regarded as a "special" method, quite separate from the classic wet-on-dry technique. In fact, although some artists do paint whole pictures wet into wet, it is perhaps more usual to see the two methods used in conjunction with one another.

Painting wet into wet is enormously enjoyable. One of the delights of water-colour is its unpredictability, and here the medium is at its tantalizing best – you never know exactly what will happen. Surprisingly, when you drop one wet colour into another, they do not mix completely. The weight of water in the new brushstroke pushes the first layers of paint away slightly, so that the colours mingle and "bleed" into one another, while still remaining separate to an extent. This can create very exciting effects, which vary according to how wet the paint is, the kind of paper you use and

Working on dry paper

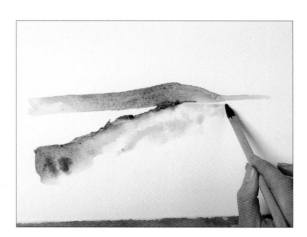

1 *Whether you work on pre-dampened or dry paper depends on how thorough you want the wet-into-wet effect to be. Here the artist needs a crisp edge at the top of the hills, and therefore uses dry paper.*

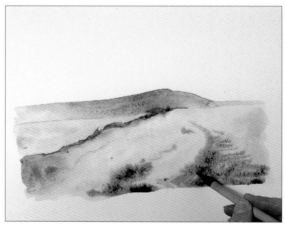

2 *Several applications of paint have by now made the paper thoroughly damp, and the green applied in the foreground spreads out and diffuses. To control the spread of colour, the artist applies the paint lightly, with the tip of the brush.*

Controlling the flow

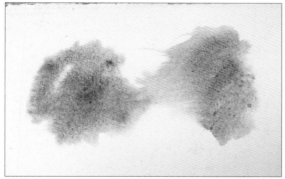

1 *The paper has been dampened, two colours laid side by side, and the paper lifted and tilted to the left so that the red runs into the blue.*

2 *(Right) A stronger blue has been dropped in at the top and the paper is now tilted so that the colours run down. The paper should normally be stretched for wet-into-wet work, but this is very heavy paper which does not buckle.*

3 *The paper has now been damped only in one area so that the blue paint does not spread below the boundary of the cloud. The tip of the brush is used to create a slightly streaky patch of sky.*

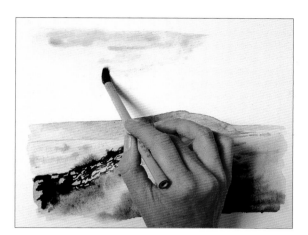

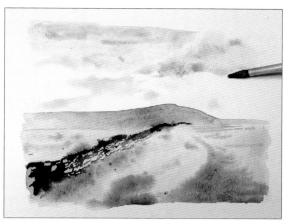

4 *(Above) The same method is used for the large cloud, with dark mauve-greys introduced into a lighter wet wash. Smaller, paler clouds are now touched in above the horizon, again with the tip of the brush.*

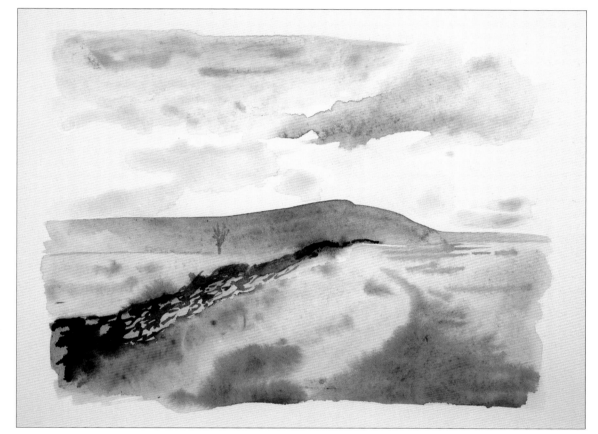

5 *(Left) The soft effect of the wet-into-wet painting is enhanced by the occasional crisp edges. Parts of the wall and the small tree have been painted wet on dry, while the cloud has formed a jagged edge where the wet paint met dry paper.*

the colours themselves (different pigments have different "behaviour patterns"). The main problem with the method is that you can't control it very precisely – the paint continues moving until it has dried, and you often find that you cannot preserve a particular effect. You can exert some control, however, by tilting the board so that the paint runs in a certain direction. Artists who paint extensively wet into wet will sometimes move the board around until they have achieved the flow of colours they want; they then use a hairdryer to hasten the drying process and thus "freeze" the picture at a specific moment.

Wet into wet can create a lovely soft atmosphere and, for this reason, is often used for landscapes and weather effects. It can, however, look *too* soft, giving the painting a distinctly woolly and nebulous appearance, so sharper details are usually painted wet on dry as a final stage. You can also add an extra dimension to any subject by working wet into wet in small areas only, thus contrasting soft, blurred edges with the crisper ones made by wet-on-dry washes.

BRUSHWORK

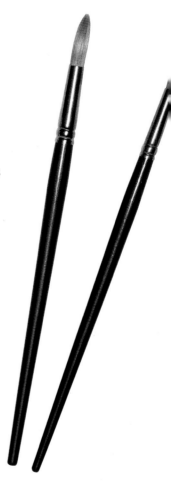

People do not always think of brushwork in connection with watercolour. So much emphasis is placed on the importance of laying flat washes that this aspect of painting tends to be overlooked, but, although brushwork in general is less obvious in watercolour than in a thick, buttery medium like oil, it still has a place. Sometimes it is restricted to the final defining details in a painting. In a mainly wet-into-wet landscape, for example, some light flicks of the brush can suggest foreground grass or the branches of trees, in contrast to softer blends of colour elsewhere in the picture.

Brushwork is more important in the classic wet-on-dry method because of the possibilities presented by the hard edges formed by overlaid washes. These "washes" can take the form of individual brushmarks: perhaps small dabs to suggest the foliage of a tree; calligraphic squiggles to describe reflections in water, or sweeps with a broad brush to follow the direction of clouds in a

windswept sky. Some artists lay almost no conventional flat washes, constructing whole paintings by means of a network of interconnected brushmarks.

Obviously different brushes make different marks, so try to discover their capabilities by practising "drawing" with a brush. You can make a wide range of marks with just one brush if you vary the way you hold it and the amount of pressure you apply. Most people tend to hold a brush as though they were writing, gripping it firmly near the ferrule, but, although this gives maximum control, it can limit the artist's expressive style. Try holding it nearer the top and varying the pressure from heavy to light, flicking it at the end of a stroke. See what happens if you use a flat brush and twist it in mid-stroke, or draw out a brushstroke as far as you can so that the brush is progressively starved of paint. This kind of doodling is never a waste of time, as you will be training your hand, albeit unconsciously.

Drawing with paint

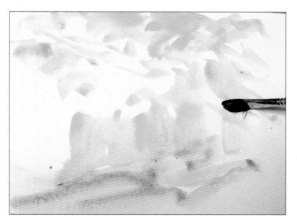

1 *The artist has chosen to work on a smooth-surfaced watercolour paper, which enables her to combine strong brushmarks with softer wet-into-wet painting. She begins with broad strokes, letting the colours run together slightly.*

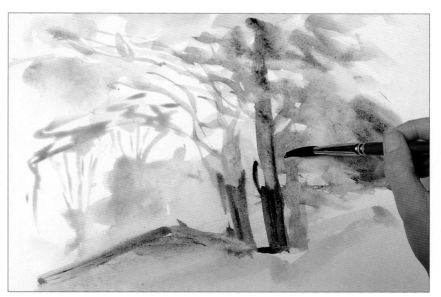

2 *The first applications of paint have now begun to dry, but are still damp enough for the next brushstrokes to spread slightly and soften.*

3 *Crisp strokes of almost undiluted colour are now worked wet on dry over the softer brushmarks. Notice the position of the brush; instead of pulling it downwards in the usual way, the artist uses an upward flick.*

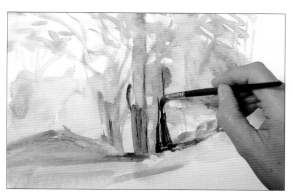

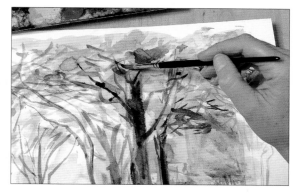

5 *A broader effect suggesting the dark green foliage is produced by flooding dark green paint into lighter green, in a modified wet-into-wet technique.*

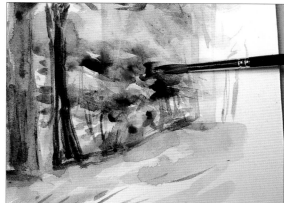

4 (Above) *At the top of the picture, the succession of criss-crossing brushmarks, where the first colours show through the later ones, creates a lively impression of light and movement.*

6 (Below) *The small backrun at the top of the tree and the jagged edges on the tree trunk and foliage formed as the washes dried out; these are typical semi-accidents which occur during watercolour work. Experienced painters exploit such effects rather than trying to correct them, and here they enhance the lively, edgy quality of the picture.*

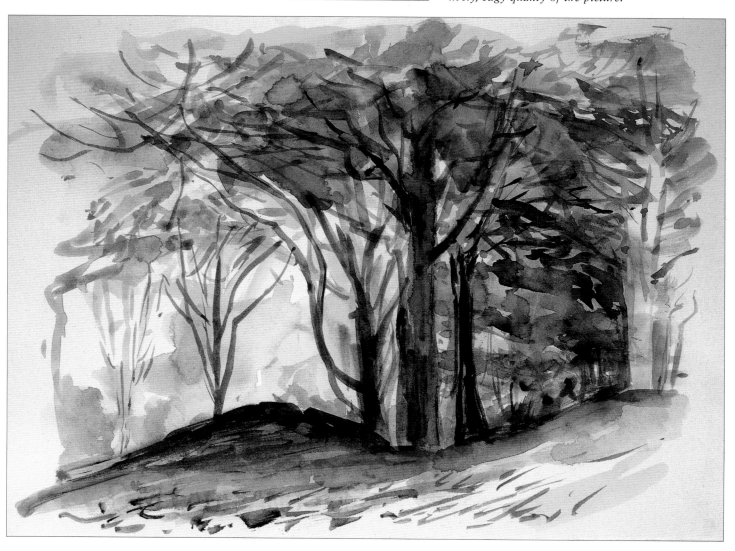

LIFTING OUT

As we have seen earlier, highlights in watercolour are normally created by painting around them. There is, however, another method, which involves putting on paint and then removing it. Highlights made by the classic reserving method have crisp, clear edges, but often a softer, more diffuse effect is required. For example, clouds or matt-surfaced objects do not have sharp highlights and would look unrealistic if painted in this way. In such cases, lifting out is the method you need.

It is beautifully easy; all you do is lay down the paint and, before it has dried, dab into it or wipe it with a very slightly damp sponge, a rag, a piece of kitchen paper or blotting paper – anything absorbent in fact. If you have ever worried about how to create the effect of white clouds in a blue sky without laboriously painting around the shapes (which looks unnatural anyway), your problems are solved. Simply lay a gradated wash and then dab into it or, for windclouds, sweep across the paper with your chosen implement. More complex colour effects can be created by lifting out one colour to reveal another. For the soft dappling of foliage, for example, you could lay a dark green wash over a lighter one which has been allowed to dry, then lift out some of the darker colour.

Small, soft highlights, such as those on matt-surfaced objects or on distant water in a landscape, can be made by allowing a cotton bud (swab) or virtually dry paint-brush to suck up some of the colour where you want the highlight to be. You can even lift out dry paint in small areas, using a firmer pressure and slightly more water. Alternatively, you can scrape into the paint with a blade. This scratching technique is commonly used for tiny, fine lines, such as those created by light on blades of grass.

Lifting out clouds

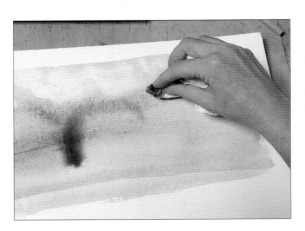

1 *Having laid a pale blue wash, allowed it to dry and then painted a multi-coloured wash on top, the artist uses a crumpled piece of kitchen paper to dab into wet paint.*

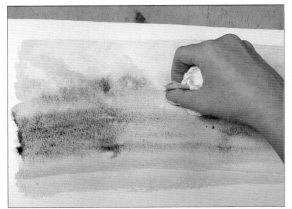

2 *To darken the undersides of the clouds, more colour has been laid on, wet into wet, and is partially removed again with kitchen paper.*

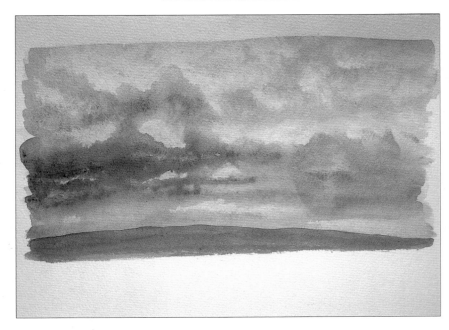

3 *The effect is very realistic and has been achieved with the minimum of time and effort. The soft clouds at the top contrast with the irregular edges formed when the darker washes dried out.*

Lifting out dry paint

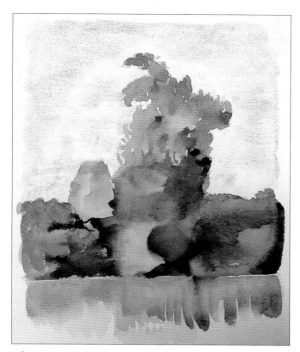

1 A series of green washes has been painted over a dry yellow one, with small areas of the yellow reserved for the sharper highlights.

2 (Right) A cotton bud (swab) dipped into water is now used to work into the green paint, creating much softer highlights than can be achieved by reserving.

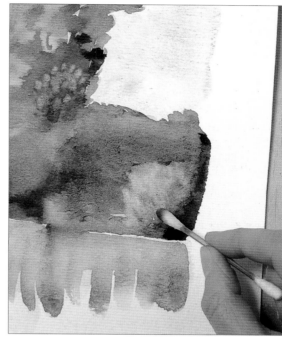

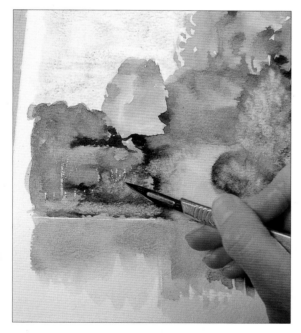

3 Finally, tiny highlights are made by scratching into the dry paint with a scalpel blade. This must always be done at a final stage in the painting because it breaks up the paper surface, making it impossible to lay colour on top.

4 (Right) The lifting-out method is ideal for the soft, diffused highlights seen on foliage or matt-surfaced objects, but is most effective when contrasted with the crisper edges achieved by reserving areas of the painting.

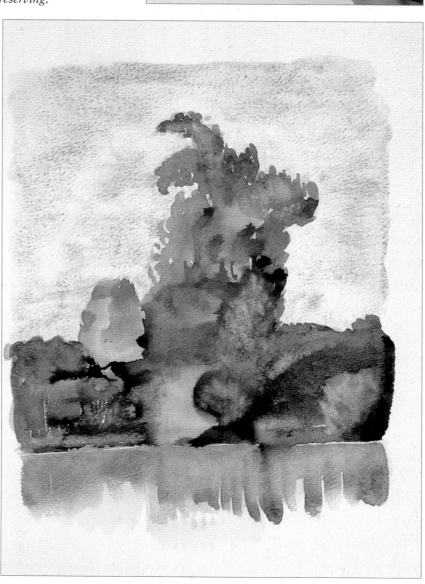

MASKING

Reserving highlights by painting around them is ideal if the required shape is reasonably large and clearly defined, but often the highlights may be small and intricate, in which case it is helpful to use masking fluid. Some watercolourists disdain the use of such methods, regarding them as "mechanical" or "tricksy", but others find them indispensable.

The great advantage of masking is that it removes the worry and allows you to paint more freely. If you have to think constantly about not taking the paint over little shapes which you want to reserve, there is a danger that your work may become tight and fussy; masking fluid allows you to work as broadly and splashily as you like, knowing that those areas are protected.

Masking fluid is a viscous solution sold in small bottles. It is either white or yellow, the latter being the best choice because you can see where you are putting it on. It is applied with a brush and, when dry, washes are laid on top. When these too are dry, the fluid is removed by rubbing with a finger or a plastic eraser. Wash the brush immediately because, once dry, the fluid is very difficult to remove from the hairs – and don't use your most expensive brush.

Highlights with masking fluid

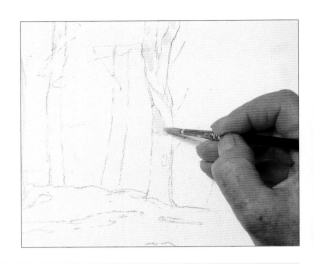

1 *Here the artist is using masking fluid to reserve small areas suggesting dappled light. She starts with a pencil drawing and then paints on the masking fluid with a small brush.*

Painting white shapes

Masking fluid not only provides a convenient means of reserving white paper for highlights, but can also be used in a more positive way to make distinctive brushmarks of white. Being thick, it holds the marks of the brush very effectively, as you can see from these examples, where the fluid was removed after the paint had dried. You are thus virtually painting with white, in a way that is otherwise impossible with watercolour alone.

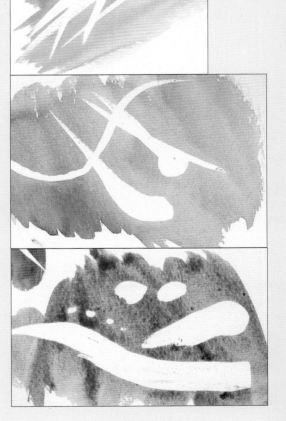

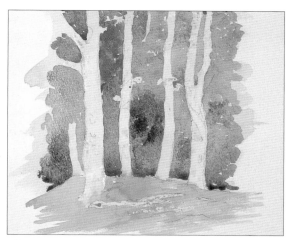

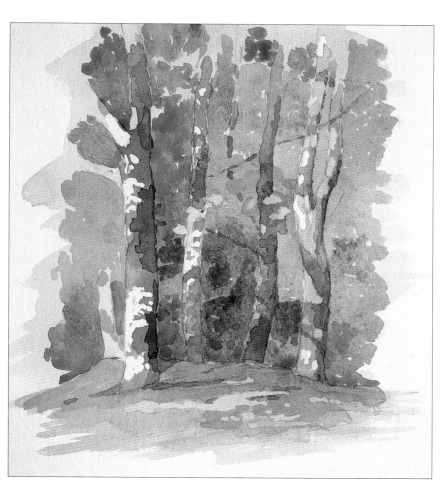

2 *A light blue-grey wash is taken over the whole area of tree trunks and foliage and allowed to dry before further greens and yellows are painted, largely wet into wet.*

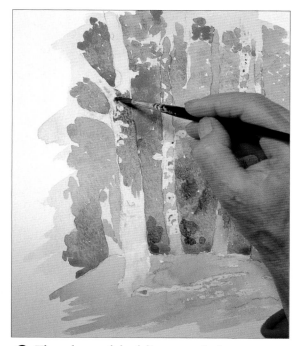

3 *The colours of the foliage must be kept separate from those of the tree trunks, so the first colours were dried with a hairdryer. Browns are now painted over the masking fluid.*

4 *(Right) The fluid is removed by rubbing with a finger. The paint must be perfectly dry before this is done, so again a hairdryer was used.*

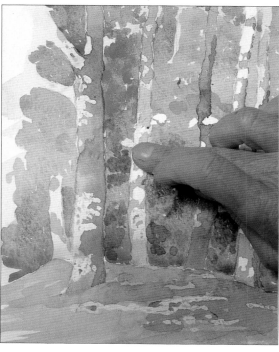

5 *(Above) When the masking fluid is taken off, you often find that some of the white highlights are too stark. In this case they have been left as white on the two left-hand tree trunks, but slightly darkened elsewhere; light yellow washes were laid over the leaves in the centre and on the lighter patch of foreground.*

USING OPAQUE PAINT

Watercolour has not always been used as a transparent medium in the past, nor is it always used as one today. Artists such as Albrecht Dürer in the Renaissance period and J.M.W. Turner in the 19th century used watercolour which was similar to today's gouache paints. Many of today's artists use gouache and watercolour together, or mix their colours with a little opaque white, which gives them body while still preserving much of their translucent quality (opaque watercolour is sometimes referred to as "body colour").

Opaque paint, like masking fluid, is frowned upon by some purists, who regard it as cheating, but this is nonsense. The point of painting is to exploit your medium to the full, to gain the effects you want; if you can do this by adding opaque white, then go ahead and do it. It is the perfect method for atmospheric weather effects, for example, such as cloud-shrouded hills or the soft lights on water.

You can add an extra dimension to your work by using coloured paper, whether or not you are adding white to the paint. Working over a base colour gives you a start in the process of building up the colours; it is particularly well suited to any paintings which are to be relatively dark overall, without bright highlights. It is now possible to buy coloured watercolour papers, but they are not easily available, so you might consider trying some of the papers made for pastel work, which come in an extensive colour range. Stretch them first, however, as they are thinner than most watercolour papers.

Working on tinted paper

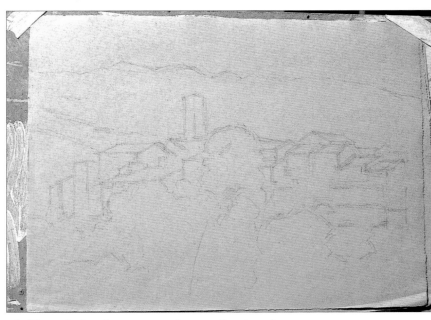

1 *The artist is using a paper whose surface is rather similar to the Ingres paper used for pastel work, but it is thicker and does not buckle when wet. He makes a careful drawing of the buildings within the landscape before putting on any colour.*

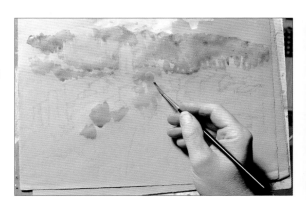

2 *The secret behind an effective opaque-watercolour technique is to add white to the paint only where necessary, and to use it sparingly. Here white has been used for the sky, but the darker paint now being applied is pure watercolour.*

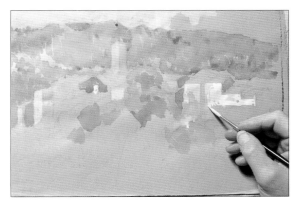

3 *For the houses, white with a small addition of crimson is painted into pure white, wet into wet, to create a slight blending of colours. Wet-into-wet effects are less dramatic and unpredictable with opaque paint, because it runs less freely.*

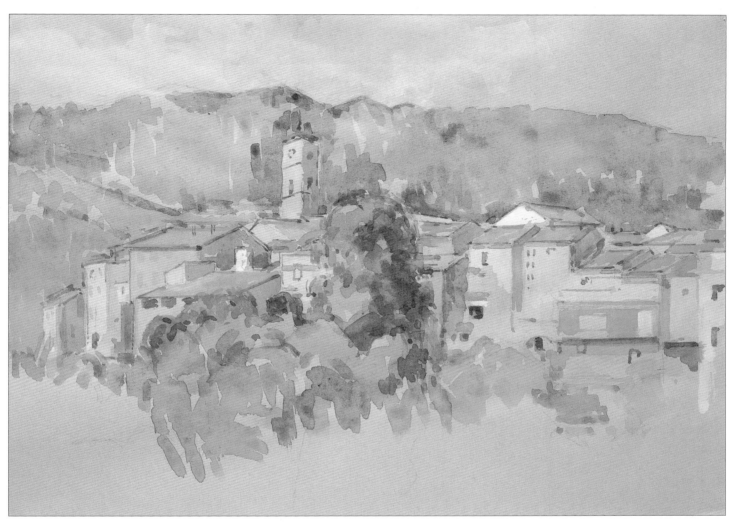

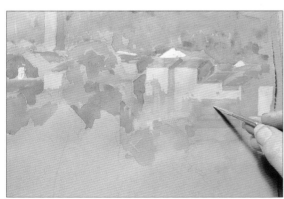

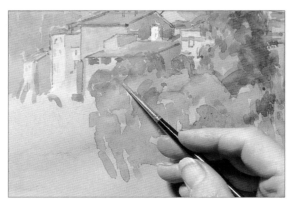

6 (Above) *The finished picture is delightfully delicate and fresh, retaining the translucent qualities associated with watercolour. The colour of the paper, deliberately left to show between brushstrokes in the background and foreground, plays an important part in the overall colour scheme.*

4 *Again opaque white is mixed with watercolour, as it was for the roofs of the houses. The white used is gouache paint, which the artist finds more satisfactory than the Chinese white sold for watercolour work.*

5 *In the final stages, a small brush was used to outline the roofs and paint in details of windows; now the foreground foliage is built up with small washes and overlaid brushstrokes of pure watercolour. The darker colours have been kept transparent throughout.*

TEXTURING METHODS

It can be hard to know where to start when describing texture in a fluid medium like watercolour. How, for instance, do you give the impression of a shingle beach or a cornfield without painting every pebble or cornhead? In fact there are a good many special techniques to hand. One is dry brush which, as its name implies, means working with the minimum of paint on the brush so that it only partially covers the paper. This method is often used for grass, the hazy effect of distant trees or the fur of animals. The best brush to use is a flat one, with the hairs slightly splayed out between thumb and forefinger and then dabbed onto blotting paper or absorbent kitchen paper to remove the excess paint.

Another popular method is spattering or flicking paint onto the paper with an old toothbrush. The toothbrush is loaded with colour and held above the work; the handle

Dry-brushed grasses

1 *As the name of the method implies, the brush must be fairly dry so, after dipping it into the paint, the artist dabs it onto a piece of kitchen paper to remove the surplus paint.*

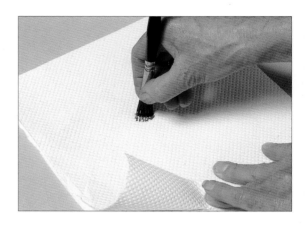

2 *Using a square-ended brush, she splays the hairs out slightly and then gently drags the brush over the paper, creating a series of fine lines.*

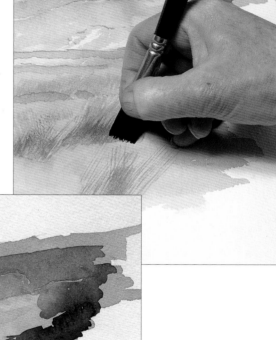

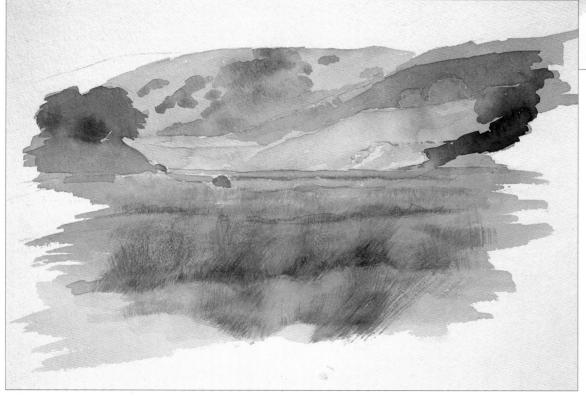

3 (Left) *One layer of dry brushing has been laid over another to suggest the different directions in which the marsh grasses lean.*

Toothbrush spatter

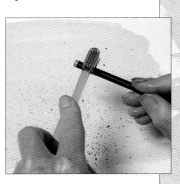

1 *A toothbrush is loaded with paint, and a pencil is pulled across the bristles to release a fine spray.*

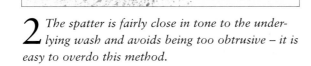

2 *The spatter is fairly close in tone to the underlying wash and avoids being too obtrusive – it is easy to overdo this method.*

Paintbrush spatter

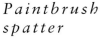

1 *This time dark paint is spattered into a light green wash using a bristle brush tapped against a pencil, producing larger droplets.*

2 *As the spattering was done wet into wet, the darker colour has spread out and blended to some extent with the lighter one.*

Salt spatter

1 *This technique works best on a non-absorbent paper, and here smooth (hot-pressed) watercolour paper is used. The salt is dropped into a wash and begins to absorb the water immediately.*

2 *(Right) These examples show some of the different effects which can be achieved; they vary according to the colour used, the wetness of the wash and the closeness of the crystals.*

of a brush, a knife or your thumbnail is drawn quickly across it to release a spray of droplets. This technique is very effective for suggesting texture without describing it too literally, but it should not be overdone, nor should it look too obtrusive. If you are spattering over a pale wash, perhaps for a sandy beach, don't make the spattered colour too dark or it will look artificial. Spattering can also be used in a purely decorative way, to create an area of colour with a stippled appearance.

A particularly exciting method, ideal for the texture of old pitted rocks or crumbling walls, is salt spatter, which involves dropping crystals of coarse sea salt into wet paint. The salt granules absorb the water while "pushing away" the pigment, leaving a pattern of pale, crystalline shapes when they are removed. The effects vary according to how wet the paint is and which colours you use – some pigments are "heavier" than others and do not move so readily. For the best results, apply the salt just after the wash has lost its sheen, which indicates that it is beginning to dry. The salt itself takes a long time to dry, but it is worth persevering with the technique.

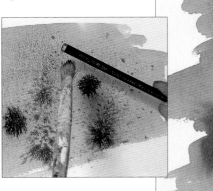

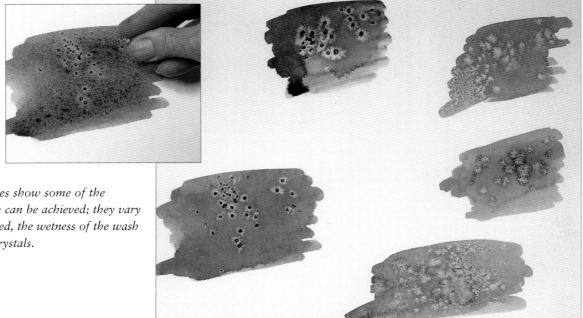

WAX RESIST

In one way this technique is similar to that of using masking fluid. Both involve creating a block which prevents the paint from reaching the paper, but wax resist gives a very different effect. It is based on the mutual antipathy of oil (the wax) and water (the paint). If you scribble over paper with a household candle or wax crayon and then apply washes, the paint will slide off the wax. Unlike masking fluid, however, which leaves perfect shapes when removed, the wax creates a subtler, lightly speckled effect. This is because watercolour paper is textured, so the wax adheres only to the top of the grain, unless you draw very heavily indeed with the candle or crayon.

Wax resist is a simple technique which can yield quite beautiful results. It is often used in landscape, for skies lightly broken by clouds or the gentle gleam of water on lakes, rivers and seas. It also provides yet another way of describing texture. The roughened surface of an old building, a crumbling cliff or an ancient gnarled tree, for example, can be quickly and easily suggested with a light application of wax under loose wet-into-wet washes.

If you want a coloured resist, you can use wax-oil crayons or the new oil bars, which serve the purpose very well. You can make the wax underdrawing as simple or as complex as you like. Some artists build up paintings in layers, applying crayon, then paint and then more crayon, sometimes even scratching into the wax before putting on more paint. It is an exciting method to try as it contains an element of surprise – you never quite know what will happen.

Watercolour and oil bar

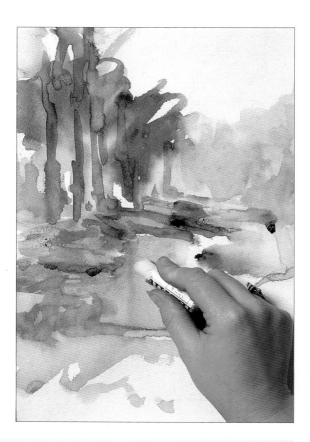

1 *This artist uses wax resist a good deal in her work, building up effects by means of a layering technique. She has begun with loose watercolour washes and now scribbles over the dry paint with a transparent oil bar.*

Types of wax

The final results depend on the texture of the paper, the pressure applied and the kind of wax used. A household candle was used for the first example and an oil bar for the other two. More delicate lines can be made with a wax-oil crayon.

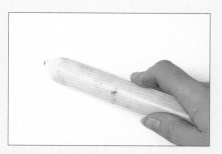

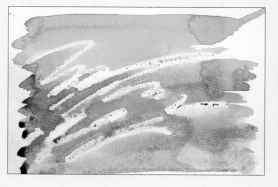

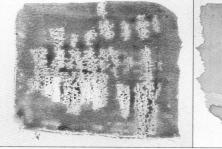

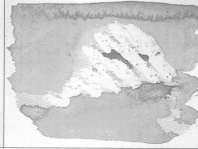

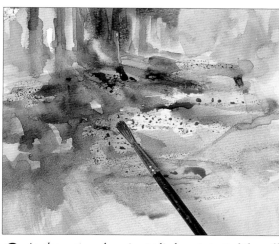

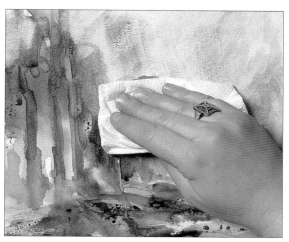

2 As the watercolour is applied on top, it slides off the wax, leaving small blobs and speckles. This method is often used to suggest texture.

3 A further application of oil bar has been followed by another watercolour wash, which is smeared down the paper to create an effect of brushstrokes.

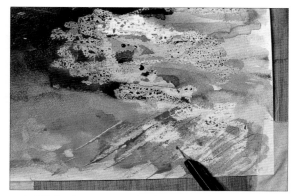

4 While the paint in the foreground is still wet, a craft knife is used to scratch into both wax and paint. Dark lines are created where the wax is removed, as the paint seeps into the slightly scuffed paper surface.

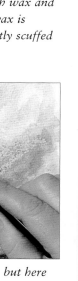

5 Lighter scratching is used for the sky, but here the effect is different: the knife removes the watercolour on top of the wax, leaving white marks.

6 (Right) The artist has not attempted a precise representation of the landscape features; the wax resist in the foreground suggests water without describing it literally. Her approach is impressionistic and, to a large extent, she allows the painting itself to dictate her procedure.

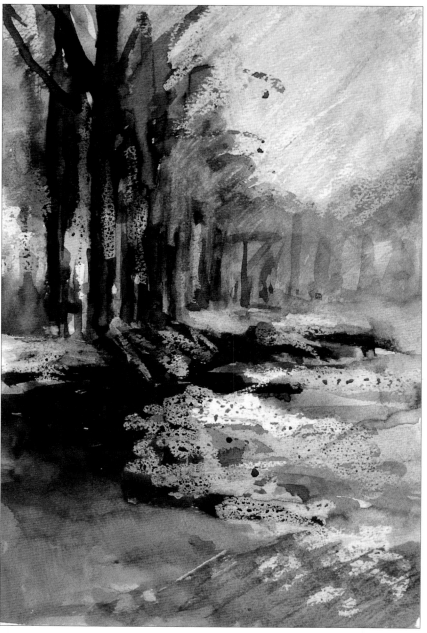

LINE & WASH

This technique, which combines drawing and painting, has been in use for a long time, but has lost none of its appeal. Traditionally it was employed by illustrators – as it still is today – as a means of introducing colour into what were basically drawings, usually in pen and ink. Nowadays artists exploit the technique of line and wash in more personal and often highly inventive ways.

Line and wash is essentially a mixed-media technique and, as in all such work, it is important to try to integrate the two media to create a unified image. Thus it is not always wise to begin with the drawing, or at any rate to take the drawing to a finished stage, before putting on colour. Generally the best and most "painterly" effects are created by developing the two side by side, adding more colour and more line as the picture demands.

You don't have to use pen for line and wash – watercolour is often combined with pencil drawing, the pencil lines providing detail and touches of definition. Pencil and watercolour marry very well together, as pencil gives a gentler and less assertive line than pen.

However, on the whole, pen is the implement most often used, so if you want to try this technique you will need to experiment with different pens, of which there is a bewilderingly large range on the market. You can use fine fibre-tipped and felt-tipped pens (but make sure they are non-fading), fountain pens or dip pens. For the beginner, the latter are probably the best, as a holder with interchangeable nibs is relatively inexpensive. Waterproof ink is normally used, but it is worth trying water-soluble ink too. This runs slightly when the watercolour washes are laid on top, which can be an effective way of softening the line.

Pen and watercolour

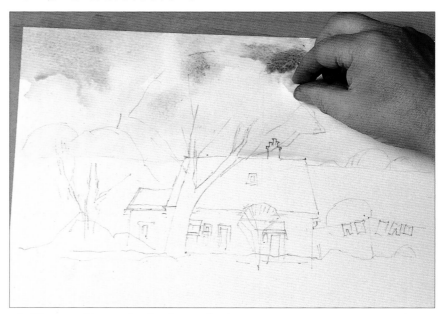

1 *The artist likes to develop line and colour together, so he has begun by making a pencil drawing to provide some guidelines for the first washes, which he applies loosely, wet into wet.*

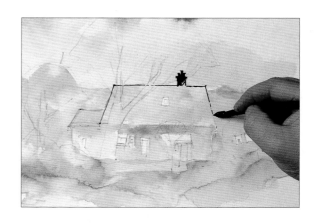

2 *With the washes now dry, he draws with a pen, using waterproof ink. He keeps the line drawing to a minimum at this stage of the work.*

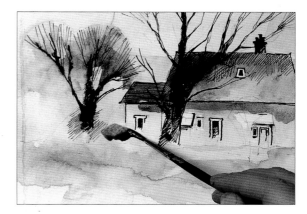

3 *The drawing has been considerably strengthened with bold lines and areas of hatching and cross-hatching. To avoid giving too much prominence to the linear element, the artist now applies darker colour.*

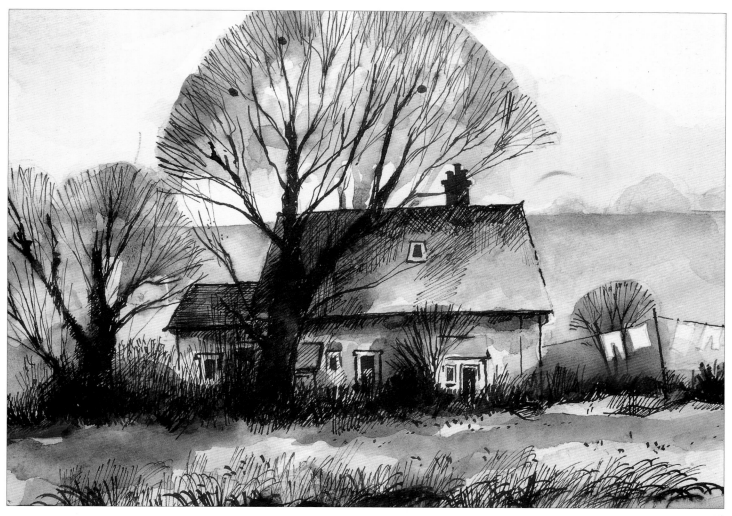

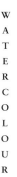

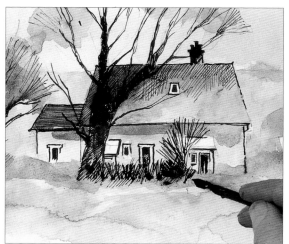

4 *The area in front of the house is defined with further pen work. Notice how the wet-into-wet washes in the foreground have dried with hard, irregular edges, complementing the pen lines.*

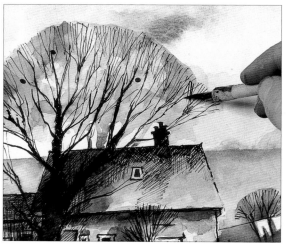

5 *A succession of washes has been laid over the large tree, again with the paint used loosely and freely; final touches are added with a finer nib than that used previously.*

6 (Above) *When the entire drawing is done at the beginning, pen-and-wash work can become rather tight and fussy, giving the effect of a "filled-in drawing". The artist has avoided this pitfall and integrated the drawing and painting media, while still providing a good contrast between linearity and boldly applied colour.*

BACKRUNS

If you have ever tried to work into a wash before it is dry, you may have come across the phenomenon of the backrun. The new paint seeps into the old, creating an odd blotch with hard, jagged edges – some people call it a cauliflower for obvious reasons. Normally backruns cause alarm and despondency because you may have to abandon a whole piece of paper, or at least wash the area down with a sponge and begin again.

However, a very important part of watercolour work is learning how to exploit accidental effects of this nature – watercolours are never totally predictable. Some artists induce backruns deliberately, or simply allow them to happen and then leave them alone because they improve the painting. The effects they create are quite different from those made by more conventional means, and the strange shapes are often highly suggestive. For example, a backrun in a sky can often look like a cloud, possibly suggesting a different treatment

from the one you originally had in mind, while one in the foreground might provide the perfect touch of additional interest. In flower painting, backruns are particularly useful, often resembling the shapes of petals and flowers.

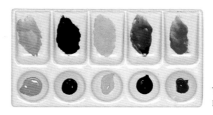

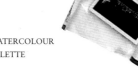

WATERCOLOUR
PALETTE

WATERCOLOUR PANS

Backruns cannot be controlled with much precision, but you are not altogether at the mercy of events. You can make them happen at will if you always use paint which has a higher water content than the original colour (thick paint on thin will not work). You can tilt the board, as in any wet-into-wet work, and then use a hairdryer to "stop" the run when you are satisfied with the effect, but remember that wet-into-wet paint goes on moving until it dries.

Accidental backruns

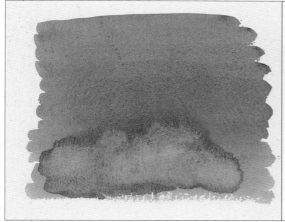
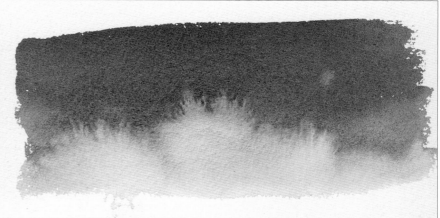

These examples show what can happen when you panic and try to work back into a wash. In the first, the wash was very wet; in the second, it appeared dry but was not.

Deliberate backruns

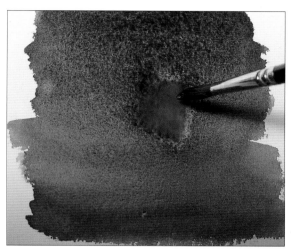

1 A dark indigo wash is laid first, and a slightly more watery solution of alizarin crimson is then dropped into the wet paint. It begins to spread immediately.

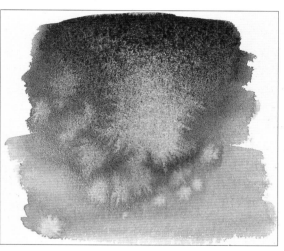

2 The paint will continue to move until it is fully dry. At this stage the first wash has begun to dry at the edges, but the central area is still wet, and the crimson continues to bleed into the darker colour.

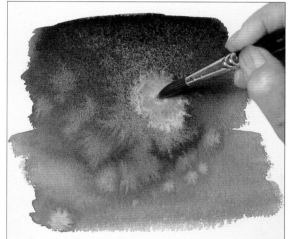

3 Yellow is now dropped into the centre; this in turn pushes the crimson away to create a pale area within the darker colours.

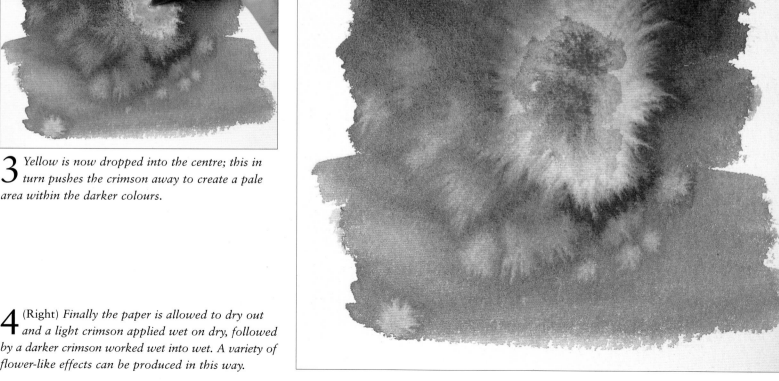

4 (Right) Finally the paper is allowed to dry out and a light crimson applied wet on dry, followed by a darker crimson worked wet into wet. A variety of flower-like effects can be produced in this way.

The pigment used to make watercolours is bound with a gum called gum arabic, which can also be used as a painting medium; it is sold in most good art shops. A little gum mixed with water (known as gum water) makes the paint more lustrous and less runny, giving it extra body. This allows you to build up an area of the picture in small separate brushstrokes which do not merge together. It is thus useful for any area of a picture where you want a lot of precise detail, particularly if you intend to use dark colours, which can otherwise become muddy and dull. It is also useful for lifting out dry paint. If you lay a colour mixed with gum water over another paler wash and let it dry before working into areas with a wet brush, the top layer of paint will come away very easily because the water dissolves the gum, revealing the paint beneath.

Using gum water

1 *The artist began with conventional water and paint washes, and has painted the trees with dark green paint mixed with gum water (about two parts of water to one of gum). Notice the richness of the colours and how each brushstroke remains separate.*

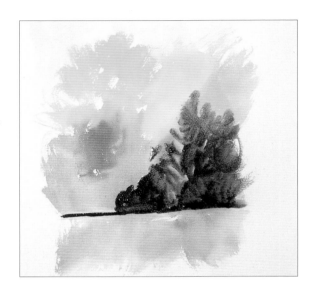

2 *Gum arabic also facilitates the lifting-out technique. The gum is water-soluble, so a wet brush dabbed into the paint removes the top layer.*

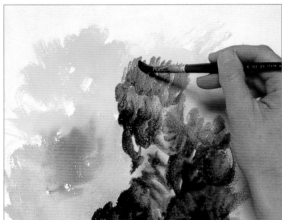

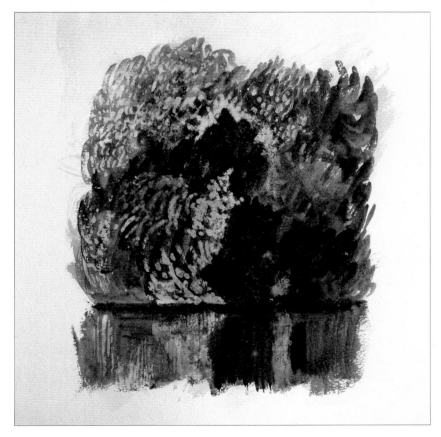

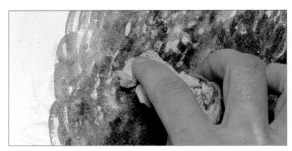

3 *A damp rag is dabbed lightly into the paint to create softer, more diffuse highlights. Note how the original yellow wash remains intact; this is because gum water was not used for the first colours.*

4 *(Left) You may find that gum water adds an extra dimension to your work; the effect of the lifted-out highlights is unlike anything achieved by standard methods. The artist herself, who had never used the technique before, was delighted.*

Mixing paint with soap

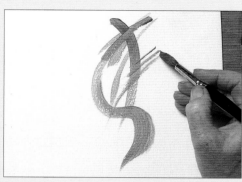

1 *The brush has been dipped into a strong solution of colour and rubbed over a bar of soap. This thickens the paint so that it holds the marks of the brush without sacrificing the transparency of the colour.*

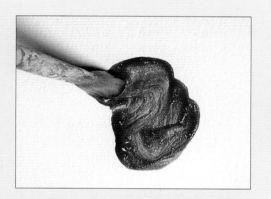

2 *A bristle brush gives a different effect because the soapy paint can be used more thickly, in swirling strokes so that it forms ridges and bubbles. These remain when the paint has dried, creating an intriguing impression of specks and small circles.*

Watercolour and turpentine

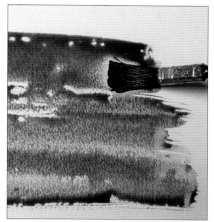

1 *The brush has been dipped first into turpentine and then into paint, thus creating a striated effect as the paint withdraws from the oily substance of the turpentine.*

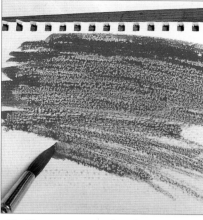

2 *Here turpentine has been scrubbed over the whole surface of the paper with a bristle brush before paint is applied on top.*

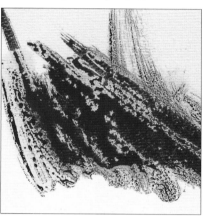

3 *The same method has been used for this example, but the brushstrokes are not as close together, having been drawn out to produce a light, scratchy texture.*

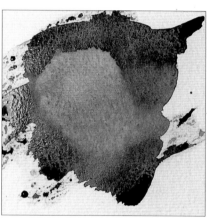

4 *In this case turpentine has been dropped into a wet wash; the water-and-paint mixture is then pushed outwards to form a pale shape.*

Ox gall, another medium sold specially for watercolour work, has the opposite effect. This makes the paint flow more freely and is therefore known as a "water-tension breaker".

So much for the conventional additives. There are some interesting "alternative" ones too, such as soap. This has a similar effect to gum arabic, thickening the paint so that it holds the marks of the brush, but with an added dimension – the bubbles, which form as you work, leave intriguing rings and blobs when dry. Soap is particularly useful for creating texture

effects and could be ideal for a dramatic stormy sky.

You can also create interesting effects in watercolour by exploiting a variation of the wax-resist technique. In this case turpentine is used which, being an oily substance, repels the watercolour. If you lay down some turpentine and then paint over it, the paint and the oil will separate, but only partially, giving a streaky or marbled appearance. Alternatively you can mix up some paint and dip your brush into turpentine before applying it. Like all such methods, this one is unpredictable but fun to try.

COMPARATIVE DEMONSTRATION

Non-professional watercolour painters sometimes restrict themselves unnecessarily by following, or studying under, one particular artist, trying to paint in exactly the same style. This can be valuable – artists have always been influenced by their teachers or by artists of the past whom they admire – but it can mislead you into thinking that there is only one way of doing things and that certain techniques are somehow wrong. To show that no two people work in the same way, we have asked two different artists to paint the same subject using their preferred method.

John Lidzey uses a combination of wet-into-wet and wet-on-dry methods, painting on smooth (hot-pressed) paper, because he likes to encourage the colours to run into each other and to form pools and backruns. Rosalind Cuthbert, on the other hand, paints on medium (Not surface) paper, using the classic wet-on-dry technique.

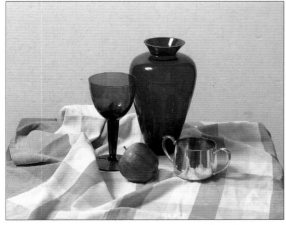

(Above) *An attractive still life of blue glass and silver objects is assembled on a checked tablecloth.*

Watercolour on smooth paper

1 *To make it easier to judge the colours needed for the silver bowl, the artist begins by laying light washes over the background. A careful pencil drawing was made first in order to keep these early washes away from the edges of the objects.*

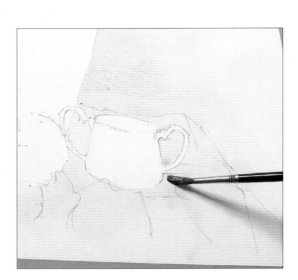

2 *For the main body of the vase, a soft effect has been created by painting wet into wet, but the white highlights must be sharply defined, so these have been reserved by painting carefully around them. Parts of this orange-yellow wash will in turn be reserved as highlights, together with the small patch on the right, which has been left white.*

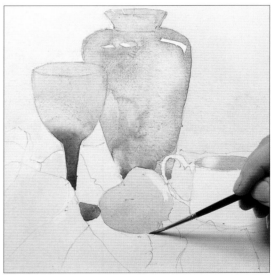

3 *The artist's method is to use wet-into-wet techniques only for certain areas of the painting; both here and on the silver pot he produces clean, clear edges by working wet on dry, drying the picture with a hairdryer between each stage.*

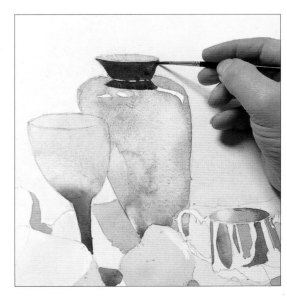

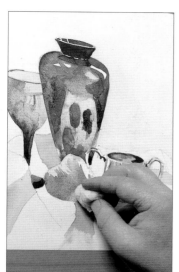 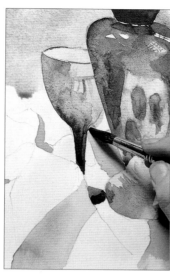 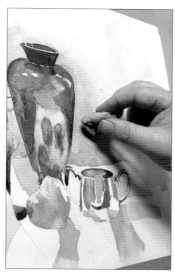 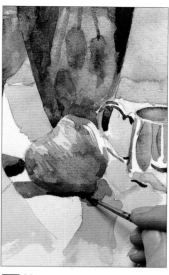

4 *A darker wash laid on the apple is dabbed with cotton wool (a cotton ball) to create a softly diffused highlight. Cotton wool (cotton balls) and a hairdryer are both important items in the artist's "tool-kit".*

5 *The background colour is taken carefully around the edges of the glass. Although the glass and vase have been painted mainly wet into wet – you can see the effect clearly in this photograph – the painting has been dried to prevent the new colour from bleeding into the blue.*

6 *To soften areas of the background and provide a slight variation in tone and colour, damp cotton wool, (a cotton ball) is again employed to lift out some of the wet paint. Granulation, one of the attractive accidental effects which watercolourists like to exploit, often occurs on smooth paper.*

7 *Here you can see how the original wash laid on the apple in Step 2 has been reserved for highlight effects, with the darker colours painted over it wet on dry. The added dark shadow gives the apple extra solidity.*

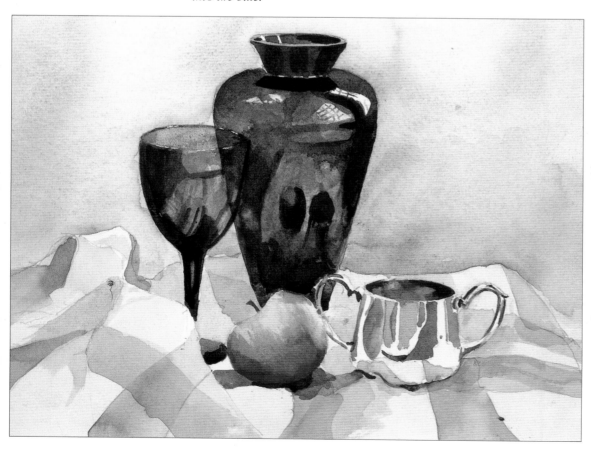

8 *The combination of soft, wet-into-wet effects and crisp, clean edges is very attractive. The treatment of the silver bowl and the top of the vase shows the importance of a preliminary drawing in watercolour work; each highlight and patch of reflected colour must be precisely placed, in order to explain the forms of the objects.*

Continued ▷

Wet on dry on medium paper

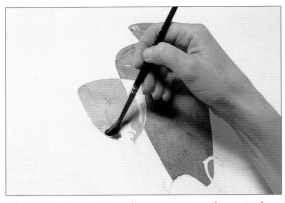

1 *As in the previous demonstration, the artist has begun with an underdrawing, although here the lines are lighter. Unlike the other artist, she does not begin with the background, but establishes the colours of the glass and vase immediately.*

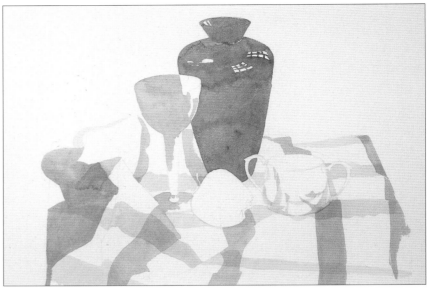

2 *(Above) As blue is the dominant colour in the painting, no other colours have yet been introduced. Two main blues have been used – ultramarine for the vase and Winsor (phthalocyanine) blue, a cooler, greener colour, for the glass and cloth.*

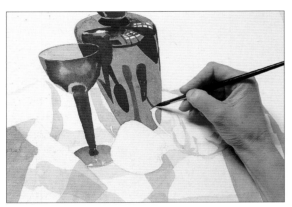

3 *The artist plans to key the background and foreground colours to those of the vase and bottle, therefore she concentrates on these first. The dark ultramarine now being used has also been laid over much of the glass, with some of the lighter blues reserved for highlights.*

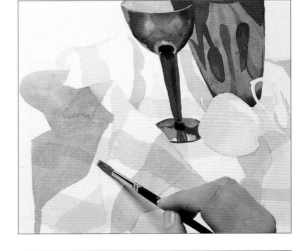

4 *(Right) Light yellow washes are laid on the cloth and apple and, where the yellow is painted over the light blue, the two colours mix to produce green. A warmer, more orangey yellow has been painted over the blue at the bottom of the vase, which reflects colour from the apple.*

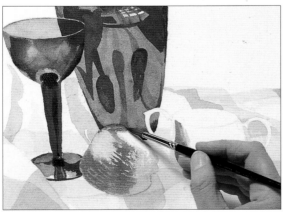

5 *By completing the vase before the other objects, the artist is able to evaluate the strength of the colours needed for the apple and its reflection in the silver bowl, which she paints next.*

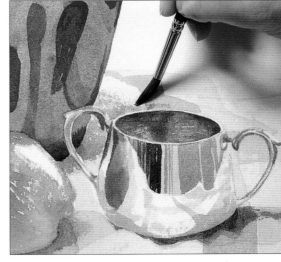

6 *(Right) The broken colour of the apple and the inside of the silver bowl have been achieved by stippling, a version of the dry-brush technique, which is used once more for this shadow. Taking up the minimum of paint with the brush, the artist dabs it lightly onto the paper.*

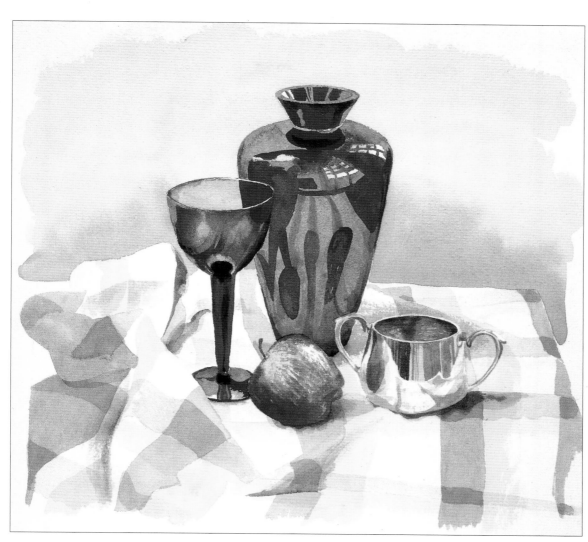

9 In the final stages, a few further light washes were laid on the tablecloth to strengthen it slightly, and the area of background behind the table was darkened with a warm blue-grey. This is the one area of the painting in which colours were blended wet into wet, to achieve the required soft effect.

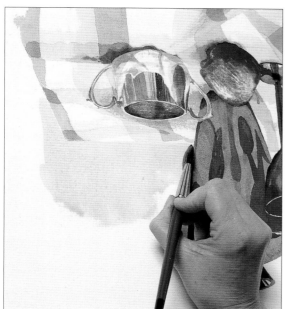

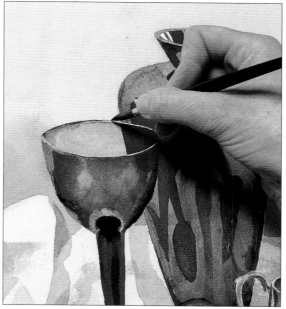

7 Leaving the background until last is often a good idea in still-life painting, as sometimes you do not know what kind of background is needed until the objects have been painted. Here a yellow similar to that of the cloth is chosen; the board is turned upside-down to facilitate the laying of the wash.

8 To give objects such as the blue glass extra definition and impact, fine highlights are added where edges catch the light.

LANDSCAPE

In most people's minds, watercolour is perhaps more closely associated with landscape than with any other subject. This may be because there is a long tradition of sketching in watercolour but, whatever the reason, there is no doubt that the fluidity and brilliance of watercolour, together with its portability, make it an excellent medium for on-the-spot painting.

Of course, you don't have to work directly from life all the time – we will be looking at alternative methods later on. If you are interested in landscape, however, it is advisable to do at least some location work, as there is no substitute for a direct response to your subject. Before you begin to translate your response into paint, you must make some initial decisions about how you are going to organize your picture in terms of composition.

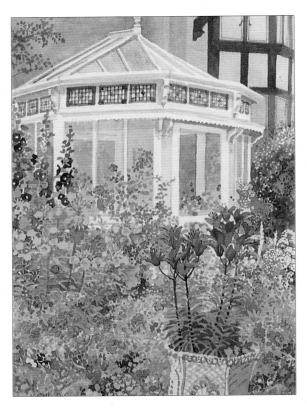

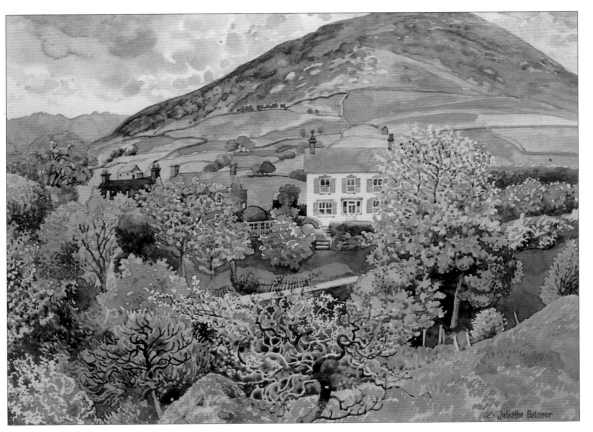

Unity and contrast
In the landscape shown below, Juliette Palmer has created visual links between the sky and the land areas by using similar shapes for both the small clouds and the trees. This has given an overall unity to her composition, with the straight lines of the houses providing contrast. In The Conservatory (left) *she has exploited this kind of contrast more thoroughly, using the geometric shapes and light colours of the architectural features as a foil for the free forms and bright colours of the flowers.*

Placing a focal point
(Left) *If there is one particular feature in your chosen view which catches your attention, such as a dark tree against a light background or a vivid area of colour, it will become the focal point in your painting, and you must decide where to place it and how to emphasize it. In Juliette Palmer's* Peak District – Springtime *the focal point (the white house) has been placed slightly off-centre, and the eye is led towards it by the curving diagonals of the foreground field and wall and the strong shape of the tall tree.*

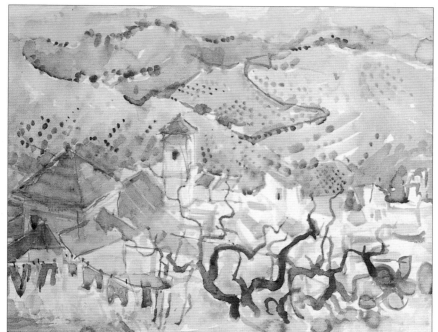
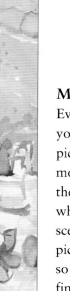

Making visual links

(Above) *Foregrounds are a frequent cause of failure in landscape composition; often they are treated in more detail than the middle distance and distance, making the picture look disconnected. In* From the Mule Path with Fig *Joan Elliott Bates has treated the foreground with the minimum of definition, but has taken care to link the fig tree to the rest of the picture both by letting the branches overlap the buildings and by using similar curving lines for the hills beyond.*

Creating movement

(Right) *A good landscape painting should encourage the viewer's eye to travel into and around the scene, to create movement in the composition. In* Road to Ronda *Pip Carpenter has achieved this quality both through her energetic brushwork and the way she has organized the picture. The area of trees and barely defined grass on the left leads towards the curving path, which the eye naturally follows. Paths, roads, streams or rivers leading from foreground to back-ground are common compositional devices.*

MAKING THE PICTURE

Even though you are simply painting what you can see, you still need to compose your picture. This doesn't mean that you have to move trees around or invent shadows where there are none, but you do have to decide what viewpoint to take, which part of the scene to concentrate on, how much of the picture you will devote to foreground and so on. Before you start, walk around a bit to find the position that gives you the most interesting angle on the subject; once you have chosen the viewpoint you are halfway to composing the picture.

However, you still need to decide where to place the horizon and to consider whether there are any elements in the scene which you can emphasize for effect, or any which you can play down or perhaps leave out altogether. You are not copying the

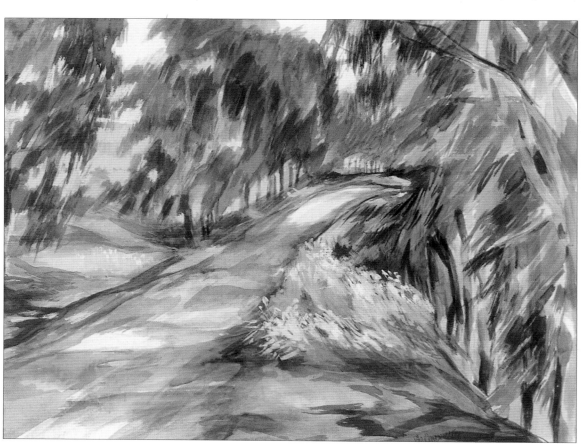

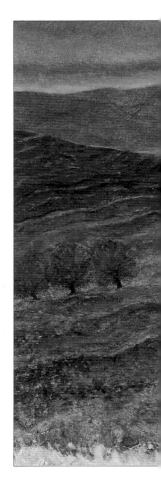

scene; you are making your own statement about it and you don't have to include everything you see. After all, you would hardly try to paint every blade of grass in the foreground – you would generalize to create an impression of grass. So if there is a small, featureless shrub in the foreground which obscures your view of a grand tree further back, ignore it; alternatively, move your position so that it is less obtrusive.

The golden rule of composition is to avoid symmetry. It is never wise to divide your picture into halves, with the horizon exactly in the middle, particularly if it is a flat horizon line, as in a seascape. Nor should you place the most important element in the painting, for example a tree, right in the middle. Symmetry is dull and static and you should aim for a feeling of life and movement in your work.

KEEPING UP WITH THE LIGHT

Changing light is a constant problem for those who work out of doors. Even if the sun does not actually go in, thus removing all the shadows and much of the colour from the scene, it moves inexorably round the sky, altering the direction of the shadows and shining first on one side of a tree and then on the other.

The only way to cope with this is to work as fast as possible without actually rushing; restrict yourself to a fairly small scale so that you can cover the paper as quickly as possible. It is helpful to make a note of the direction of the light as soon as you begin. Either put a small pencil cross in a corner of the picture or block in the main shadows first – in this way, you won't be tempted to change them.

Do not try to work on the same painting over a whole day, unless it is overcast, because the scene you saw in the morning will be quite different from the one you see in the evening. It is better either to give yourself a definite time limit – say three hours – or to work on two consecutive days at the same time. Experienced painters can

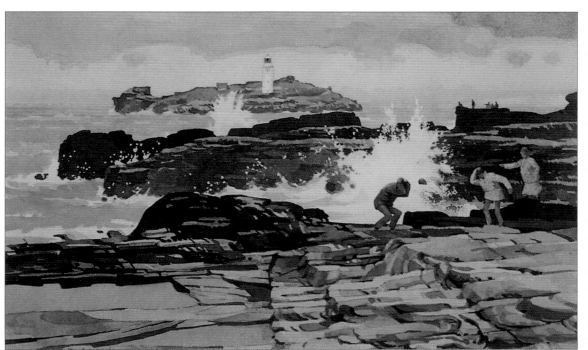

Human interest
(Left) *You can often give additional interest to a landscape, or stress a centre of interest, by including one or two figures. In Ronald Jesty's* A Wild Day, *the men shielding their heads against the spray from the breaking wave and the woman pointing her hand in warning introduce an element of narrative, and both these and the surrounding dark rocks provide contrasts of tone which draw attention to the picture's focal point.*

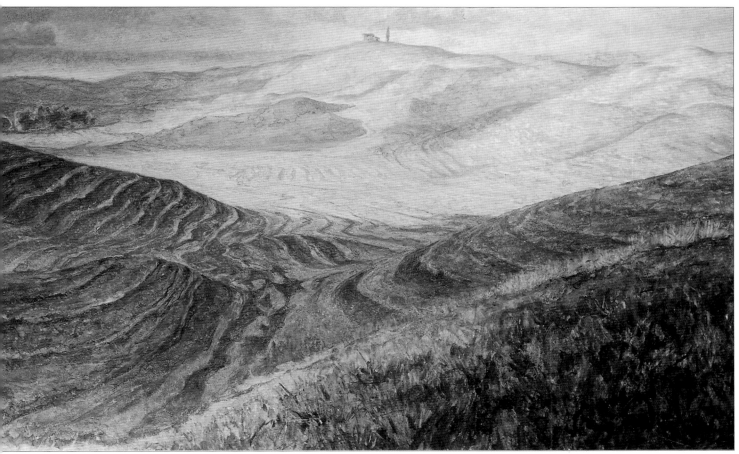

often continue in the face of changing conditions, but only because they have well-trained visual memories and are sufficiently disciplined to stick to what they originally saw.

WORKING INDOORS

It is not really practical to paint big pictures out of doors, but a good method is to make a series of drawings and small colour sketches on location, then to compose and paint the actual picture indoors. This has the dual advantage of giving you direct experience of the subject and allowing you to paint at your own pace, incorporating any special techniques which you feel might improve the picture.

Making sketches for a painting, as opposed to simply sketching for the fun of it, is rather a special skill, as you must learn to give yourself sufficient visual information from which to work. Artists often make written notes about colours, shapes and so on in their sketchbooks, to help jog their memories when they are recreating a scene

later. Even when making colour sketches, try to back these up with suggestions to yourself – it is better to have too much information than too little.

You can also use photographs as a basis for painting. You may have been told that you should never work from photographs, but this is not realistic. Most painters have limited time at their disposal and the weather often makes outdoor work impossible, so it is better to paint from photographs than not to paint at all.

There are problems, however. The camera is seldom reliable over colour; it loses many subtle nuances and often reduces dark colours to a formless mass with no detail. Photographs also tend to flatten out perspective and reduce the feeling of three-dimensional space.

To give themselves a wider choice of possibilities, artists who use photographs usually take several versions of the subject, which they can then combine in their own composition. Sometimes they make sketches as well.

Studio paintings
(Above) *Patrick Cullen paints large-scale watercolours in the studio from sketches: this painting,* Landscape in La Crete Region, Tuscany, *is over five feet wide. Referring to sketches and drawings done on the spot, and sometimes making a working drawing to plan the composition, he paints area by area, building up deep, rich colours with a series of overlaid brushstrokes and occasionally washing down the paint to achieve soft gradations of tone and colour.*

DEMONSTRATION

Hazel Soan is known primarily as a watercolour landscape painter, although she does work in oils on occasion. She likes to paint on the spot whenever possible but, if time does not permit this, she composes her paintings in the studio, making extensive use of photographic reference. She seldom works from just one photograph, but uses a combination of several, selecting different elements from each and editing out unwanted features. The photographs are put away when she has reached a certain stage of work so that the painting can develop independently.

COLOURS

USED *mauve, permanent rose, cobalt blue, cerulean blue, ultramarine, yellow ochre, cadmium yellow, new gamboge, Winsor green, burnt sienna and a tiny amount of cadmium red*

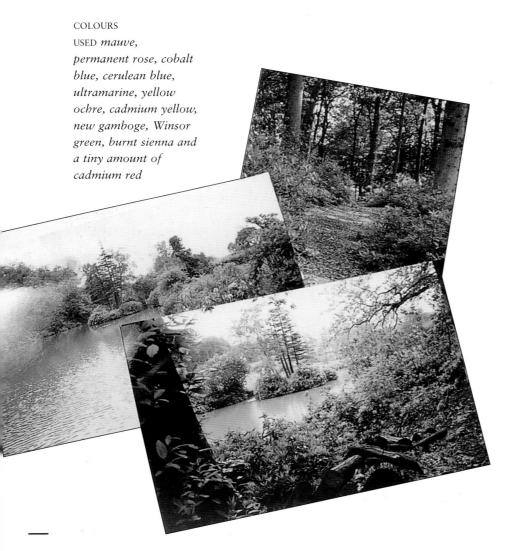

1 *The artist generally uses masking fluid to reserve highlight areas; here she begins to paint it in, referring to the photograph and guided by her initial light pencil drawing.*

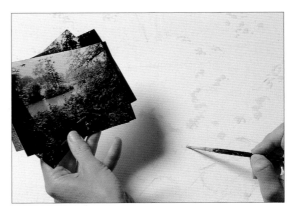

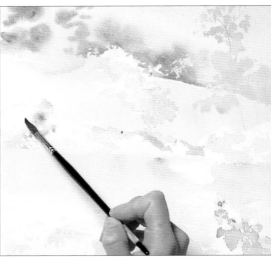

2 *She builds up gradually from light washes to darker ones in the classic watercolour technique, working mainly wet on dry but using wet-into-wet methods in certain areas. A light rose pink and mauve mixture is laid over the masking fluid on the left of the picture to be rubbed into later on.*

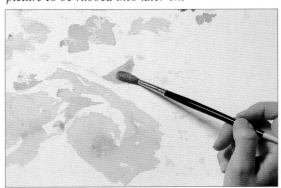

3 *The colours of the flowers and the vivid red-brown of the foreground set the key for the overall warm colour scheme, so these are blocked in at an early stage.*

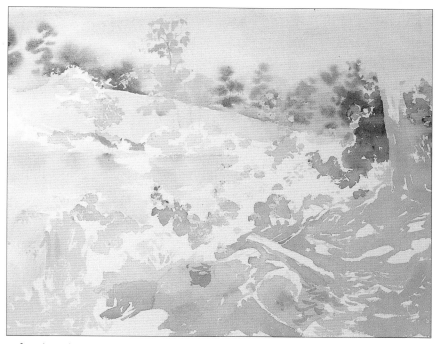

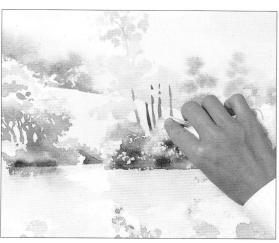

5 *With the distant trees now complete, the artist turns her attention to the area on the far side of the lake. Here the colours are stronger but, for a relatively soft effect, the wet colours are blotted lightly so that they are not so saturated.*

4 *After about an hour's work, the main colours have been established, to be darkened and strengthened in places with further washes. The wet-into-wet method has so far been used only in the background, where soft effects are appropriate.*

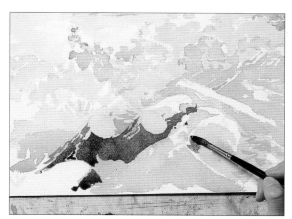

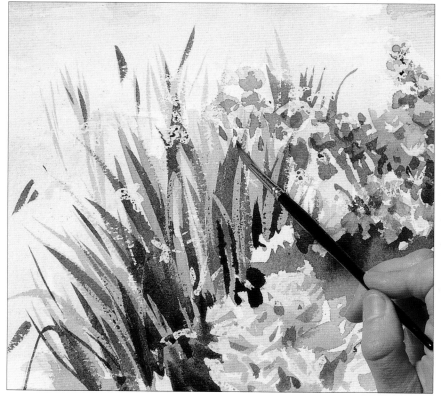

6 *To strengthen the foreground, a dark mixture is painted over the light pink and red-brown washes. This area is worked wet on dry to achieve crisp edges, giving the foreground a sharper focus than the more distant parts of the landscape.*

7 *(Right) The masking fluid has been removed from some of the flowerheads, which are now touched in with pink. The fluid is removed at various stages during the painting, depending on how strong the highlights are to be.*

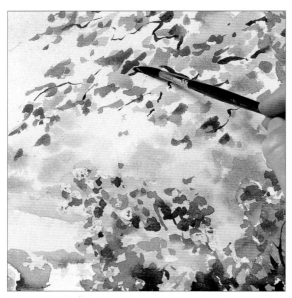

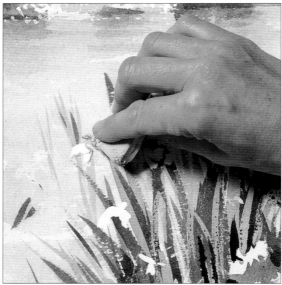

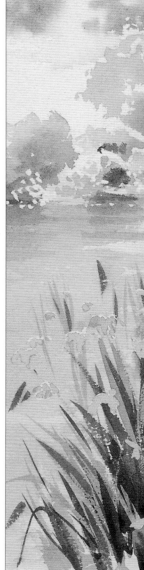

8 *The foliage of the large tree on the right had previously been painted wet into wet to give gentle blends of colour, with yellows merging into blue-greens. Crisp brushmarks now define those leaves nearer the foreground.*

9 *The masking fluid is removed from the flowerheads in the foreground by gently rubbing with a putty eraser. On the reeds it will be left in place, creating an attractive speckled texture similar to the effect of wax resist.*

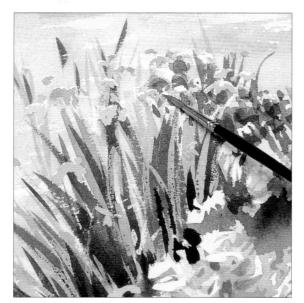

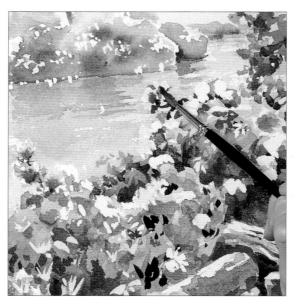

10 *The flowers are now painted in yellow, with tiny patches of the white paper left uncovered. They could have been painted over the light blue of the water, without the use of masking fluid, but even the palest of underlying colours would have compromised the purity of this brilliant yellow.*

11 *Touches of deep pink are added to the flowerheads in the foreground of the picture.*

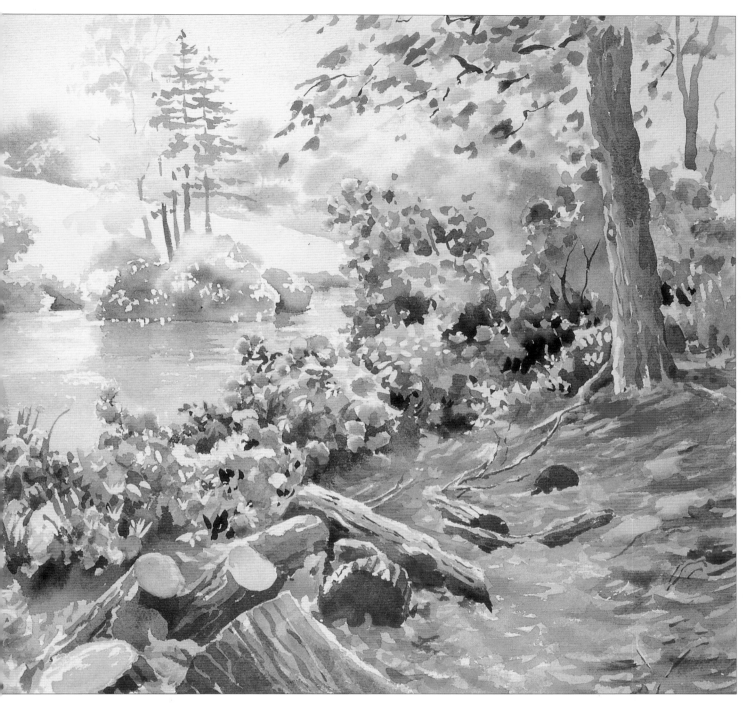

12 (Right) *In the final stages, the tonal contrasts in the foreground are strengthened to bring this area forward and increase the feeling of depth in the painting. The artist drops in dark colour wet into wet, using the tip of the brush.*

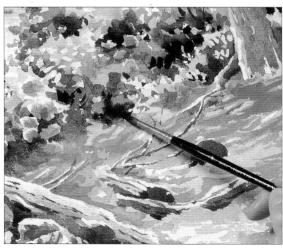

13 (Above) *The artist deliberated over whether to make more of the reflections, which were clearly visible in one of her photographs of the scene, but she decided against it, preferring to emphasize the triangular shape made by the pale expanse of water.*

FLOWERS

If landscape is the most popular subject for watercolour painters, flowers are not far behind. Sometimes, of course, the two subject areas overlap. When you are painting flowers in their natural habitat, perhaps in a garden or a park, you are painting a "mini-landscape", whereas flowers in a vase or bowl indoors become a floral still life.

Whether you paint flowers indoors or out (or both) is up to you, but for those who are new to flower painting it is perhaps best to avoid the problems of changing light, unreliable weather and discomfort. It demands concentration and patience to paint flowers. By setting up your own floral still life, you can take time to arrange it and then work at your own pace.

ARRANGING THE GROUP

Arranging any still-life group takes careful thought, and floral groups are no exception. First you must consider the balance of colours – in general you don't want too many different blooms, with all the shapes and colours fighting for attention. The most effective flower paintings are often those with one predominant colour. You could choose all white flowers, for example, or a selection of blue ones, perhaps with one yellow flower for contrast.

Choose a receptacle which suits the flowers, making them look neither cramped nor swamped. Aim for a natural look and avoid the kind of formal, official arrangement that you sometimes see in churches and public places. Let some of the flowers overlap; have some higher than others, some turned away and others facing you.

PUTTING IT ON PAPER

You will paint more confidently if you start with a good drawing, but, before you begin,

Keeping it simple

(Below) *The kind of elaborate groups beloved of florists do not always make the best paintings, so when you begin to arrange your flowers see if you can improve the composition by limiting their number. In Poppies Elisabeth Harden has given impact to the shapes and colours of the poppies by concentrating on a few flowerheads, including one or two small white flowers and seedheads for contrast. As the red against the dark green foliage in the foreground makes such a dramatic statement, she has wisely left the background unpainted.*

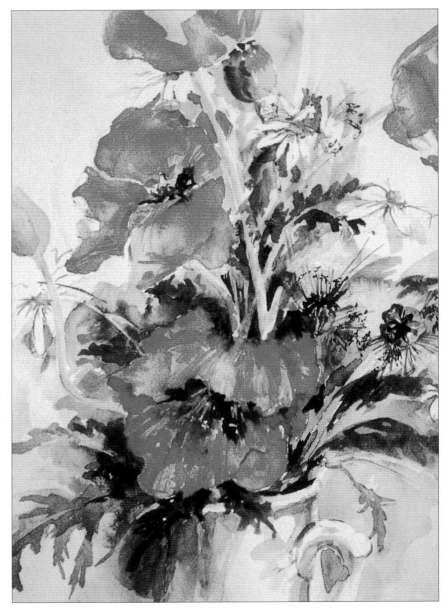

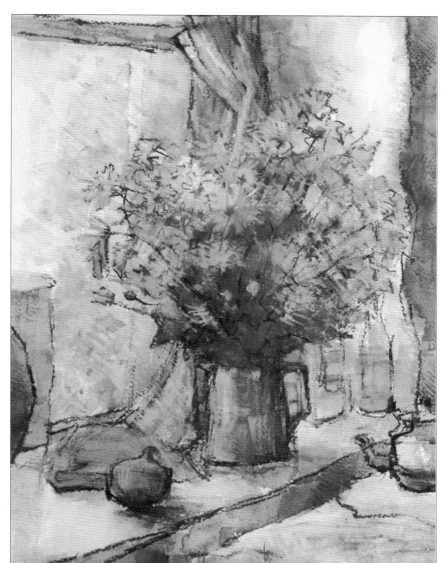

Flowers in still life

(Left) *Flowers do not have to be painted on their own; they can form part of a more general still life, as in* Still Life, Welsh Kitchen *by Joan Elliott Bates. The flowers are the main centre of interest, but the objects and curtain have been carefully arranged, as they play a subsidiary but vitally important role in the composition. Notice particularly the way the curtain sweeps around and upwards, creating a strong curve which provides a foil for the flowers and vase. This is a mixed-media painting, in which watercolour has been combined with Conté crayon and pastel.*

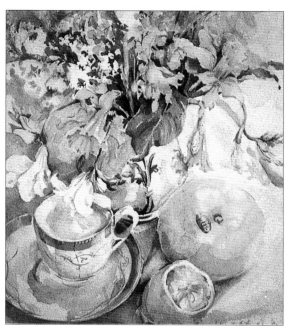

consider how to place the group of flowers on your paper. Again, try to avoid symmetry; don't place the vase exactly in the middle of the picture unless there is enough asymmetry in the arrangement itself to balance this. Decide how much of the group you are going to include. A device often used is "cropping", which means allowing one or two blooms and stems to go out of the picture at the top. This can be very effective if you are painting tall flowers, while a wider group could be cropped at one side or the other.

The foreground and background need consideration too. Avoid leaving a blank space on either side of the vase. Sometimes this can be done by making a positive element out of the shadow cast by the vase; other alternatives are to put the vase on a patterned cloth or to take out one or two of the flowers and place them in front, to one side of the vase.

Backgrounds in watercolour flower painting are often left vague and undefined, but they don't have to be. If there is a window behind the group you could lightly suggest it, thus giving a geometric framework to the composition. Or you could set the group against a patterned wallpaper, which might echo and reinforce the pattern made by the flowers themselves. As a general rule, however, it is best to

Colour unity

(Above) *In* Daffodils and Fruit *Elisabeth Harden has paid attention to the colour schemes, ensuring that links are established between the flowers and objects. The lemon and grapefruit echo the yellows of the daffodils, and similar blues and greys appear in the vase, cup and saucer, and tablecloth. The muted greens of the leaves give greater prominence to the whites, yellows and greys.*

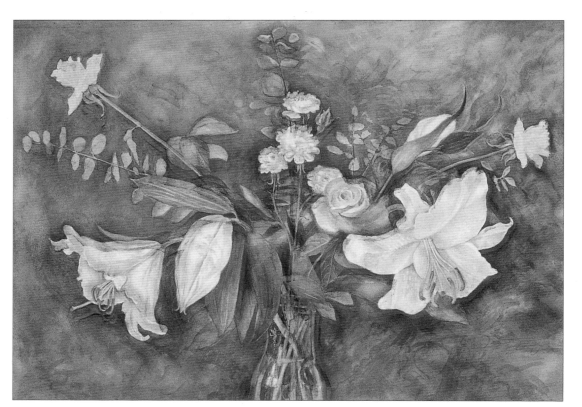

Making a pattern
(Left) *There is a strong built-in pattern element in floral subjects, which has been exploited to the full in Audrey Macleod's* Casablanca Lilies. *Although the forms of the flowers and leaves have been built up carefully so that they are completely realistic and three-dimensional, the painting makes its initial impact as a pattern of light on dark. The soft effects on the leaves and in parts of the background were achieved by washing down the paint.*

avoid too much detail in the background or foreground – the flowers are the centre of interest in the painting, and, by introducing too many other elements, you could rob them of their importance.

THE PAINTING

The essence of flower painting is lightness of touch; if you overwork the paint the freshness of the colours will be lost. Try to work broadly and freely, at least initially, blocking in the main shapes and colours and reserving detail for the final stages. Masking fluid can help you here. If you are painting white or light-coloured flowers against a mass of green foliage, you can mask the flowers and leave them until a later stage in the painting.

Try to set up contrasts between hard and soft edges, using the wet-into-wet technique in some places and painting wet on dry in others to form crisper areas (perhaps for certain well-defined petals or leaves). Don't be tempted to put in small details until you are sure that all the shapes and colours are working as they should – only in the final stages should you bring your tiny, fine brush into play.

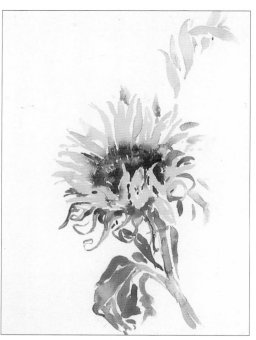

Single blooms
(Above) *Although flowers are more generally painted as an arrangement in a vase, individual flowers make equally rewarding subjects. The artists of China and Japan brought flower painting of this kind to a high art, and Vicky Lowe's lovely* Sunflower *owes much to the Oriental tradition, both in the composition and in the technique, with each petal described by one swift, sure brushstroke. The soft effect where the dark centre of the flower merges into the petals has been achieved by dampening selected areas and dropping in wet paint.*

Using colour
(Opposite) *The way you treat flowers, or any other subject, depends on what it is that particularly interests you. For Gerry Baptist, colour is all-important; in* Clandon Garden Flowers *he has made the most of the brilliant reds and yellows by contrasting them with cool blues, mauves and dark greens. He has also paid attention to the flower shapes, however, and the pansies in the foreground in particular are clearly recognizable.*

Foregrounds and backgrounds

(Right) *When painting a tall floral group it can be
difficult to know what to do with the area below and
beside the vase. In Elisabeth Harden's painting of
poppies, Audrey Macleod's* Casablanca Lilies *and this
watercolour-and-wax-resist painting,* Roses, *by
Debra Manifold, the artists have solved the problem
by cropping the vase at the bottom of the picture.
Here, the way in which the flowers merge into
the dark background is also important to the
composition, with the dark shape seeming to push
upwards away from the pale foreground area,
almost like a firework exploding.*

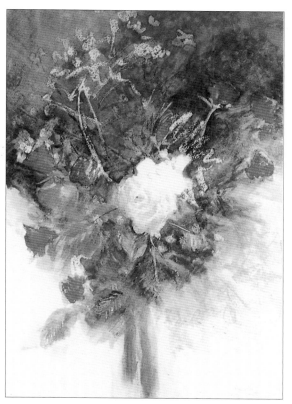

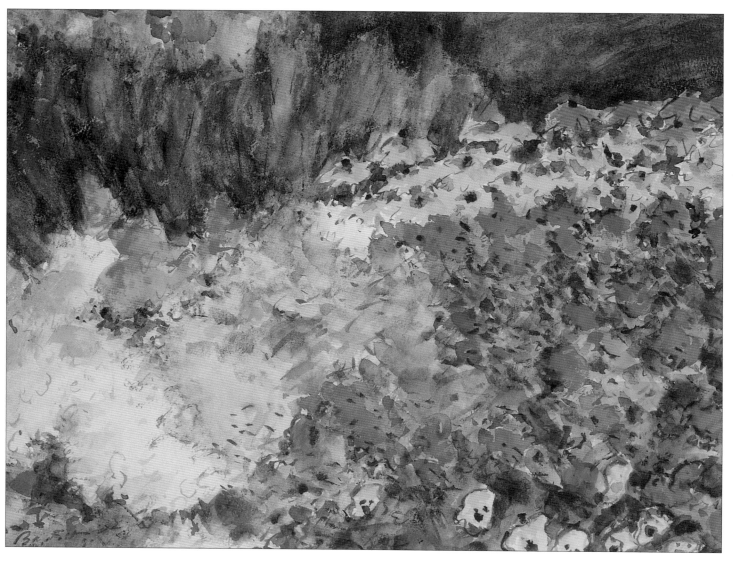

DEMONSTRATION

John Lidzey works entirely in watercolour, enjoying the challenge of its unpredictable nature and the way it encourages the painting to develop in its own way. He paints mainly landscapes and lovely light-filled interiors, the latter often including still lifes and flower groups. He is self-taught and has evolved a highly personal style, at which he arrived through experiment rather than the study of any other artist's methods. He enjoys wet-into-wet effects, although he controls them carefully, and usually paints on smooth-surfaced (hot-pressed) paper to allow the paint to move around more freely.

COLOURS USED *yellow ochre, aureolin yellow, cadmium yellow, ultramarine, cadmium red, carmine, indigo, Payne's gray*

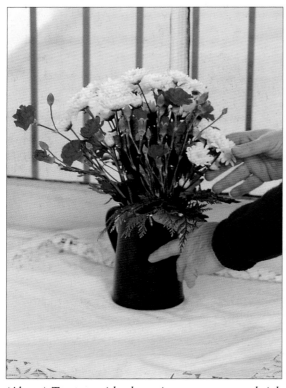

(Above) *To start with, the artist arranges some bright, contrasting flowers in a vase.*

1 *The artist begins with a detailed drawing in 4B pencil. He takes considerable care with this, measuring to check the relative proportions of flowers to vase and so on, and making small marks across the paper to establish key points.*

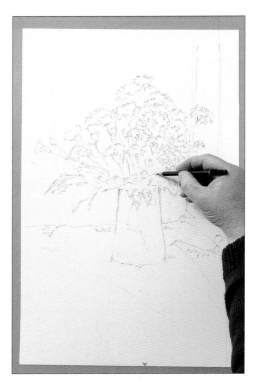

2 *The vase and the shadow beneath are painted wet into wet, with one colour dropped into another so that they merge and mingle. A piece of cotton wool (a cotton ball) is used to control the flow of the paint.*

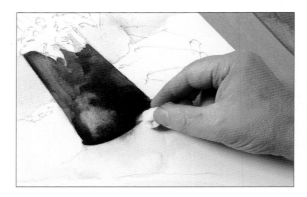

3 *The initial applications of paint are allowed to dry slightly; darker colour is then painted on top and dabbed with cotton wool (a cotton ball) to create soft highlights.*

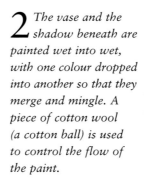
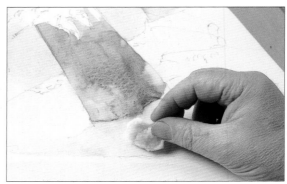

4 *It is unusual to begin with the darkest colour – darks are generally built up gradually. In this case, however, the artist wanted to establish the deep blue of the vase in order to assess the strength of colour needed for the leaves.*

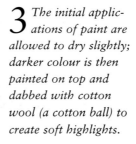
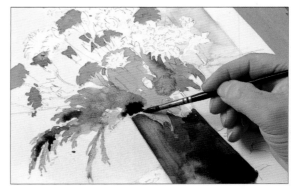

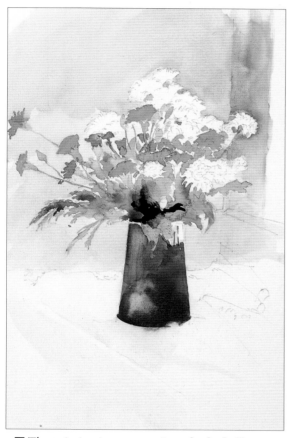

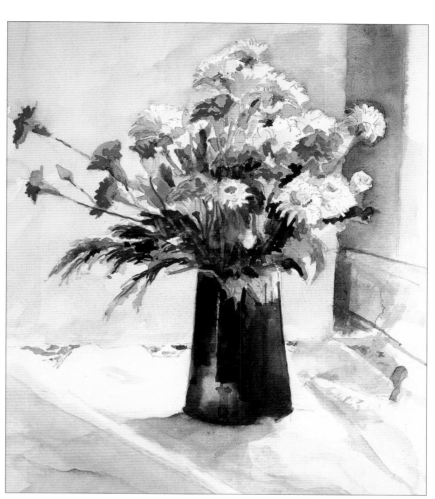

5 *The painting is at approximately the halfway stage, with the darkest colours in place and the white flowers reserved as bare paper.*

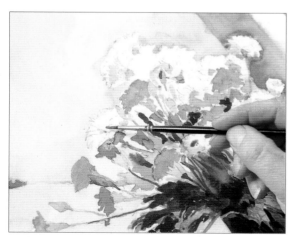

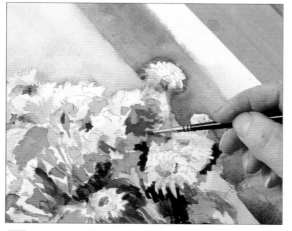

6 *A good deal of the paper is to be left uncovered for the flowers, but they must be given sufficient detail to suggest their structure. A fine-pointed brush is used to touch in the blue-grey shadow.*

7 *Carnations have a very distinctive petal formation; only a few touches of darker paint over the original pink wash are needed to describe their forms and character. The artist is working wet on dry here, to achieve the necessary crisp edges and strong tonal contrasts.*

8 *(Above) Finally, the flowers and leaves are built up with further wet-on-dry work. The pencil marks on the white flowers have been deliberately left showing, to provide further suggestions of detail. The artist subsequently improves the composition by placing paper masks at top and bottom to cut down the rather featureless expanses of foreground and background; look back at Step 5 to see what a difference this makes.*

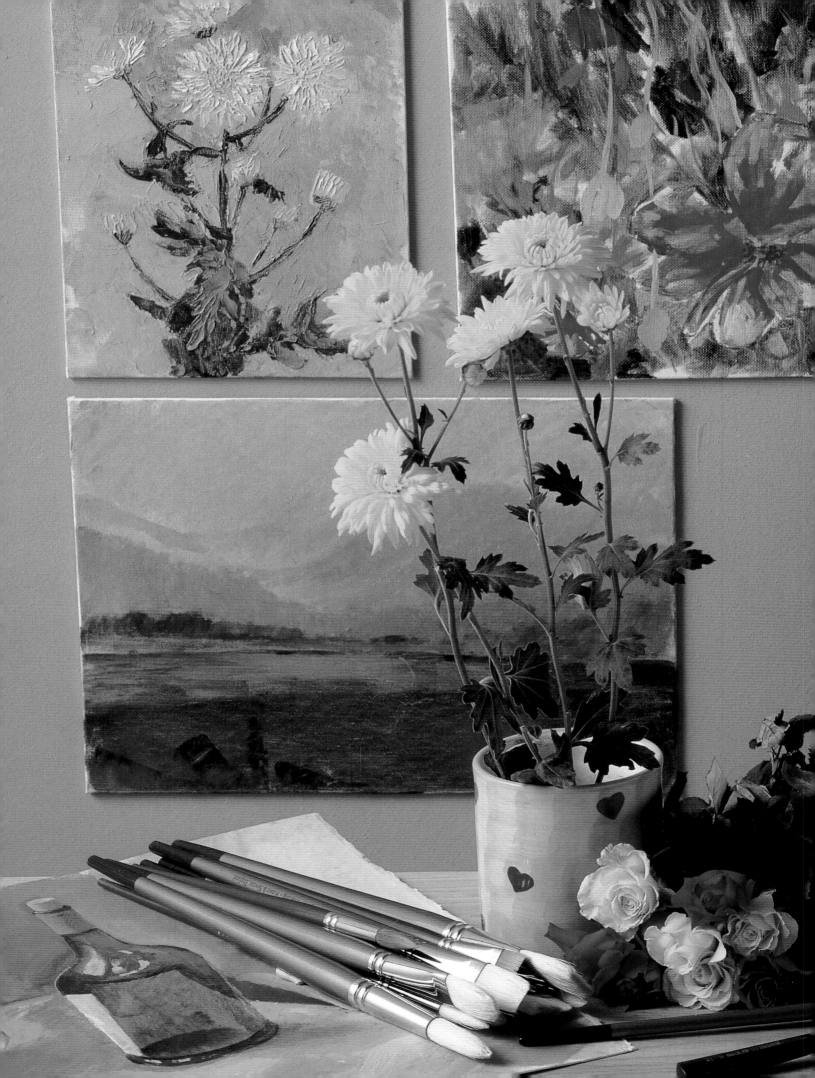

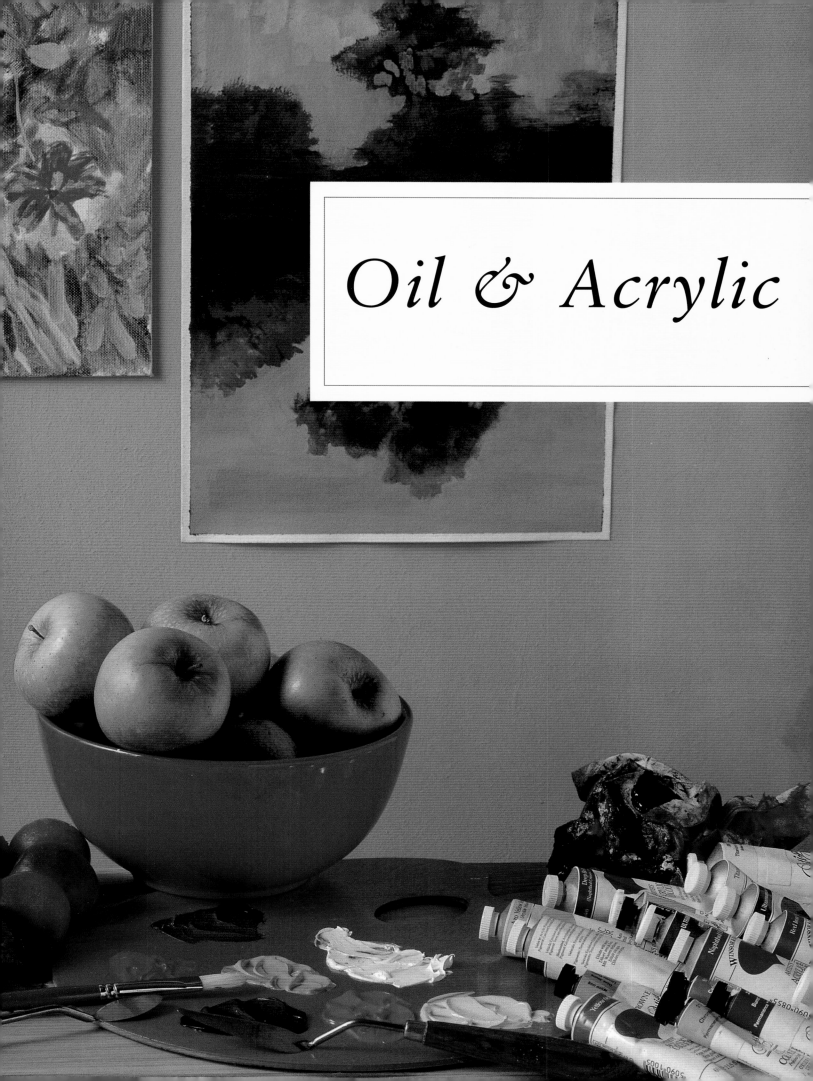

Oil & Acrylic

ABOUT OIL & ACRYLIC

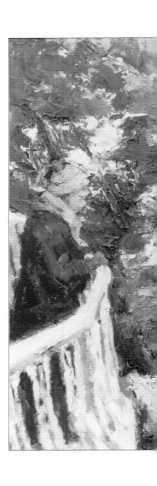

Oil paint, although often seen as the traditional painting medium, is in fact younger than watercolour – or at any rate than a form of watercolour. The tempera paints which preceded oil and were used for both panel paintings and frescoes (wall and ceiling paintings) were made from pigments suspended in water and mixed with some form of glue, usually either egg yoke or casein, made from the curd of milk.

The idea of binding pigment with oil is often credited to the Flemish painter Jan Van Eyck in the early 15th century, but it is probable that other artists had experimented with similar ideas. Whatever the origins of the medium, it rapidly became popular. Tempera was a difficult medium to use, and the potential of oil-bound pigment quickly became obvious.

In the early days of oil painting, the paint was in the main used thinly, rather as tempera had been, but the colours were much richer, achieved by a layering technique called glazing. The surface was smooth, with no brushmarks visible. Later on, however, artists began to use the medium with more appreciation for its inherent qualities, and the marks of the brush (and sometimes of the knife) became an important part of the finished picture. Rembrandt's paintings, for example, demonstrate a love for the paint itself and what it can do, while in the works of the Impressionists, the brushwork and manner of applying the paint are inseparable from the subject matter.

OIL PAINTS TODAY

A walk round an exhibition of oil paintings instantly reveals the versatility of the medium, and it is this quality which has made it so popular from its inception to the

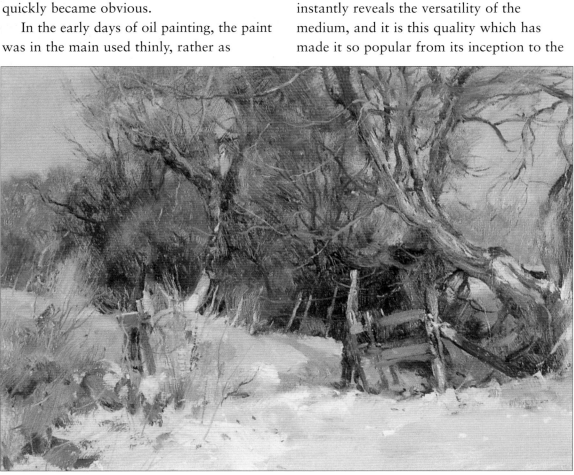

DAVID CURTIS
RED LANE,
NEAR DRONFIELD
(Left) *Brushwork is an important element in this oil painting on canvas; the brushstrokes follow the direction of the tree trunks and branches, describing them with great economy of means. Depth and recession are suggested by the contrast between thick and thin paint: on the right-hand tree the paint is thick and juicy, while for the area of blue distance it has been brushed lightly over the surface.*

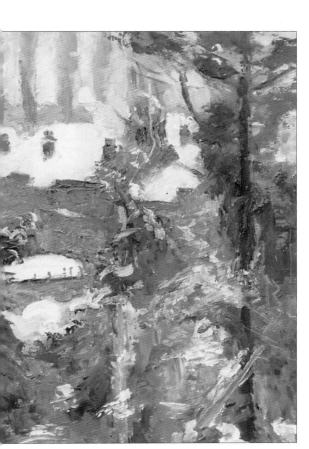

GERRY BAPTIST PINES ON BEAUVBALLA
(Below) *This painting is also acrylic on canvas, but here the paint is slightly diluted with water to a consistency similar to that of gouache paint. The artist controls the juxtapositions of colour carefully, using complementaries such as yellow and mauve to create maximum impact while giving a realistic account of the landscape.*

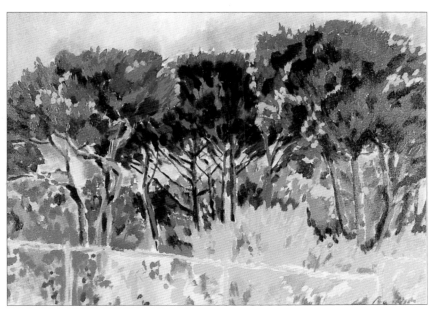

TED GOULD
SNOW SCENE
(Above) *While David Curtis has juxtaposed warm golden browns with the blues and greys of the snow, the colour scheme in this painting is cool throughout; the yellow of the hat and scarf provides the only touch of contrast for the blues, blue-greens, greys and grey-browns. The painting is in acrylic, used thickly on canvas. This artist works mainly in oil, and applies the same methods to his acrylic work.*

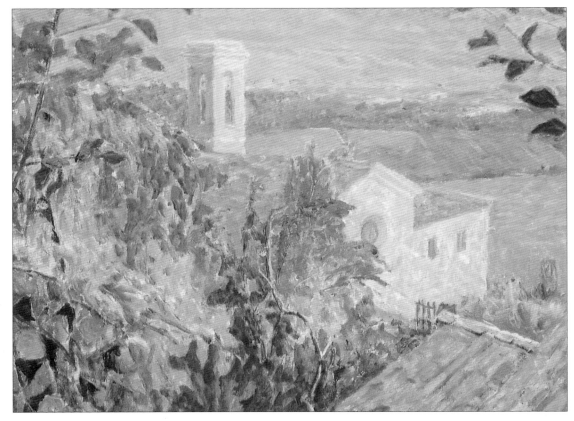

PATRICK CULLEN CHURCH, SAN DONNINO
(Above) *Some artists like to paint on a coloured ground, but when the paint is used thinly, as in this lyrical oil painting, the white of the canvas reflects back through the colours to give a luminosity more often associated with watercolour.*

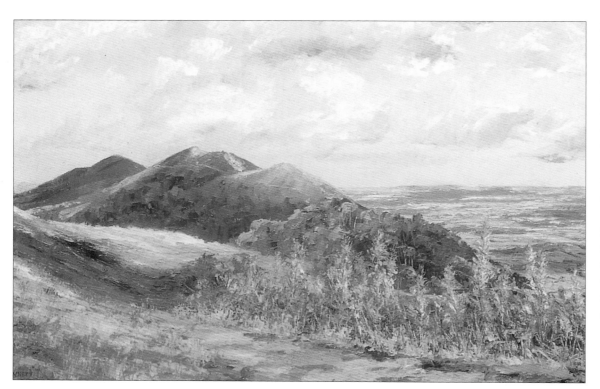

present day. Any painting medium should be seen as the servant of the artist, and oil paints behave in such an obedient manner that no two artists need paint in the same way. Oils can be used thinly or thickly, applied with knives or brushes – or even your fingers – and you can work on a large or a small scale. You can also move paint around on the picture surface, and, best of all for inexperienced painters, you can scrape the paint off and start again.

In times gone by, artists had to employ assistants to grind the pigments laboriously to make up the paint, but today we have no such chores to perform. The paint comes to us in convenient tubes, so that outdoor work presents no problem. The colours are all manufactured to the highest standards possible and there is a wider choice than ever before. There are ready-made canvases and painting boards, as well as brushes to suit all styles and ways of working. Furthermore, new mediums to use with oil paints have made it possible to revive some of the old techniques, such as glazing, which had been largely abandoned by the late 19th century. The oil painter has never been in such a fortunate position.

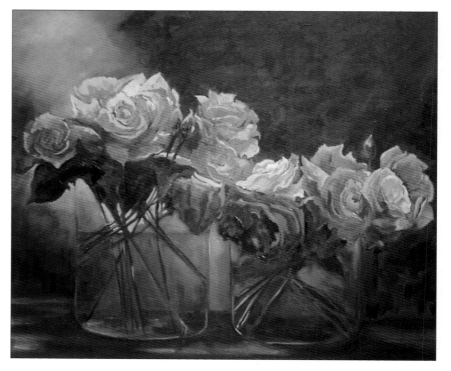

MADGE BRIGHT
VICTORIAN ROSES IN GLASS
(Above) *Once more, oil paint is the medium used for this lovely painting, which provides a perfect example of the skilful exploitation of a limited colour scheme consisting almost entirely of pinks and dark greens. In spite of its apparent simplicity the painting is meticulously planned and composed, with the mass of the flowerheads creating a strong, irregular shape across the picture, and the stalks arranged to introduce a contrasting linear pattern.*

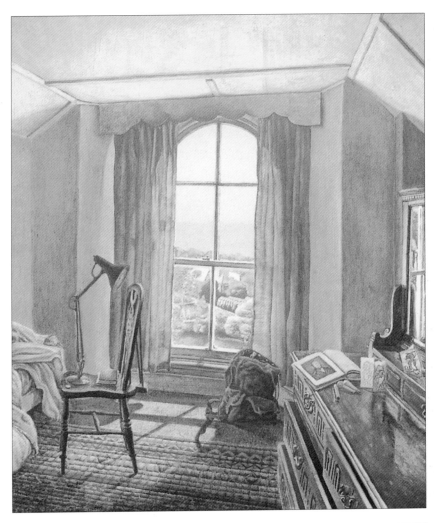

PAUL BARTLETT
ROOM 15, KATHMORE HOUSE, FALMOUTH
(Left) *Light is the primary theme of this picture, painted in oil on canvas. The colour scheme is similar to that of Karen Raney's painting (below),* but here the artist has used a very different technique. The brushstrokes are almost invisible and every detail and texture is described in minute detail.

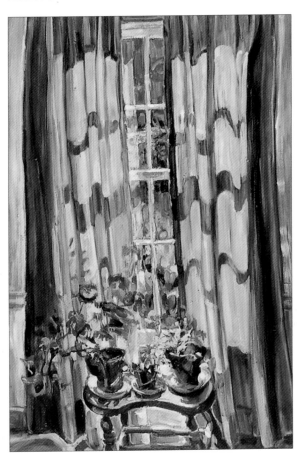

KAREN RANEY
CLAIRMONT ROAD
(Above) *Room interiors can make exciting painting subjects, providing opportunities for exploring the effects of light.* In this painting, also in oil on canvas, the shadows thrown on the curtain by the window bars have created an intriguing pattern of light on dark, which the artist has made her central theme. She has chosen a tall-format canvas in order to stress the vertical thrust of the composition.

STEWART GEDDES
ROSE-COLOURED HOUSE, PROVENCE
(Left) *In certain lights, brick and stonework can appear surprisingly rich in colour;* the building here, which might have looked dull under a grey sky, has provided the artist with the inspiration for an essay in colour. Colours always appear more vivid by contrast, and he has introduced neutral colours to enhance the warm, glowing hues. The painting is done in oil on board.

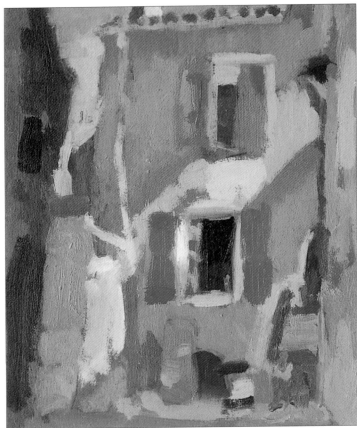

OLIVER BEVAN
SHARP CORNER
(Right) *Bevan paints both landscapes and urban scenes, using colour in a way that is not strictly naturalistic but which invokes a powerful atmosphere. In this oil painting, strong contrasts of tone and colour produce a highly dramatic effect, with a slight sense of menace reinforced by the two dark figures and the gravestone shapes in the foreground.*

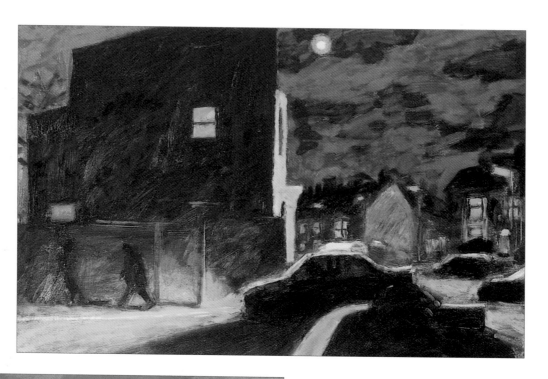

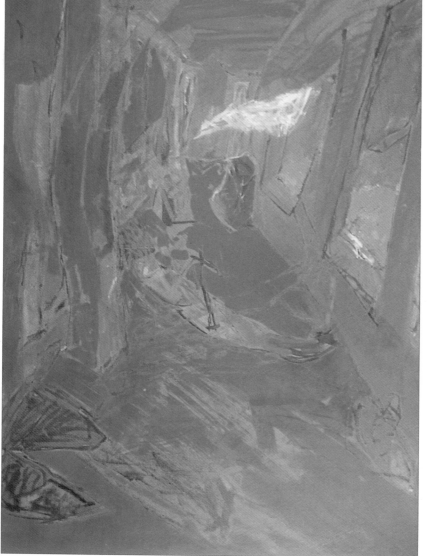

ANNE VANCATOVA
BLUE INTERIOR
(Left) *Painted in oil on canvas, this evocative and intriguing painting of an interior is a celebration of colour. An intense sky blue is used to cover most of the canvas, and form is picked out with a minimum of dark, linear marks which convey the composition's perspective and touches of yellow-green, red and white which hint at details of the scene such as the evening light outside the windows.*

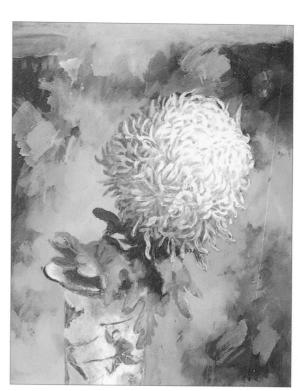

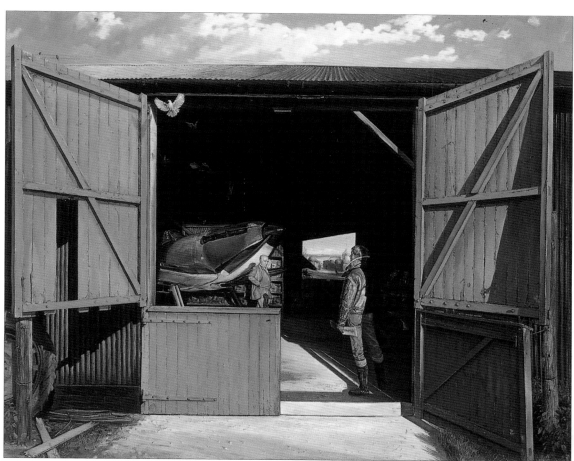

TIMOTHY EASTON
RESTORATION
(Right) *The degree of control in this oil painting is breathtaking, with every detail and texture minutely described – notice especially the peeling paint on the open doors and the leather jacket worn by the figure in the doorway. When figures are included in a painting they generally become the centre of interest, but here the power of the geometric pattern of brilliant blue, near-black and golden brown is such that the figures play a minor role; the painting can almost be read as an abstract composition in colour.*

ROSALIND CUTHBERT
GIANT CHRYSANTHEMUM
(Opposite) *One of the beauties of acrylic is that, because it is not oil-based, it can be used in conjunction with other water-based paints as well as with various drawing media. Working on paper, the artist has used acrylic with gouache paint, exploiting the contrast of thick and thin paint and adding touches of texture and detail to the flowerhead and vase by using the effective sgraffito technique.*

ACRYLICS

A by-product of the new plastics industry, acrylics were invented in the 1950s. Perhaps because they are such newcomers to the art scene, a certain amount of prejudice against them still exists in some quarters, which is a pity, as they are as versatile as oil paints and have some unique qualities of their own.

One of these – vital from the amateur standpoint – is that they dry very quickly, so that you can overpaint as much as you like. You can, of course, overpaint with oils but, because they are slow-drying, there is always a risk of churning up the colours and creating a muddy mess. Acrylics, once dry, are immovable, so that each new layer completely covers the one below without picking up any colour from it. Another advantage is that you can paint on more or less anything, from paper and board to canvas, and the surface needs no advance preparation, or "priming".

Acrylic paints can be used as "imitation" oils because they behave in much the same way, but there are differences between the two, both in handling and in make-up. All paints are made from fine-ground pigment particles suspended in liquid and bound with a glue of some kind. In the case of acrylics the liquid is water and the binder is a form of plastic – a polymer resin to be precise. Acrylics are thus water-based, not oil-based and, if they need to be thinned, you use water not oil. Likewise, brushes used with acrylics come clean in water, not white spirit.

The disadvantages of acrylics are that changes to the picture can only be made by overpainting, and the paint dries so fast that it cannot be moved around on the surface to any degree like oil paints can. Also, brushes must always be left in a container of water or washed regularly, otherwise they will be ruined. However, the virtues of acrylics far outweigh these minor vices, and those new to painting could find them the perfect medium with which to begin.

PAINTS, BRUSHES & MEDIUMS

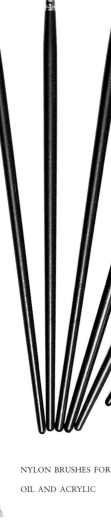

O I L & A C R Y L I C

Both oils and acrylics come in tubes, though some manufacturers of acrylics also produce them in pots, of about the same size as those used for poster paints. Tubes are the usual choice, but pots have the advantage of minimizing wastage. When

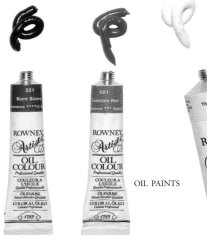

OIL PAINTS

acrylic paints are squeezed onto the palette at the beginning of a working session, some paint is usually left at the end which is wasted, having become hard and unworkable. With pots, you can dip in as needed and replace the lid immediately. However, the paint is thinner than that in tubes and is thus less effective for thick, oil-painterly effects.

BRUSHES

Long-handled bristle brushes are traditionally used for oil painting and are equally satisfactory for acrylic. They are made in three basic shapes: flats, rounds and filberts, all of which make a different kind of brushstroke. Only experience will tell you which ones you prefer, so as with paint colours it is wise to begin with a small range – perhaps two of each type.

Most artists' kits include one or two soft brushes, which are used for small details as

well as for any flat, smooth areas of paint. Sables are the best, but they are expensive (and very easy to ruin), so start with one of the many synthetic substitutes, or a sable and synthetic mixture. There is an excellent range of white nylon brushes specially

NYLON BRUSHES FOR OIL AND ACRYLIC

formulated for acrylic painting, and these can also be used for oils.

MEDIUMS
Both oils and acrylics can be used straight from the tube, but often some medium is used to thin the paint or change its quality. Acrylics are water-based and are thus

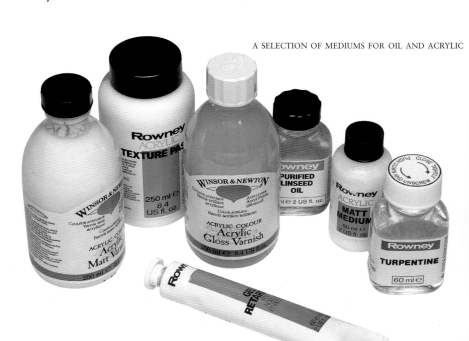

A SELECTION OF MEDIUMS FOR OIL AND ACRYLIC

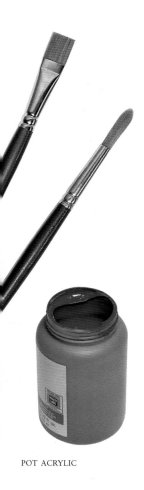

POT ACRYLIC

BRISTLE BRUSHES FOR
OIL AND ACRYLIC

thinned with more water, while oil paints are diluted with turpentine, a mixture of turpentine and linseed oil, or with linseed oil alone.

Various special mediums are made for particular methods of painting. For both

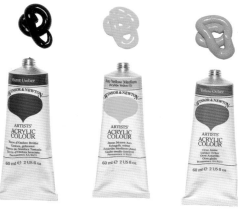

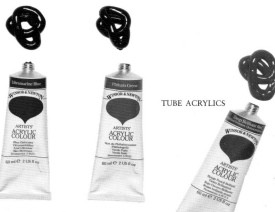

TUBE ACRYLICS

oil and acrylic, for example, there are glazing mediums which make the paint more transparent and thin it without causing it to become runny. For those who like to paint very thickly, impasto mediums bulk the paint out. You won't need any of these

initially, but you may want to try them later on, so we will be looking at their uses in the section dealing with techniques.

However, if you intend to try acrylics, there is one special medium you may find useful from the start. This is a retarder, which slows the drying time of the paint, allowing you to manipulate it more easily. It is only used for thick paint, as water affects its performance, but it is a great help for acrylic used in the "oil mode".

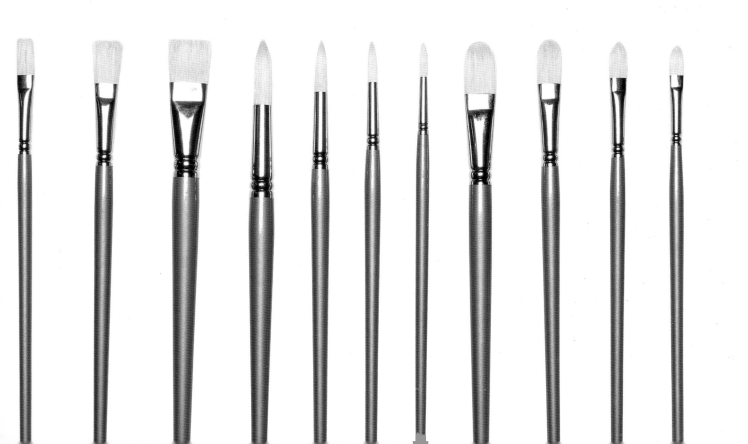

PALETTES & PAINTING SURFACES

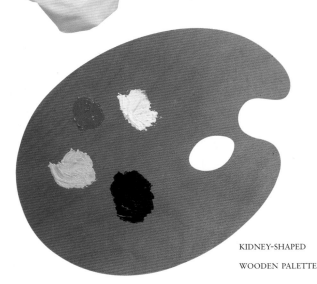

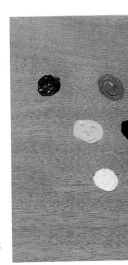

O
I
L

&

A
C
R
Y
L
I
C

The palettes normally used for oil are made of wood and are either kidney-shaped or rectangular (to fit into the lid of a paintbox). Both have a hole for the thumb so that you can hold them comfortably when you work in the traditional standing position. But you do not have to work standing up, nor do you have to hold the palette. Many artists prefer an improvised palette such as a piece of thick glass or hardboard, which they place on a surface beside them, such as a low table or stool.

Glass is a popular choice for acrylic. Wooden oil-painting palettes are not suitable because the paint cannot be removed easily when dry; you need a non-absorbent surface. The palettes sold especially for acrylic are white plastic. Some people find these satisfactory, but others dislike them, as the glaring white surface makes it difficult to judge the colours when mixing them.

There is one other special palette made for acrylic work, which is particularly useful if you are painting out of doors. This "Stay-Wet" palette is a shallow plastic tray in which there is a top layer of non-absorbent paper and a lower layer of blotting paper. Water is poured into the tray below the blotting paper, the paints are laid out on the top layer, and enough water seeps through from the blotting paper to keep them moist. There is also a transparent plastic lid that fits over the tray, keeping the paint fresh more or less indefinitely.

WORKING SURFACES

The best-known surface for oil painting (also used for acrylic) is stretched canvas – that is, some form of cotton or linen material supported by a wooden frame. Canvases are not cheap, but you can stretch your own quite easily. The larger art shops sell canvas

KIDNEY-SHAPED
WOODEN PALETTE

RECTANGULAR
WOODEN PALETTE

by the metre, and stretchers can be bought in pairs. Another method is to stick the material (which does not have to be canvas; you can use old sheets) onto a stiff board such as hardboard (Masonite). You can do this with animal skin glue (size) or with PVA medium diluted with water.

A primer, or ground, is a layer of paint on top of the canvas or board which, in the case of oil paint, prevents the oil from seeping into the material and damaging it. Most canvases and painting boards now made are intended for both oil and acrylic.

There is a variety of different boards sold for oil and acrylic painting, the best of which are canvas-textured. They form an inexpensive alternative to canvases. You can also paint on hardboard (Masonite) or tough cardboard, but for oil painting you need a primer. The best all-purpose one is acrylic gesso.

You can paint on paper too. For acrylic applied fairly thinly, ordinary cartridge (drawing) paper is fine, but for oil, or acrylic built up thickly, use something more solid, such as heavy watercolour paper.

1 CANVAS BOARD

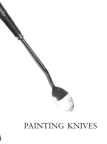

PAINTING KNIVES

Stretching unprimed canvas

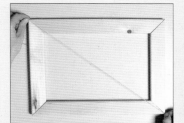

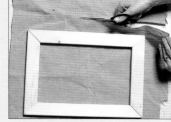

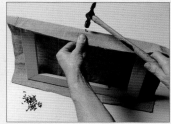

1 When you have assembled the stretchers, use a piece of string to check both diagonal measurements, taking it across one way and then the other. If the second measurement differs from the first, the rectangle is out of alignment.

2 Place the stretcher on the canvas, make pencil marks all the way round at least 5 cm (2 in) from the stretcher, and cut out the canvas.

3 Hammer a tack into the centre of the first long side, and then another one on the opposite side; continue from the centre outwards. You can use a staple gun, but tacks are easier to remove if re-using the stretchers.

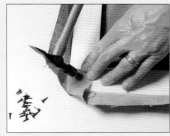

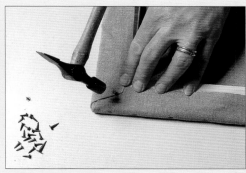

4 There are various ways of dealing with corners, but this is one of the simplest. Fold in the corner of the canvas neatly and then hammer in a tack to hold it in place.

5 Fold in the remaining flaps of canvas and tack again. Unprimed canvas should not be stretched too tightly because the priming will shrink it. To stretch ready-primed canvas, you need canvas pliers.

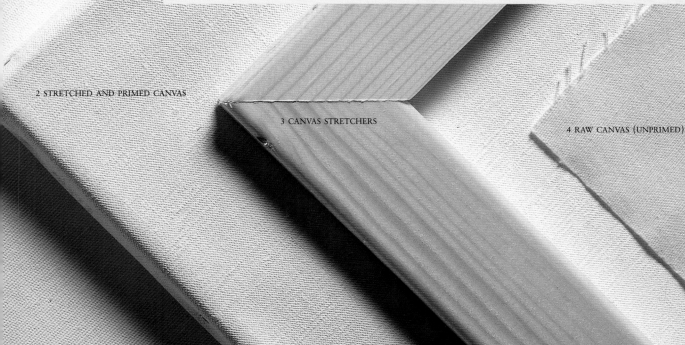

2 STRETCHED AND PRIMED CANVAS

3 CANVAS STRETCHERS

4 RAW CANVAS (UNPRIMED)

Mixing

PRIMARY &
SECONDARY COLOURS

Most non-painters know something about colour, for example many people can name the colours of the spectrum (which are those you see in a rainbow). There are seven of these: violet, indigo, blue, green, yellow, orange and red; they are produced by the dispersal of white light through a prism – different colours have different wavelengths. But while this kind of knowledge may have its uses in photography or colour printing, it cannot be applied usefully when it comes to painting. The colours of light are absolute, there is just one red, yellow, blue and so on, but artist's pigments are not.

MIXING SECONDARIES
The spectrum colours have given rise to the well-known belief that it is possible to mix

any colour under the sun from the three primary colours alone: red, yellow and blue. The colour pictures in this book are indeed produced from just these three colours (plus black), but paints simply do not work in this way. In colour printing a series of tiny dots of pure colour mixes in the eye (optical mixing), but paints have to be physically combined. More important still, pigments are not pure; there are different versions of each primary colour, so which red, blue and yellow would you choose for mixing up another colour?

The first step to successful colour mixing is to recognize the differences between the primary colours; only then can you discover how to mix the best secondary colours – mixtures of two primaries. If you look at the reds, yellows and blues on the starter

Mixing secondary colours
(Opposite) The top row shows mixtures of "like" primaries – those with a bias towards each other – and the bottom row shows the more muted colours produced by mixing unlike pairs of primaries. In each case the primary colours are shown on the right and left, and the mixtures in the three central divisions. The mixtures nearest to the primary colours have a higher proportion of this colour, while for the central division the colours have been mixed in equal proportions.

A STARTER PALETTE

As a general rule it is wise to begin with as few colours as possible and build up gradually. As you become more experienced you will discover which colours you find difficult or impossible to mix, and you can add to your range accordingly. It is virtually impossible, for example, to achieve good purples and mauves by mixing colours, so artists who specialize in flower painting usually have one or two purples as well as some special reds. The colours shown here will be quite adequate to begin with. They are available in both oils and acrylics, although some acrylic ranges use different names for the colours. For example, some makes of acrylic do not include viridian, but there is a similar colour called phthalocyanine green.

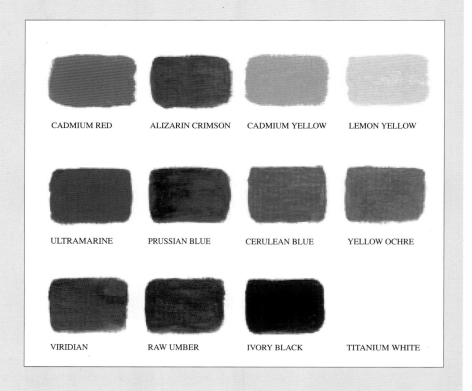

CADMIUM RED   ALIZARIN CRIMSON   CADMIUM YELLOW   LEMON YELLOW

ULTRAMARINE   PRUSSIAN BLUE   CERULEAN BLUE   YELLOW OCHRE

VIRIDIAN   RAW UMBER   IVORY BLACK   TITANIUM WHITE

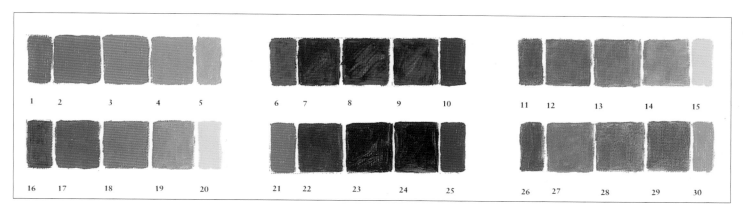

1 CADMIUM RED 2, 3 AND 4 MIXTURES 5 CADMIUM YELLOW 6 ALIZARIN CRIMSON 7, 8 AND 9 MIXTURES 10 ULTRAMARINE 11 CERULEAN

12, 13 AND 14 MIXTURES 15 LEMON YELLOW 16 ALIZARIN CRIMSON 17, 18 AND 19 MIXTURES 20 LEMON YELLOW 21 CADMIUM RED

22, 23 AND 24 MIXTURES 25 ULTRAMARINE 26 CERULEAN 27, 28 AND 29 MIXTURES 30 CADMIUM YELLOW

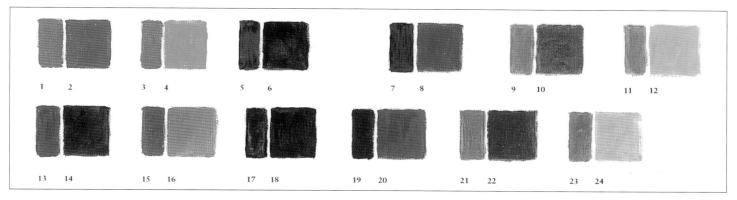

1 ORANGE (CADMIUM RED AND YELLOW) 2 PLUS BLACK 3 ORANGE 4 PLUS WHITE 5 PURPLE (ALIZARIN CRIMSON AND ULTRAMARINE) 6 PLUS BLACK 7 PURPLE 8 PLUS

WHITE 9 GREEN (CERULEAN AND LEMON YELLOW) 10 PLUS BLACK 11 GREEN 12 PLUS WHITE 13 MUTED ORANGE 14 PLUS BLACK 15 MUTED ORANGE 16 PLUS WHITE

17 PURPLE BROWN 18 PLUS BLACK 19 PURPLE BROWN 20 PLUS WHITE 21 GREEN 22 PLUS BLACK 23 GREEN 24 PLUS WHITE

Adding black and white
(Above) These "swatches" give an idea of the large range of colours which can be made by adding black or white to mixtures. The 50:50 mixtures of primary colours shown in the chart above have been taken as the basis, with first black and then white added.

palette, you will see that they have different biases. One red leans towards purple or blue, and the other is more orange; lemon yellow is greener than cadmium yellow; ultramarine is slightly redder than cerulean or Prussian blue. The most vivid secondary colours are made by mixing primaries which are biased towards each other. You cannot make a good, bright orange, for example, with lemon yellow and alizarin crimson, or a good purple with cadmium red and ultramarine.

Making charts like the ones shown here, using the six basic primary colours, first on their own and then with the addition of black and white, will teach you a great deal about colour. As well as finding out how to make bright secondary colours, you may discover some useful mixtures for more muted effects. If so, try to remember them, as many paintings are spoilt by muddy, characterless neutrals. For example, an interesting grey is often made from a mixture of colours, not black and white.

USING A RESTRICTED PALETTE

O
I
L
&
A
C
R
Y
L
I
C

Painting with a limited range of colours is an exercise often set in art schools. In this case the idea is to use only the six basic primary colours: cadmium red, alizarin crimson, cadmium and lemon yellow, ultramarine and Prussian blue; plus white. You are not allowed black because, although a useful colour, it is also a seductive one; you may feel tempted to take the easy way out by adding it whenever you want to darken a colour, and this can lead to muddy, dull mixtures. White is permitted because there is no other way to lighten colours when you are using opaque paints, but you may discover that white is not always the answer. Adding white to red, for instance, turns it pink, so it is sometimes better to add yellow instead.

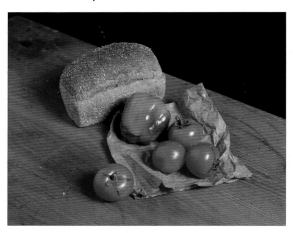

Choose a simple still-life group like the one shown here, but make sure you have plenty of colour contrast and some good dark areas to test your ability to make dark colours without black. You can use either oil or acrylic – the exercise is about mixing colours rather than handling paints.

COLOURS USED (OIL PAINTS) *titanium white, Prussian blue, alizarin crimson, ultramarine, cadmium red, lemon yellow, cadmium yellow*

Still life in six hues

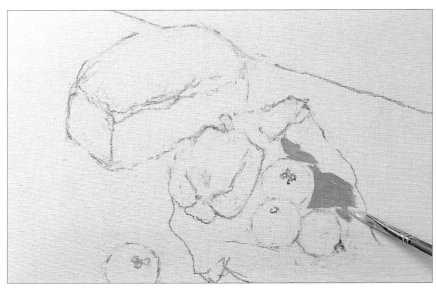

1 *The colour used here, which looks very similar to yellow ochre, has been mixed from white, lemon yellow and a little cadmium red.*

2 *For the tomatoes, the artist uses a mixture of both reds, with an added touch of lemon yellow for the lighter areas. He leaves the white of the board to show through for the highlights.*

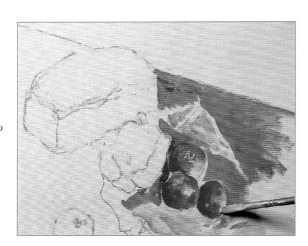

3 *The basic green for the pepper is ultramarine and cadmium yellow, two colours which can be mixed in varying proportions to produce a good range of greens.*

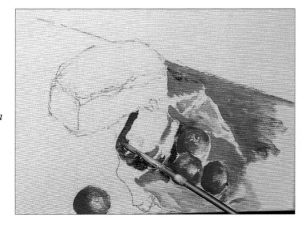

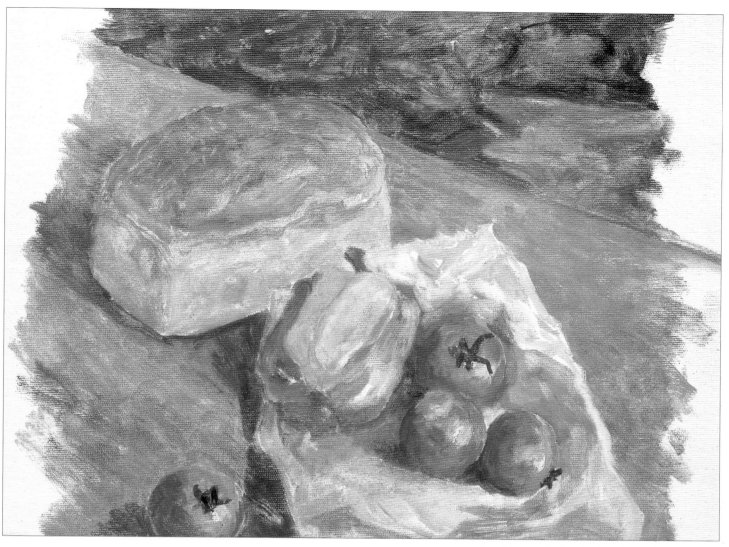

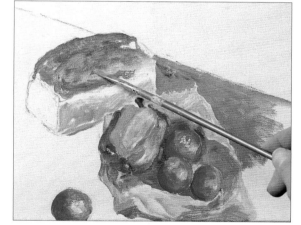

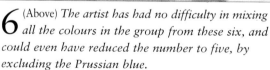

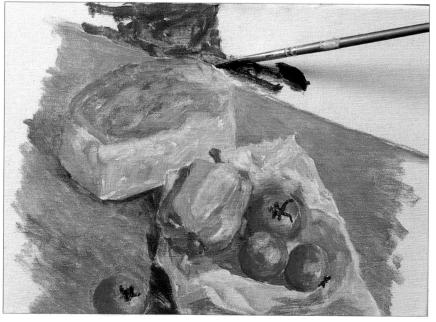

6 (Above) *The artist has had no difficulty in mixing all the colours in the group from these six, and could even have reduced the number to five, by excluding the Prussian blue.*

4 *The brown for the loaf of bread is similar to the colour used in Step 1, but slightly darkened with small additions of alizarin crimson and ultramarine.*

5 (Right) *Prussian blue, a very strong, dark colour which must be used sparingly, is now mixed with both reds and yellows for the background. A similar mixture, but with more Prussian blue, was used for the leaves on the tomatoes.*

COLOUR RELATIONSHIPS

Establishing how to mix colours similar to the ones you observe is a vital step in the business of learning to paint, but you also need to understand something about how colours relate to each other. No colour exists in isolation – it is defined by juxtaposition and contrast with other colours. An orange or lemon placed on a neutral-coloured or dark cloth shines out because of the strong contrast, but the same fruit on an orange or yellow cloth forms no contrast, and thus creates little impact.

The fruit on a dark cloth would make use of contrasts of tone, which means the lightness or darkness of a colour. Tonal contrasts are important in painting, but there are other kinds of contrast too. Bright colours can contrast with neutral ones, and so-called "warm" colours with "cool" ones.

TEMPERATURE

Artists often describe colours in terms of "temperature", a visual and partially subjective quality that cannot be measured. Blues, blue-greens and blue-greys are cool, while reds, yellows and colours with red and yellow in them are warm.

Warm–cool contrasts are a way of creating the impression of space and recession in a painting. This is because the warm colours tend to advance to the front of the picture and the cool ones to recede further into the background.

But everything in colour is relative; even a colour ordinarily described as cool may lose its recessive habit if there is an insufficient contrast of warm colours. To complicate matters further, there are warm and cool versions of each colour. Ultramarine, which has a red bias, is warmer than cerulean or Prussian blue, and cadmium yellow is warmer than the slightly acid lemon yellow, which leans towards green.

NEUTRALS

These colours, the greys, browns, beiges and all the indeterminate ones in between, are often dismissed as unimportant. But, in fact, they have a vital role to play: they act as a foil for the bright colours and provide a framework for them.

The trouble with neutrals is that, because they are often difficult to analyse, it is hard to know which colours to start mixing. Furthermore, they are only neutral by virtue of contrast; for example, a greenish grey that takes a definite back seat when juxtaposed with red can look quite vivid when set against the ultimate neutral – a mixture of black and white.

Apart from the latter, which has no colour at all and should seldom, if ever, be used in painting, all neutral colours have their own colour biases. Greys are yellowish, brownish, slightly blue or tending towards mauve. This means that they must fit in with the colour bias of your painting. A useful device is to scrape your palette with a palette knife halfway through a working session and use this subtle colour mixture for neutrals. This ensures that the neutrals, being a mixture of all the colours used, will work in the context of the painting. You can do this only in oil, unfortunately, as acrylic dries too quickly on the palette.

Another good way of neutralizing a colour is to use its complementary. Complementary colours are those that are opposite each other on a colour wheel: red and green, violet and yellow, orange and blue. When these pairs of vivid opposite colours are mixed together they cancel each other out, making subtle neutrals that vary according to the proportions of the colours used. Successful neutrals always give a painting much more impact.

Warm and cool colours
As can be seen here, the warm colours, the reds, oranges and yellows, push forward in front of the cooler greens and blues. However, the orange does not advance as much on warmer blue.

Relative values
The colours in the centres of the first two squares are cool, but do not recede because the surrounding colours are cooler still. In the second pair, all the colours are warm, but the alizarin crimson and lemon yellow are cooler than the orange.

Neutrals
All the colours shown in the swatches are neutral, made from black and white with small additions of other colours. Seen in isolation they do not seem to be any particular colour, though some have biases towards red, green or blue. However, the squares at the bottom show how differently they appear depending on their surroundings. In the first and third squares a neutral colour is shown against a vivid background, while in the second and fourth the background is a neutral grey made from black and white.

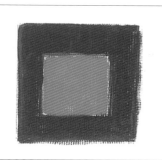

ORANGE ON ULTRAMARINE

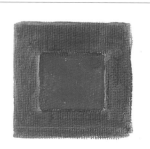

CADMIUM RED ON BLUE-GREEN

ORANGE ON CERULEAN BLUE

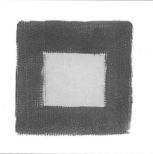

LEMON YELLOW ON GREEN

ULTRAMARINE ON PRUSSIAN BLUE

YELLOW-GREEN ON BLUE-GREEN

ORANGE ON ALIZARIN

CADMIUM YELLOW ON LEMON YELLOW

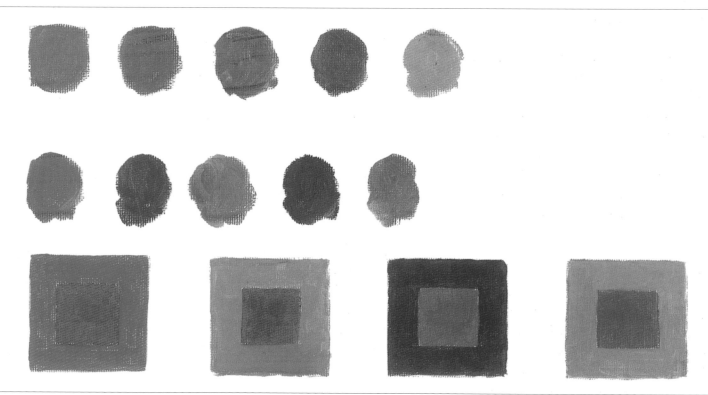

NEUTRAL BROWN ON CADMIUM RED   SAME COLOUR ON GREY   NEUTRAL GREY ON ULTRAMARINE   SAME COLOUR ON GREY

PAINTING WHITE

There is no better way of learning how to analyse and mix neutral colours than by painting one or two bright-coloured objects on a white background. You will also discover how radically light affects colour. Dark colours absorb the light but white is reflective, so when you look at a white object you see a marvellous range of subtle colours and probably very little pure white, or even none at all. The colours vary according to the kind of light you are working under, and on the objects, which can throw colour into the nearby shadows. Unfortunately, as the light changes so do the colours – a particular problem if your group is set up near a window. But it is a challenging task and well worth trying.

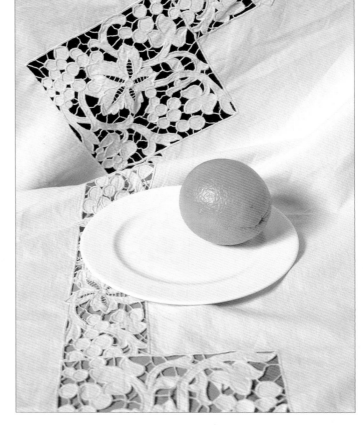

COLOURS USED *black, ultramarine, cerulean blue, Indian red, cadmium red, Venetian red, burnt umber, yellow ochre, cadmium yellow, lemon yellow, titanium white*

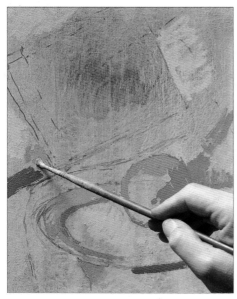

1 *As the orange is the brightest colour in the group, it has been blocked in first. This provides a key, enabling the artist to assess the grey-greens and blue-greens for the plate and background.*

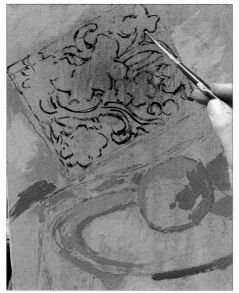

2 *He moves on to the area of strongest tonal contrast, drawing in the pattern of the cloth with a fine sable brush.*

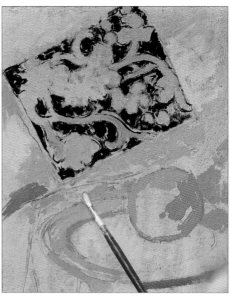

3 *As he works, he carefully assesses one colour against another. The greys of the cloth are far from being colourless, although they are neutral in comparison with the orange.*

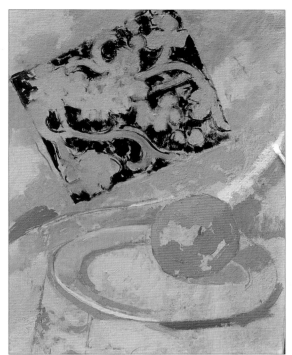

4 *The middle tones of the cloth have been established before the lightest areas, where the folds of the cloth catch the light. Here the artist has used pure white, but has painted lightly so that the brushstroke is broken up by the texture of the canvas, and a little of the underlying colour shows through.*

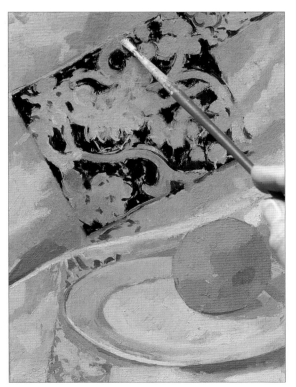

5 *The orange and the plate have been solidly built up and final touches are now given to the background. The tonal contrasts here must not be too strong, so the white is mixed with a little yellow and red to darken and warm it.*

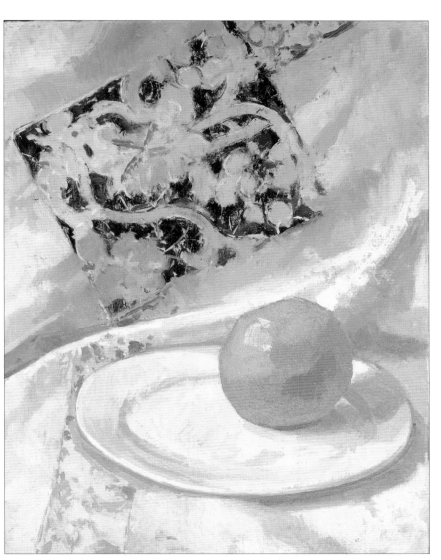

6 *The artist has worked on fine canvas stretched over board and lightly tinted with a wash of watercolour. He finds that a coloured ground makes it easier to judge the tones of his mixtures, and in a subject such as this, with a predominance of light tones, it is particularly helpful.*

WORKING ALLA PRIMA

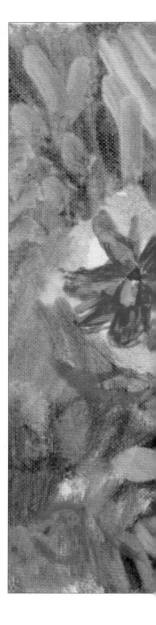

Students often want to know how to build up an oil painting – where should they start and what are the stages? These are not easy questions to answer, as there are so many different ways of doing things. Oil-painting techniques have changed through the centuries; besides which, individual artists have their own methods.

A REVOLUTION IN TECHNIQUE

The most important change in technique was brought about by the French Impressionists in the 19th century, who overturned many earlier ideas, not only about methods but also about the whole nature of art. Previously, oil paintings had been built up in layers, beginning with a monochrome underpainting on a mid-toned ground. This established the composition, the modelling of forms and the whole tonal structure of the work. The colour was added only as a final stage. These paintings were done in the studio, with location work restricted to small studies.

The Impressionists worked out of doors direct from their subject, abandoning the complex layering method entirely and always completing a painting in one session. This method, known as working "alla prima", which means "at first", rapidly became the norm, particularly for outdoor work, where speed is vital. However, many of the older methods are now being revived in modified forms and some artists prefer to work over an underpainting, a method which is discussed on the following pages.

WET INTO WET

The term "alla prima" does not describe one specific technique because there are different ways of starting and completing a painting in one go. There is, however, one feature that characterizes alla prima paintings: that of blending colours wet into wet. When paint is allowed to dry before further layers are added, each new brushstroke is crisp and well-defined, but laying one colour over and into still-wet

Working wet into wet

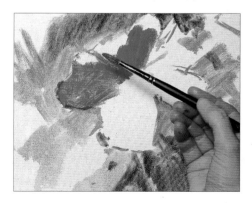

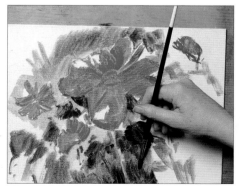

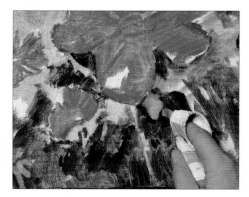

1 *Working in oil on canvas board, the artist begins with the paint used thinly, diluted with turpentine alone. White spirit can also be used, but turpentine, being slightly oily, gives a more lustrous surface.*

2 *Having blocked in the flowers, still with fairly thin paint, she blends dark green into the still-wet paint beneath. She uses a sable rather than a bristle brush, as this makes a softer impression.*

3 *A soft, blurred highlight is now created by wiping into the paint with a rag. The first layer of blue-green, which is now dry, remains in place.*

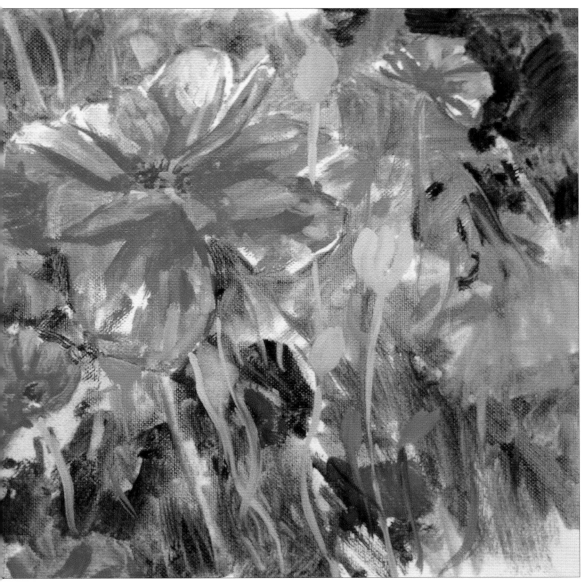

6 (Left) *In any oil painting, but particularly for wet-into-wet methods, it is best to begin with thin paint and build up gradually to thicker applications, otherwise the paint becomes unmanageable. Here the thickest colour has been used for the red flowers.*

4 (Right) *The paint is now used more thickly, slightly diluted with a mixture of linseed oil and turpentine, and the brushstrokes are gently blended into one another.*

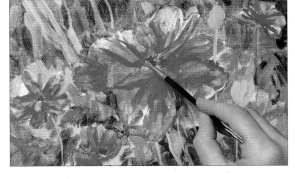

5 (Right) *White is applied lightly over the wet red paint so that the two colours mix together on the surface, to produce a gentle pink highlight.*

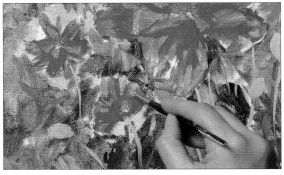

paint creates a gentler, less decisive effect, as each new colour is modified by the one below. The Impressionists painted wet into wet extensively – the soft, slightly blurred effects you see in Monet's beautiful paintings of water and foliage were achieved in this way.

The method is not quite as easy as it sounds; you need a light touch and it's best to avoid too much overworking. Too many colours laid one over another can result in a churned-up mess of paint, with no colour or definition. If this happens, scrape the area back with a palette knife and start again. It is only possible to work wet into wet in acrylic if you use a made-for-the-purpose retarding medium to keep the paint moist and workable.

UNDERPAINTING

Most artists make a drawing on their working surface before they begin to paint; this can be a brush drawing or one made with pencil or charcoal. Some take this framework for the painting one step further, making a full-scale underpainting in monochrome. This allows them to plan the composition and the tonal structure of the picture before putting on the colour.

A monochrome underpainting need not be in shades of grey – monochrome simply means one colour. Another function of the underpainting is to provide contrasts of colour; sometimes areas of underpainting are left to show through in the finished work, or the paint is applied thinly enough to be modified by the colour of the underpainting – a method often used in conjunction with glazing techniques in either oil or acrylic. The Renaissance painters liked to use a green underpainting, building up warm skin tones with thin layers of colour. In the same way a warm red or yellow underpainting could be tried for a subject in which greens and blues predominate.

More than one colour can be used – underpainting simply means a layer of paint below the top layer. Some artists begin their paintings by covering the whole canvas with "washes" of very thin paint, heavily diluted with turpentine; they allow this to dry and then build up gradually to thicker paint. Because oil paints can be used over acrylic (but not vice versa), acrylic is sometimes used for the earlier stages of paintings built up in this way, although oil paint thinned with turpentine also dries quite quickly.

Underpainting in acrylic

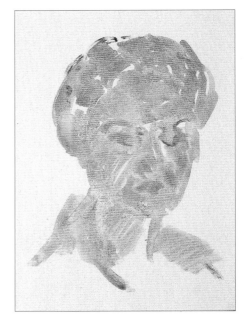

1 *The artist begins with thin washes of diluted grey-green acrylic, gradually building up the basic forms of the face and head. She is working on canvas board.*

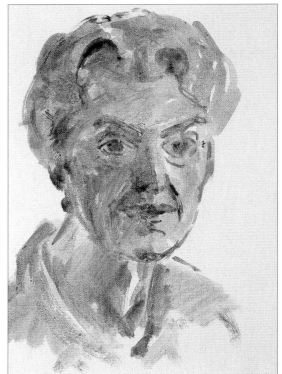

2 *The underpainting is now complete, providing a tonal basis on which the colours can be applied. Although working in acrylic, she uses the traditional method of beginning with thin paint.*

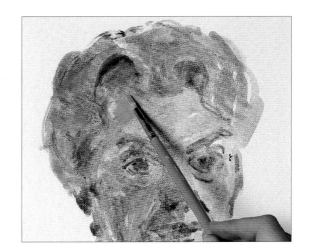

3 *She now turns to oil paint, still using it thinly for the hair and then slightly more thickly for the warm colour of the forehead.*

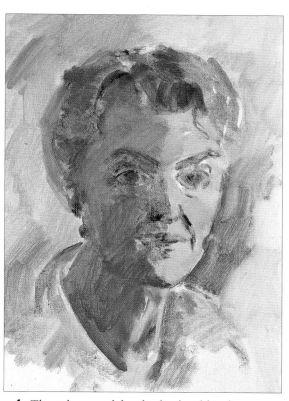

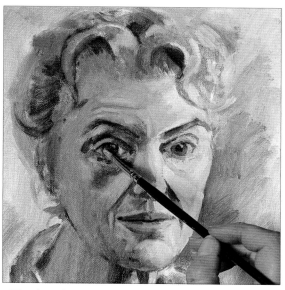

5 *The oil paint is thicker for the highlights and details of the features, but in places the underpainting is still visible; you can see the original grey-green on the hair and beneath the left eye.*

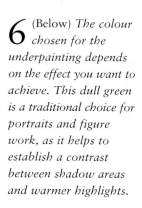

6 *(Below) The colour chosen for the underpainting depends on the effect you want to achieve. This dull green is a traditional choice for portraits and figure work, as it helps to establish a contrast between shadow areas and warmer highlights.*

4 *The colour used for the forehead has been blended lightly into the underpainting to give a soft gradation of tone. The mauve-blues of the background have been kept thin by diluting the oil paint with turpentine.*

FROM LEAN TO FAT

Nowadays there are few hard-and-fast rules in oil painting but, if you are building up a painting in layers, you must always work from "lean" to "fat", or from thin paint to thick. When diluted (lean) paint is laid over thick, oily (fat) paint, cracking may occur due to the top layer drying before the bottom one, which shrinks slightly as it dries. Apart from these technical considerations, saving the thick paint until last also minimizes the risk of churning it up by subsequent painting over the top.

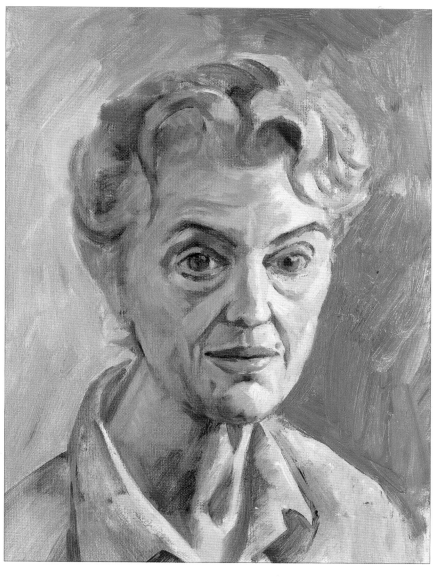

WORKING ON A TINTED GROUND

Up until the middle of the 19th century it was standard oil-painting practice to work on canvas which had been given an overall tint, called an *imprimatura*. The Impressionists abandoned this practice, as they did so many others, and worked on white canvas, which they found increased the brilliance of the colours (though Monet returned to coloured grounds at various stages in his career).

Today's artists are divided on this issue, but there is no doubt that a coloured ground can be very helpful. White is an artificial colour (there is little or no true white in nature) so beginning with a white surface makes it difficult to judge the strength of the first colours you apply. You may make them too light, because any colour looks dark against white. Colouring the canvas provides an average tone, allowing you to work up to the lightest areas and down to the dark ones. The choice of colour will influence your painting from the start. The most usual

choices are neutrals such as browns, yellow-browns, greys and blue-greys. These are useful base shades on which to apply brighter colours. Some artists like a ground which contrasts with the overall colour scheme, for example warm brown for a painting in which blues will predominate; others prefer one which harmonizes. In either case, small areas of the ground colour are sometimes allowed to show through between brushstrokes, which has the effect of pulling the picture together, or unifying it, by creating a series of colour links. In this way a coloured ground can act very much like an underpainting.

Laying a ground is very easy and you can use either acrylic, watercolour or oil paint thinned with white spirit – obviously one of the first two if you are working in acrylic. Spread the paint over the surface either with a large brush or with a rag. It doesn't matter if you create an uneven, streaky effect; a completely flat colour tends to look mechanical and unappealing.

Acrylic on a blue ground

1 *The ground colour chosen for oil paintings is most frequently an unobtrusive brown or grey, but acrylic encourages a bolder approach; a deep blue is used here. The artist, working on watercolour paper, applies the ground with a large nylon brush for quick coverage of the surface.*

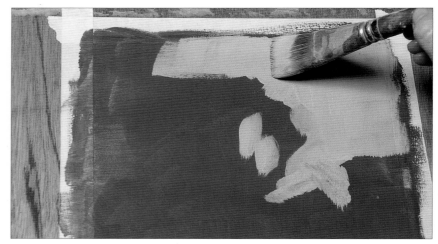

2 *She begins with the light area of sky, painting boldly with another large, square-ended nylon brush. The paint is used quite thickly, mixed with just enough water to make it malleable. She has not made a preliminary drawing because acrylic can easily be corrected by overpainting.*

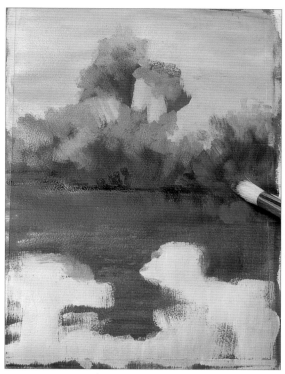

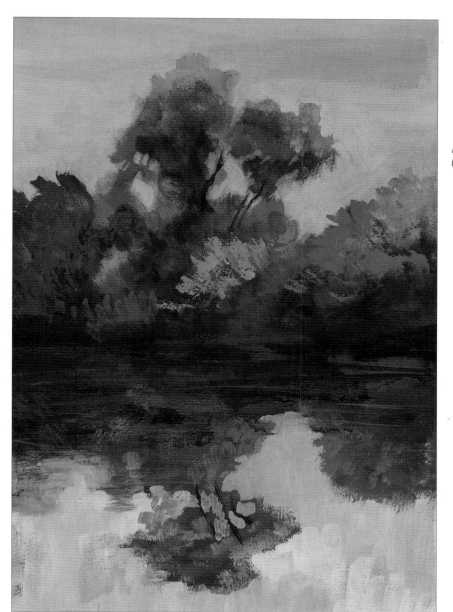

3 Dark green is now painted over the blue, this time using a smaller bristle brush to make dabbing brushstrokes which do not completely cover the blue ground colour. The paint is also used quite thinly to modify the blue without obscuring it.

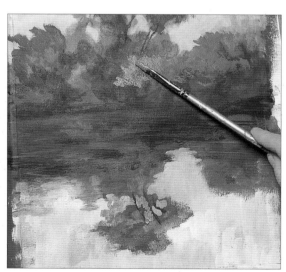

4 To create the blurred effect of the water, black paint is lightly scrubbed over the underlying colours, which are now dry. Again, care is taken not to cover all of the blue underpainting.

5 In the final stages, a definite centre of interest is created by introducing a vivid yellow-green into the small tree.

6 (Above) The dark reflections beneath were slightly blurred by glazing over them with well-watered paint, applied with a large, soft brush.

BRUSHWORK

As the natural consistency of both oil and acrylic paints is thick and creamy, they hold the marks of the brush very well and, for any paintings except those built up in smooth layers or glazes, brushwork is an integral part of the painting. The idea of exploiting the physical presence of the paint began with artists such as Titian in the 16th century and Rembrandt in the 17th; it was developed further by the Impressionists and further still by Cézanne and Van Gogh – the two artists one automatically associates with brushwork.

Many promising paintings are spoiled by inattention to brushwork. This is understandable when there are so many other things to consider, such as working out how to mix the colours, getting the drawing right, and the general business of depicting your subject. But brushwork needs as much consideration as any other aspect of the painting; in fact, it can help you in the task of description. If you are painting a tree trunk, for example, or you want to suggest the sweep of a hill or field, it is easier to use a large brush and let it do the work by following the forms and directions than it is to build up the shape with a series of small, fussy strokes.

One thing you need to guard against is inconsistency of brushwork. Your brushstrokes do not all have to go in the same direction or be the same size (though they can be), but you must use the same approach throughout. If the sky in a landscape is painted flatly, and bold, sweeping brushstrokes are used to depict trees and hills, the picture looks disjointed. Skies can be problematic because they do appear flat, but here you must use artistic licence. Paintings by Cézanne clearly reveal individual brushmarks in the sky area as well as a variety of different colours.

Exploiting the brushmarks

1 *Working in oil on oil-sketching paper, the artist uses her bristle brush as a drawing implement, making sweeping strokes to describe the shapes of the hills.*

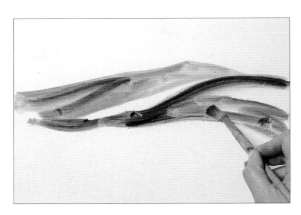

2 *It is not necessary to use thick paint to exploit brushmarks, and here it is quite thin (it has been diluted with turpentine). This gives the brushstrokes an uneven striated quality, with the white paper showing through in some areas.*

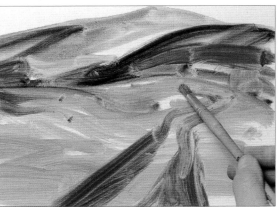

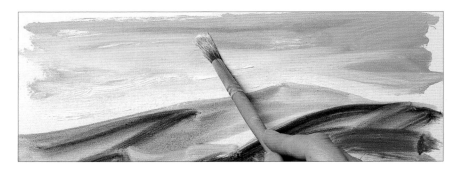

Brushes are made in different shapes as well as different sizes, and it is worth experimenting with them to discover the kinds of mark they can make. Cézanne used mainly large flat brushes, which give a brick-like stroke, whereas Monet favoured pointed ones, applying the paint in smaller dabs. Try out all your brushes, holding them in different ways and varying the pressure to make different kinds of strokes. This kind of doodling will help you to discover your own painting style.

3 (Above) *The paint is used more thickly here, but the brushwork is similar to that depicting the land area. The artist uses long, sweeping strokes, letting the brushmarks follow the direction of the hills.*

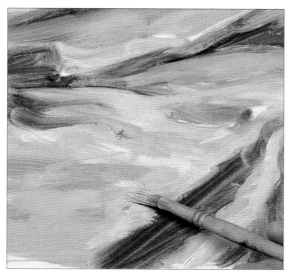

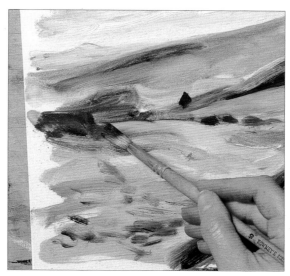

4 *The paint was used thinly in the early stages and the first applications are now dry; consequently, brushstrokes of thicker paint can be laid without disturbing those below.*

5 *The brush is used in a different direction, with more upward strokes, again of thicker paint, suggesting the stone wall in the middle distance without describing it literally.*

6 *(Below) The brushwork is consistent throughout the painting, and not only describes the forms of the landscape but also imparts movement and energy to the picture.*

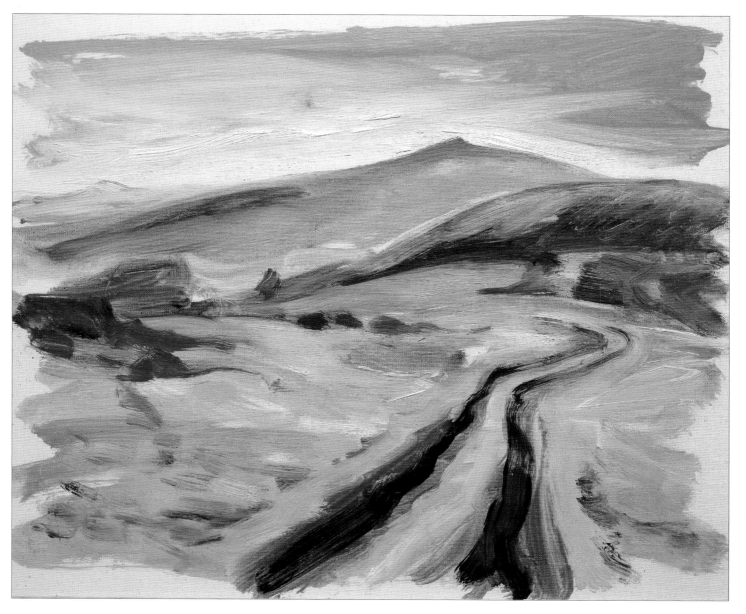

IMPASTO

Impasto means thicker-than-usual paint. For some artists, one of the main attractions of oil and acrylic is that they can be built up thickly to create a range of exciting surface textures.

Impasto techniques are far from new. Both Rembrandt and the great 19th-century landscape painter, J.M.W. Turner, used thick, solid paint in some areas of their paintings, contrasting this with thinner applications elsewhere. In some of Rembrandt's portraits, too, the faces, particularly the highlight areas, are so solidly built up that they resemble a relief sculpture. Van Gogh was the first artist to use uniformly thick paint, applied in swirling or jagged brushstrokes; since then many artists have exploited the expressive and dynamic qualities of thick paint, sometimes squeezing it on straight from the tube and then modelling it with a brush, or applying it with a knife or even fingers.

Impasto of this nature requires a great deal of paint, so it is a good idea to bulk it out with one of the special media sold for impasto work in both oil and acrylic. This is particularly necessary for acrylic, as it is slightly runnier than oil. The media are effective, enabling you to produce two or three times the amount of paint without changing the colour. The only other way to bulk up paint is to add white.

Impasto used selectively, for specific areas of the painting, is usually reserved for finishing touches, highlights or any small areas of vivid colour in the foreground. There is a good reason for this: thick paint, having a more powerful physical presence than thin paint, tends to advance to the front of the picture.

Using thickened paint

1 *This photograph shows the oil paint being mixed with special impasto medium (the brownish substance on the left). Similar mediums are available for working in acrylic.*

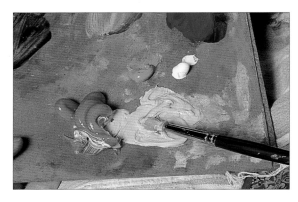

2 *Sometimes impasto is reserved for certain areas of a painting, usually added in the final stages, but here thick paint is used throughout. At this stage, each area of colour is kept separate to avoid mixing and muddying.*

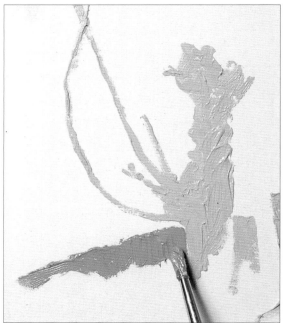

3 *In this sky area, the brush is taken in different directions, creating ridges and swirls of paint which reflect the light in varying degrees.*

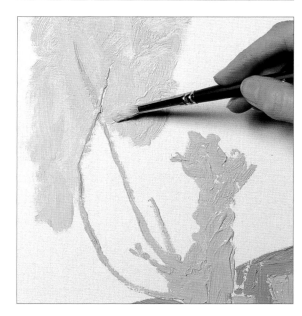

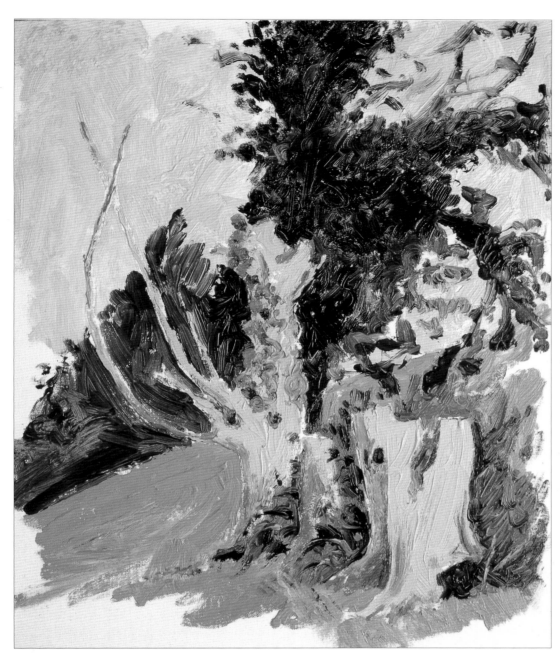

6 (Left) *Finally, with deft touches made with the tip of the brush, darker colours were laid over and into the light yellow-browns on the tree trunks. Paint applied as thickly as this takes several days to dry out thoroughly.*

5 (Right) *To produce a soft blend of colours, dark green is worked into a lighter one, wet into wet. The top and edges of the dark green foliage have also been softened by painting over the light grey of the sky.*

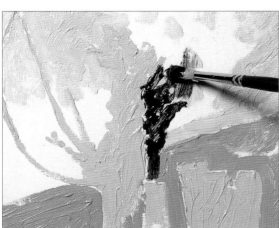

4 *Again, the artist takes care to keep each new colour separate. If the thick dark green paint were allowed to mix with the lighter colour, both would become muddied.*

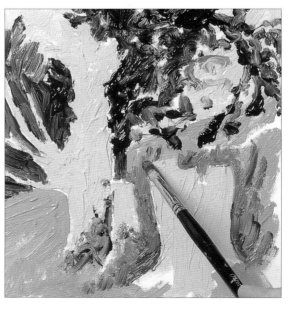

KNIFE PAINTING

A brush is the most obvious implement for applying paint, and the most commonly used, but paint can also be put on with a knife made for the purpose. Knife painting is an exciting and expressive technique, and it creates effects quite different from any which can be achieved with a brush. The knife squeezes and flattens the paint on the surface, producing a smooth plane with ridges at the edges.

These small ridges and lines of thicker paint catch the light and, when a whole painting is built up with knife marks, they create an energetic and lively effect. Like brushstrokes, the marks can be varied according to their direction, their size, the amount of pressure you apply and the thickness of the paint. But take care not to overwork; too many knife strokes laid over one another will sacrifice the crispness which characterizes the method, creating a muddled impression.

Like any other impasto technique, knife painting can be used selectively to emphasize certain areas of the painting. For a floral subject, you might use a flick of the knife to suggest a highlight on the vase or a leaf catching the light, while in landscape you could enliven a dull foreground with some fine strokes made with the side of the knife, depicting long stems of grass, or make small dabs with the point of a knife to create colourful flowerheads.

Painting knives are surprisingly delicate and sensitive instruments. They are not to be confused with the ordinary straight-bladed palette knife used for general cleaning up. These knives are specially made for the job; they have cranked handles and highly flexible forged-steel blades, and are produced in a wide variety of different shapes and sizes.

Knife-painted flowers

1 *To provide a background for the colours of the flowers and leaves, the artist has begun with thin "washes" of oil paint, which she has allowed to dry before putting on the first knife strokes.*

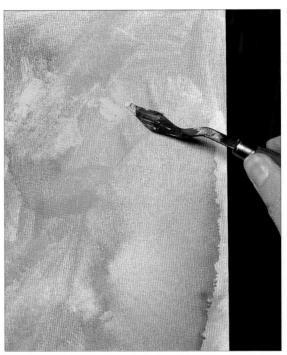

2 *Using the point of the knife, she now flicks on thick, dark colour for the stems. The flowers are still essentially a thin veil of colour, achieved by laying on paint and then scraping it back with the side of the knife.*

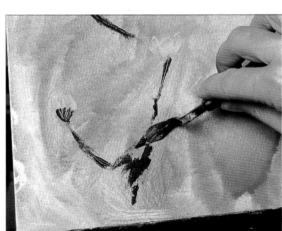

3 *A light blue-green is laid over the darker colour with the flat of the knife. Notice how this flattens and pushes the paint so that it is thinner in the centre of the stroke, only lightly covering the canvas.*

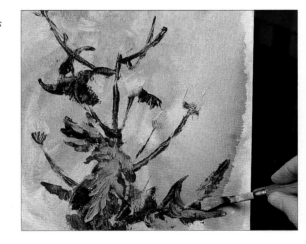

4 (Right) *The flowers are built up with a combination of strokes using the point and side of the knife. This small triangular knife is ideal for chrysanthemums and similar flowers, as each petal can be quickly created with a single sharp flick.*

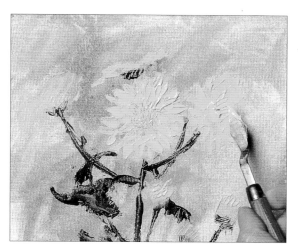

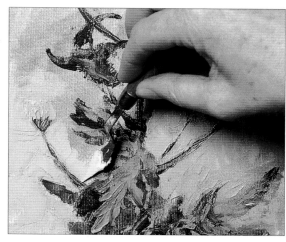

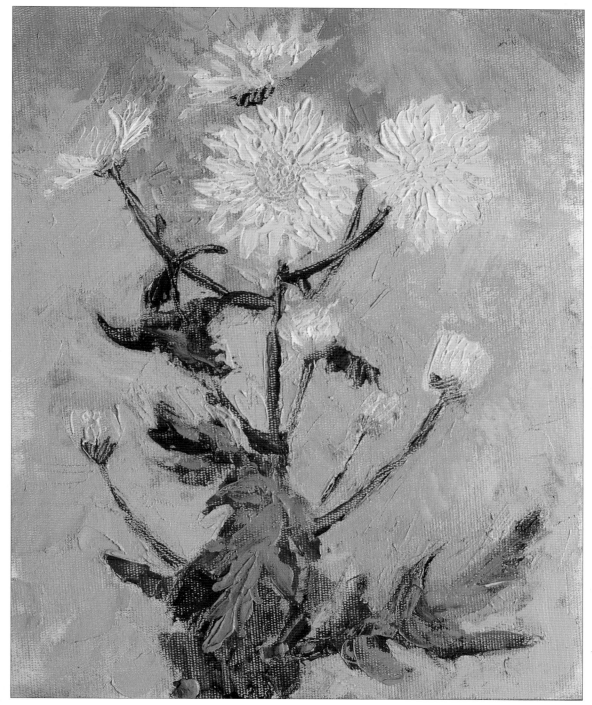

5 (Above) *Grey-green background colour is now "cut in" around the stems and leaves with the flat of the knife. If the flowers and leaves had been painted over thick, wet background paint, the colours would have mixed together and lost their brightness.*

6 (Left) *The flowers and leaves are convincingly depicted, and the liveliness of the picture is increased by the contrast between thick and thin paint. The knife work stands out from the surface, while in some areas of the background the canvas is only lightly stained with colour.*

GLAZING

Glazing is one of the traditional techniques that is regaining popularity – and for good reason, as it can create beautiful effects. The painters of the early Renaissance used oil paints very thinly, building up layers of transparent colour. The brilliant blues and reds you see in the gowns of madonnas and saints were achieved by this method.

Glazing used to be a slow process because each layer had to dry before the next one was applied, so when alla prima painting became the most usual way of working, glazing was largely abandoned. Now, however, the paint manufacturers have brought out special glazing media which cut down the drying time of oil and make the colours more transparent.

In acrylic, glazing takes no time at all because the paints dry so fast, and so the method is particularly popular with acrylic painters. The paint can be thinned with water, or with acrylic medium (matt or gloss). The latter is usually preferable, as paint thinned with water alone dries to a dull, matt finish, while the medium gives it a slight or high gloss – depending on which one you use – which enriches the colours.

Glazes can also be laid over thick paint, as long as it is dry. In acrylic particularly, thick impastos made with a brush or knife are often modified by glazes, which give a touch of delicacy to the heavy surface. This is also a good way to suggest texture, because the colours settle into the crevices.

If you intend to experiment with glazing you may have to consider buying some extra colours. Although both oil and acrylic are technically opaque, some pigments are relatively transparent. As the essence of glazing is the way one layer of colour shows through another, the best results are achieved by sticking to the more transparent colours.

Building up colours

Instead of using full-strength opaque colour from the start, it is possible to build up with a series of glazes. The "swatches" shown here are in acrylic, but similar effects can be achieved in oil, or oil can be glazed over acrylic.

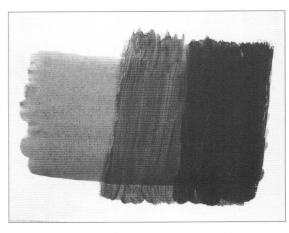

Changing colours

One colour glazed over another produces a third colour by modifying the one below. Here the top colours have been thinned with acrylic medium, which makes them more transparent.

Toning down

If colours appear too bright in one area of a painting they can be neutralized by laying a light glaze of acrylic diluted with water. Water glazes cannot, of course, be used in oil painting, but oil paint can be thinned with glazing medium.

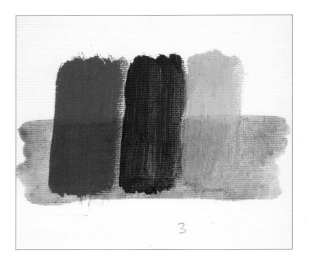
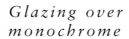

Glazing over monochrome

In either oil or acrylic, a picture can be started in monochrome – black and white or shades of one colour – and glazes subsequently laid on top.

BROKEN COLOUR

When you drag oil or acrylic paint lightly over a textured canvas or a layer of dry paint, it adheres only to the peaks, thus breaking up the brushstroke and allowing some of the earlier colour to remain visible. This method, called dry brush, is particularly suitable for creating veils of colour or for suggesting texture. It is frequently employed in landscape, for example, for light on water, distant trees or the texture of grass, while in portraiture it is useful for hair and textured clothing. The trick is to apply the minimum of paint to the brush and to use a fairly thick, dry mixture.

A similar method, scumbling, gives you less control and is more suitable for large areas than for fine detail. It involves scrubbing thick, dry paint over another colour, either with a rag, a stiff bristle brush or even your fingers. You can scumble dark colours over light, but light over dark usually achieves the best results. You might use the method for skies in a landscape (scumbling light blue over deep blue to produce a shimmering effect), or for richly coloured fabric in a portrait or still life.

The effects of these methods are sometimes described as "broken colour" – a term which has an alternative meaning, referring to an area built up with small brushstrokes of separate colours. This technique was more or less invented by the Impressionists, who found that they could make areas of grass or foliage appear brighter by juxtaposing blues, yellows, greens and sometimes purples, which from a distance would be interpreted as green.

4 (Right) *As well as being the ideal method for suggesting texture, dry brush also creates a livelier effect than flat areas of colour. It is best to work on a textured surface – this picture has been done on canvas board.*

Dry brush in acrylic

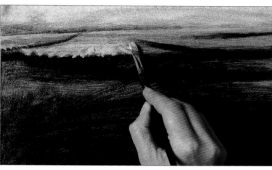

1 *The artist has begun with an underpainting of rich blue-green for the land, with transparent washes for the sky. She now drags thick paint lightly over.*

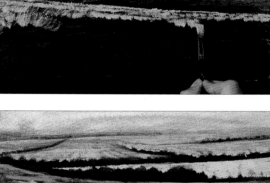

2 *For the foreground she uses the same brush but makes shorter, more upright strokes, varying them to suggest both the texture and movement of the grass.*

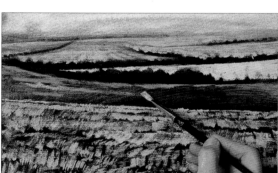

3 *The field in the centre is the deepest area of colour in the picture; not wanting to cover too much of the underpainting, the artist uses a colour which is only slightly lighter, applying it with horizontal sweeps.*

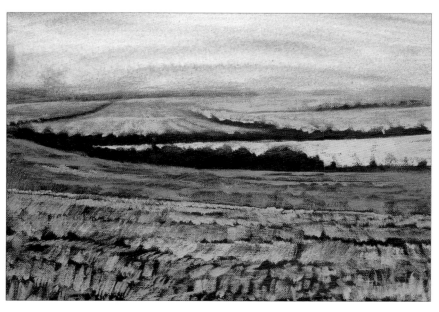

REMOVING PAINT

O
I
L

&

A
C
R
Y
L
I
C

The first two methods described here are not suitable for acrylic, as they rely on the slow-drying nature of oil paints.

SCRAPING BACK

When something goes wrong with an oil painting, you can scrape back the offending area or even the whole painting with a palette knife – as long as the paint is still wet – and repaint it. If you have ever done this, you may have noticed that the effect of the scraped painting is rather attractive – a misty ghost image of the original picture.

Scraping back need not be limited to correcting mistakes; it can be a technique in its own right. It has been employed by several well-known artists, most notably the 19th-century American-born artist James Whistler, who often scraped back his portraits at the end of each day's session in order to avoid overworking his paint and, on one occasion, observed that this gave him exactly the effect he wanted for the gauzy dress of his young girl sitter.

Scraping back is a layering technique, similar in some ways to glazing, as each new application of colour, after scraping, reveals something of the colours below. You can use it to build up subtle colour effects, or to create the impression of a misty landscape. If you work on a textured surface such as canvas or canvas board, the knife removes the colour only from the top of the raised grain, leaving a deposit of paint in between the weave.

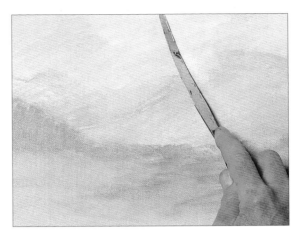

1 *Working on canvas board – stretched canvas could be damaged by scraping – the artist lays thick paint on the sky and hills and scrapes over it with the side of a palette knife.*

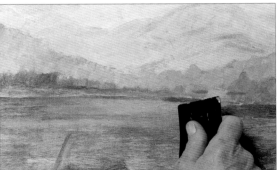

2 *Having begun with a wash of yellow-green which has now dried, she then laid darker, thicker colour which she partially scrapes away. This time she uses a plastic credit card, a useful if unusual painting tool.*

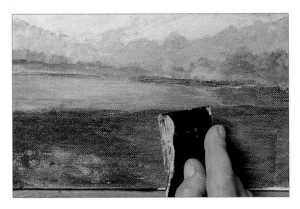

3 *The foreground has been darkened with successive applications of paint, each subsequently scraped back. The artist now used the card first to apply paint and then to scrape it back in diagonal strokes.*

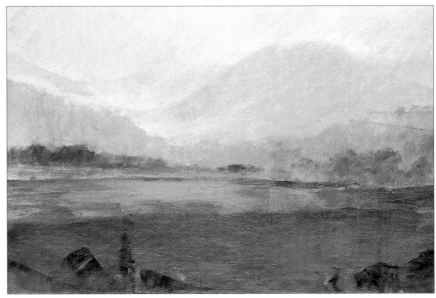

4 *(Right) The technique is particularly useful for atmospheric effects and subtle blends of colour. Finger smudging has been used in places, and the shapes in the foreground were made by using the plastic card as a painting knife.*

Scratching into paint

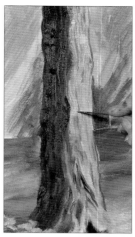
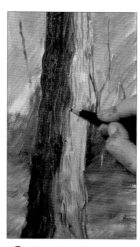

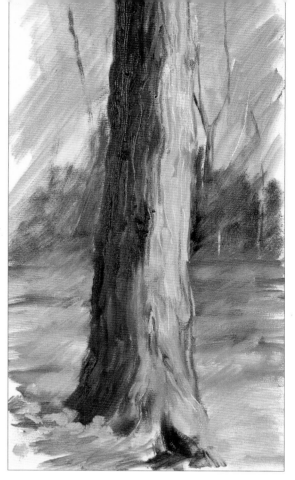

1 *Having laid a foundation of relatively thick oil paint on canvas board, a paintbrush handle is used to draw into it, creating ridges and indentations.*

2 *The point of a scalpel removes the paint more cleanly and thoroughly, revealing the surface of the canvas beneath in a series of fine white lines.*

3 *Drawing into wet paint with a pencil is a variation of sgraffito. The pencil makes dark lines as well as similar indentations to thoses produced by the paintbrush handle.*

SGRAFFITO

This involves scoring or scribbling into the paint while it is still wet – the word comes from the Italian *sgraffiare*, to scratch. Rembrandt used to scribble into thick, wet paint with a brush handle to suggest the hairs of a moustache or the pattern and texture of clothing. Working into thick paint in this way produces an indented furrow, with slight ridges where the paint has been pushed upwards. This can be a useful method for describing textures.

Sgraffito can also be used in a purely decorative way to add a pattern element to your work. If the top application of paint is thin, you can scratch into it with a sharp implement to reveal the white of the canvas, or another dry colour below. For example, the objects in a still life could be outlined with fine white lines or you could create the pattern on a piece of fabric by scratching back to another colour. Although sgraffito is easier in oil, it can be done with acrylic too, as it is possible to scratch into dry paint providing you work on a rigid surface such as a painting board.

TONKING

Invented by Sir Henry Tonks, one-time professor at the Slade School of Art in London, tonking is another correction method which can be utilized as a technique. An oil painting often reaches a stage where it is unworkable because there is such a heavy build-up of paint that any new colours simply mingle with the earlier ones, producing a muddy, churned-up mess. Tonks recommended removing the top layer of paint by laying a sheet of newspaper over the painting and rubbing gently to transfer the paint to the paper. The resulting softened image can be a basis for further work, but often the effect is pleasing in itself; you can leave the tonked painting alone, or perhaps add touches of further definition in certain areas. Tonking is particularly useful for any painting in which you have tried to add too much detail too early on, such as a portrait, where the eyes and mouth tend to attract a concentration of paint.

4 (Above) *This method is useful for textures and ideal for making the kind of very fine lines which are difficult to achieve with a paintbrush, such as stalks of grass or tiny twigs catching the light.*

COMPARATIVE DEMONSTRATION

Oil and acrylic paints can be used in many different ways. One of the best ways of learning, at least initially, is to attempt to emulate the methods of artists whose work you admire. In order to provide a stimulus as well as to show something of the possible variations in approach, we have asked three artists to paint the same still life subject. James Horton is working in oil, on fine canvas stretched over board, primed with whiting and rabbit-skin glue and tinted with watercolour, giving a slightly absorbent and lightly coloured surface. Patrick Cullen is also working in oil, but on white canvas board. Rosalind Cuthbert is painting in acrylic on paper, making considerable use of glazing methods.

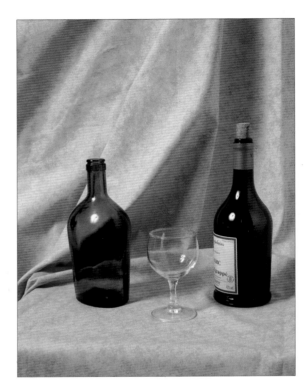

Oil on primed and tinted canvas

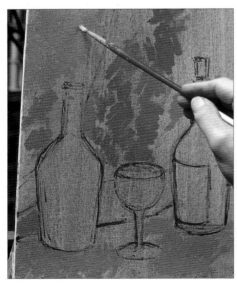

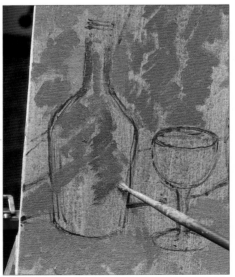

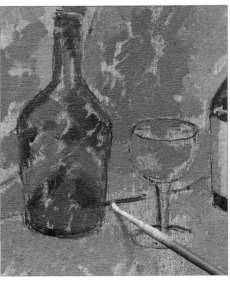

1 *The artist has begun with a brush drawing (in a mixture of Venetian red and raw umber) to establish the shapes and position of the bottles, and now works on the warm colours of the background. It is important to have some of this colour in place before painting the bottles.*

2 *His method is to place small patches of colour all over the picture surface in order to assess the relationships of colour and tone at every stage in the painting.*

3 *Darker tones have now been introduced into the bottles, and he returns to work on the background, using a lighter colour to bring out the dark greens.*

(Right) *Various artists' palettes give an interesting insight into their various working methods. In this case the "brushstrokes" used to mix the colours reflect those in the painting itself.*

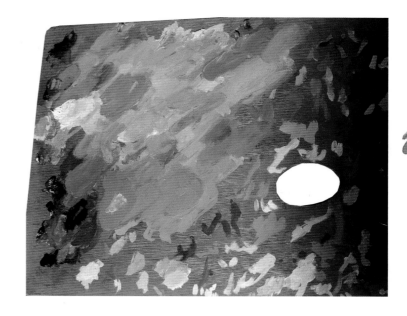

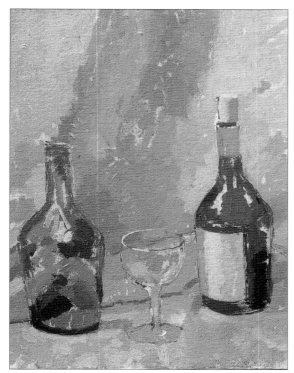

4 *With the painting at about the halfway stage, the brushwork is still loose, with the surface not yet fully covered. The paint is used at the same consistency throughout, slightly thinned with a mixture of turpentine, linseed oil and Damar varnish.*

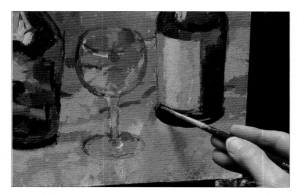

5 *Ellipses are always tricky and, in spite of careful initial drawing, have to be maintained through the course of the painting. Here the edge of the label is defined by cutting in darker paint around the bottom.*

6 *(Right) In the final stages, details were added, such as the suggestion of printing on the label, the cork of the bottle and the ellipse of the glass. Notice how varied the brushwork is, and the many different colours used in each area of the picture.*

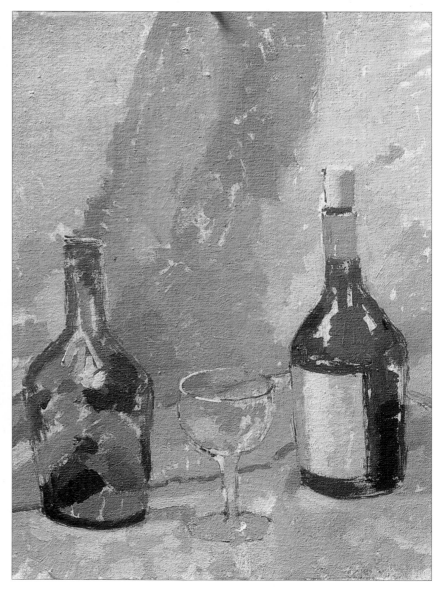

Continued ▷

167

Oil on canvas board

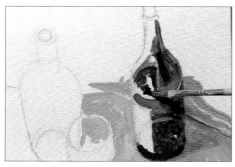

1 *The artist began with a drawing in soft pencil, erasing from time to time until it was correct. He uses the paint quite thinly, diluting it with a 50:50 mixture of synthetic medium and turpentine.*

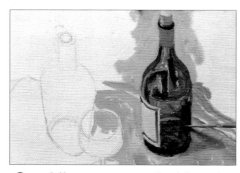

2 *A difference in approach in the early stages is immediately apparent. This artist takes each part of the painting close to completion before beginning on the next; here he works extensively on the bottle.*

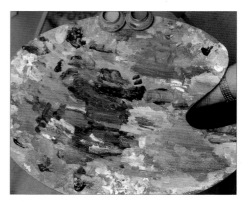

The artist prefers a large kidney-shaped palette to the small rectangular type which fits into the lid of a paintbox. Once more, the brushwork in the painting is echoed in the palette.

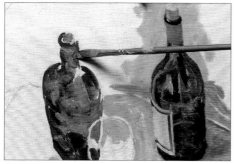

3 *The first bottle is now virtually finished, and the second one is painted before the background. The white board shows through the thin paint in places to suggest the transparency of the glass.*

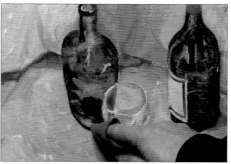

4 *With the background and the wine glass now painted, finishing touches are given to the bottle. A soft highlight is created by rubbing into the wet paint with a clean rag.*

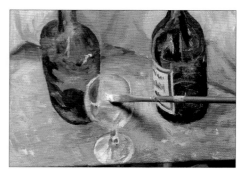

5 *When painting transparent objects it is vital to ensure the continuity of the background, so this has been painted first, leaving the highlights and shadows of the glass until last.*

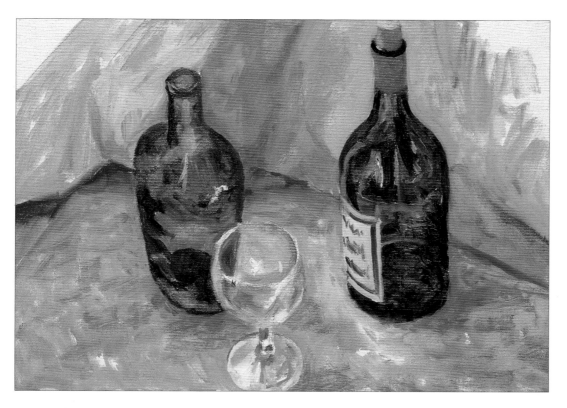

6 *The biggest difference between this and the previous painting is in the consistency of paint, which here has been wiped off to create highlights rather than added as thicker paint. The brushwork in both paintings is lively and varied, but each artist has a distinctive style.*

Acrylic on watercolour paper

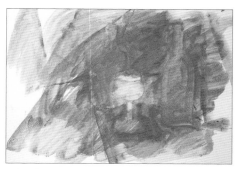

1 The artist begins with a thin under-painting diluted with water, lightly sketching in the shapes of the bottles. She seldom makes an initial drawing when using opaque paints.

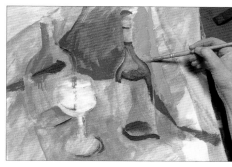

2 Her method is to build up the more subtle colours by glazing in successive layers over a brightly coloured base, so initially she uses blue for the bottles and a rich red for the background.

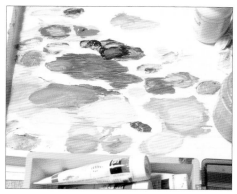

These Stay-Wet palettes look far from attractive after a day's work, but they are ideal for preventing acrylic paint from drying out.

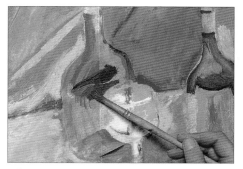

3 Paint mixed with matt medium is laid over the blue. While still wet the colour looks opaque, but it becomes more transparent as the medium dries.

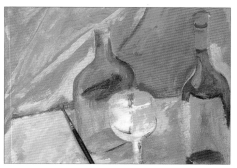

4 On the left-hand bottle you can see the effect of the glazing method clearly – the paint has now dried and each colour shows through the other. Slightly thicker paint is now used for the background.

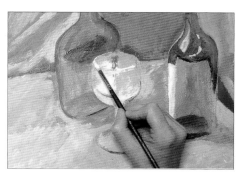

5 As in the previous two demonstrations, the glass is left until last. The highlights on the ellipse are painted, again with a fine sable brush, but this time with thicker paint, straight from the tube.

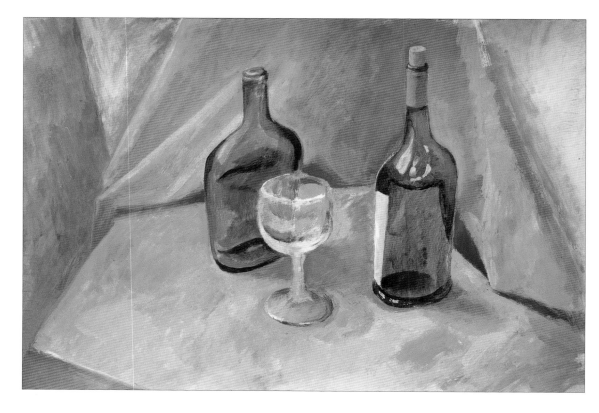

6 This artist has taken a less literal and more personal approach to the group than the other two, inventing a blue 1background and keying up the colours. She has also deliberately distorted the right-hand bottle to improve the composition.

STILL LIFE

Throughout the history of painting, still life has gone in and out of fashion, mainly according to the whims of buyers. Still-life paintings were particularly sought after in 16th- and 17th-century Holland, while in France and England they were less popular nationally, although there were certain areas where this branch of painting flourished. In the 19th century, when more humble, down-to-earth subject matters began to replace grandiose historical works, still life came into its own; since that time many artists have painted still life in addition to other subjects, and some have made it their speciality.

There is no better way of practising your skills and working out ideas about colour and composition than by choosing and arranging your own subject. When you are painting landscape on the spot, the arrangement of shapes and colours is dictated by nature, but with still life you are the one in control – you have a captive subject. You can set up the group in any way you choose, decide on the best lighting and take as long as you like over the

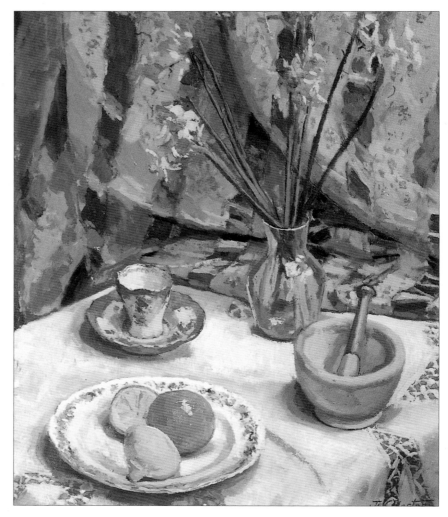

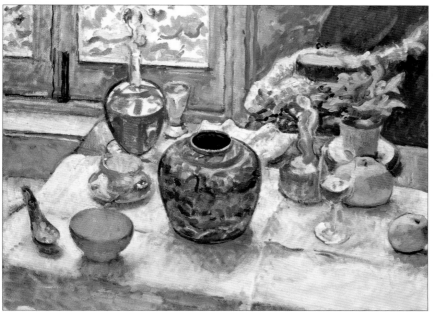

Setting up the group

(Above) *In still-life painting, much of the composition is done before you begin to lay paint on paper, so it is wise to take time at this stage. In James Horton's oil painting* Still Life with Narcissi *the objects, the tablecloth and the background drapery have been arranged with great care. By overlapping the mortar and the flower vase, a link is established between them, while the pattern on the tablecloth draws the eye into the composition.*

Repeating colours

(Left) *Elizabeth Moore's lovely* Objects on a Table *(oil) is also carefully arranged, although she has aimed at a more natural-looking effect. When painting a wide assortment of objects, some unifying factor is needed, and here she has created relationships of colour by taking the mauve-blues through the painting.*

Pattern and viewpoint

(Right) *The viewpoint you choose for your still life depends on your personal approach and interests. Seen from above, objects become flattened to some extent, creating a clearer pattern than at eye level. In* Still Life with Aubergines *(oil) Robert Maxwell Wood has exploited this element to the full, choosing and arranging the objects so that they echo the bold motifs of the fabric – notice the pansy, which appears both as living flower and as printed pattern.*

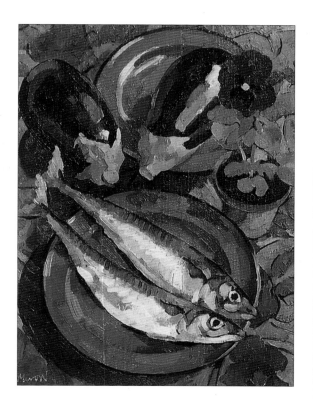

Composing with light

(Below right) *Light and shadow can play a vital role in any still life illuminated by natural light, and in* Lilies and Straw Hat *(oil) by Timothy Easton the shapes made by the shadow of the window bars and flowers are as important as the objects themselves. The use of carefully controlled, pale colours, with the only dark tone being the foliage glimpsed through the window, beautifully expresses the theme of light, which is further illustrated by the hat in the foreground – sunlight by association.*

CHOOSING A THEME

Most still lifes have some kind of theme, with the objects linked by association. An ill-assorted group of objects with nothing in common creates an uneasy feeling – the Surrealist painters used odd juxtapositions for this very reason. Still lifes with a culinary theme are a common choice: for example, fruit and vegetables placed on a kitchen table.

But the theme can be simply one of colour or shape. For example, you might choose a group of predominantly blue objects, placed on a yellow or pink cloth for contrast. You might be attracted by the vertical emphasis of bottles, or long-stemmed flowers in a tall vase, or be interested in an arrangement of plates and bowls which make a series of intersecting circles and ovals.

Still lifes can also tell a story, or hint at one. Artists may choose a subject close to their hearts, or something which has associations for them, such as favourite books, or a hat worn during a successful holiday. Van Gogh, when he was working as a peasant in the fields, painted a pair of battered, work-stained boots, which spoke volumes about the desperation of his life at the time.

painting. You are not at the mercy of the weather, as you are with landscape; indeed, still life is something you can always fall back on when it is too cold, wet or dark to paint anything else.

ARRANGING THE GROUP

It must be said that still life is not an easy option. You have to take as much care over choosing and arranging the objects as you do over painting them. Cézanne, who produced some of the most beautiful still lifes in the history of art, sometimes spent days over the initial arrangement.

Try to aim at a natural-looking grouping of the objects; although still life is highly artificial, it should not look that way. Let

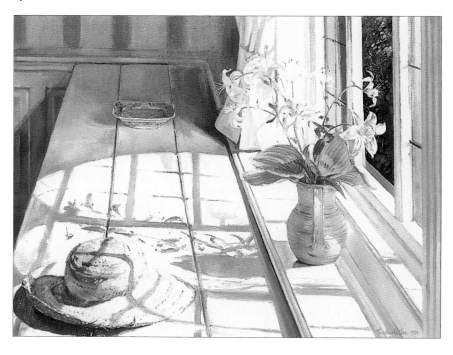

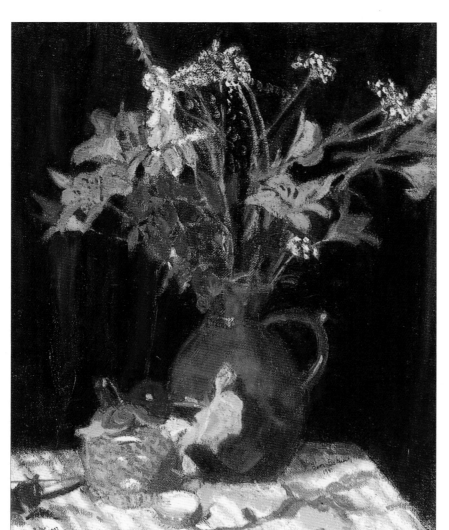

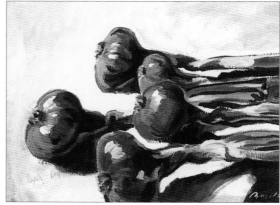

Floral still life

(Left) *The foreground can be a problem in floral groups, as the spaces beside and in front of the vase can become dull and empty if they are not filled in some way. Common devices are to introduce some other object or place one or two of the blooms in front of the vase, and in Ben Baker's colourful* Still Life with Flowers *(oil) he has done both. He has treated the foreground very broadly, however, so that the objects are mere suggestions and do not detract from the painting's centre of interest, which is emphasized by the use of a dark background.*

some of the objects overlap, but be careful how you do this. Avoid obscuring one shape with another or leaving too small a part of one showing, as this can create an awkward, cramped feeling.

Consider too the spaces between things – wide gaps between objects may make them look disconnected, in which case some kind of link needs to be established. Depending on the source of light, shadows can provide a link between objects; another well-known device is drapery, often seen in still lifes, curving round behind, between and in front of objects to unite them.

Drapery also gives a sense of movement to the group. In any good painting, whatever the subject, the composition is arranged to lead the eye from one part of the picture to another. For this reason, avoid placing objects so that they "look" out of the picture. If the spout of a teapot,

for example, is pointing outwards instead of inwards towards the other objects, the eye will naturally follow its direction.

PLANNING THE PAINTING

It often happens that a group that has taken time to set up causes problems when you start to paint, or to make your preliminary drawing. You may now notice that one object is too tall, giving you a featureless area of background on both sides of it, or that there are too many objects crowded to the front. You can always make adjustments; it is better to get things right before you have gone too far than to paint something you don't like.

Once satisfied with the arrangement, you must consider how you are going to place it on the canvas. This means deciding what angle to paint from, what viewpoint to take and how much space to leave around the

Unusual treatments

(Above) *One of the exciting aspects of still-life painting is that the objects you choose can often suggest new approaches, in terms both of composition and treatment. Gerry Baptist initially chose this bunch of onions for his acrylic painting* Red Onions *because he liked their rich colours, but their shapes suggested movement, so he has arranged them in such a way that they appear to be rushing across the paper, an effect he has played up by using strong shadows and long, sweeping brushstrokes.*

Found still life

(Below) *Although most still-life paintings are the result of planning, occasionally something makes a natural painting subject. Examples could be clothes left on a chair, shoes in the corner of a room – indeed almost anything in your home environment. In his oil painting,* Decorated Tree, *Robert Maxwell Wood studies shapes, colours and textures not normally associated with still-life painting.*

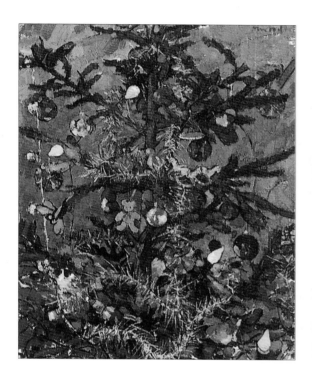

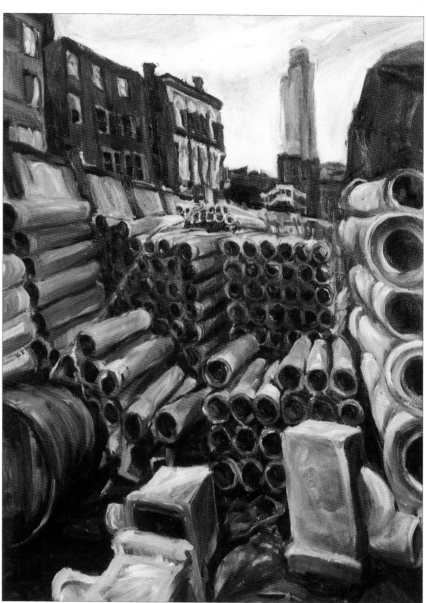

objects. If your group is on a table top and the front of the table is in the picture, it is best to avoid a straight-on view, as this creates a horizontal in the foreground. Horizontal lines give a static impression, whereas diagonals lead the eye inwards, so study the group from different angles.

It can be interesting to look down slightly on the group you are painting, particularly when circles (plates and bowls) are an important part of the theme. From a high viewpoint, you see a rounder ellipse – the term for a circle in perspective – than you do at eye level. The viewpoint you choose depends very much on what you are painting; experiment with high and low viewpoints as well as different angles. Some artists find it helpful to settle all these questions before they begin to paint by making a series of rough sketches of the group, seen in various ways.

Outdoor still life

(Above) *A still life can be broadly defined as anything that is not capable of movement, so it follows that you may find ready-made groups outside as well as in your home. Stones on a beach, plant pots, a group of chairs in a garden, or glasses and bottles on a café table are just some of the many possibilities. In* East End Pipes *(oil) Karen Raney has found an exciting and unusual subject which has allowed her to explore strong contrasts of tone and relationships between shapes and colours.*

STILL-LIFE DEMONSTRATION

James Horton regards himself primarily as a landscape painter, although he also paints portraits and often turns to still life when the weather does not permit outdoor landscape work. He enjoys still-life painting because it allows him total control of the subject, enabling him to work out ideas on composition and colour. He works in oil on a small scale, painting on canvases he prepares himself by stretching cotton fabric over board. They are then primed with a home-made recipe consisting mainly of whiting and rabbit-skin size.

1 (Right) The artist dislikes working on white canvas, so, after priming, he tints it with a wash of watercolour. He has chosen a warm yellow ground colour which will help to establish the overall colour scheme. For the initial drawing, made with a fine sable brush, he uses an equally warm red-brown.

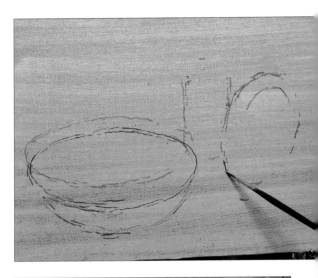

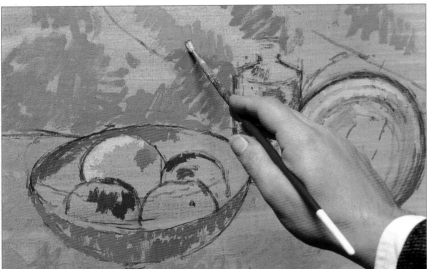

2 (Above) He begins by placing brush-strokes over the entire picture surface, working up the foreground and background at the same time in order to relate one colour to another.

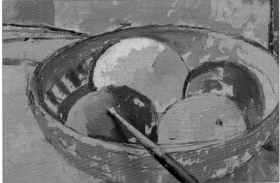

3 Light and dark tones must be related in the same way, and the highlight of the grapefruit provides a key for judging the strength of colours needed for the apple.

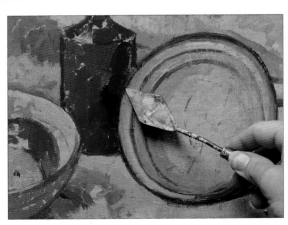

4 Here, a painting knife is used, not to apply paint but to scrape it off, thus blending and softening the colours on the edge of the plate.

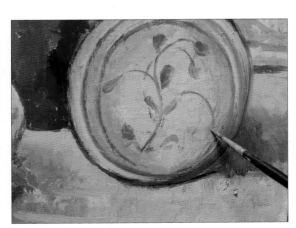

5 The pattern of the plate is drawn in with a fine sable brush. This stage also demonstrates the positive role played by the coloured ground, patches of which show through the light, cool, neutral colours.

6 *With the pattern complete, highlights have been added to the plate, but the ground is still visible in places and will not be completely covered, even in the final stages.*

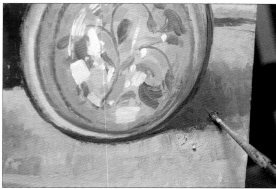

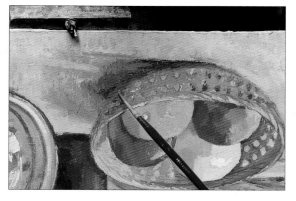

7 *Too much detail in the background would detract from that in the foreground, so the artist suggests the pattern with small dabs of the brush. The pattern of holes in the weave of the basket was created by working small brushstrokes of light green over the brown.*

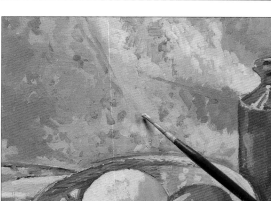

8 *For the final details on the basket, the painting is turned upside-down to give better access to this area, and a fine sable brush is used to touch in the lines of the weave.*

9 *(Below) In the finished painting, small patches of the coloured ground are still clearly visible, particularly in the blue-green foreground. This has the effect of linking this area with the warm colours of the background and objects.*

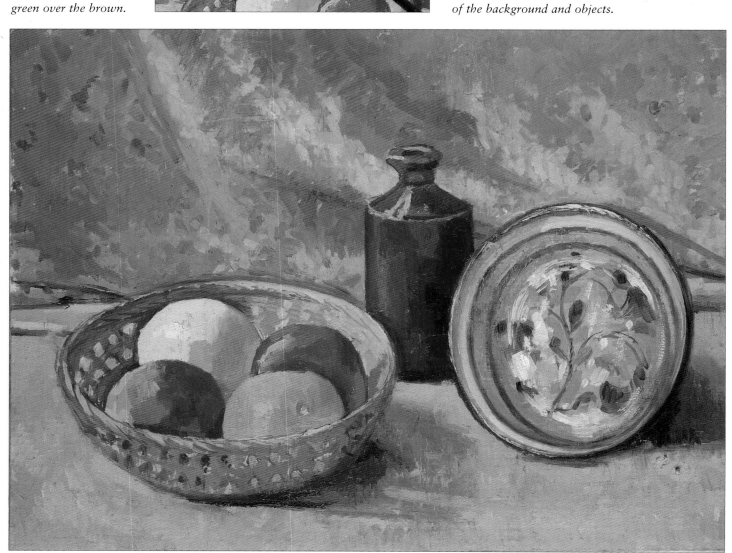

LANDSCAPE

Landscapes need not be painted on the spot – many fine paintings are made from sketches and photographic reference – but when weather permits there is nothing more enjoyable than working direct from the subject out of doors.

Both oil and acrylic are excellent for outdoor work. With acrylic, of course, the paints could dry out on your palette before you are halfway through but, if you use a Stay-Wet palette, this will not happen. The advantage is that the painting will be completely dry when you want to stop work; you can also work on paper instead of canvas or board if you prefer. With oil,

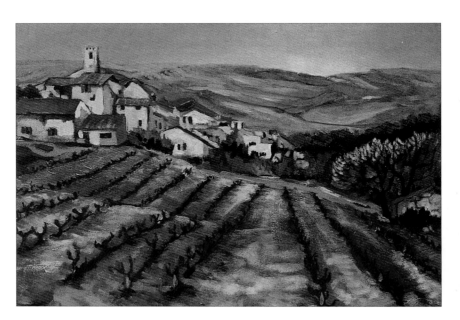

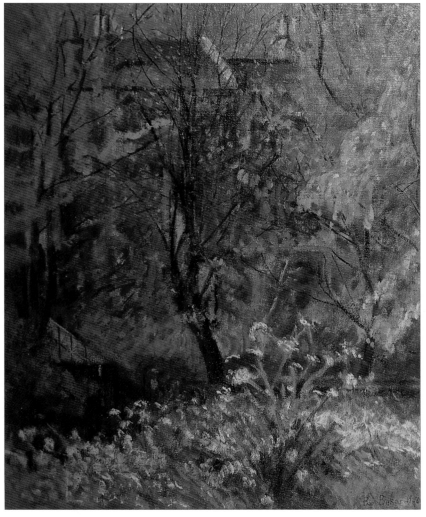

Leading the eye

(Above) *A good landscape gives you the feeling that you can walk into and around it, so the artist must consider ways of leading the eye into the picture. A common device is to use a curving path or river travelling from foreground to middle distance, and in* Vineyard in the Languedoc *(oil) Madge Bright has used the lines of the vineyard in the same way, so that they act as signposts towards the painting's centre of interest: the group of houses.*

Restricting the space

(Left) *The word landscape generally conjures up an image of a wide panorama or perhaps a dramatic mountain view, but anything that is out of doors is a landscape; for those who have no access to open countryside, parks and gardens are an excellent choice. Restricting himself to a landscape in microcosm in his* View of Back Gardens, *Ben Baker has achieved a lively composition in which he has explored contrasts of colour, shape and texture.*

Human interest

(Opposite) *Another way of drawing the eye into the painting is to introduce a figure or figures in the middle distance, as David Curtis has done in* Poppyfield over Misson *(oil). It is a curious fact that, because of the way we identify with them, fellow humans always attract attention. The other function of figures in landscape is to provide scale; here they emphasize the wide expanse of poppy-strewn field.*

Creating space
(Right) *If you are painting a small section of landscape in close-up you do not have to worry unduly about creating a sense of space, but in a panoramic landscape like Timothy Easton's* The Ploughed Edge *it is vital. He has done this in two main ways: firstly by exploiting the perspective effect of the converging lines of ploughing; and secondly by using paler, slightly cooler colours in the distance.*

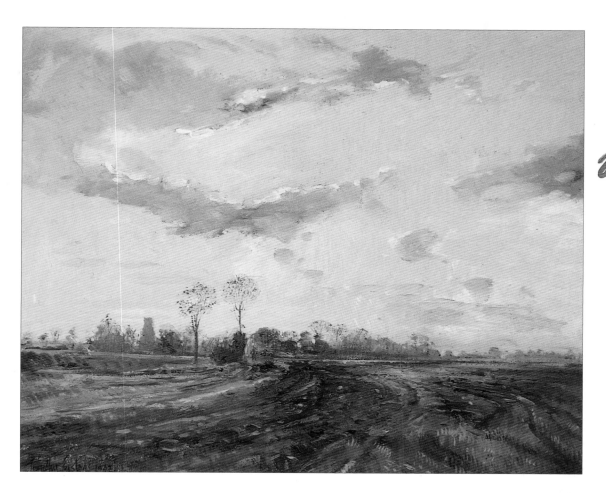

you will always have a wet painting to carry home, which can be a problem if the painting is large and it is a windy day.

PLANNING THE PICTURE
One of the commonest faults in paintings done on the spot is poor composition –

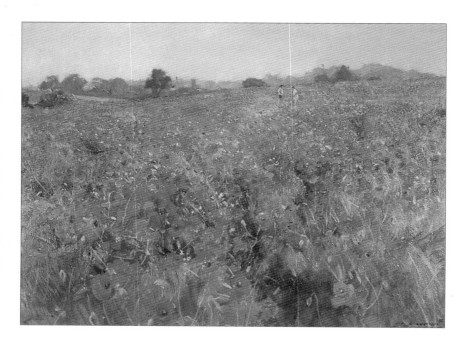

sometimes even professionals get it wrong. First you must decide what format your painting should take and, secondly, how much of the view you should include.

A further advantage of working with acrylic on paper is that you can let the composition grow "organically". Without much time for planning, because of changing light and so on, mistakes can easily occur; when you are well into a painting you often find that you should have included a certain tree on the right, for example, or made the picture vertical instead of horizontal. The answer is to take a larger piece of paper than you need and leave generous margins when you begin to work; this allows you greater flexibility and the freedom to make any necessary changes.

You cannot do this with oil paintings, unfortunately, because they have to be fitted into the confines of your canvas or board. It is wise to take several working surfaces with you so that you can decide which one best suits the subject. Using a

The foreground

(Right) *This can be a problem area in landscape paintings. Because this part of the view is closest to you it is seen in sharp focus, so the natural tendency is to treat it in detail. This can, however, be unwise, as it can act as a block, discouraging the viewer from looking beyond it into the picture. In Timothy Easton's* Dwarf Firs and Cottage *(oil) he has solved the problem by contriving a strong focal point – the figure in front of the house – so that although the foreground flowers claim attention first, the eye then travels over and beyond them.*

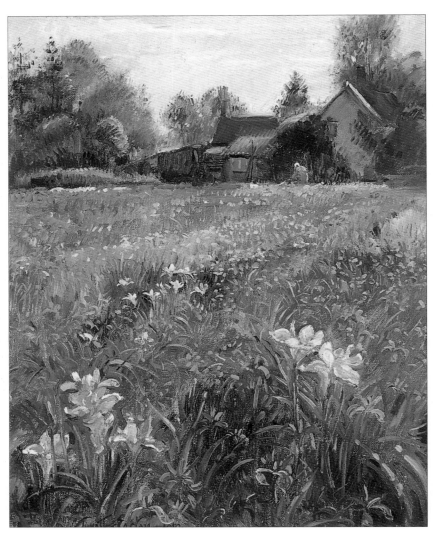

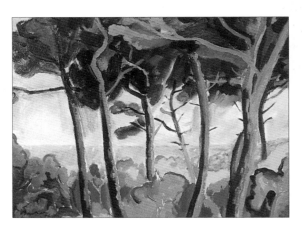

Cropping the foreground

(Above) *Sometimes the foreground in a landscape serves to introduce the view beyond, with a focal point in the middle distance, but it can be the* raison d'être *of the painting, as in Gerry Baptist's* On the Coast of Provence *(acrylic). In order to create space and recession he has employed a traditional compositional device, that of cropping the trees at the top and bottom of the picture. This has the effect of bringing them to the front of the picture, while everything beyond recedes.*

viewfinder is also a good idea, to help you to decide how much of the scene to include. This device is easily made by cutting a rectangular aperture in a piece of card; you can then hold it up at different angles and at different distances from your eyes in order to isolate various sections of the landscape. This can help when you are faced with a wide panoramic view and you cannot decide which bit to focus on, or where the centre of interest lies.

THE FOCAL POINT

Most landscapes have a centre of interest, or focal point, to which the eye is drawn. How obvious this is depends on the scene. Examples of an obvious focal point might include a group of buildings in a landscape, a tall tree, or some people sitting down having a picnic – people always grab our attention because we identify with our fellow humans. A less obvious focal point might be a ploughed field making a pattern in the middle distance, a particular hill, a gleam of light on a lake or river, or a light tree set against darker ones.

Try to orchestrate the painting so that you set up a series of visual signposts towards the focal point. These will probably already exist, although you may have to exaggerate them. Diagonal lines or curves invite the eye to follow them, and a device frequently used in landscape is a curving path leading from the foreground in towards the middle distance – where the focal point is often located. Alternatives are receding lines of trees, lines of ploughed fields or the stripes of a newly cut hay field. Do not make the foreground too dominant. If the focal point is in the middle distance or the far distance, too much detail in the foreground will detract from it.

CREATING SPACE

A landscape will not look convincing unless you give the impression of space, and there are two principal ways of doing this. One is to observe the effects of linear perspective correctly. Everyone knows that things become smaller the further away they are, but it is easy to underestimate this effect. You know that a field or a far-away lake is a certain size and you fail to realize that it is actually tiny in relation to the rest of your picture. It is wise to measure such landscape features when you make your preliminary drawing. Hold a pencil or paintbrush up at arm's length and slide your finger and thumb up and down it; in this way you can establish the size of the distant lake in comparison, for example, with a field which is closer.

The other way to create space is to use aerial perspective. Tiny particles of dust in the atmosphere create an effect rather like a series of ever-thickening veils, so that far-away objects are paler than nearby ones. There is far less contrast of tone (light and dark) and the colours change, becoming cooler and bluer. Again, this effect is easy to underestimate, particularly for features in the middle distance. You know that a tree trunk on the other side of a field is dark brown, so you paint it that way but, in fact, it will be much lighter in tone than it would be if it were in the foreground.

When it comes to far distance, colours can be very pale, although sometimes they appear dark in relation to a still-lighter sky. The contrasts of tone are minimal, sometimes barely distinguishable. A ray of sunshine lighting up part of a distant hill looks dramatic, but the tonal contrast is still relatively limited. These subtle nuances of colour and tone can be tricky, but with practice you will master them.

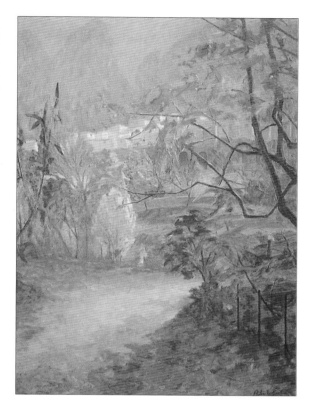

Controlling tones
(Left) *Patrick Cullen's* Landscape in Provence *is first and foremost a painting of light, with the landscape illuminated by the soft, pearly glow of early morning. This reduces contrasts of tone, so the relative lightness and darkness of colours must be controlled extremely carefully. Notice that there are no dark colours here – even the foreground tree and railings are pale whispers of golden brown and green, and the composition is unified by the repetition of delicate mauves, yellows and golds.*

Light and colour
(Below) *The effects of light can completely transform a landscape: colours that looked vivid on a sunny day may seem flat and dull under an overcast sky, and the differences between evening light and a high midday sun are equally striking. Stewart Geddes's lovely* Le Rocher Dongle, Evening *(oil) is as much about light as it is about the landscape itself, and the artist has wisely treated both the buildings and the landscape features very broadly to give full rein to the golden evening colours.*

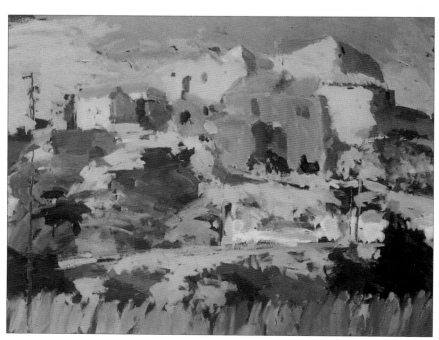

LANDSCAPE DEMONSTRATION

Karen Raney is an experimental artist who works in a number of media and paints a variety of different subjects – indeed, anything which excites her interest. Although she works direct from the subject whenever possible, she also uses photographs as an extensive reference; here she re-creates a landscape from her own photographs, aided by memories of the place, which she has painted many times. She is working in oil on a commercially prepared stretched and primed canvas.

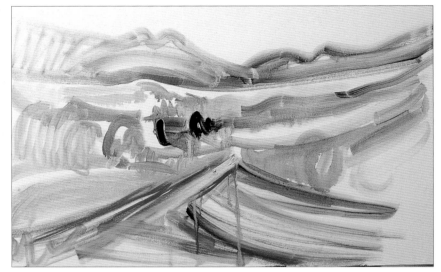

1 *Brushwork is an important element in this landscape, and the artist has begun to exploit it immediately, employing a flat bristle brush to make sweeping strokes of paint diluted with turpentine.*

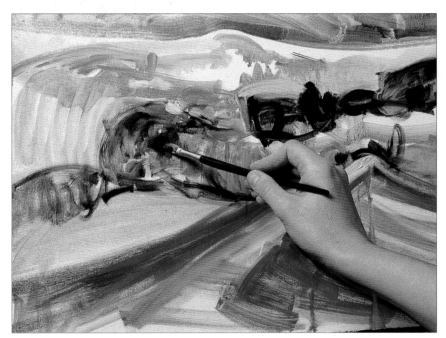

2 *Once the composition has been established with the diluted paint, she begins to use it more thickly, adding a little linseed oil to the turpentine and painting darker colours into the thin washes.*

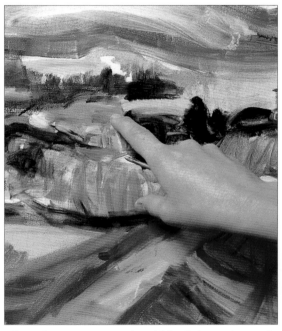

3 *Colours are smeared and blended together with a fingertip. She likes to move paint around as she works, and oil paint, which remains wet for a considerable time, encourages such manipulation.*

4 (Right) *To create the rounded blobs of the trees, a bristle brush is loaded with paint, pushed onto the picture surface and twisted slightly. The paint is then built up more solidly all over the picture; here it is used straight from the tube, with no added medium. Notice the way in which the artist uses the brush-marks to describe the shapes of the roof tiles.*

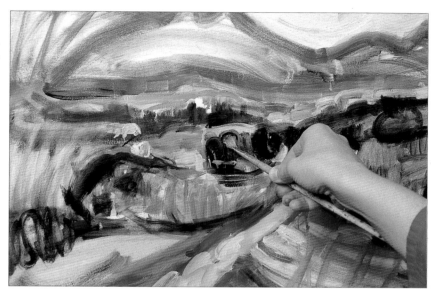

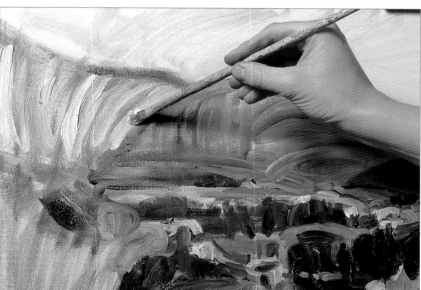

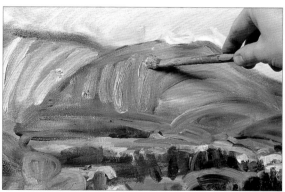

6 (Above) *She takes a less deliberate approach to painting than some artists, letting the picture dictate what she should do next, and experimenting to see what happens. Here she uses upward-sweeping brushstrokes once more, later modifying them slightly.*

5 (Above) *The artist has wiped into the thin paint with a rag to create a striated effect, which she now reinforces with thick white brushstrokes. She works instinctively, seeing that the sweeping roof lines need to be echoed in this area of the painting.*

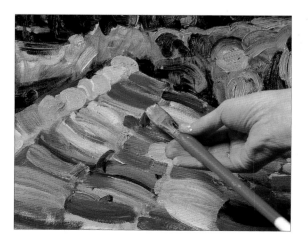

7 (Right) *Having built up the middle ground and distance, she returns to the foreground and introduces darker, richer colours into the roof, using the side of a flat bristle brush to suggest the shadowed divisions between the tiles.*

Continued ▷

8 *The distant village, which is the focal point of the picture, is left until a late stage; it is now treated in the same way as the rest of the painting, with bold brushstrokes describing the shapes and forms.*

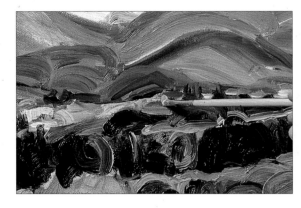

9 *The brushwork depicting the houses can be seen clearly here – vertical strokes for the walls and horizontal for the roofs. The hills behind are now built up more decisively.*

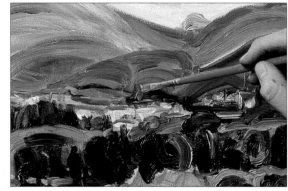

10 *A fingernail scratches into the light paint to reveal a little of the darker colour beneath, which is now completely dry.*

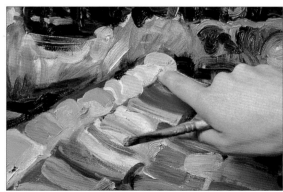

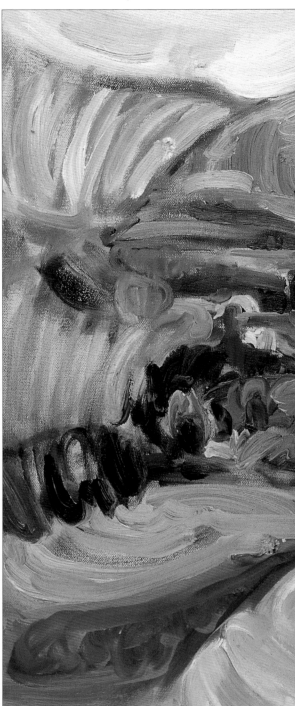

11 *It is important to create visual links between one part of the picture and another, and a little of the light green in the middle ground is now taken into the blue of the hills.*

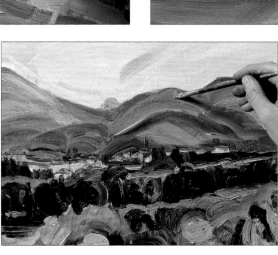

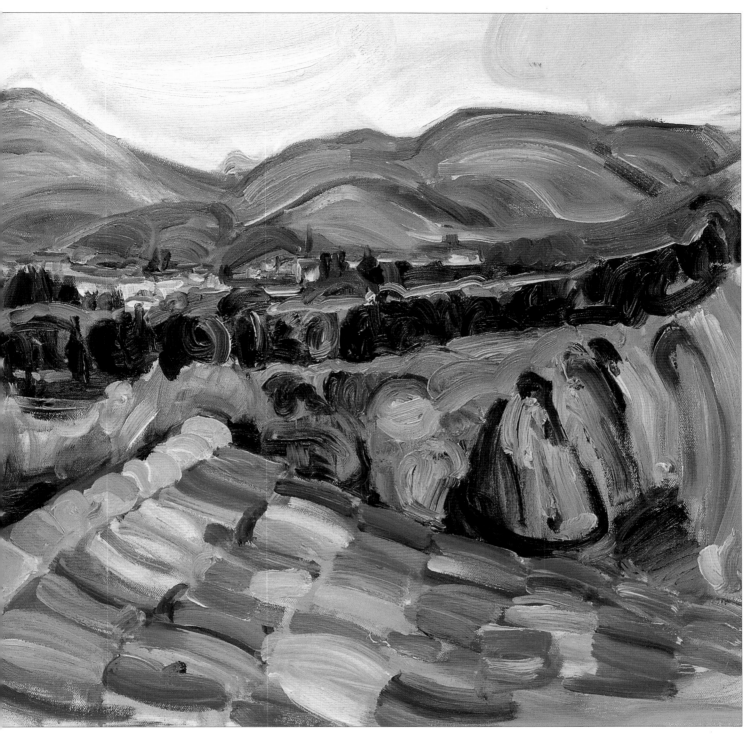

12 (Right) *Strokes of thick, light paint are swept across the sky, with sufficient pressure applied to the broad flat brush to create a series of tiny ridges in each stroke.*

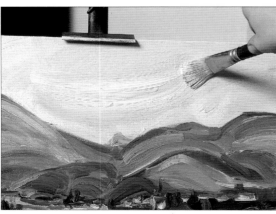

13 (Above) *The finished painting illustrates beautifully what is meant by creating a sense of movement in a composition. The eye is led into and around the painting by the wing-like shape of the foreground roof and by the directional brushwork.*

FIGURES & PORTRAITS

The human figure, whether painted as a portrait, a full-length study, a clothed figure or a nude, presents a greater challenge to the artist than any other subject. A still life may be quite satisfactory even if the ellipse on a vase or plate is not right or the table top is out of perspective. But in figure painting such things do matter – we are all familiar with the general structure and proportions of our fellow humans.

It has to be said that the human figure is not easy to portray; the interaction of forms is complex and subtle. Figure and portrait work relies on drawing as much as on painting. This does not mean that you must make a painstaking and detailed drawing and then fill it in, but you must think about the underlying structure – the drawing – all the time as you work and be prepared to make corrections. Working in opaque paints is a considerable advantage here. With oil you can scrape areas back and repaint them, while with acrylic you can easily correct the drawing by overpainting.

STUDYING THE SUBJECT

Drawing the nude is one of the best ways of studying the figure, and even if you intend to paint only portraits and clothed figures it pays to join a life class. It is not essential, however. What is important is to practise drawing people whenever you can. Ask friends to pose for you; draw yourself in the mirror; take a sketchbook with you and make studies of people walking in the street, sitting at café tables, reading or simply relaxing.

PLANNING THE PICTURE

Whether you are painting a head-and-shoulders portrait, a full-length portrait or a nude figure study, never lose sight of the fact that you are also producing a picture.

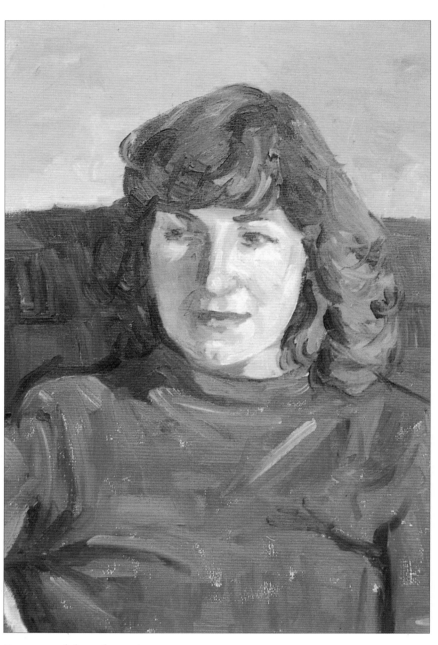

Form and brushwork

(Above) *As the human face and head are complex and difficult to paint, even before you have considered how to achieve a likeness of the sitter, there is a tendency to draw lines with a small brush. This is seldom satisfactory, however, as hard lines can destroy the form. In Ted Gould's Sue (oil), the features, although perfectly convincing, are described with the minimum of detail and no use of line, and the forms of face, hair and clothing are built up with broad directional brushwork.*

Form and colour

(Right) *As a general rule, the colours in shadows are cooler, that is, bluer or greener, than those in the highlight areas, and Gerry Baptist has skilfully exploited this warm/cool contrast to give solidity to the head in his acrylic* Self Portrait. *Although all the colours are heightened, they are nevertheless based on the actual colours of flesh, and the picture is successful in its own terms.*

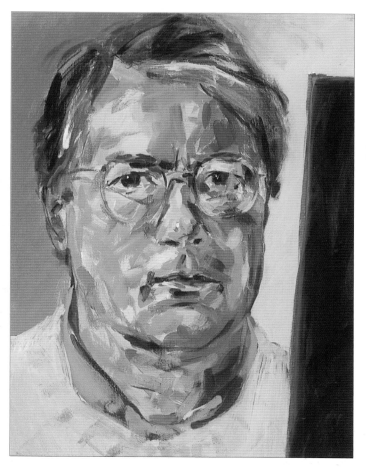

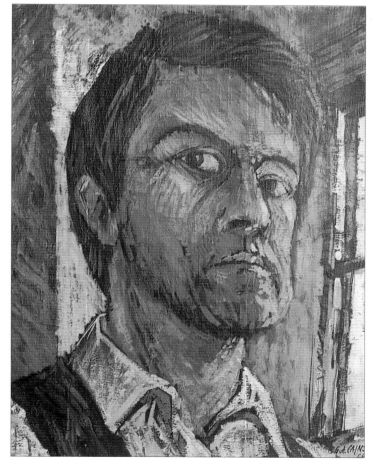

Painting in monochrome

(Left) *In this unusual oil painting,* Self Portrait at 32 Years, *Gerald Cains has taken a diametrically opposite approach to Gerry Baptist and ruled out colour altogether, while using highly expressive brushwork. The effect is extraordinarily powerful. It can be a useful discipline to work in monochrome, as it helps you to concentrate on composition and tonal balance without the distraction of colour.*

In a portrait, particularly, the desire to achieve a likeness can be so all-consuming that you may forget about all the other aspects of the painting.

Much the same applies to figure paintings. The model is often placed right in the middle of the canvas or, worse still, with the feet cropped off at the ankles because they would not fit in. Too much attention is given to the figure and not enough to any other elements in the picture, such as the background. This is understandable, as the figure is the most difficult thing to paint, but it gives a disjointed effect – a good composition is one in which everything is given equal consideration.

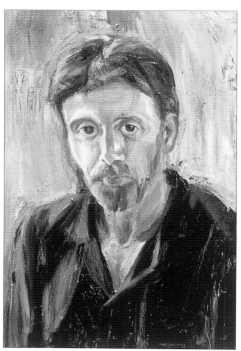

Colour and mood

(Left) *Portraiture involves more than simply achieving a likeness through correct observation of the shapes of noses, eyes and mouths. The best portraits give a feeling of atmosphere and express something of the sitter's character. In Karen Raney's* David *a sense of melancholy and introspection is conveyed through the sombre colours and heavy, downward-sweeping brushmarks as well as by the sitter's intense but inward-looking gaze.*

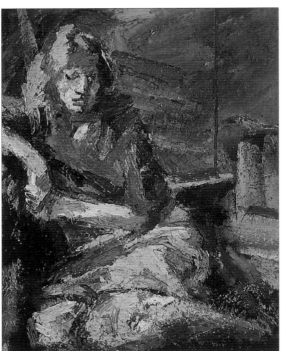

Before you start to paint, consider how you are going to place the head or figure on the canvas. A central placing generally looks stiff and unnatural, as does a direct, face-on approach. Heads in portraits are usually placed slightly off-centre, with the sitter viewed from a three-quarter angle; one shoulder thus appears higher than the other. In this case, more space is often left on the side towards which the sitter is looking, and the near shoulder is sometimes cropped by the canvas edge. Consider how much space to leave above the head. Too much and the head can appear pushed down; too little and it will seem cramped.

LIGHTING

Lighting is vital in portraiture and figure work. The play of light and shade not only describes the forms but also provides the all-important element of tonal contrast. If you look at a face under a harsh, direct light, it looks flat and dull with very little depth, but if the light comes from one side it strikes parts of the face while throwing others into shadow, immediately creating a more interesting configuration. The form of lighting most favoured for portrait and figure work is called three-quarter lighting – the illumination comes from one side,

slightly to the front of the model, thus lighting three-quarters of the face and body.

If you can control the lighting set-up, think also about the strength of the light. Those who paint out of doors will have noticed that bright sunlight casts very positive, heavy shadows. Although strong light can create dramatic effects in a portrait and many artists deliberately choose it, it is not suitable for all subjects. In a painting of a young woman or child, for example, a diffused light is more suitable, as this brings out the subtlety of the flesh tones. If you are painting by a window, you might consider some form of diffuser, such as a net curtain or tracing paper placed over the window. Over-hard shadows on one side of the face can also be lightened by using a reflector. By propping up a white board or piece of paper by the side of your sitter, opposite the source of light, you can bounce some light back onto the dark side of the face, giving touches of colour to the shadow while still preserving tonal contrast.

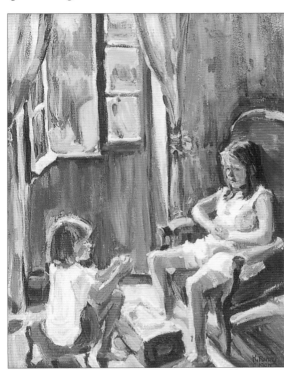

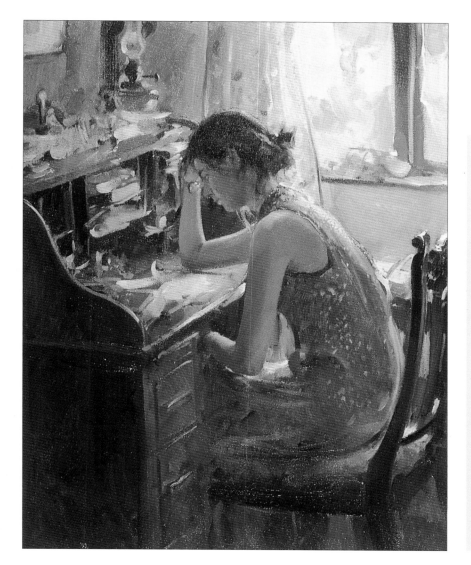

THE FIGURE IN CONTEXT

In a head-and-shoulders portrait, the background is frequently left deliberately vague and undefined in order to focus attention on the face, but a whole figure must be put into a believable context, so some of the room should be included. If you are painting the nude in a life class, you may not have much control over background and other elements, but for a clothed figure painted in your own home or theirs, you will have a wider choice. Particular props are often used in portraiture to help describe the character and interests of the sitter. A writer or someone fond of reading might be shown with a selection of favourite books, or a musician with his or her instrument. Try to convey something of the atmosphere surrounding your sitter.

Full-length portraits

(Above) *When you intend to paint the whole figure rather than just a head and shoulders, you must consider what other elements to include and what props will help to enhance your description of the sitter. If you are painting the subject in their own home, you can show them in familiar surroundings and with personal possessions, as David Curtis has done in his lovely* Interior with Jacqueline *(oil), which is both a portrait and a visual essay on light.*

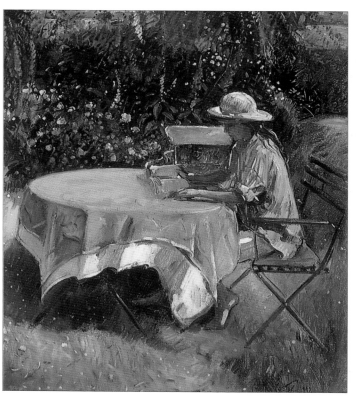

Outdoor settings

(Right) *Light is also an important element in Timothy Easton's* The Summer Read *and, like David Curtis, he has described the sitter more by posture, clothing and general shape than by detailed depiction of features, indeed the features are barely visible. With careful observation, you will find that it is perfectly possible to paint a recognizable likeness of a person without showing the face at all.*

PORTRAIT DEMONSTRATION

Elizabeth Moore paints landscapes, portraits and still lifes, working in all the painting media, but with a tendency towards oil. She often works from photographs, particularly black-and-white ones, which leave her free to interpret an idea in her own way. This oil painting was initially based on a photograph, but the colours are the product of her imagination and experience.

1 (Right) *The sketches, two in pencil and one in oil pastel, were made to explore possible compositions and work out ideas about the general colour scheme for the portrait.*

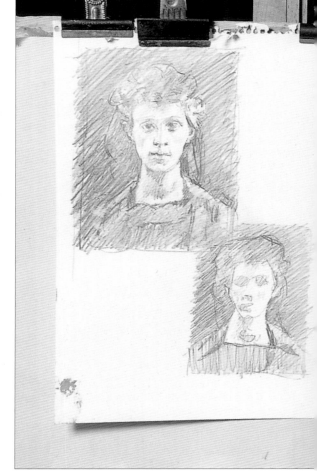

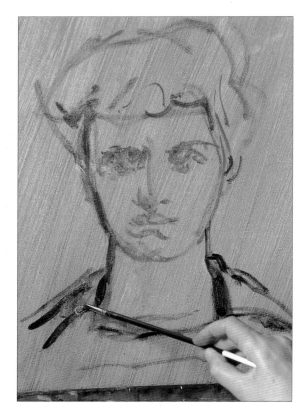

2 *The artist is working on primed and stretched canvas, which she has coloured with a rich yellow-brown to provide a foundation for the flesh tints. She begins with a brush drawing in green, the colour to be used for the dress.*

3 (Right) *The deep, rich purple of the background is painted first, in order to assess the colours needed for the face. Without a live sitter, the artist is working blind in a sense, and must relate the colours to each other rather than to reality.*

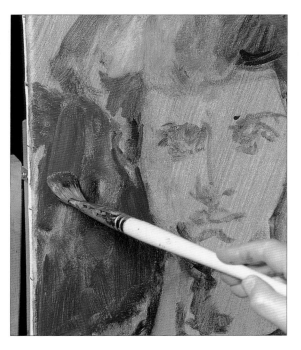

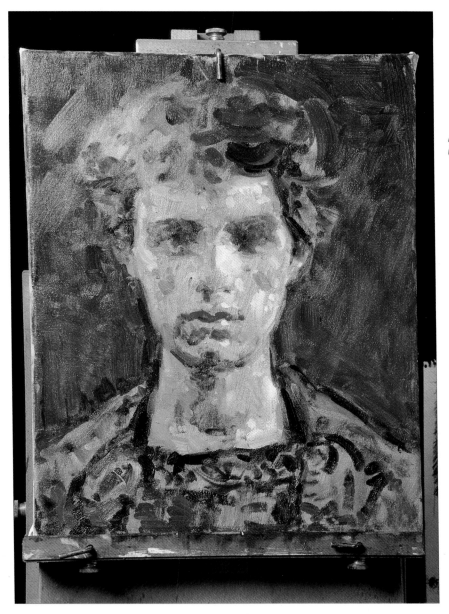

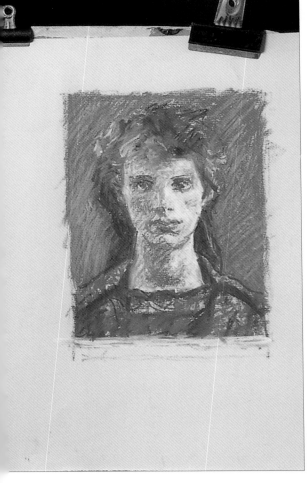

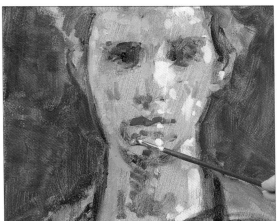

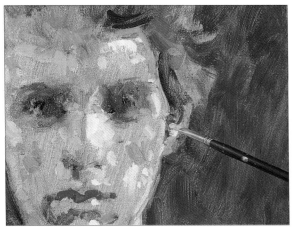

6 (Above) *At this stage in the painting, the artist takes a break for assessment, standing well back from her easel to check whether the colours work when viewed from a distance.*

4 *She proceeds to lay down patches of colour on the face, neck and garment, concentrating on the lightest and darkest tones. She keeps the colours as pure as possible, doing the minimum of mixing and employing an unusually large palette of colours to capture the subject accurately.*

5 *Having used a modified version of the background purple for the shadowed eye sockets, she builds up the light side of the face. To avoid these pinks merging into the darker colour, she places them carefully with a small pointed bristle brush, which gives more control than a flat brush.*

Continued ▷

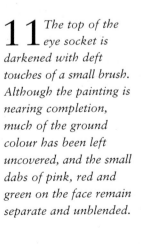

7 *In any portrait, but particularly one in which the subject is looking straight ahead at the viewer, the eyes are the focal point; the eyes and eyelids are defined carefully here with delicate touches of a filbert brush.*

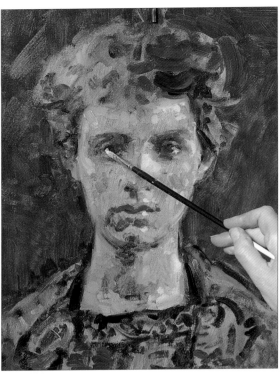

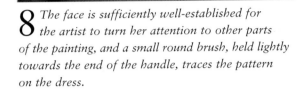

8 *The face is sufficiently well-established for the artist to turn her attention to other parts of the painting, and a small round brush, held lightly towards the end of the handle, traces the pattern on the dress.*

9 *The purple of the background was too warm a colour and needed some variation, so deep blues are introduced. In the classic fat over lean method, the paint now used is thicker and oilier than in the early stages.*

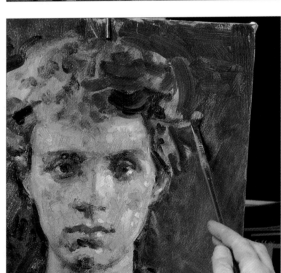

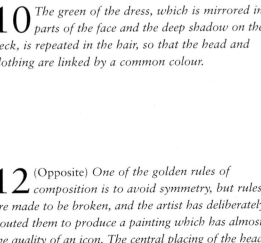

10 *The green of the dress, which is mirrored in parts of the face and the deep shadow on the neck, is repeated in the hair, so that the head and clothing are linked by a common colour.*

11 *The top of the eye socket is darkened with deft touches of a small brush. Although the painting is nearing completion, much of the ground colour has been left uncovered, and the small dabs of pink, red and green on the face remain separate and unblended.*

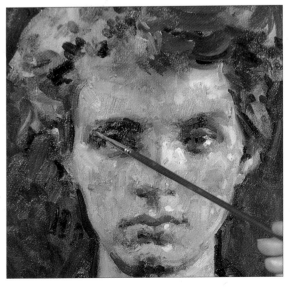

12 *(Opposite) One of the golden rules of composition is to avoid symmetry, but rules are made to be broken, and the artist has deliberately flouted them to produce a painting which has almost the quality of an icon. The central placing of the head on the canvas and the solemn outward gaze impart a sense of strength and dignity to the image.*

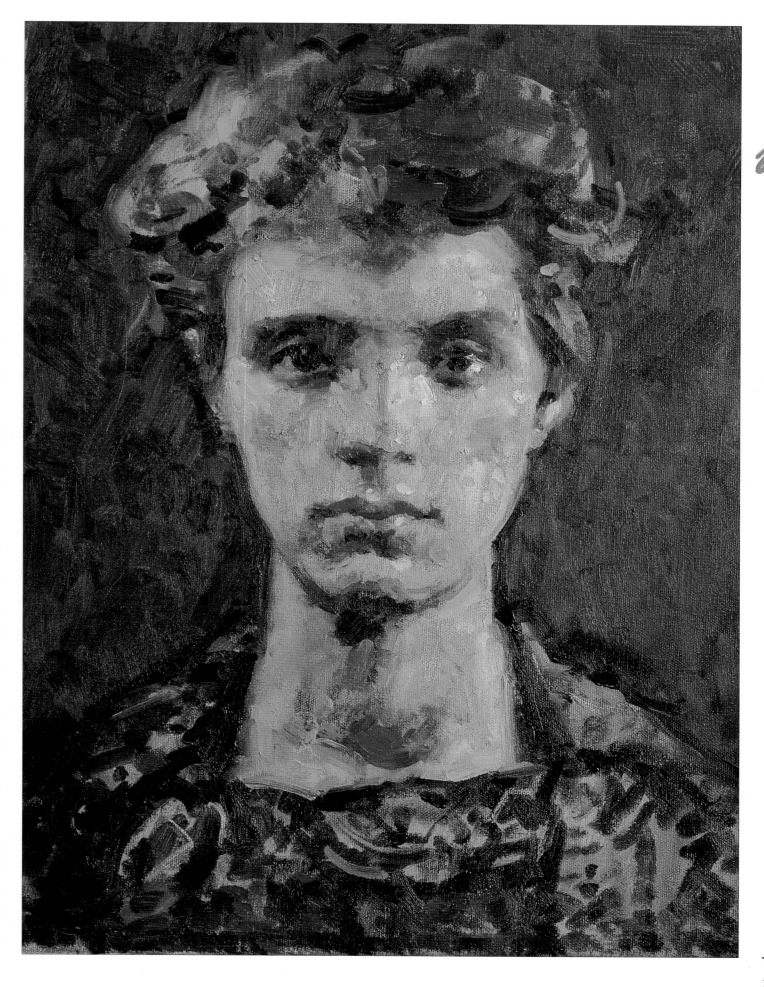

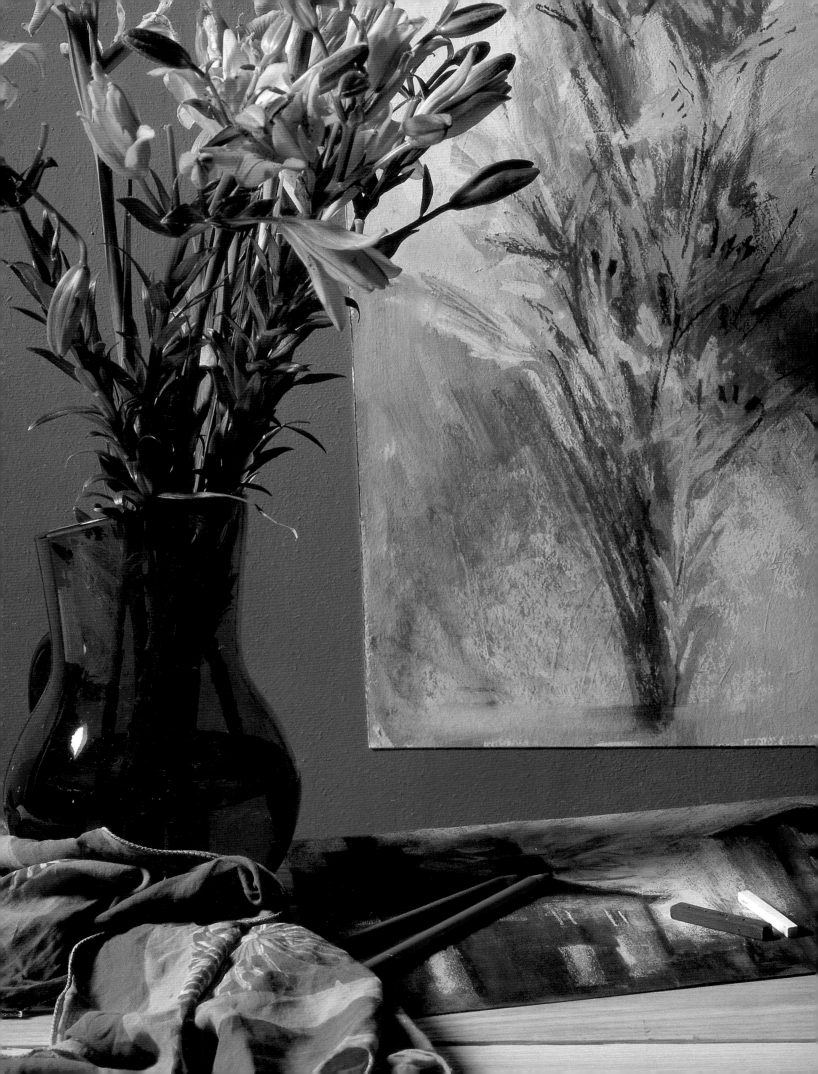

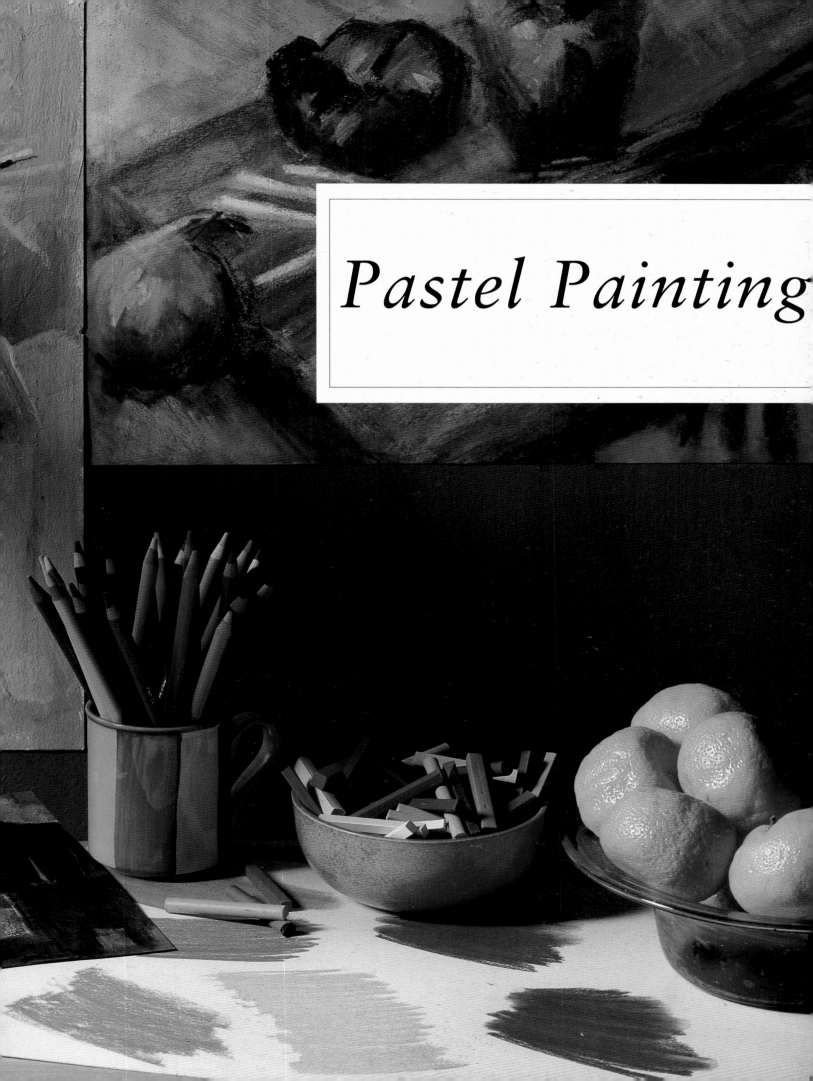

Pastel Painting

Introduction
ABOUT PASTELS

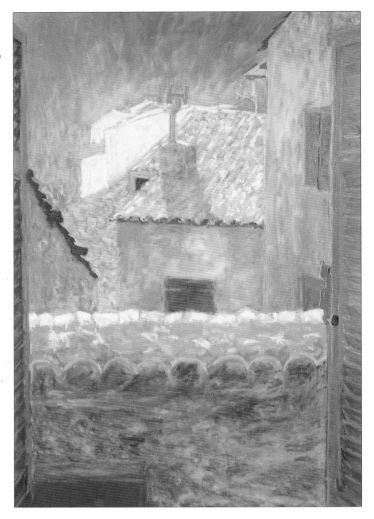

Pastel is unique in that it is both a drawing and a painting medium. It tends to be associated with drawing because the colours are not applied with a brush, but the medium's malleability and richness of colour invite a painterly approach. Many of today's artists exploit this effect in pastel to produce works which at first sight look almost like oil paintings.

Pastel is rapidly becoming one of the most favoured painting media, vying with watercolour for popularity. One of the reasons for this is probably that pastel sticks simply look so beautiful – open one of the boxed sets of pastels in an art shop and you will see a rich array of colours, which seem to offer a direct invitation to the artist. A tube of paint is a poor thing by comparison because you can't see the colour until you have squeezed it out.

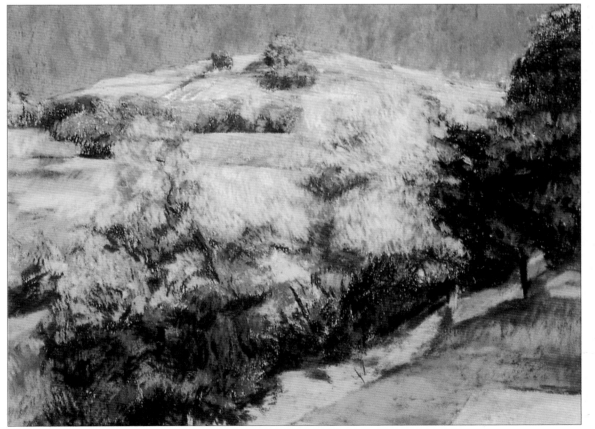

JAMES CRITTENDEN
SUMMER HILLSIDE
(Left) *Pastel is often associated with delicate colours, hence the term "pastel shades", but this powerful landscape shows that considerable depth of tone can be achieved by laying one colour over another. The artist has given a lovely feeling of life and energy by the way he has used the pastel strokes; in the trees, particularly, the effect is very much like brushstrokes in an oil or acrylic painting.*

PATRICK CULLEN

WINDOW IN PROVENCE

(Opposite) *The colours are also built up thickly in this painting, but the technique is very different, with short pieces of pastel used to make broader marks. To create the gentle but luminous colours, the artist has restricted himself to light and mid-tones, controlling them carefully, and changing the direction of the strokes to give variety to the different surfaces.*

KEN PAINE

HEAD OF A YOUNG WOMAN

(Right) *This artist exploits the directness and expressive qualities of pastel in his portraits. He works with great rapidity, usually beginning by building up the tonal structure with a monochrome "underpainting" made with broad strokes of short lengths of pastel. Linear definition and bright colour accents are left until the final stages. The coloured paper is still visible in areas.*

MAUREEN JORDAN

ROSE AND GERANIUM TEXTURES

(Below) *The artist has exploited the whole range of pastel techniques in this vivid and lively picture, combining solid, thickly applied colour, blended in places, with fine-line drawing to pick out individual flowers and petals. In the foreground, an area which can become dull in a floral group, a series of strong, decisive marks creates its own pattern and interest.*

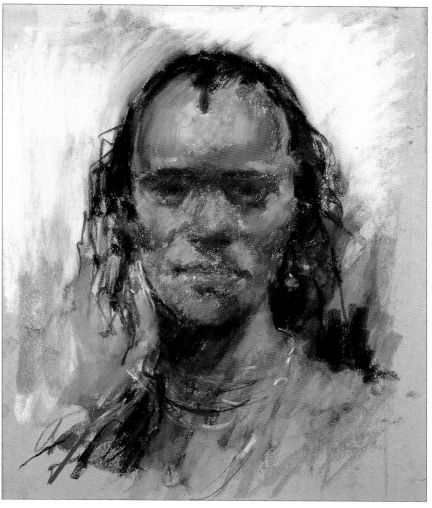

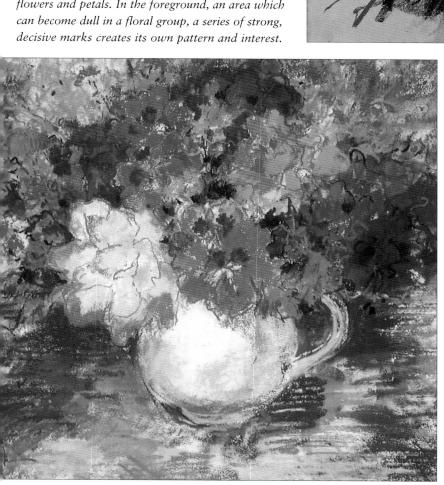

PROS AND CONS

The immediacy of pastel is also appealing. These sticks of colour form a direct link between your hand and the paper. You don't have to mix colours on a palette and you need no brushes. Like any drawing medium, pastels are responsive, easy to manipulate and quick to use, which makes them ideal for outdoor work and rapid effects; but because of their loose, crumbly texture and brilliance of colour – pastels are almost pure pigment – they can also be built up thickly in layers just as paints can. As you will see from the small gallery of paintings shown here, pastels are a versatile medium and there are many different ways of using them.

No medium is perfect, however, and those who are not accustomed to pastels may experience some problems until they become familiar with techniques involved, and learn what pastels can and cannot do.

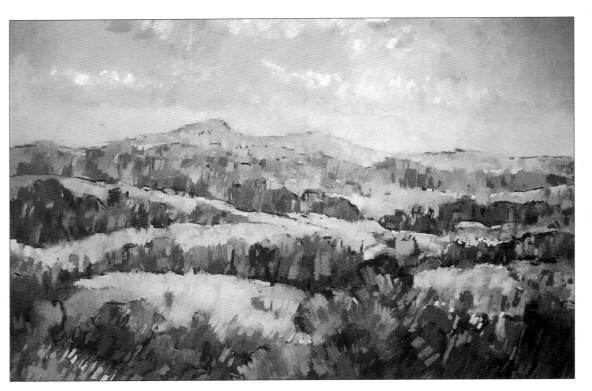

GEOFF MARSTERS
LANDSCAPE IN THE AUVERGNE
(Left) *When he first took up pastels, Marsters was determined to use the medium as a painting rather than a drawing technique, and through constant experiment he has evolved his own methods of working. He achieves his rich, dense colours by working on abrasive (pumice) paper, rubbing the pastel into it, fixing and then applying further layers on top. He loves the brilliance of pastels, and exploits this quality by "keying up" the colours.*

One of the advantages of pastels – that you do not have to pre-mix colours – can also work against you. Any mixing has to be done on the working surface but, because it is not possible to try out mixes in advance as you can with paints, it is all too easy to make mistakes. You cannot erase pastels easily, although you can correct mistakes to some extent by laying more colours on top. If you do too much of this, however, you will clog the paper surface and may end up with a tired-looking, muddy painting.

One of the greatest exponents of pastel, the 18th-century portrait painter Maurice Quentin de La Tour, mentioned the possibility of spoiling work by over-mixing; he had one or two other complaints, too – about the dust generated by working with pastels, for example. It has to be admitted that it is not a medium for those who like to keep their floors clean. It is hard on the hands too, as they become covered with colour as soon as you pick up a stick.

A more serious problem is the fragility of pastels, in particular soft pastels. The sticks break very easily under pressure, added to which it is very easy to smudge finished work. Even when sprayed with fixative, the pigments tend to fall off the paper, especially if they rub up against another surface. Unless you can frame and glaze your work immediately, it is vital to store it carefully, laying it flat with pieces of tissue paper on top.

Despite these minor problems, pastel is a wonderful medium to use. Few who have taken it up, whether amateur or professional, feel inclined to abandon it.

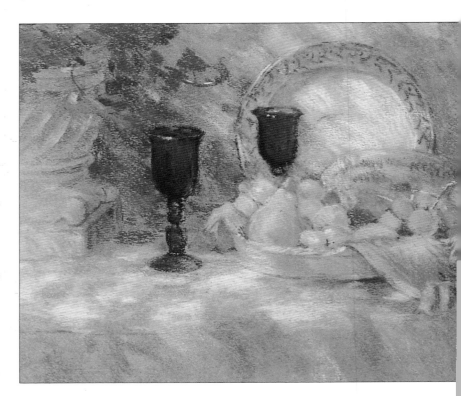

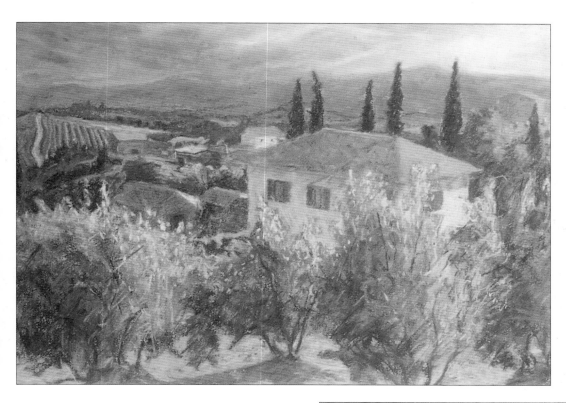

PATRICK CULLEN
CASA DE LIDO

(Left) *In this atmospheric painting, the approach to colour is more naturalistic than in the landscape opposite, but there are some similarities in technique, with the pastel again applied thickly and layered in places. Cullen usually works either on sandpaper, or on heavy watercolour paper on which he first lays a ground of watercolour.*

GEOFF MARSTERS
INTERIOR OF BOATHOUSE

(Right) *This subject, with its angularity and profusion of detail, might not seem suitable for a soft, crumbly medium such as pastel, which is usually considered better for broad effects, but the artist has treated it with great assurance. If you look closely you can see that the lines and edges are in fact quite loose and free; the impression of sharp linearity is created by the strong contrasts of tone and colour.*

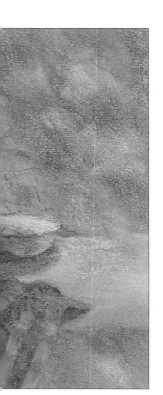

JACKIE SIMMONDS
STILL LIFE WITH BLUE SPANISH GLASS

(Left) *In this gentle and tranquil painting the artist has made clever use of pastel's capacity for creating a variety of textures. For the glass, deep blues have been blended to imitate the smoothness of the material, but the central area of the plate has been left slightly rough, while in the background several colours have been dragged lightly over one another.*

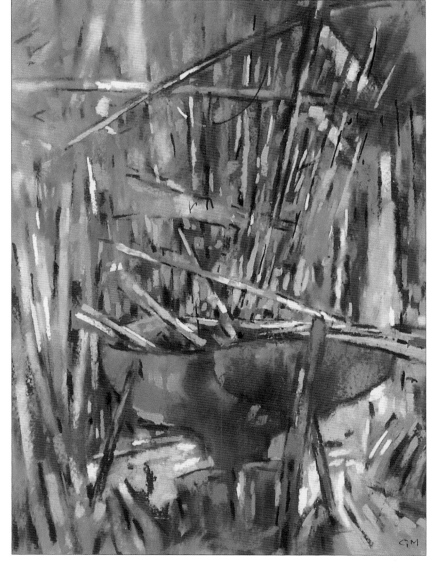

197

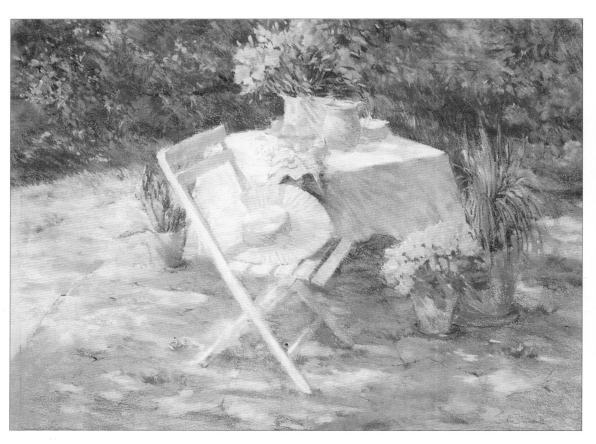

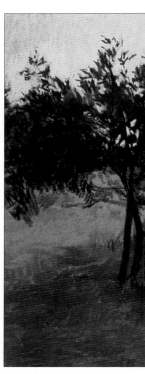

JACKIE SIMMONDS
TEA ON THE PATIO
(Above) *This delightful painting probably comes closest to most people's idea of pastel – the colours are light and fresh, in keeping with the airy subject, and the handling is delicate. In fact, however, these qualities owe more to the artist's skill in controlling the medium than to its inherent properties; it needs a light touch and a sound knowledge of both colour and technique to achieve such effects.*

ELIZABETH MOORE
STILL LIFE WITH PEARS AND PLUMS
(Below) *For this still life, the artist has worked in oil pastel, which she likes because it is related to oil paint, the medium she uses most frequently. She also finds it more controllable than soft pastel. Here it has allowed her to build up deep, rich colours as well as very subtle effects, notably the bloom on the plums.*

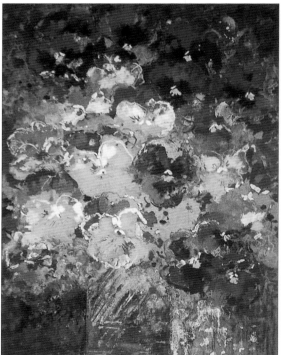

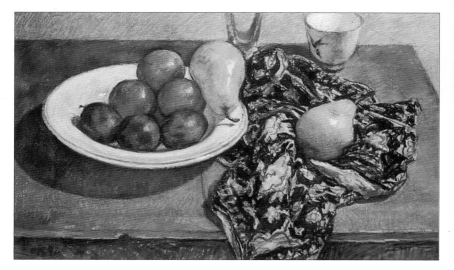

MAUREEN JORDAN
PANSY TEXTURES
(Above) *The characteristic crumbly texture of pastel can benefit from contrast with a smoother medium, and here the artist has used pastel in combination with acrylic. The acrylic underpainting has also allowed her to establish deep, rich colours from the outset without a heavy build-up of pastel.*

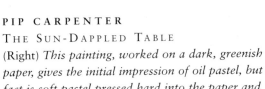

JAMES CRITTENDEN
ORANGE GROVE IN THE EVENING

(Left) *As in most of his pastel paintings, this artist skilfully combines the drawing and painting qualities of pastel to produce an interpretation of the landscape that is both realistic and highly personal. What appear at first glance to be solid areas of colour – the sky and grass – are in fact a complex network of overlaid lines and marks made with the tip of the stick, while the leaves of the trees are expressed by rapid calligraphic dashes and squiggles.*

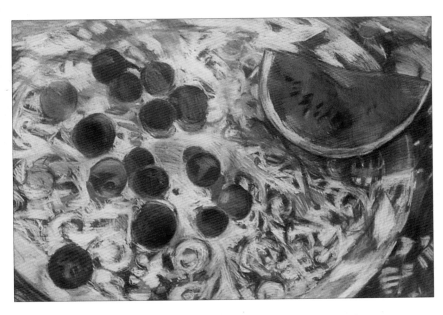

PIP CARPENTER
THE SUN-DAPPLED TABLE

(Right) *This painting, worked on a dark, greenish paper, gives the initial impression of oil pastel, but in fact is soft pastel pressed hard into the paper and fixed between stages to allow one colour to be laid over another. The artist was particularly excited by the effect of the light on the different surfaces – the volume of the fruit and the flat plane of the ornamental iron table.*

JUDY MARTIN
BANDSTAND SERIES

(Left) *Vivid colour was of primary importance in this painting, and here, too, acrylic has been used in combination with pastel. The underpainting, which set the colour-key for the picture, was mainly in shades of red and yellow, with contrasting colours of pastel applied on top in vigorous strokes. You can see this effect clearly in the sky, where strokes of blue pastel overlay bright red paint.*

PASTELS

There are four main types of pastel: soft (also known as chalk pastels), hard pastels, pastel pencils and oil pastels. All pastels are made in the same way. Ground pigment is bulked out with a "filler" such as chalk and held together with some sort of binder, the traditional one being gum tragacanth.

SOFT PASTELS

Very little binder is used in the manufacture of soft pastels, which are almost pure pigment, hence their brilliance of colour, fragility and powdery texture. Although the majority of pastel painters use soft pastels, you may find hard pastels and pastel pencils form a useful complement to these.

HARD PASTELS

Hard pastels contain more binder and have a finer consistency. They do not break so easily and can be sharpened to a fine point for detailed work. Some artists use the side of a hard pastel stick to block in large areas of colour in the preliminary stages of a painting. Because they are less crumbly than soft pastels, they are easier to work over with other colours as the work progresses. They can also be used on their own, but in general they are better suited to pastel drawing, where the approach is more linear, than to pastel painting. The range of colours is also quite limited, at least in comparison with soft pastels, where the colour variations are truly awesome.

PASTEL PENCILS

These are also more of a drawing than a painting tool, but a few pastel pencils will form a useful addition to your kit; they are ideal for small areas of detail in a painting as well as for making preliminary drawings. Ordinary graphite pencils should never be used for underdrawings for pastel, as

graphite is slightly greasy and will repel any pastel colour laid on top. In terms of softness and hardness, pastel pencils lie somewhere in the middle. The colour ranges are similar to those of hard pastels.

OIL PASTELS

These can't be used in combination with ordinary pastels, as they are bound with oil rather than gum. They are, however, an excellent alternative to soft pastels and are capable of very exciting and painterly effects. What is particularly intriguing about them is that the colour can be "melted" with turpentine or white spirit, then spread across the paper with a brush. You can even dip a brush moistened with turpentine into the sticks of colour and apply it, just as you would put on paint. The colours are rather more restricted than those of soft pastels but, as the medium grows in popularity, manufacturers are beginning to respond to demand.

DIFFERENT SHADES

In oil, watercolour and acrylic painting, you can manage with very few basic colours because you can obtain so many more by means of mixing. Pastels, however, can't be premixed, so you will need many more sticks of pastel than you would tubes of paint. Choosing a range of colours which gives you sufficient scope for colour matching, without incurring vast expense, can be a problematical business. Some ranges contain literally hundreds of colours, so where do you start?

Fortunately many manufacturers help you here, producing "starter" sets tailored to particular subject areas. There are, for example, large and small boxed sets, with a range of suitable colours for either landscape or portrait work. One of these

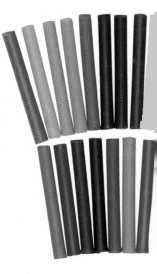

OIL PASTELS

PASTEL PENCILS

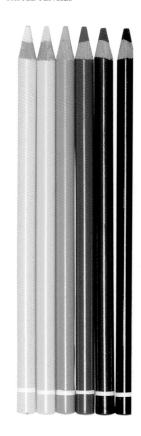

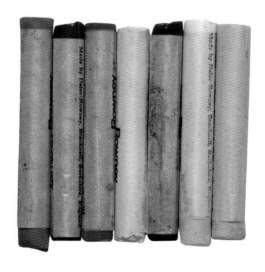

SOFT PASTELS

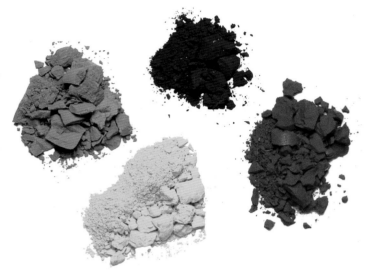

CRUMBLED SOFT PASTELS

could make a good starting point. You can add more colours when you know which ones you need – all pastels are sold singly as well as in boxes.

If you already know something about colour, you can simply rely on choosing by eye. As you look through drawers of pastels, you will notice that some of the colours bear a name and a number. The latter denotes the tone of the colour,

whether it is a light or dark version of ultramarine, for example. All pastel colours are made in a pure hue plus light and dark versions, the former achieved by adding white and the latter by adding black. Unfortunately, there is no standard naming or numbering system among manufacturers but, as you become more experienced, you will be able to pick out the colours you want quite quickly.

VARIATIONS

There are considerable differences in colour from one range of pastels to another so, when you have reached the stage of adding colours, it's always worth trying out several different kinds. Experienced artists become familiar with the different ranges and often have one or two favourite colours made only by one particular manufacturer. They will thus have a selection of different makes in their "paintbox".

The textures vary too. Some "soft" pastels are relatively hard, while others are so crumbly that they break as soon as you pick them up and have to be spread with your fingers. You can find these things out only by experience, but it's all part of the learning process.

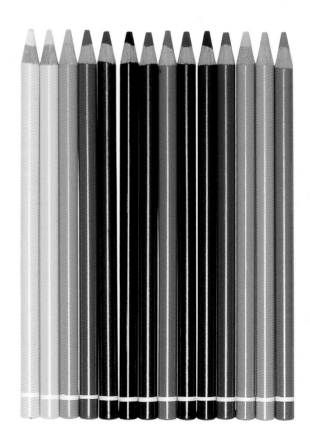

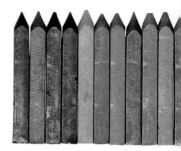

HARD PASTELS

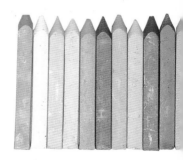

PASTEL PENCILS

The choice of paper is extremely important in pastel work because both the colour and the texture play an important part in the overall effect. Pastels are usually done on a coloured surface; the paper must also have some texture in order to hold the pigment (this is known as "tooth"). If you work on too smooth a surface, the pigment will tend to slip about and fall off, making it impossible to achieve any layering of colour in your picture.

PAPER AND TEXTURE SHADE

The reason for working on coloured paper is that it is very difficult, sometimes impossible, to cover the whole surface with pastel. Even if you use a pastel stick fairly heavily on its side, some of the paper will still show through. Small flecks of white paper appearing between pastel strokes create a jumpy effect, as well as devaluing the colours. Thus it is usual to work on a colour that either complements or tones in with the overall colour scheme of the picture. There are artists who like to work on white paper, but they are very much in the minority.

There are two standard papers made for pastel work: Ingres and Mi-Teintes (these are not manufacturers' names; they describe a type of paper). Both are made in a wide range of colours and both have a texture to hold the pigment in place. Ingres is a laid paper, with a pattern of fine, even lines, while Mi-Teintes has a pattern of dots slightly resembling fine chicken wire. It is worth trying both of these, as you will only discover which one you like best by hands-on experience. You can also use the "wrong" side of Mi-Teintes paper if you find the grain too obtrusive.

The choice of colour is more difficult, as it involves knowing what your picture will look like before you start. Some artists choose a paper which will be one of the key colours in the painting, and leave areas of it

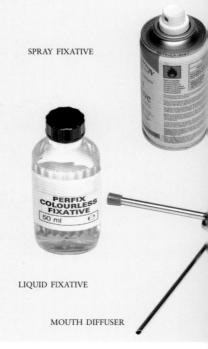

1 AND 2 MI-TEINTES

3 AND 4 INGRES

5 SANDPAPER

6 AND 7 SANSFIX PAPER

8 WATERCOLOUR PAPER

FIXATIVE

Although some artists dislike fixative and use it as little as possible or even not at all, you will certainly need it when you are starting out in pastel. Unless you can frame and glaze your pictures immediately, there is a serious risk of smudging them if you fail to spray them with fixative before putting them away. Even after fixing, you will still need a sheet of tissue paper on top of the picture to protect it.

The problem with fixative is that it does tend to darken the colours slightly; you may also lose something of the delicate, fragile texture of pastel pigment. However, for any painting built up thickly in layers, it is essential to spray at regular stages, in order to overwork with new colours without disturbing earlier ones. Keep the spray as light as you can – several sparing applications are better than one heavy one – and don't continue working until you are sure the fixative is completely dry.

You can either use a bottle of fixative with a mouth diffuser or an aerosol can; the latter are all now "ozone friendly" and produce a suitably fine spray. They are quite expensive, however, so you might like to consider using odourless hairspray as an alternative – the ingredients are much the same.

SPRAY FIXATIVE

LIQUID FIXATIVE

MOUTH DIFFUSER

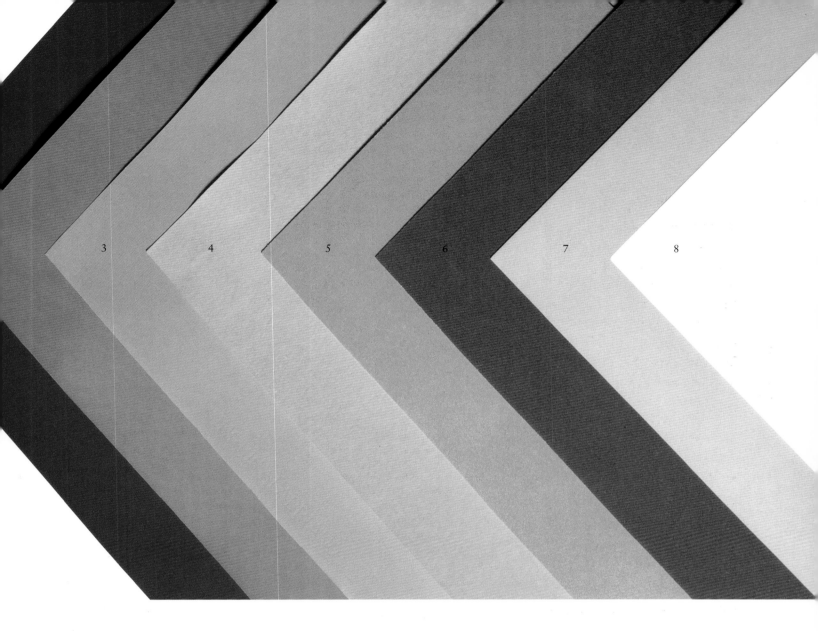

uncovered. For example, a blue-grey might be chosen for a landscape or seascape seen under a cloudy sky, with parts of the paper left for areas of sky and water. Other artists like to work on a contrasting colour, choosing, for example, yellow for a snow scene consisting mainly of blues and blue-greys. To start with, it is probably best to choose a neutral mid-toned colour such as light grey or beige; very bright or very dark colours are hard to manage until you know what you are doing.

OTHER PAPERS

You can also work on a variety of papers not actually designed for pastel work, such as medium (Not surface) watercolour paper (CP paper). This has a very pronounced texture, which breaks up the pastel strokes,

while also allowing for heavy build-ups of colour. If you use watercolour paper, you can tint it in advance by laying a watercolour wash. There are also three special papers produced for pastels, used by artists who like to build up colours very thickly: sandpaper, velour paper and Sansfix paper.

Sandpaper is the same as the fine sandpaper sold for carpentry and other work around the home, but the artist's version comes in much larger sheets. Velour paper, as its name implies, has a velvety texture and gives an attractive soft line. The third alternative, Sansfix (also called Rembrandt paper depending on who makes it), is similar to sandpaper but slightly less abrasive. There is no need for fixative when using any of these papers.

LINE STROKES

Pastel is a drawing medium as well as a painting one, in as much as the pastel stick, like a pencil, is the direct intermediary between your hand and the paper. Although it is possible to produce a pastel painting in which all the colours are smoothly blended and there are no visible lines or marks, this is something of a lost opportunity, as the way in which pastel bridges the gap between drawing and painting is one of its major attractions. In the 18th century, when pastel painting became very popular, artists such as Jean-Etienne Liotard and Maurice Quentin de La Tour produced works whose smooth finishes emulated contemporary oil paintings. However, nowadays most artists prefer to exploit the mark-making aspect of pastel, to give free rein to its energetic, linear quality.

In order to do this successfully, you will need to develop your own "handwriting" in pastel. The tip of a pastel stick can produce a wide variety of different marks, depending on the pressure you apply, the sharpness or bluntness of the point and how you hold the stick. To practise mark-making, don't try to draw actual objects, but just doodle or scribble as the mood takes you. Try applying heavy pressure at the start of a line and then tapering off towards the end, or twisting the stick in mid-stroke so that it trails off in a narrow tail.

Although pastel is soft and crumbly, you will find that you can make surprisingly fine lines if you break a stick in half and use the edge of the broken end. However, hard pastels are the ones for really crisp details, so if you have these in addition to soft pastels, experiment with them too.

SIDE STROKES

The way to cover large areas of the paper in pastel painting is to sweep the side of the stick across the paper, thus depositing a

(Below) *These swatches show the variety of marks that you can make with the tip and side of a pastel stick.*

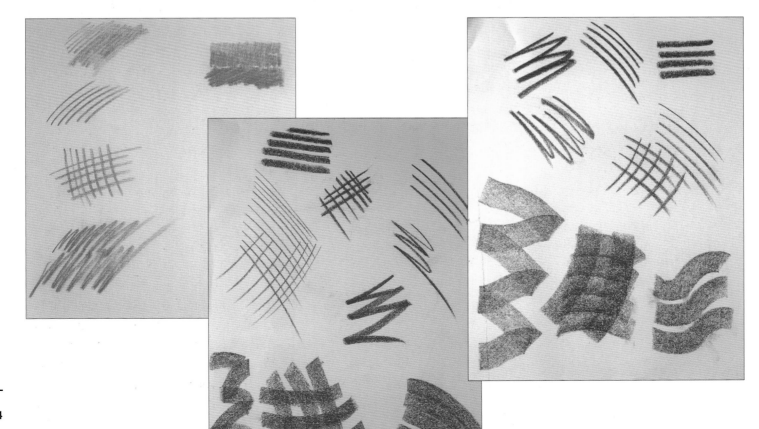

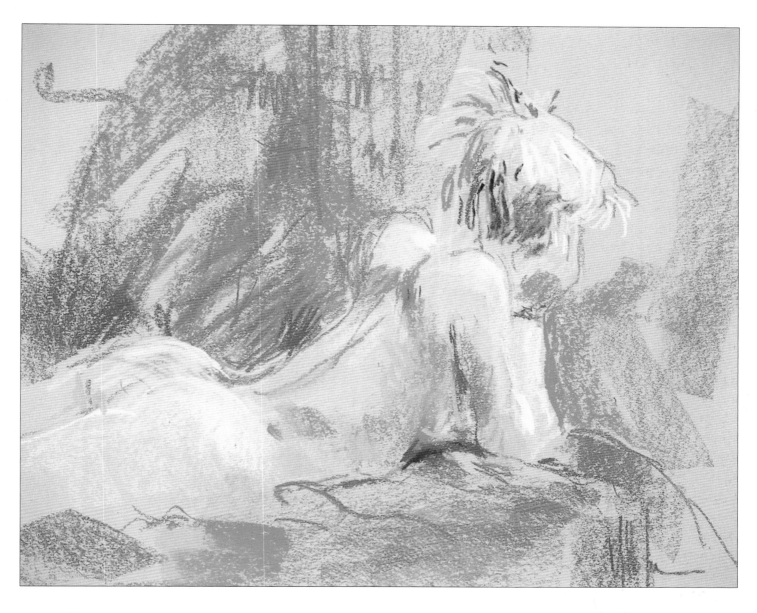

MAUREEN JORDAN
NUDE AGAINST PINK

A classic combination of line and side strokes can be seen in this lively figure study. Notice how the artist has used the pastel sticks in a descriptive way, following the directions of the shapes and forms.

broad band of colour. Side strokes can, however, be much more than just a means of "blocking in" – they can be as varied, beautiful and expressive as line strokes. Many different effects can be created by varying the pressure and direction of the stroke, by laying one stroke over another, by blending in some areas and by laying one colour over another.

The length of the pastel stick also affects the kind of stroke you make. Unless you are using hard pastels, which are relatively tough, you will nearly always have to break the stick. If you try to make side strokes with the whole length of the stick, it will probably break under pressure anyway, added to which a short length is more controllable. Usually the length should not

be more than 5 cm (2 in), but you can use much smaller pieces of pastel than these to make short, jabbing strokes, similar to linear marks.

The other factor which affects side strokes, even more than linear ones, is the texture of the paper. A heavy texture such as watercolour paper will break up the stroke, producing a grainy effect, with the colour deposited only on the top of the weave. On smoother paper, the colour will be denser and, if you apply the pastel heavily, it will cover the paper thoroughly. Be warned that, if you intend to use side strokes as a means of colour mixing, with one colour laid over another, the pressure should be kept light initially, or the paper will quickly become clogged.

MIXING PASTELS

However many pastels you have – and professional pastel painters may have hundreds – you will nearly always have to mix them to reproduce the colours you see. Nature provides far more subtle and varied nuances of colour than could be matched by any manufacturer of artist's pigments.

LIGHTENING AND DARKENING COLOURS

As mentioned earlier, all pastel colours are made in light and dark versions. Further variations of tone (the lightness and darkness of colours) are produced by controlling the amount of pressure you apply to the pastel stick – the heavier the pressure, the more solid the colour will be. However, you will frequently have to lighten or darken colours by mixing. A pale blue sky, for example, may call for a combination of blue and white, or blue and pale grey; dark areas of foliage or heavy shadows may need a mixture of dark blue or black with green and other colours. Black is particularly useful in pastel work as the colours are brilliant and generally not very dark, so it is hard to achieve any depth of colour without using black.

METHODS OF MIXING

One of the best-known techniques for colour mixing is blending. Two or more colours are applied to the working surface and rubbed together with your fingers, a rag, a piece of cotton wool or an implement called a torchon (a rolled paper stump made specially for the purpose). If you choose your pastel sticks carefully, you can achieve almost any colour and tone in this way. However, although blending is ideal for areas of a picture where you want a soft effect, you should not rely on it too much, as over-blending gives a bland impression.

Lightening

1 *When very pale pastel colours are required, it is sometimes necessary to mix on the paper surface by adding white. Here white is laid over a mid-blue.*

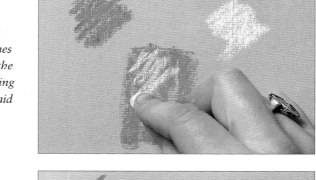

2 *The pastel pigments are gently blended together with a fingertip. Be prepared to use your fingers a good deal in pastel work; they are the best "implements" for blending in relatively small areas.*

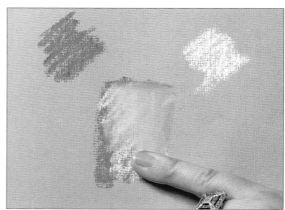

Darkening

1 *Black is a useful colour in pastel work, as it can be difficult to achieve really dark colours without it. Here the black is laid down first, with the green on top.*

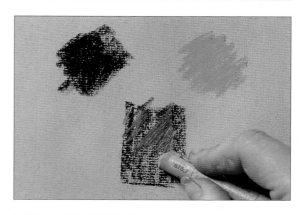

2 *With experience you will discover which colours can be successfully darkened with black. In this case, the mixture is rather muddy and the light green has lost much of its character.*

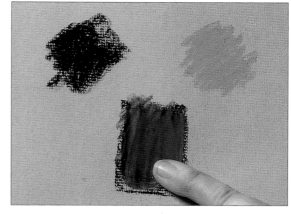

Mixing greens

To reproduce the wide range of greens in nature, you generally need to mix colours to some extent. Here, ultramarine is laid over a lemony yellow. The two colours are blended lightly to produce a strong green. Yellows and blues can also be added to ready-made greens to modify them.

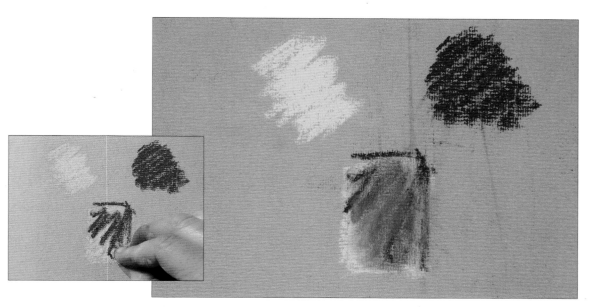

Mixing oranges

To mix a pure orange, choose the strongest red and yellow in your pastel set, and lay the yellow over the red. Even when the two colours are blended, the darker colour will dominate if it is laid over the lighter one. Experiment to discover the effect of light-over-dark and dark-over-light mixtures.

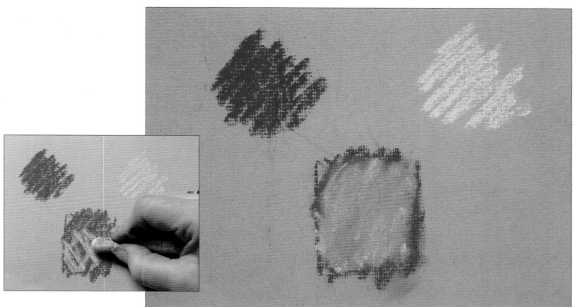

Mixing greys

Most pastel ranges include a good selection of greys, but they can easily be mixed from black and white. Other colours, such as blues and greens, can be added for interest. The result will be affected by the order in which the colours are laid: white over black will produce a lighter mixture, particularly if the colours are only blended gently.

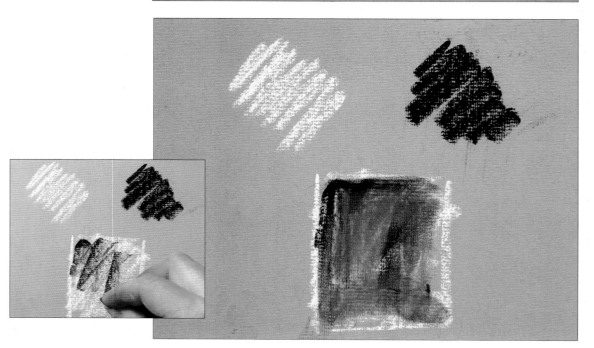

Blending large areas

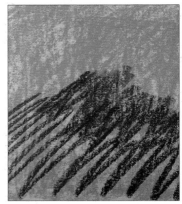

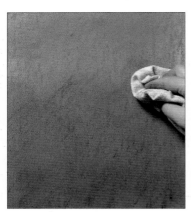

Feathering

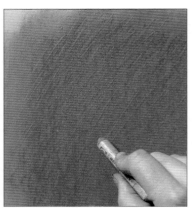

1 *For a subtle blend which would be suitable for a large area of sky, blue and black are first lightly scribbled together.*

2 *The rag used to blend the colours knocks some of the particles of pastel off the paper, producing a lighter mixture than finger blending, which pushes the pigment into the paper.*

This is a useful method for rejuvenating an area of colour which has become flat and dull, or for toning down an over-bright colour. Here light feathering strokes are made in green over an area of red.

A light, unblended application of one colour over another makes a more vibrant and exciting alternative because the first colour shows through the second, producing an attractive sparkle. Pastels are opaque, and so light colours can be laid over dark ones as well as the other way round, to modify the tone of colours.

For many artists, one of the main attractions of pastel is its vigorous linear quality, with the marks of the pastel stick forming an integral part of the image (like brushwork in painting). For this reason, colours are sometimes mixed by building up a network of linear strokes which merge when seen from a distance. A related method is feathering, which is often used to revive an area of colour which has become flat and dull through over-zealous blending. It involves dragging light strokes of colour over the offending area with the tip of the pastel stick and provides a useful means of modifying colours which do not look quite right. For example, a solid area of red which seems too bright in the overall context of your painting can be feathered over lightly with strokes of green, or a too-blue sky can be transformed with greys or pale mauves.

CHOOSING PAPER

When one colour is laid over another it produces a third colour – yellow over blue makes green; red over yellow makes orange and so on. Thus it follows that the colour of the paper will influence the applied colour. If you choose a neutral mid-toned paper the effect will not be dramatic, but a light application of yellow on a rich blue paper has a similar effect to laying yellow over blue pastel. It is important to remember this, as the paper always acts as a third colour in any two-colour mixture, unless the pastel is applied heavily. On the following pages you can see some of the effects of the paper colour on mixtures.

GEOFF MARSTERS
FEN LIGHT
(Above) *Rich painterly effects have been achieved by laying one colour over another, with the work fixed between stages. For the bright patches of highlight in the fields, the artist has used the tips of the pastel sticks, applying thick colour over softer blends.*

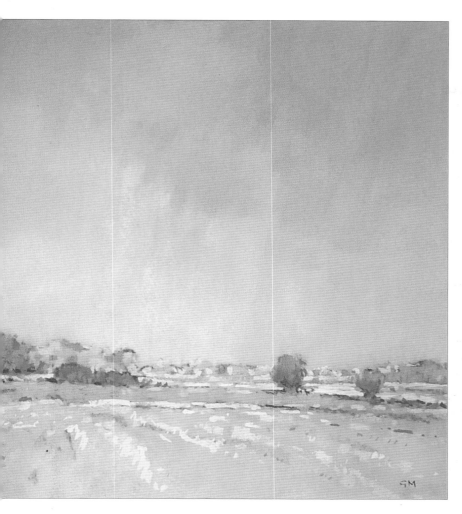

Using the paper colour

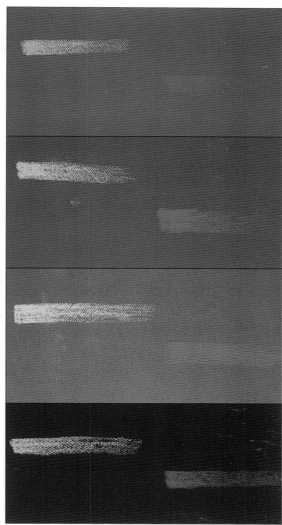

(Above) *As you can see in these examples, even when pastel is applied thickly, small specks of the paper will show through, affecting the appearance of the applied colour. The colour of the paper also influences the way you work, acting as the "key" against which you must judge the first colours you put on. Working on black or very dark blue paper makes it difficult to assess the lighter colours, because even a brilliant green or red will look pale in comparison. Until you have gained some experience, it is wise to choose a mid-toned neutral colour, thus avoiding the possibility of the base colour working against you.*

Overlays

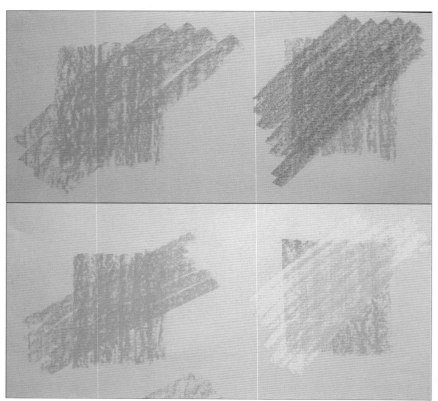

(Left) *Thoroughly blended colour mixtures may be necessary in certain areas of a painting, but the effects of unblended colours are often more exciting. In these examples you can see how one colour shows through another to produce a lively, sparkling effect.*

EXERCISE: EXPERIMENTING WITH DIFFERENT PAPERS

It requires a good deal of experience to know which colour of paper to choose, so it is not a bad idea to start by painting the same subject on two different colours. Set up a simple still-life group, making sure that whatever objects you choose have a predominant colour theme. You might decide on blue, in which case you could paint a bunch of blue flowers, perhaps with one or two yellow ones for contrast. Or you might set up a still life consisting of green bottles, again with one other colour for contrast – perhaps an orange or apple.

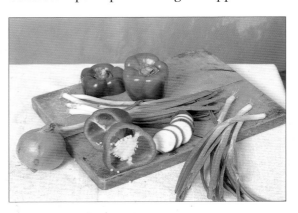

Paint the still life first on a colour which is the opposite of the main colour in the group. This is orange-yellow if you have chosen blue as the predominant colour, and red or red-brown if you have decided on green. These opposite colours are called complementaries; there are three pairs of them: red and green, blue and orange, and yellow and violet. For your second painting, choose a paper which represents one of the colours in the subject. For the blue flower group you could use a dark or mid-toned blue, or a blue-grey. You should find that you don't have to cover the entire paper with pastel colour.

Some artists always use a complementary coloured paper, while others prefer one which tones with the key subject colour.

Painting on toning paper

1 *Working on dark green paper, chosen in order to represent the dominant greens of the still life, the artist begins with the opposite colour, making a light drawing in red-brown pastel.*

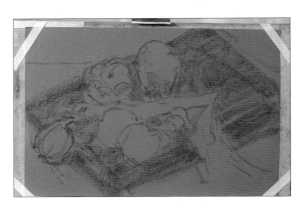

2 *Initially, she concentrates on covering the green paper in the non-green areas, establishing the contrasting warm browns and blue-whites. Notice that she does not attempt to cover the paper entirely; the paper colour still shows through.*

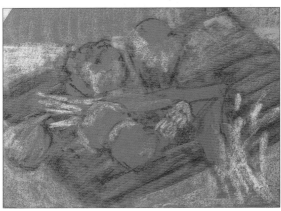

Painting on contrasting paper

1 *In this case the paper picks up the yellow-brown of the board, but is in opposition to the greens of the vegetables.*

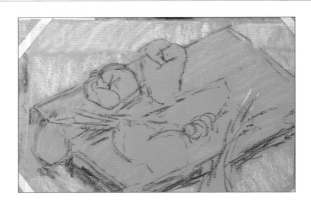

2 *To counteract the colour of the paper, the artist has to use a different selection of greens and yellows from those she chose for the first painting. Here the colour scheme is warmer and the greens are also less dominant.*

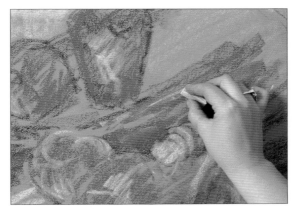

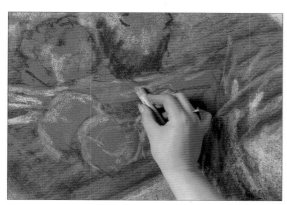

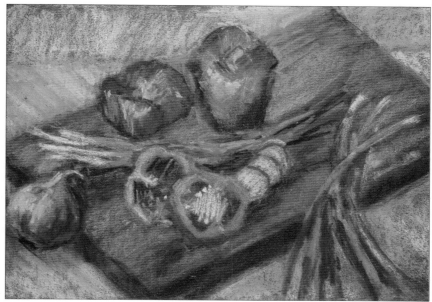

3 Leaving the paper colour to stand for the mid-tones of the vegetables, she now builds up both the dark shadows (the pepper in the background) and the brighter green highlights. Touches of the warm browns and yellows used for the chopping board have also been introduced into the vegetables, so that the green-brown theme runs through the picture.

4 The finished picture shows the importance of the role played by the colour of the paper. Large areas have been left uncovered on the vegetables; elsewhere in the painting, streaks and flecks of the green base colour show through the light pastel strokes. Repeating colours from one part of a picture in another area makes a series of visual links, creating an overall unity in the composition.

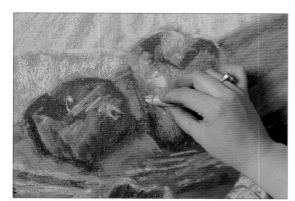

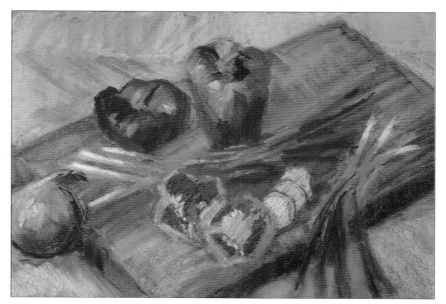

3 In the first painting, the greens of the vegetables were applied quite lightly because the paper did not need to be covered completely. Here, however, the greens have to be built up heavily to prevent too much of the paper from showing through.

4 There are a number of differences between this and the first painting. The dominant colour here is orange-brown rather than green, with the paper colour showing through most clearly on the board and in the background. The method of working has also been affected by the need to build up the greens heavily; the vegetables look darker and more solid, forming a stronger contrast with the wooden board. Both paintings are on the "wrong" – smoother – side of Mi-Teintes paper, chosen in preference to the more obtrusive texture of the "right" side.

TINTING YOUR PAPER

The two standard pastel papers, Ingres and Mi-Teintes, are produced in a vast range of colours. However, some artists, particularly those who like to build up their colours thickly, prefer to work on watercolour paper, which has a distinctive texture, and which they generally tint in advance with their chosen colour.

LAYING A TINTED GROUND

There are two ways of doing this. One is by laying a wash, either of watercolour or thinned acrylic paint, which is quick and easy. However, if you work exclusively in pastel you won't have these paints to hand, in which case you can prepare the paper with what is called a dry wash of pastel. To do this you first reduce a pastel stick to dust by holding it over a bowl or plate and scraping the long edge with a sharp knife. When you have sufficient colour, simply dip a piece of cotton wool (a cotton ball) or a rag into it and spread it over the paper surface, using an even pressure.

If you want an all-over colour, spread the pastel dust evenly across the paper. This method also allows you to introduce tonal variations by applying the colour more thickly in some areas than others. You can also use more than one colour, perhaps using a blue dry wash for a sky in a landscape and a brown or yellow ochre one for the ground. Indeed, dry washing need not be restricted to colouring the ground or sky, it is also a useful method for creating hazy effects of soft colour. If you intend to work over the wash, however, spray it with fixative first. The advantage of the watercolour or acrylic method is that you need not do this.

Laying a dry wash

1 *A knife is used to scrape the side of the pastel stick, producing a fine dust. The method may seem wasteful, but in fact you don't need a great deal of colour.*

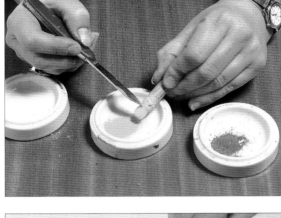

2 *This dry wash is for a landscape, using two colours: blue for the sky and yellow for the land. The blue powder is applied lightly on watercolour paper with a piece of cotton wool (a cotton ball).*

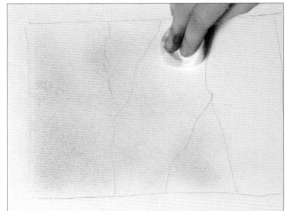

3 *Some of the blue has been taken into the land area, and the yellow applied on top, so that the two colours overlap to produce a yellow-green mixture. Before starting the painting proper, the dry wash should be sprayed with fixative.*

Wet brushing with a bristle brush

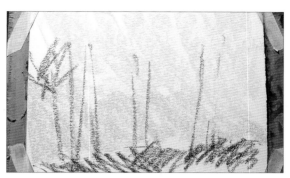

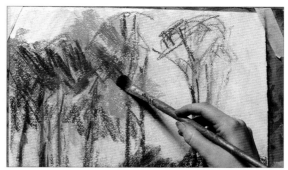

1 *Working on watercolour paper, the artist began by sketching out the composition. Having blocked in the large areas with side strokes, she then used a pastel tip to sketch in the shapes of the trees.*

2 *A bristle brush dipped in water is used to spread the colour. This type of brush, being harder than a watercolour brush, creates a more thorough spread of colour, dislodging more particles.*

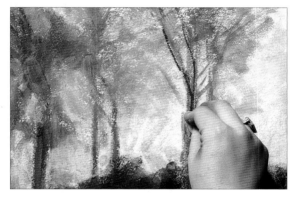

3 *She proceeds to draw over the wet-brushed areas with the tip of the pastel stick to add touches of crisp definition to the tree trunks and branches. In places, she has also drawn on still-damp paper to create softer lines and strokes.*

Wet brushing with a soft brush

Clean water taken over pastel marks with a soft brush releases some of the colour to form a watercolour effect, leaving the marks of the pastel stick intact. Watercolour paper rather than pastel paper should be used for this method, as the latter may buckle.

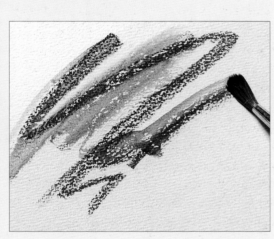

WET BRUSHING

If you go over soft pastel marks with a brush dipped in clean water, it releases some of the colour while leaving the pastel strokes clearly visible. You can use this technique only on watercolour paper, as the standard pastel papers are quite thin and would buckle under the water. If you like to work on watercolour paper, however, wet brushing forms a useful alternative to tinting the paper in advance. It allows you to cover the surface quickly with colour, obliterating the distracting white specks you see between strokes on white paper.

Wet brushing over side strokes produces a granular wash, which is ideal for suggesting the texture of objects such as rocks, cliffs or the barks of trees in a landscape. Over linear strokes, the effect is somewhat similar to that of line and wash in watercolour, with the wash a paler version of the original line. Wet brushing is often used to "pull together" lines and marks made with soft pastel or pastel pencil; it can also create light and shade effects to suggest form.

The idea of wetting pastel colour is not new. Edgar Degas, who took to pastel painting when his eyesight began to fail, was one of the greatest technical innovators in the medium. He would make a paste of his pastels, sometimes steaming his board or spraying warm water over the colours and then working into them with stiff brushes, before overlaying further linear marks.

UNDERPAINTING

The practice of working over an under-painting, usually done in either watercolour or acrylic, is rapidly gaining acceptance in pastel-painting circles. It stems from the same idea as colouring the paper in advance, but goes several steps further. By making a full-scale underpainting, you can introduce as many colours as you like before laying on any pastel, and so relate the colours to the shapes in your picture. Alternatively you can make a monochrome underpainting to establish the drawing and main tonal structure of the painting, perhaps choosing a colour which contrasts with the overall colour key of the subject.

The advantage of a multi-coloured underpainting is that you can carry out at least some of the colour mixing at the painting stage. This helps to avert one of the potential dangers of pastel painting: over-mixing and clogging the surface of the paper. You can also work on smoother paper than usual; as you will not be laying so many layers of pastel colour, there will be less risk of the pastel pigment slipping off the surface. As a general rule pastel paper should be textured, but it can be exciting to work on a smoother surface, such as Hot-pressed watercolour paper. This does not break up the pastel strokes as much as the medium-surface (Not, or CP) paper normally used for watercolour work, thus allowing you to lay thick, solid areas of smooth colour.

Pastel over paint

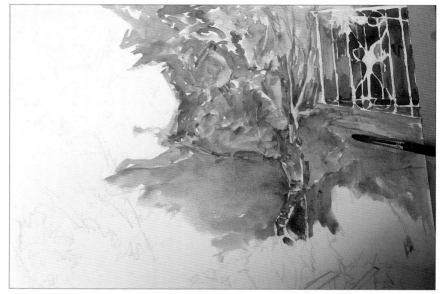

1 *Working on medium-surface watercolour paper, the artist begins with watercolour. He allows the brushmarks to show in order to complement the pastel strokes.*

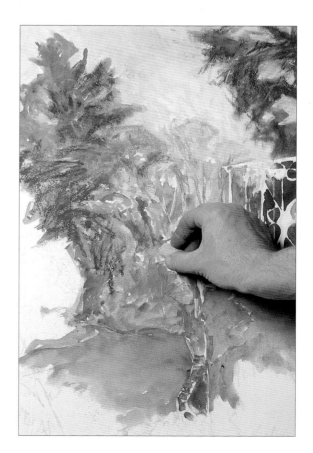

2 *Light pastel marks now overlay the paint in the foliage and sky areas, and pale grey is used to draw into the darker blue-greys.*

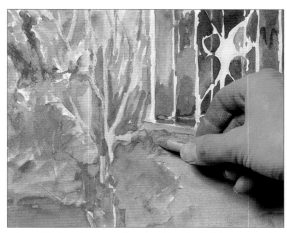

3 As he wishes to achieve a blend of the two media, the pastel colours chosen are close to those of the watercolour beneath. There is no attempt to cover the first colours completely.

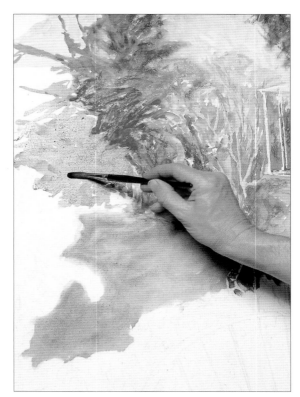

4 The artist works from the centre of the picture outwards, and now lays down more watercolour, again using brushstrokes which suggest the movement of the foliage.

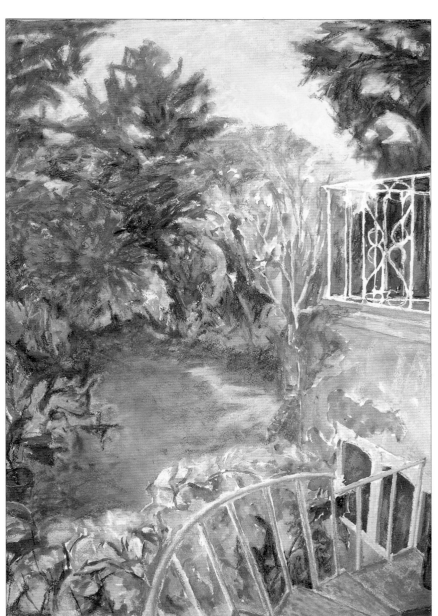

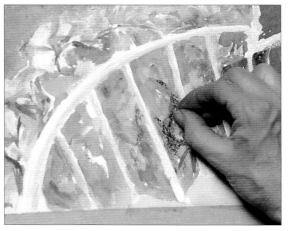

5 The railings have been reserved as highlights, with the watercolour painted around them and later light applications of grey pastel giving a suggestion of modelling. The central area of foliage is now darkened so that the whites stand out clearly.

6 (Above) Some artists use a water-colour underpainting much as they would a coloured ground, cover-ing most of it with pastel. In this case, however, the two media work together, with the water-colour playing an important part in the overall effect.

WET BRUSHING OIL PASTEL

Oil pastel is an exciting medium to use, although it is very different in character from soft pastel, being bound with oil rather than gum. Its dense, rather greasy quality means that it fills the grain of the paper relatively quickly, making it less suitable for colour mixing by layering.

However, this is only true if the medium is used "dry" like conventional pastel. The great advantage of oil pastel is that the colour can be melted with an application of turpentine or white spirit and spread with a brush or rag over the paper (with canvas or oil-sketching paper as possible alternatives). This allows you to lay broad areas of colour very quickly and you can then work over these with more linear strokes, building up the picture with a succession of wet and dry layers. If the paper becomes clogged, you can remove whole areas of colour by applying more turpentine and rubbing gently with a rag. On oil-sketching paper you can make as many such corrections as you like, without harming the surface.

Oil pastels come in a more limited colour range than soft pastels, but this wet-brushing method allows you to achieve very subtle colour mixes on the working surface. As with paints, you can even mix colours on a palette before putting them on. Simply moisten the tip of a pastel stick with a brush dipped in turpentine to release the colour and transfer this to the palette.

As oil pastels are quick to use, easy to correct and, best of all, do not need fixing they make an ideal medium for outdoor sketching. However, they do have a tendency to melt under a hot sun, becoming very soft and buttery, which makes them hard to manage; it is best to work in the shade wherever possible.

Oil pastel and white spirit

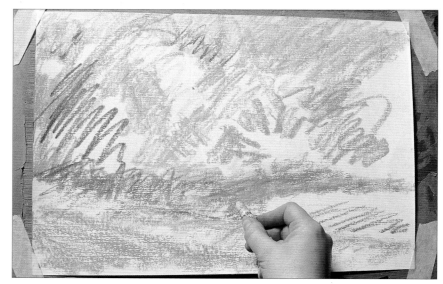

1 *Working on oil-sketching paper, the artist blocks in the composition lightly with very soft oil pastels. You can also work on ordinary pastel paper, such as Ingres, but there is a slight possibility of the oil in the pastels causing deterioration over time.*

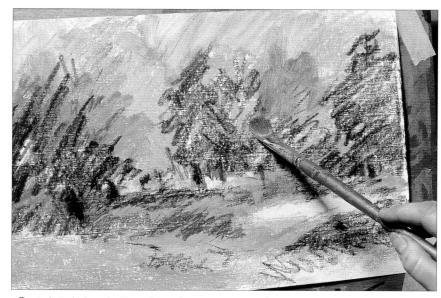

2 *A bristle brush dipped in white spirit is used to spread and mix the colours. The mixture is relatively transparent because the first colours were applied lightly. If colour is built up too thickly in the early stages, mixtures can become muddy and dull.*

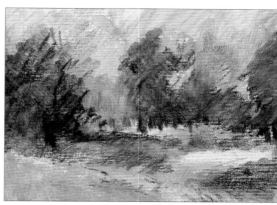

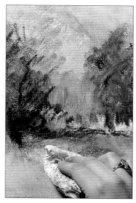

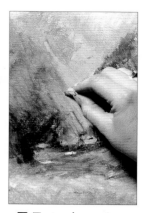

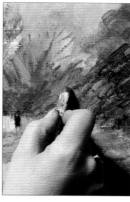

3 Further brushwork over the whole picture has now firmly established the form and colours of the trees. Again, you can see how the artist has avoided over-mixing and churning up the colours; blues and yellows can be clearly distinguished in the dark and light green areas.

4 The beauty of this method is that amendments can be made simply by wiping off colour with a rag, dipped in white spirit. The foreground needs to be softened, so the whole area is wiped down prior to re-working.

5 To produce a textured effect on the foliage, the artist works into a still-wet area with firm strokes of the pastel stick. This creates distinctive marks and slight ridges rather similar to the effects of sgraffito.

6 For colour contrast and a suggestion of the trunks and branches, dark red oil pastel is now used to draw over the earlier colours. The artist keeps the marks very broad and free; her approach is impressionistic.

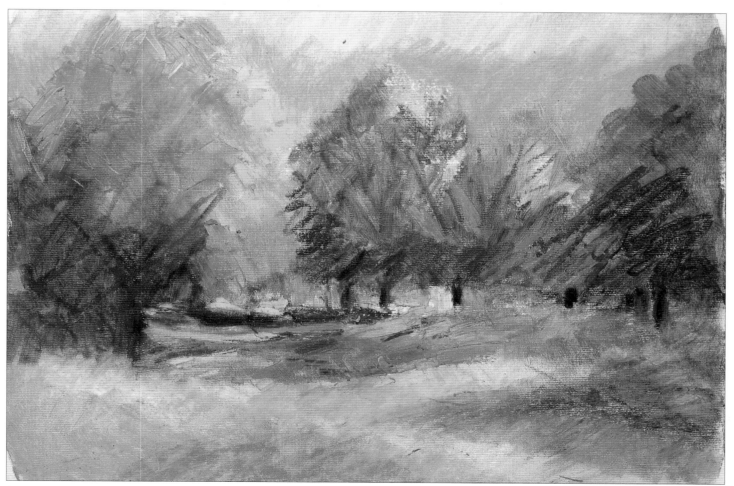

7 As the pastel has been used in a series of thin washes, rather like glazing in oil painting, the colours are beautifully luminous, an effect enhanced by the white paper reflecting through the colours. When using oil pastel in this way, white paper can be a better choice than coloured.

CHARCOAL AND PASTEL

Charcoal and pastel are frequently used together; they are natural partners because both have a similar texture. As underdrawings for pastel work should never be done in pencil – the greasiness of graphite repels the pastel colour – charcoal is often used to make the preliminary line drawing. Any loose dust is then brushed away and the charcoal is fixed before the pastel colour is applied on top.

In this case the charcoal is largely obliterated by the overlaid colours and plays no part in the finished work. However, it can also be used in a more positive way, with the charcoal complementing the pastel colour. As charcoal gives a clearer, crisper line than soft pastel, it is sometimes used to define detail and provide a linear structure, with the pastel used for the broader colour areas (like line and wash in watercolour painting).

Another approach, sometimes used for figure work and portraiture, is to make a tonal underdrawing, using the side of the charcoal stick to establish light and dark areas. This is suitable only for paintings which are to be relatively "low-key" in colour, as, even when the charcoal is fixed, the pastel laid on top picks up a little of the black dust. This has the effect of muting the pastel colours, which can be very effective for certain subjects.

Charcoal can also be used hand in hand with pastel colours and, because it is less dense than black pastel, it is particularly useful for the subtle mid-toned colours which are often hard to mix successfully. The grey-greens or grey-blues seen in the middle distance of a landscape, for example, can often be achieved by mixing charcoal and green or blue pastel, or by dragging a light veil of charcoal over a pastel colour to tone it down.

Making a charcoal underdrawing

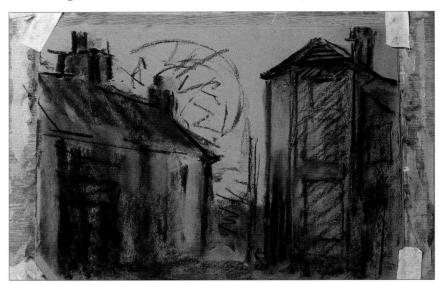

1 *The colour scheme planned for this picture is relatively sombre, with a predominance of dark tones, so the charcoal drawing is made on a mauve-blue paper chosen to set the key for the later colours. The paper is Mi-Teintes, used on the smoother side.*

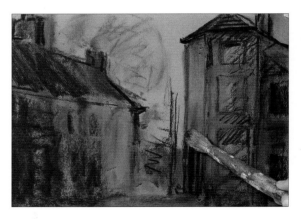

2 *With the underdrawing complete, the excess charcoal dust is flicked off the paper with a bristle brush. The drawing is sprayed with fixative before the pastel colours are applied, so that the charcoal does not muddy the colours.*

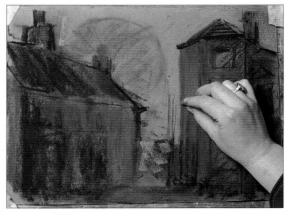

3 *The artist's method is to build up her colours gradually with a series of overlays. The bright pink used for the sky at this stage will be modified by later applications. Although dark in tone, the colours chosen for the buildings are very rich.*

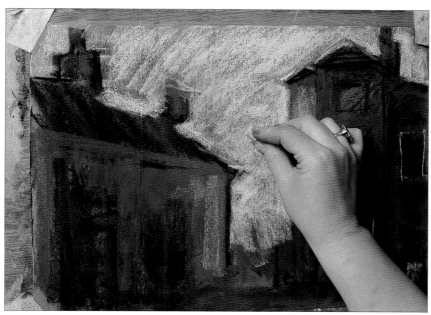

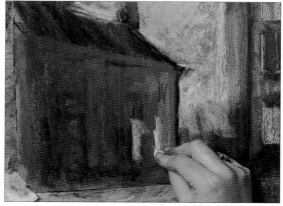

4 *The side of a short length of white pastel is now dragged lightly over the earlier pink; some of this is still visible, as is some of the paper colour. The sides of the buildings nearest to this sky area have also been lightened slightly.*

5 *The highlights have been left until the final stage, because pastels are opaque and it is therefore possible to cover dark colours with light ones. Notice the variety of colours used for the walls of the houses, from deep greens to reds and pinks, plus a mauve produced by the paper colour showing through the original charcoal drawing.*

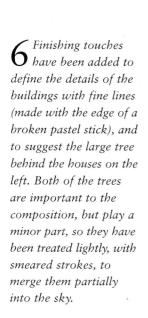

6 *Finishing touches have been added to define the details of the buildings with fine lines (made with the edge of a broken pastel stick), and to suggest the large tree behind the houses on the left. Both of the trees are important to the composition, but play a minor part, so they have been treated lightly, with smeared strokes, to merge them partially into the sky.*

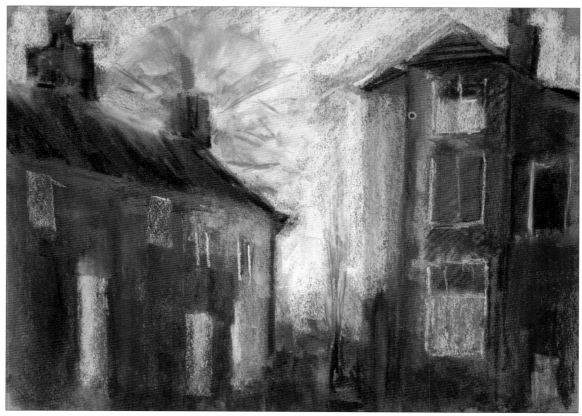

BUILDING UP PASTEL

Although the standard pastel papers are versatile and allow for a certain amount of layering, you cannot build up colours really thickly on them. For those who like truly painterly effects, it is worth trying one of the special papers produced for pastel painting: sandpaper, velour paper and Sansfix paper.

These papers handle very differently from the normal pastel paper. Sandpaper in particular grips the pastel pigment so firmly that it is virtually impossible to blend colours by spreading them with either your fingers or a rag; for the same reason you cannot move colours around on the surface. However, the paper's firm hold on the pastel pigment means that you can go on layering colours more or less indefinitely. This creates very subtle mixtures and great depth of colour as well as effects similar to that of impasto in oil painting, where the brushstrokes stand proud of the surface. In fact, some pastel paintings on sand-paper look very much like oil paintings.

These papers all have one disadvantage: they are very "greedy" with the pastel colours and you will get through your pastels at a faster rate than when working on Ingres or Mi-Teintes paper. This is partially balanced by the fact that you won't need much – if any – fixative, which is fairly expensive. If you find the paper beginning to clog you can use fixative, but it is not normally necessary. It is best not to fix the finished painting, as this will tend to darken the colours.

Working on Sansfix paper

1 *This paper grips the colour more firmly than the standard papers and is ideal for creating painterly effects in pastel. Here, the artist begins work on the lightest areas.*

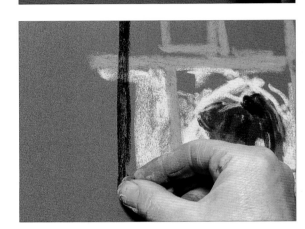

2 *A solid line of black is now pulled down the paper to define the pole leaning against the windowsill, which provides a visual balance for the artist's easel.*

3 *The colours on the face and body have been built up more thickly, and both grey and yellow added to the original application of white on the window. The paper allows for a considerable amount of building up by such layering methods.*

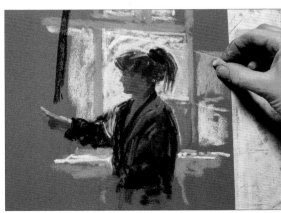

4 *Using a small piece of pastel, the artist now lays light grey over the white. He has deliberately allowed small patches of the dark grey paper to show through to create a lively broken-colour effect.*

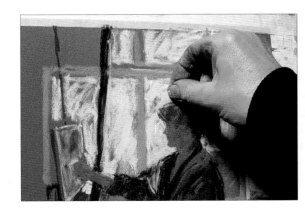

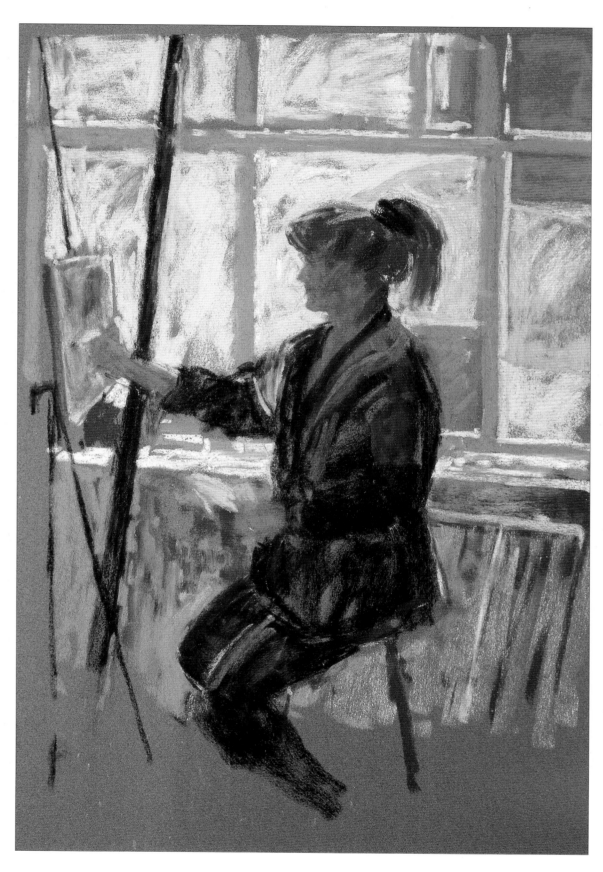

5 *The finished picture, with its thick and heavy pastel marks, is reminiscent of an oil painting. This paper is not suited to very delicate approaches or to blending techniques.*

LAYING A TEXTURED GROUND

The underlying texture of the paper is always an important factor in pastel paintings. Some artists like to work on a texture of their own making, rather than relying on the mechanically produced overall texture of the paper. A "home-made" texture can take any form you like, but the most usual one is a series of irregular diagonal or vertical brushstrokes, which give a directional emphasis to the overlaid pastel strokes. Such grounds can be laid with acrylic paint, used fairly thickly so that it holds the marks of the brush, with acrylic gesso, or, for a really heavy texture, with a substance called acrylic modelling paste, thinned with water. The latter is only sold in large pots, however, and is quite costly, so make sure you like this way of working before you invest in it.

The advantage of using acrylic paint is that you can colour the ground as well as texturing it. You can even combine the texture element with a coloured under-painting, varying the colours and textures from one area of the painting to another. Don't overdo it, however, as you don't want to introduce too many different elements before you even begin to apply the pastel. This method is best suited to thick applications of pastel; you will need to work on a tough paper, such as heavy watercolour paper – don't try to lay a ground on ordinary pastel paper, as it will buckle under the weight of the paint.

A tinted and textured ground

1 *Acrylic gesso, which is sold primarily for preparing boards and canvases for oil and acrylic painting, makes an excellent textured ground for pastel work. It is slightly thicker in consistency than tube acrylic and it dries fast. Here it has been mixed with black acrylic paint and applied to thick watercolour paper with a large bristle brush.*

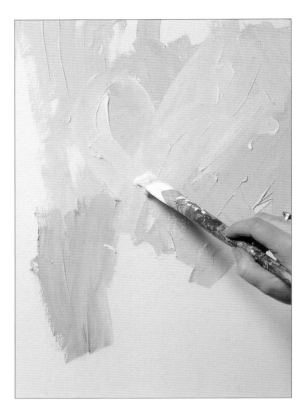

2 *The deliberately uneven application of the ground creates a surface which will break up the pastel strokes in interesting ways. This gives an exciting element of unpredictability, allowing you to exploit semi-accidental effects.*

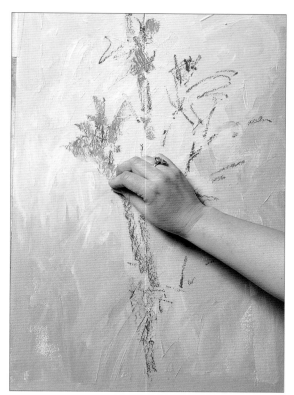

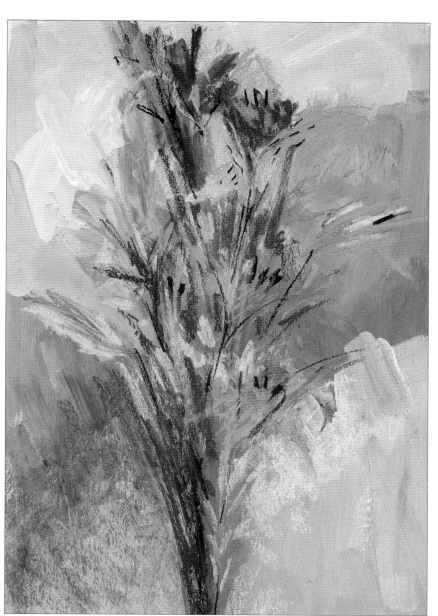

3 *As colour is scribbled over the brushstrokes of acrylic gesso, it catches only on the raised areas, creating a series of strongly textured marks. This is a method which is best suited to broad, impressionistic approaches; with a heavy underlying texture it is not possible to achieve fine detail.*

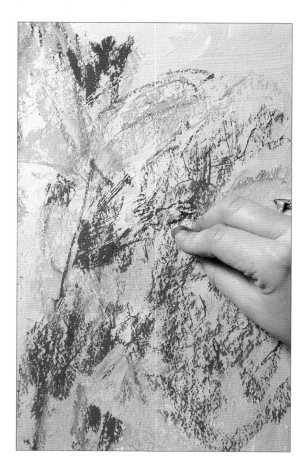

4 *(Left) Here the artist uses broad strokes of pastel to capture the essential colours and shapes of the flowers.*

5 *(Above) As the pastel cannot completely cover the brushmarks of the gesso ground, in the final stages the artist turned to a painting method, dipping a brush into gesso and painting over the pastel. This mixed with and spread the colour, giving a broad painterly effect.*

SGRAFFITO

This technique, in which one layer of colour is scratched or scraped into to reveal another one below, is sometimes used in oil painting. It is now also one of the recognized techniques in oil pastel, which is really oil paint in solid form. You can scratch into soft pastel, too, provided that you work on a tough surface, such as watercolour paper, and spray the first layer of colour with fixative before applying the second.

However, the effects are more dramatic and exciting in oil pastel and, because oil pastel colours cling to the surface very firmly and do not need fixing, they are tailor-made for the method. The effects that you can achieve are many and various, depending on the tool you use for the scratching, the amount of pressure you apply, the thickness of the colours and the texture of the painting surface. For example, if you work on a fairly smooth paper which doesn't break up the pastel strokes, lay one colour thickly over another and then scratch into the top layer with a sharp point, you can make a fine, delicate line drawing. Working on a more heavily textured paper and scratching into a layer of colour with the side of a knife, on the other hand, will give a broader, more generalized effect of broken colour, as the knife will remove only some of the colour. You can work either dark over light or light over dark, building up several different layers of colour then scratching into each one in turn; alternatively you can vary the colour combinations from one part of the picture to another – the possibilities of this technique are endless.

Sgraffito landscape

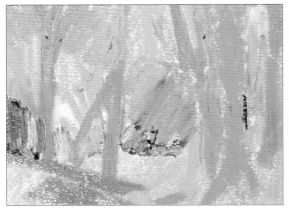

1 *Working on heavy watercolour paper, the artist has laid a foundation of light, bright colours which she will partially reveal by scratching back later colours with a knife or scalpel.*

2 *(Right) Dark greens, blues and red-browns have now been laid over the first colours, and a knife used to scratch into the central area and the tree at top left. To reinforce the broken-colour effect, much of the yellow has been left showing between strokes of green. This gives added vibrancy.*

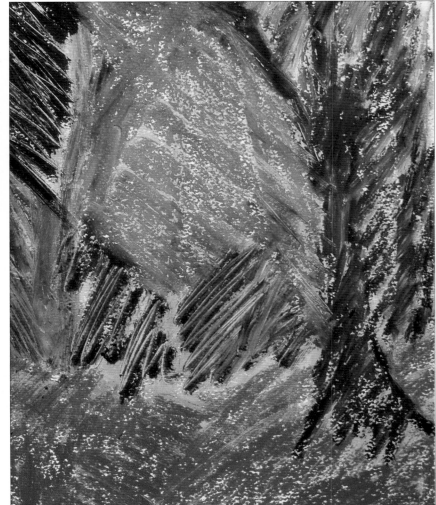

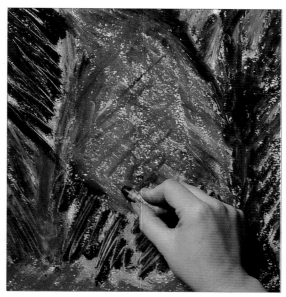

3 *Heavy diagonal strokes of deep blue are now laid over the green area in a loose cross-hatching technique. The pastel marks follow the same direction as the earlier scratch marks in order to integrate the sgraffito technique fully into the picture.*

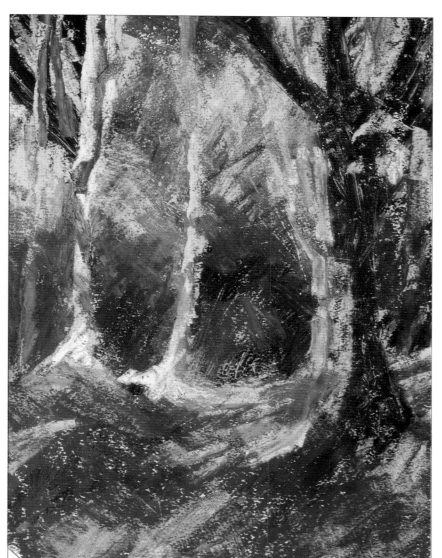

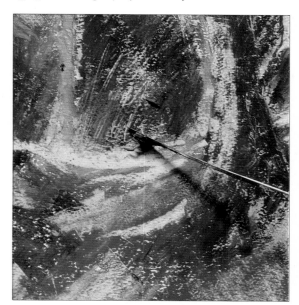

4 *With the point of a loosely held scalpel, the artist lightly scribbles into the layers of oil pastel. There is now a considerable build-up of different colours, and the scratching reveals brilliant blues and greens as well as the original yellow.*

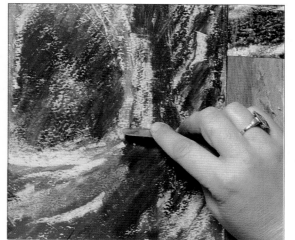

5 *Although the technique is most often associated with fine lines, broader effects can also be achieved; here, the side of a palette knife is pulled down the tree trunk. The palette knife has also been used to remove parts of the top colour in the foreground beneath the trees to suggest patches of strong sunlight filtering through the leaves.*

6 *(Above) The successive layers of scraped-back colour combined with the vigorous pastel marks create a lovely effect of shimmering light. The sgraffito has been carefully handled so that its effects are neither over-obtrusive nor self-conscious; this technique should never be allowed to dominate.*

COMPARATIVE DEMONSTRATION

If you visit an exhibition of pastel paintings you may well notice an amazing diversity of styles, even when the subject matter is similar. Three pastel landscapes by different artists, for instance, would probably bear little resemblance to each other, except in the medium used. Too often, amateur painters feel that there is a definite set of rules which must be followed, but, although hints can be given, there is really no right and wrong way of doing things. It is,

instead, up to each person to develop their own methods and artistic "handwriting". To demonstrate this, we have asked three artists to paint the same simple subject. The first, Patrick Cullen, whose work is shown on these pages, paints on watercolour paper. Debra Manifold, the second artist, works in oil pastel on oil-sketching paper, while Hazel Harrison uses standard pastels and a more conventional surface – Mi-Teintes paper.

Pastel on watercolour paper

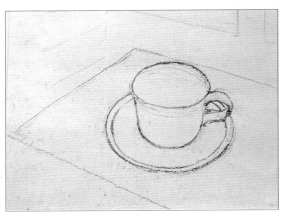

1 *The artist began by laying a light watercolour wash to tone down the white of the paper and make it easier to assess the first colours. When the wash was dry, he made a careful charcoal drawing.*

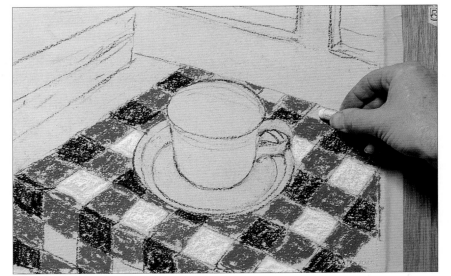

2 *(Above right) His method of working is unusual: instead of laying down broad areas of colour at the outset and modifying them later, he proceeds methodically across the picture, treating each area separately. He is now completing the tablecloth, which will provide a context for the other colours.*

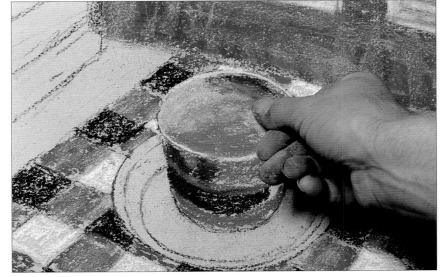

3 *(Right) To link the tablecloth to the bottom of the windowframe, which was painted next, the same grey was used. The cup and saucer provide the warmest colour area; the artist begins work here by defining the ellipse at the top and then blending the colours with his thumb.*

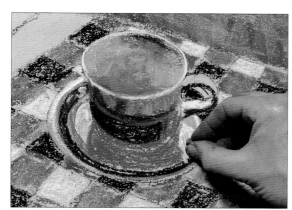

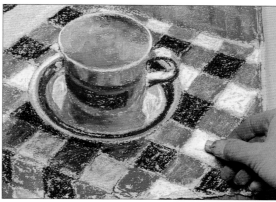

4 The highlights on the saucer, like the ellipse on the top of the cup, define its shape, so they have been drawn in firmly in white. Few highlights are pure white, however, so they are now modified with light strokes of brown laid on top.

5 Although the tablecloth was more or less complete in the earlier stages, there was insufficient contrast between the shadowed area below the cup and this right hand side where the light falls. This is now lightened with pure white.

6 (Below) *In spite of the simplicity of the subject and the limited colour scheme, the picture is satisfying and well-balanced, with the dark shapes of the window and the boxes on the left making a frame for the cup and saucer.*

Continued ▷

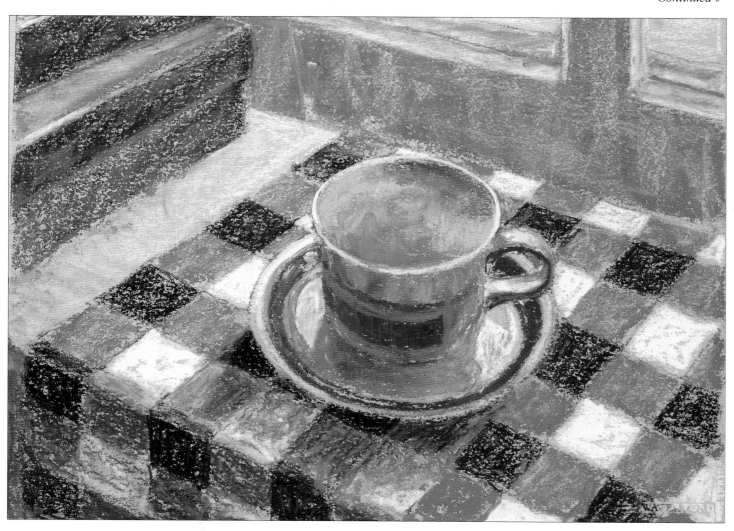

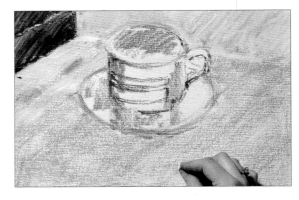

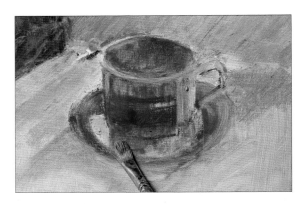

2 (Right) *The colours have been built up, and a brush dipped in white spirit is used to blend them. In order to balance the warm pinks and browns of the cup, similar colours have been introduced into the background.*

1 (Above) *The artist begins with a rough drawing in grey oil pastel and then applies light veils of colour with the side of the stick. Her drawing need not be as detailed as that of the previous artist because oil pastel can so easily be corrected.*

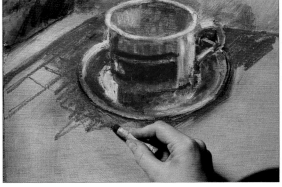

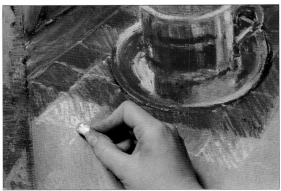

3 *This artist is always more concerned with the colour relationships in her painting than with the actual colours of the subject; here she chooses a vivid blue to contrast with the cup and saucer.*

4 *Having mapped out the grid of squares for the tablecloth, she now scribbles white pastel lightly over the blue, using diagonal strokes which blur and soften the lines to avoid too precise an effect.*

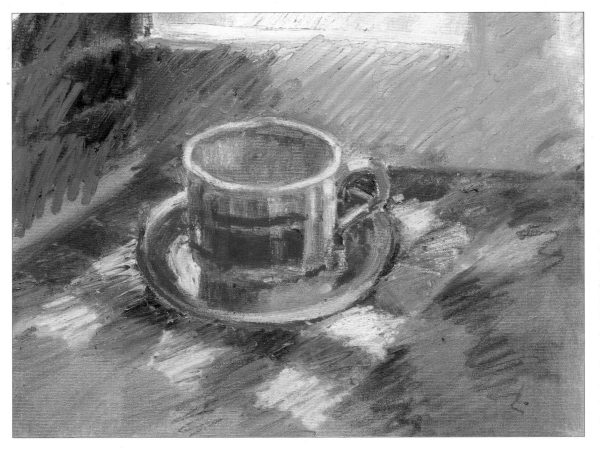

5 *The painting, with its vivid array of colours in the background and greenish blue in the foreground, is quite unlike the previous artist's interpretation. The style is very different too; the tablecloth has been treated in a much broader way and plays a less important role in the composition.*

Pastel on Mi-Teintes paper

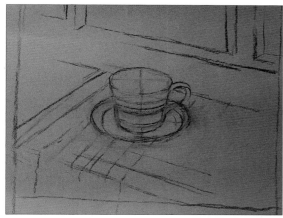

1 *A dark blue paper has been chosen to pick up the colour of the tablecloth. Working on the smooth side, the artist has begun with a charcoal drawing.*

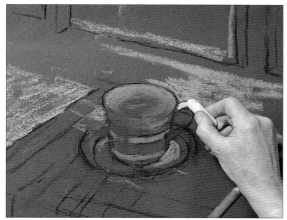

2 *The cup and saucer are seen as the key colour area, so she concentrates on this, finding it easier to assess the colours in the subject when working on a contrasting paper.*

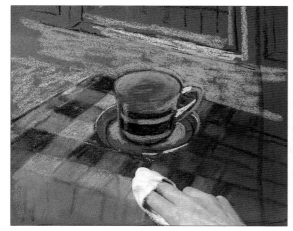

3 *At this stage it becomes apparent that the perspective of the tablecloth is wrong, so the whole area is wiped down with a rag. Pastel cannot be erased completely, but removing the loose pigment makes it possible to over-work.*

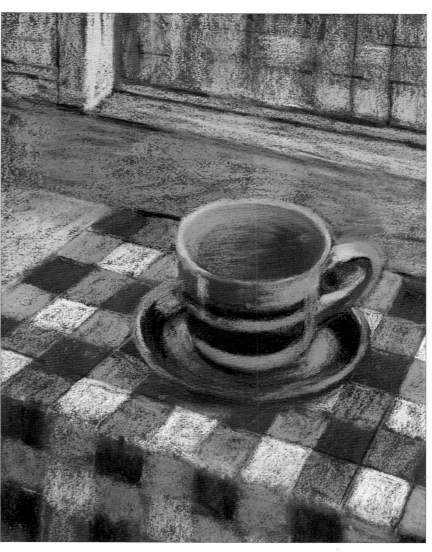

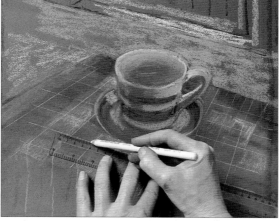

4 *A ruler and white pastel pencil are now used to re-draw the grid of squares. Straight lines are not easy to draw, and rulers can save a lot of frustration.*

5 *(Above) The artist changes the composition from a horizontal to a vertical format by placing masking tape around the central area. The ellipse of the cup is then re-defined with white pastel. Finally, the artist lightly sketches a grid of squares on the window to echo the tablecloth and introduces some touches of mauve-blue into the background.*

LANDSCAPE

Both soft pastels and oil pastels are ideal for landscape work. The range of marks that you can make – from soft blends and sweeping strokes made with the side of the stick to sharp, linear marks – is capable of matching virtually any effect seen in nature. Both types of pastel are quick to use, allowing you to build up areas of colour very rapidly, and are perfect for capturing fleeting effects of weather and light.

Best of all, if you are working outside directly from the subject, you will need far less equipment than you would with paints. The only basic requirements are your box of pastels, some paper and a drawing board. However, there are one or two other items that you may find useful.

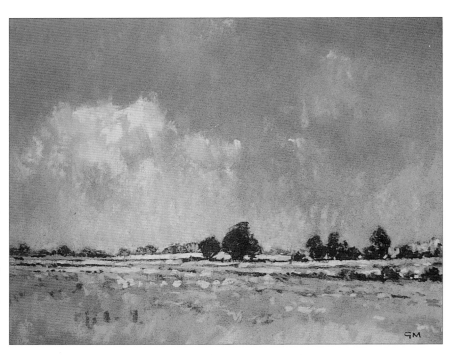

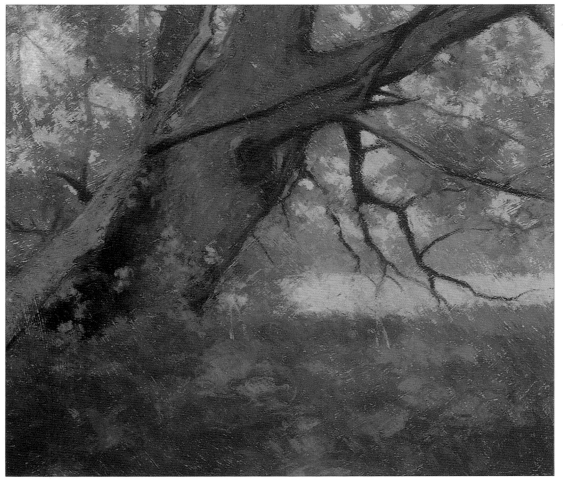

Landscape in close-up
(Left) *One of the most difficult decisions to make when faced with a large expanse of countryside is how much to include and what to focus on. You can often make a more expressive statement by moving in close, as Doug Dawson has done in* The Edge of the Meadow. *The strong diagonal thrust of the tree across the picture is balanced by the horizontal bands of colour formed by the foreground and by the light field in the middle distance.*

Tonal contrast

(Right) *A common cause of failure in landscape paintings is lack of attention to tones – the relative lightness and darkness of colours. In James Crittenden's* Spanish Landscape *the contrasts of tone not only convey the heat and strong sunlight, but also create a pattern of light and dark which gives a structure to the composition.*

Placing the horizon

(Opposite) *In a wide, panoramic landscape it is important to consider how to divide up the picture space, and how much prominence to give to the sky. The area of England in which Geoff Marsters works is very flat, with the great expanse of sky one of its most noticeable features, so in* Fen Landscape *he has given it three-quarters of the picture.*

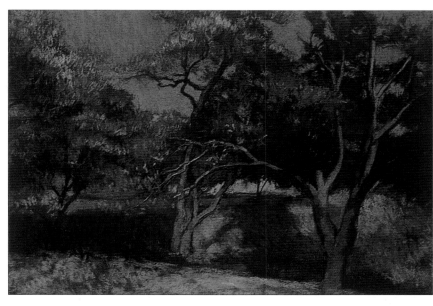

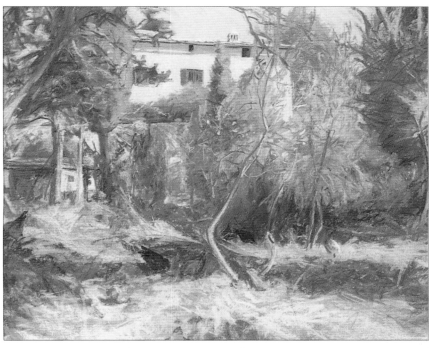

Varying the greens

(Above) *Landscapes are frequently spoiled by poor observation of colours, particularly greens. Greens are extraordinarily varied, and you must further take into account the many nuances caused by light and shade. In Patrick Cullen's* Chickens, Petrognano, *the "greens" vary from silver-greys and creamy yellows to near-browns.*

If you work on a large scale using soft pastel you may need to invest in a portable sketching easel. You will quickly be covered in pastel dust if you try to work with your board propped on your lap, and an additional advantage of an easel is that you can step back from your painting periodically to assess it.

You will get your hands dirty whether you use an easel or not, so take some rags or, better still, a packet of moistened hand wipes. For oil pastel you will need white spirit and rags to clean your hands, plus brushes if you intend to spread the colours. You will not need fixative for oil pastels but you will do for soft pastels, as it is easy to smudge unfixed, finished work when you are carrying it home.

PLANNING IN ADVANCE

Even though time is usually limited when you are painting on the spot, it always pays to do some initial planning: choosing the best viewpoint, deciding how much of the scene in front of you to include in the picture and considering where to place the horizon. There is a natural tendency to divide the picture into two distinct areas of sky and land. This is not usually the best approach, however, particularly if it creates a central division – over-symmetry should always be avoided as it makes pictures look both dull and disjointed.

Give particular consideration to skies which are vitally important in landscape; not only are they the primary light source, they also play a major role in creating space. In a wide, panoramic landscape, for example, you can often increase the sense of depth and space by letting the sky occupy more of the picture area than the land – perhaps three-quarters of it. Conversely, with a mountain scene in which you want to express the upward thrust of the land, you could give minimum space to the sky.

Foregrounds are another important area – a painting can be easily spoiled by a weak or over-dominant foreground. As a general

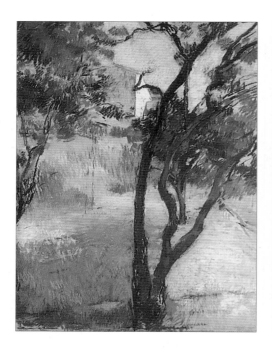

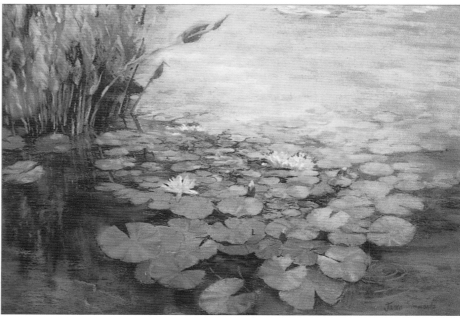

Mark-making

(Above) *The marks you make with your pastel sticks are as important as brushstrokes in an oil painting. As well as helping to describe the forms, they add an extra dimension to the picture, giving it a life and movement of its own independent of the subject it represents. In James Crittenden's* Looking through the Blue Trees, *short directional strokes play a practical role in describing the leaves of the trees, but even in the foreground shadow individual marks are visible, "lifting" an area which might have become dull if treated in a flat way.*

rule, foregrounds should "introduce" the rest of the picture and lead the eye into it. Too much detail or very strong shapes in the foreground can sometimes have the opposite effect, acting as a block, or a closed door rather than an open one. You can often solve the foreground problem in advance by choosing the best position from which to work – how much of the foreground you see is directly related to whether your viewpoint is high or low. If you look at a scene first standing and then sitting down, you will notice how it changes completely. In a flat landscape, particularly, some feature in the foreground which you may have scarcely noticed suddenly becomes dominant, while objects in the middle distance are diminished in importance. There is no reason why you should not choose a low viewpoint – for a subject such as mountains it could be ideal – but it is often better to stand at an easel to paint, or to find a vantage point such as a low wall.

MAKING CHANGES

As pastels are opaque and one colour covers another quite easily, you can often change the composition in the early stages, perhaps by lowering a horizon or generally moving things around. However, it is a good idea to

guard against possible failure by taking a larger piece of paper than you think you will need and letting the composition grow as you work. Leave generous margins around the edges so that you can expand the picture at the top, bottom or sides if you need to – this is one of the many advantages of painting in pastel.

You can also make changes to the composition afterwards by cropping, a device often used by photographers to work out which area of a negative to print. When you re-assess your work a day or two later indoors, you may feel that it is not entirely satisfactory, although you are not sure why. Usually it is a compositional problem: for example, you may have placed some feature too centrally or included too much sky. If you cut four "corners" of thick paper or cardboard and move them around on the picture, you will be able to visualize possible improvements. A small change such as taking an inch or two off the foreground on one side can change the whole feel of the picture and bring it to life. Some artists do not bother over-much about composition when they are working on location, but do it all afterwards by cropping. Don't actually cut the painting, though – just make a mount (matt) which covers the unwanted areas.

Painting water

(Opposite) *Water is one of the most attractive painting subjects, but it is not as easy to paint as it seems. Although many different colours and tones can be discerned, particularly in reflections, they must be carefully controlled. In Jackie Simmonds's* Waterlilies and Reeds *the strongest contrasts of tone are those between the lilies and the foreground water – a deep, rich blue reflected from the sky.*

A focus for the eye

(Right*) Not all landscape paintings have an obvious centre of interest, or focal point, but often you will find that you are drawn to a particular view because of some dominant feature. In James Crittenden's* Almond Blossom in the Evening *the focal point is the pale tree, and he has drawn attention to it by using dark neutral colours for the hills beyond. To balance the light tone of the tree, he has introduced strong highlights on the grass on the left of the picture.*

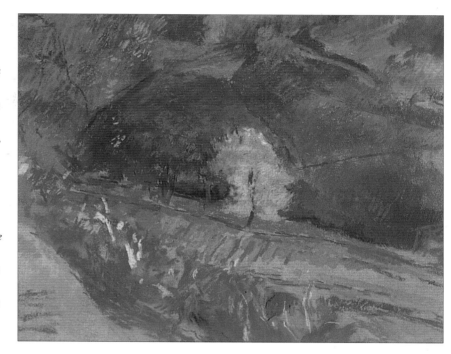

Preliminary sketches

(Left) *Some landscape painters always work out of doors directly from their subject, taking the composition as they find it, while others prefer to compose their paintings in the studio from sketches, notes and sometimes photographs. Patrick Cullen's* Landscape in Le Crete *is a sketch for a very large-scale watercolour painting, which would have been impossible to complete on the spot. The directness of pastel makes it an ideal sketching medium.*

WORKING INDOORS

As it can be so difficult to compose paintings in front of the subject, a traditional way of working is to make a sketch or a series of sketches on the spot and compose the actual painting indoors. Often something you haven't quite pulled off can become the basis for a successful composition, so never throw away sketches, even if you are not happy with them. Working indoors removes some of the pressure, giving you the opportunity to think about how best to plan the painting, mix the colours and use the range of pastel marks in the context of the picture. Like brushstrokes in an oil painting, pastel marks are an important ingredient in composition; they are not just an "extra". Vigour and movement in a landscape painting can be conveyed by varying your strokes to include, perhaps, some sweeping directional side strokes, juxtaposed with more linear marks, short jabs and calligraphic squiggles (made with the tip of the pastel).

DEMONSTRATION

Artist Patrick Cullen specializes in landscapes, particularly the scenery of Tuscany, the subject of this painting. He works in oil and watercolour as well as pastel, usually on a large scale, composing his paintings in the studio from sketch references made on the spot. This pastel painting on sandpaper was done from colour sketches and a large charcoal "working drawing" in which he planned the composition.

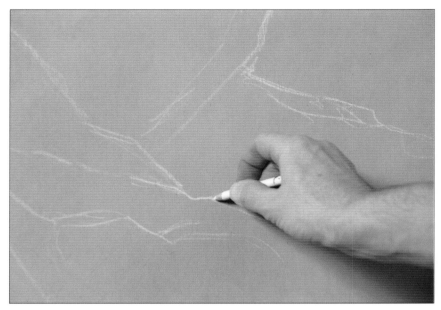

1 *Referring to his charcoal drawing, which is the same size as the painting, the artist begins by mapping out the composition in pastel pencil. He works carefully, as it is impossible to erase pastel marks on sandpaper.*

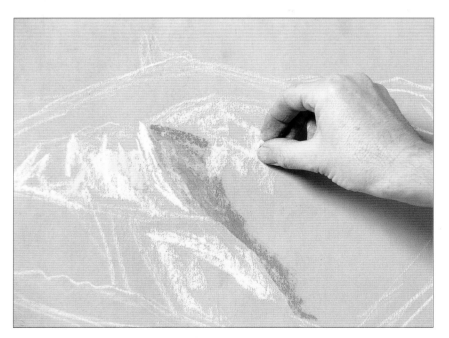

2 *Sandpaper is unlike the standard pastel papers in that colours cannot be moved around to any great extent on the surface. Consequently, the artist works on each section of the picture separately, beginning with the mountains in the centre.*

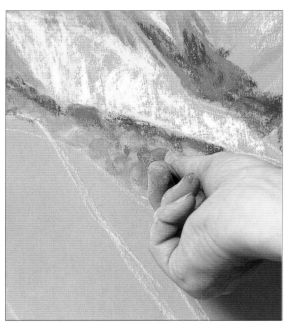

3 *To create the textured effect of the foliage, he pushes his thumb into the pastel colour and twists it. He uses his fingers a good deal in the course of a painting.*

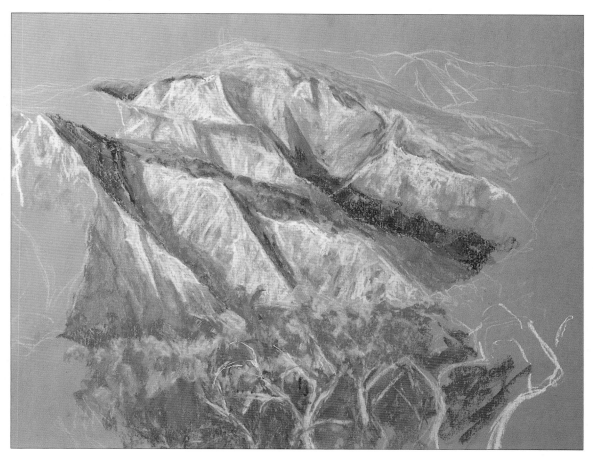

4 *The marks made by the pastel sticks are as important as brushwork in an oil painting; here you can see a wide variety of different strokes, from short jabs to tapering side strokes and crisp linear marks. These impart a lively energy to the picture as well as suggesting shapes and textures.*

5 *This illustration clearly shows the artist's method of working from the centre outwards. This piece-by-piece approach is unusual and is not recommended for beginners, as it involves having a clear vision of how the finished picture will look.*

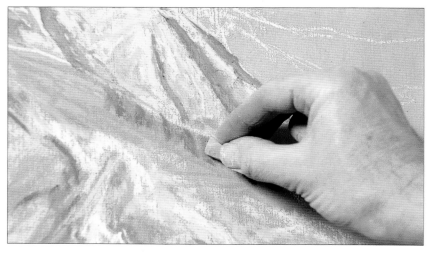

6 *The edge of a broken pastel stick is used to make short, jabbing marks, contrasting with the long sweeping strokes elsewhere. Notice how the paper shows through between strokes, contributing to the overall colour effect.*

Continued ▷

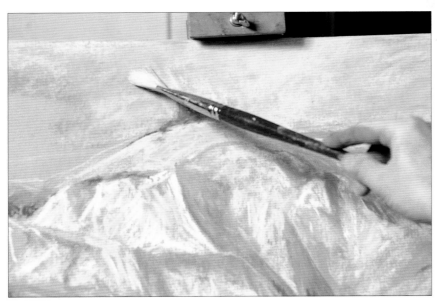

7 *Leaving the sky until a late stage enables the artist to assess it in the context of the whole painting. He chooses yellows and pale blue-greys which echo the colours of the mountains. A bristle brush is used to blend the colours together slightly.*

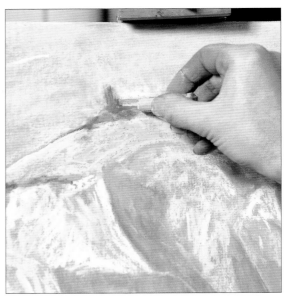

8 *Further pale colours have now been dragged lightly over the original ones in the sky area, and the house is drawn with the tip of a pastel stick. Although small, the building is important to the composition because it provides a focus for the eye; you can see this in the finished painting.*

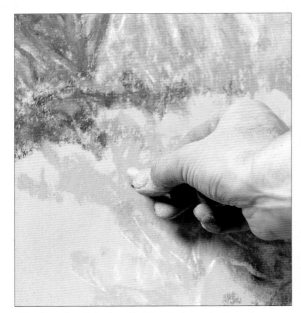

9 *On the right-hand side of the painting, the area above the white trees is developed with short strokes of green and yellow, following different directions to create a sense of movement.*

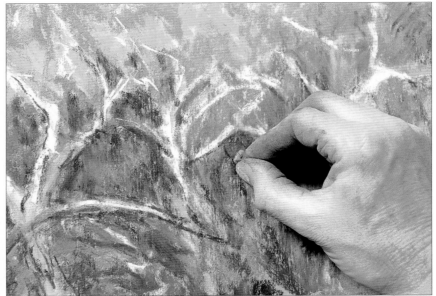

10 *The painting is now nearing completion, but requires some crisp touches and bright colours in the foreground to bring it forward in space. Vivid green is used both to suggest leaves and to outline some of the branches.*

11 (Right) *Again the artist exploits the contrast between hard and soft edges, now using the side of a short length of pastel to drag colour lightly above and around the branches.*

12 (Below) *Although the painting was virtually completed in one working session, the artist re-assessed it a day or two later and made some adjustments. The most significant of these was to increase the height of the trees on the right so that the white branches lead the eye in towards the dark tree-clad crevice, thus creating a visual link between foreground and distance.*

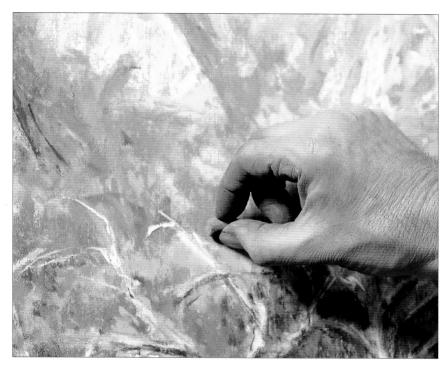

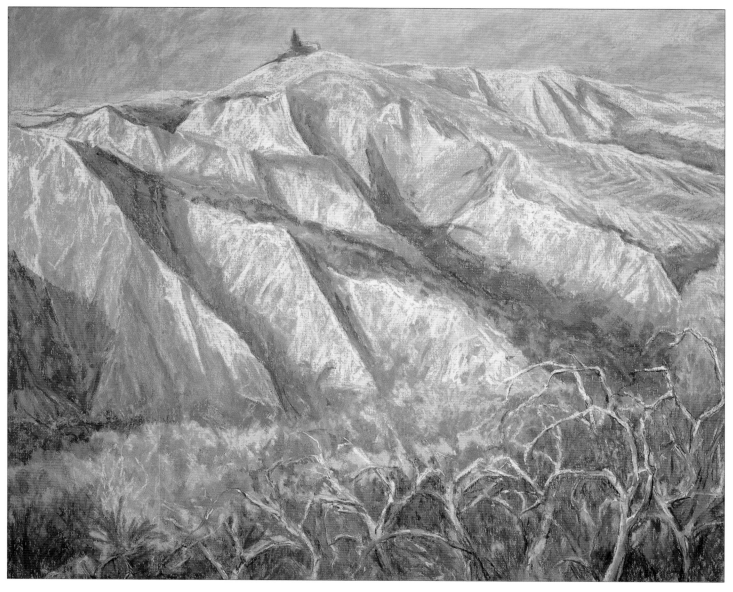

FLOWERS

When you open a new box of pastels you see an array of brilliant colours which suggests flowers, even before you have begun to put them on the paper. The soft, velvety textures also seem to emulate many of those seen in nature.

DRAWING

Flowers are certainly a wonderful subject and there are few pastel painters who have not at some time tried their hand at them. But, of course, there are problems – there always are. One of the most serious is that flowers are quite complex in shape and structure, both individually and *en masse* in an indoor arrangement and, therefore, you need to concentrate on the drawing. In a vase of flowers, for example, where there are many different shapes and colours as well as the vase itself, it is easy to go wrong and produce a painting in which the flowers and stems don't seem to relate to the container, or the flowerheads to the stems. In a watercolour or oil painting you can make a drawing in pencil first, erasing until you are sure you have it right, but you can't do this in pastel as the colour won't cover pencil marks.

You can, however, draw lightly in charcoal or in pastel pencil; the latter may be preferable in some cases as the charcoal could pollute the pastel colours. When working on coloured paper, choose a light-coloured pastel pencil for the drawing, or one that tones in with the overall colour scheme, and keep the drawing as simple as possible. If you are painting flowers in a vase, don't try to draw each individual bloom and stem; look for the overall shape made by the group.

Once you start to lay on the pastel colour, keep it light initially, as you will certainly find you have to change and redefine some

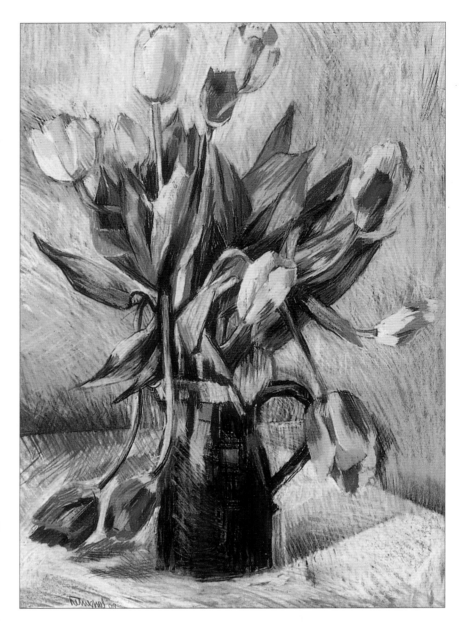

of the shapes. Try to build up the painting in large blocks of colour, leaving the details until last. It is difficult to achieve a high degree of detail with soft pastels, and pastel pencils or hard pastels may be helpful, when you come to the final stages. Meticulous attention to detail sometimes proves unnecessary anyway; pastel is essentially a medium for broad effects and it is often enough just to crispen the edge of a leaf or stem, here and there.

PATTERN

Flowers have an innate pattern element, hence their extensive use as motifs in all the applied arts, from embroidery and printed fabric to ceramics and china. Flowers in a

Unity through technique
(Above) *Pip Carpenter has carried the shapes of the flowers and leaves through into the background by using the same kind of strokes for both. This sets up a lively pattern all over the picture surface which enhances the feeling of movement. Jackie Simmonds has used a different technique in her still life* (opposite, above), *linking various elements by repeating colours.*

Unity through colour

(Below) *Although a large mixed bunch of flowers makes an attractive display, it is not always easy to tackle in a painting, as too many colours tend to fight with each other. It is often advisable to set up a group which has one dominant colour, as Jackie Simmonds has done in* Blue Marbles. *To maintain the coherence of the composition, she has repeated the deep blue of the marbles in various places on both of the pots, and has introduced blue into the background.*

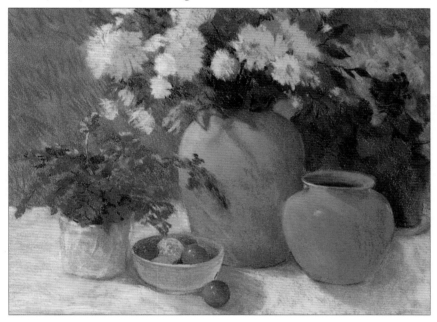

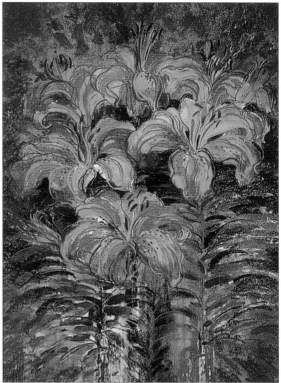

Avoiding overworking

(Above) *The essence of flowers is freshness, and overworked or clogged colour can quickly destroy the impression. In* Orange Lilies, *Maureen Jordan has avoided the necessity of a heavy build-up of pastel by working on an acrylic underpainting. This has allowed her to establish the main colours with thin washes of paint, over which she has worked crisp, linear pastel strokes which beautifully describe the convoluted shapes of the petals.*

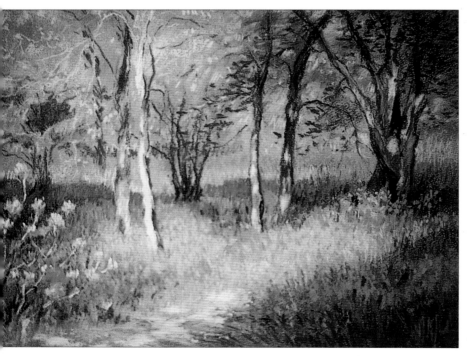

Flowers in landscape

(Left) *When flowers form only one element in a picture they usually need to be treated more broadly and simply than they would in an indoor group. The important features are the overall colour and the growth habit of the flowers. In* Bluebells at Isabella *by Maureen Jordan there is very little detail; even the flowers in the foreground are no more than small dots and dashes of pastel, yet they are immediately recognizable to anyone who has seen a bluebell wood.*

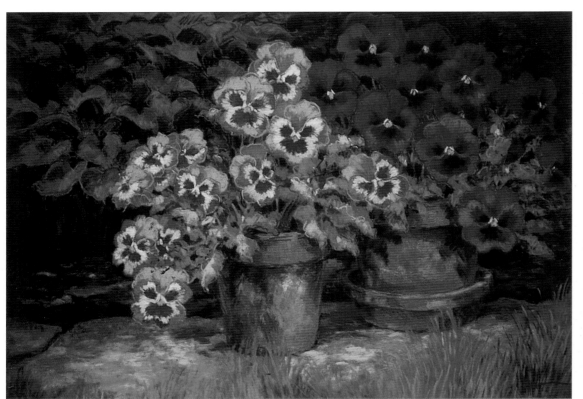

Light on dark
(Left) *A traditional way of painting white or light-coloured flowers is to set them against a dark background, which allows the artist to make the most of their delicacy and subtle nuances of colour. In* Jokers by the Pond, *Maureen Jordan has used the same idea but in an outdoor setting, with the sun and shade providing both excellent definition and contrasts of tone.*

vase create a pattern through the interaction of the various shapes and colours; you can stress this in your painting in a variety of ways. Attention can be drawn to the colour and pattern of an elaborate floral arrangement by setting it against a plain backdrop, perhaps even working on dark-coloured paper and leaving it uncovered in some areas. Alternatively, you can carry the pattern element right through the painting, choosing a decorated container for the flowers, and setting them against a wallpaper or some draped fabric with its own patterns and textures.

The way in which you use the pastel is also important in this context. You can create pattern as well as a sense of movement by letting the pastel strokes show in an active and positive way, rather than blending colours together. You might use strong, directional strokes for leaves and stems and, in the background, let the pastel stick follow the direction of the flowers to create a network of curving or vertical lines in different colours. As flowers are soft and delicate, there is always a tendency to over-blend, but bear in mind that this is not always the best approach.

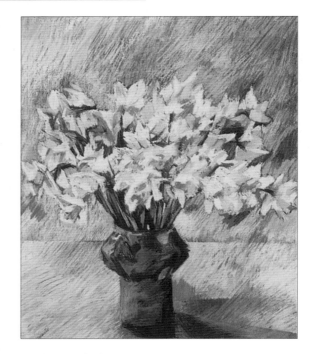

Light on light
(Above) *An alternative approach for white or pale flowers is to set them against a white background and exploit the tonal contrasts in the flowers themselves, as Pip Carpenter has done in* White Daffodils. *Although the vase and the stems are the only genuinely dark areas, she has cleverly made use of shadows on the petals and subtle contrasts in the background, and has also played up the foreground shadow to balance the dark vase. It is surprising how many dark and middle tones can be seen in white.*

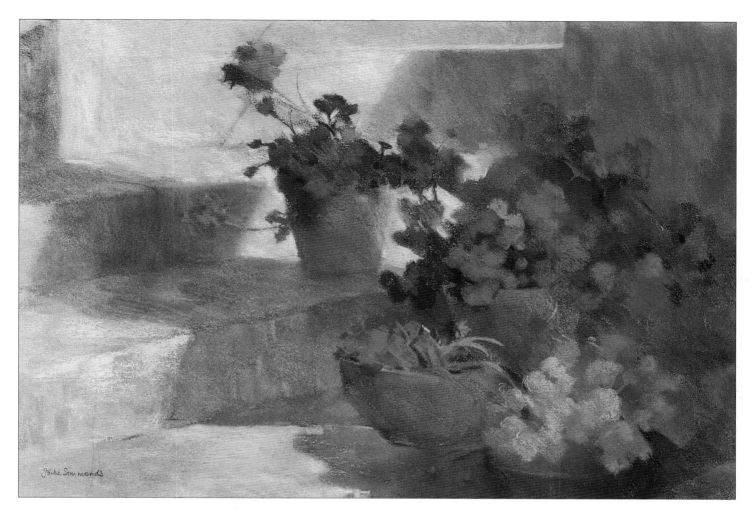

Complementary colours

(Above) *The colours opposite one another on a colour wheel – red and green, yellow and violet, orange and blue – are called complementaries, and they play an important part in painting as they set up exciting contrasts when used together. In Jackie Simmonds's* Tuscany Steps, *the red and green complementary pair was built into the subject, but she has also used yellow/ violet contrasts for both the plant pots and the steps to create areas of vibrant colour.*

HABITAT

Although the phrase "flower painting" tends to conjure up images of indoor arrangements, flowers in their natural setting can also make a rewarding subject. Whether it be garden flowers or wild flowers in a field, woodland or a patch of urban wasteland, the choice is yours. You cannot, of course, control the set-up or plan the colour scheme in advance, but you have a wide range of options with regard to composition and general approach.

Flowers in a garden or field, for example, could be treated as broad masses of colour or as colour accents in a landscape; alternatively, if you are interested in the shapes and colours of individual flowers, you could focus in

more closely, making one or two blooms the subject of your painting. If you decide to make outdoor "portraits" of flowers, you must be aware of possible changes in the light but, as pastel allows you to build up colour effects very quickly, the problem is less acute than it might be in watercolour or oil painting.

Finally, don't ignore the fact that trees have flowers too; few subjects have more appeal than an orchard or a single blossom tree in spring. Here too you could take a close-up view and paint a single bough of blossom – the Oriental painters loved such effects. Trees with large and well-shaped flowers, such as magnolia, are particularly well-suited to this kind of treatment.

DEMONSTRATION

Rosalind Cuthbert works in a number of different media and subject areas – flowers are one of her interests, but she also paints portraits and landscapes. Her light and delicate pastel style is well suited to this elegant and colourful arrangement of tall flowers. She is working on smooth-surfaced watercolour paper, which she prefers to the medium-textured paper because it does not break up the strokes to the same extent, thus allowing for clear, crisp lines.

1 *The paper has been tinted using the dry-wash method. Yellow is the dominant colour in the painting, so the artist has chosen a deep yellow for the ground. She now draws the main shapes lightly in charcoal.*

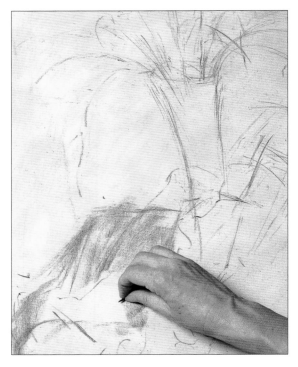

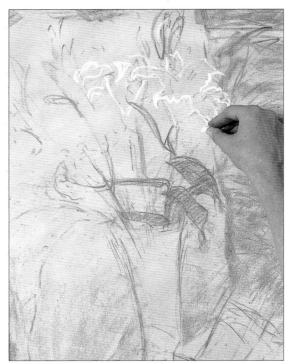

2 *Having sketched in the leaves lightly with linear strokes of blue, she now draws the outlines of the two pink-and-white lilies with the tip of the pastel stick. Her method is to build up colours with a series of light overlays; the blue leaves will be modified later using other colours.*

3 (Right) *It is important not only to define the shape of the vase at an early stage but also to establish a balance of light and dark colours. In this area she works with the tip of the pastel, although some light side strokes can be seen in the background, where softer effects are needed.*

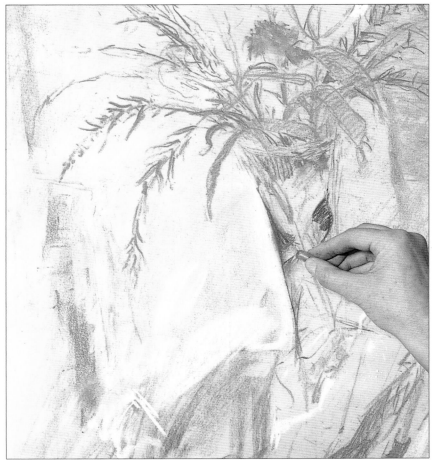

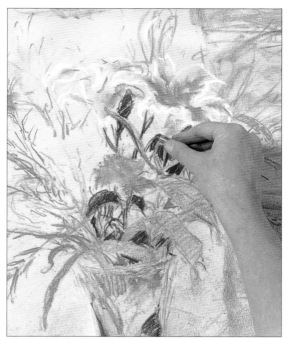

4 *These dark leaves play an important part in the picture, as the light-dark contrast between them and the flowerheads draws the eye to this central area.*

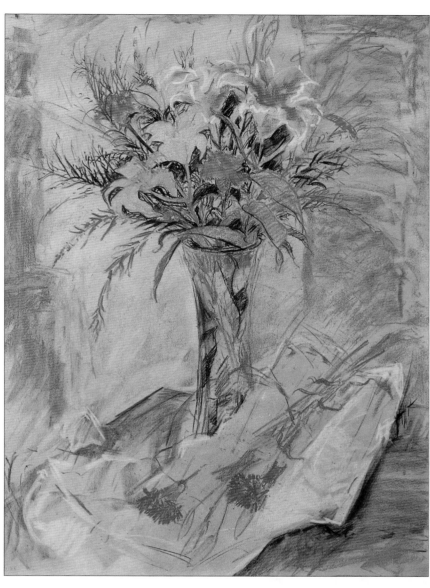

5 (Right) *The painting has now reached approximately halfway stage, with all the colours blocked in. The artist has been careful to work lightly and loosely to allow for later applications of colour and refinements of detail.*

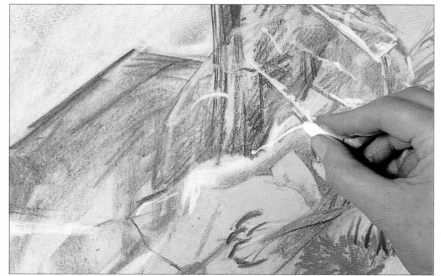

6 *The foreground, which had been left relatively undefined, is now sharpened up with a crisp drawing of the piece of crumpled wrapping.*

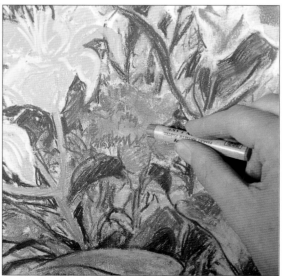

7 *The frilly-edged petals of these carnations are suggested by linear marks drawn with a darker version of the original pink.*

Continued ▷

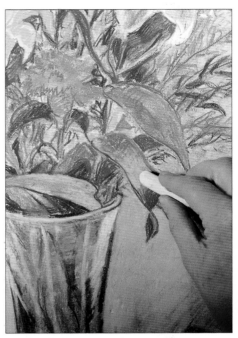

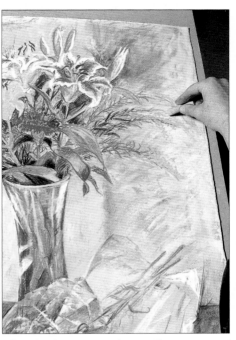

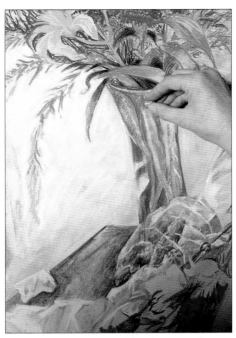

8 *The original blue used for the leaves has been overlaid with other colours and blended slightly to imitate their smooth texture. The pale grey, here used thickly for the highlights, also appears on the vase.*

9 *The dominant colour, yellow, is carried right through the painting, appearing in a paler version in both background and foreground. The pale grey background allows these small flowers to stand out, but they are treated lightly because the central flowers are the main focus for the eye.*

10 *The colours of the vase were too smoothly blended and were losing their liveliness and freshness, so small linear strokes are laid on top. This treatment has also set up a relationship between the vase and the leaves above.*

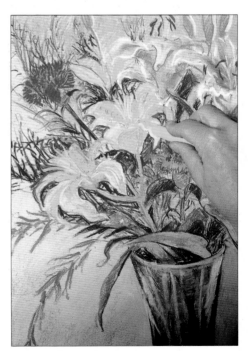

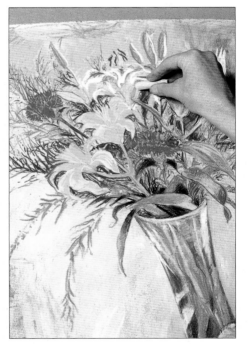

13 *(Opposite) Painting a group of tall flowers can cause problems of composition unless there is something in the foreground to create interest and to balance the shape of the vase. The artist has solved this by using the table top and the shape made by the wrapping paper as positive elements. The background, although lightly treated, is also carefully contrived, with the grey and red shapes at either side both balancing and enclosing the flowers and vase.*

11 *The flowers have been built up with layers of colour and occasional soft outlines, some made with hard pastel. A soft deep yellow pastel is now used to work carefully within the paler yellow edges of the petals.*

12 *A stick of hard pastel has been used to create a series of little broken lines on the petals of the pink-and-white lily. The underside is now toned down with grey, which mixes with the underlying pink to form a delicate mauve.*

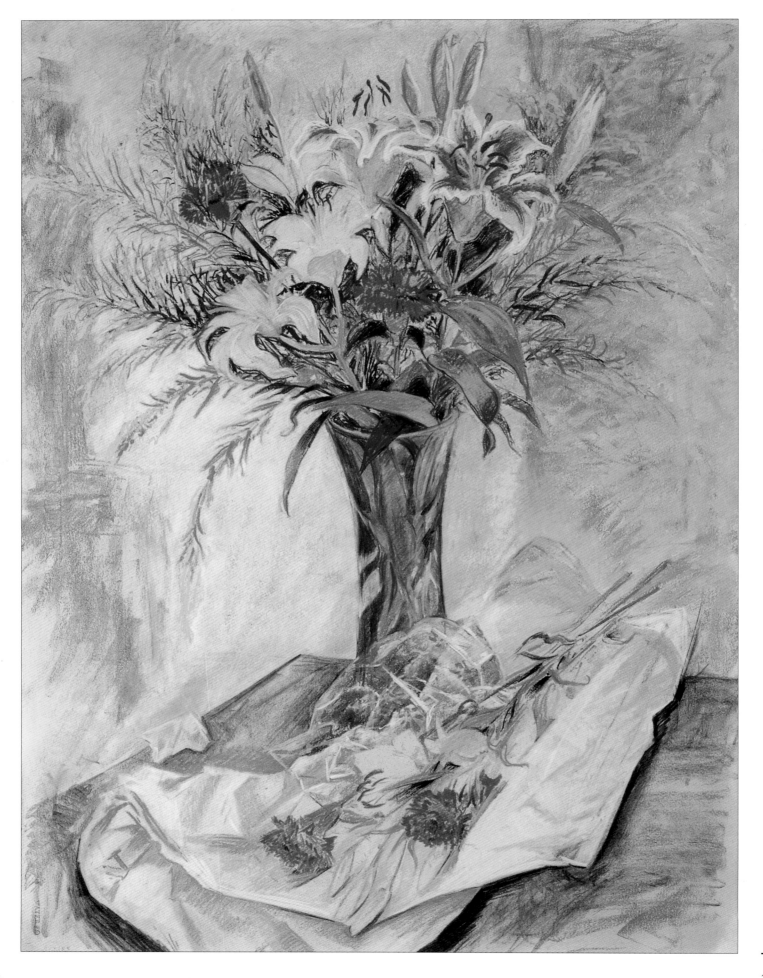

FACES & FIGURES

Pastel seems tailor-made for portraits and figure paintings because of the way in which it doubles as a drawing and a painting medium. The range and versatility of pastel enables you to build up forms with broad areas of colour as well as to exploit different kinds of lines and marks. It is also suited both to full-scale finished compositions and to quick sketches.

PORTRAITS

Pastel has been a favoured medium for portraiture since the 18th century, when artists such as Rosalba Carriera and Maurice Quentin de La Tour became fascinated by its capacity for creating soft and delicate effects. Many of today's artists also find it an excellent medium for faces and figures, though the current emphasis is less on the subtle blending of colour than on the expressive quality of pastel marks.

Embarking on a portrait in pastel does require a degree of skill and confidence, as major changes cannot be made. If you find

Using the paper colour
(Right) *In portraiture and figure work it is particularly important to choose the right colour of paper, especially if you intend to leave areas of it uncovered, as in Ken Paine's superb* Young Girl. *The painting is almost monochromatic, with the lights and darks built up from the mid-tone of the brown paper.*

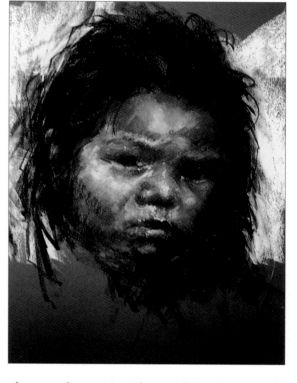

that you have misunderstood the shape and proportion of your subject's features, there is not, unfortunately, a great deal you can do about it. There are, however, some methods that you may find helpful initially, one of these being to work over a tonal underdrawing in charcoal. You can make as many changes as you like to the charcoal drawing because charcoal is easy to rub off and re-apply. Once you are happy with the drawing, you can spray it with fixative and apply the pastel colour on top.

Working on one of the pastel papers which allows you to make corrections by laying one colour over another may also boost your confidence. You can do this to some extent on any paper, but with Sansfix paper or sandpaper you can make quite major alterations.

PRACTISING PORTRAITURE
One of the difficulties with portrait painting is finding someone who is willing to sit for

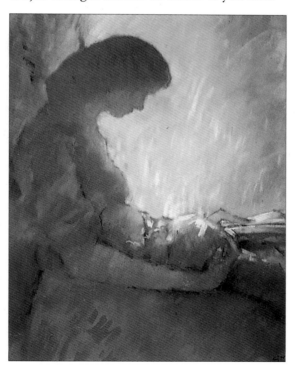

Light and mood
(Left) *For a portrait or figure painting in which it is important to describe features and forms accurately, it is best to choose side or three-quarter lighting, but backlighting can create lovely effects, silhouetting the figure, softening the colours and reducing the tonal contrasts. In his lovely* Mother and Child *Geoff Marsters has exploited this kind of lighting to create a gentle and meditative mood that is entirely in keeping with the subject.*

Painting flesh tones

(Below) *In* Seated Nude *Robert Maxwell Wood has also chosen the paper wisely; it is almost the same colour as the mid-tone of the model's flesh, allowing him to use the pastel lightly and delicately. He has used blending methods in places, but has avoided over-doing this, as it can make the image appear bland and dull. Instead he has contrasted soft blends with crisp diagonal hatching lines and fine outlines made with the tip of the pastel to describe the fall of light on the head, neck and arms.*

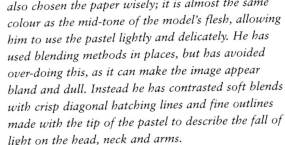

Dramatic light

(Left) *Maureen Jordan has called her painting* In the Spotlight *and, as the title implies, the main subject is light rather than the figure itself, which is treated as a bold, broad generalization. She has applied the pastel thickly, working on textured watercolour paper, which allows a considerable build-up of pigment.*

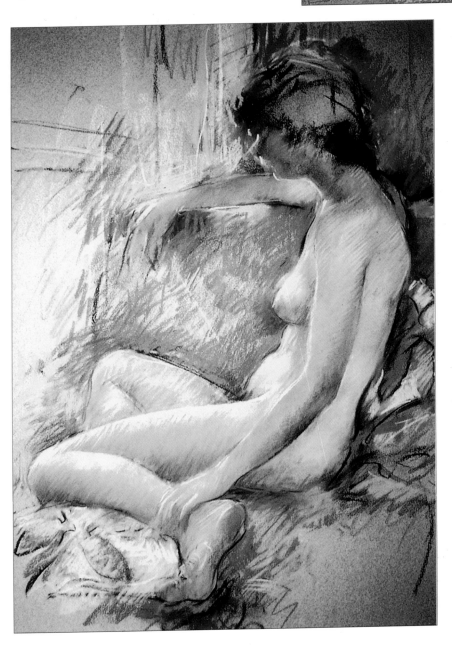

you and who won't be insulted by early and possibly inept attempts! You always have one model on hand, however – yourself. Most artists have painted and drawn self-portraits at times during their careers; this is an excellent way of gaining practice in handling the medium, as well as acquiring confidence in the basic skills of portraiture.

Another good way of learning is to copy another artist's work; up until the end of the 19th century most artists considered this an essential part of their education. It is best to make what are known as "transcriptions", which means choosing a work in another medium, such as oils, as your model. If you try to make a faithful copy of someone else's pastel portrait, it will hinder the development of your own style, added to which, colour mixing will create additional problems because you are unlikely to have the same palette of colours.

You can also learn a lot about composition by copying. Do not only concentrate on trying to reproduce the forms and colours accurately; ask yourself why the artist has arranged the picture in a particular way. You might try making small pencil sketches from several different portraits, which will give you ideas about types of portrait composition. Some portraits, for example, show the whole

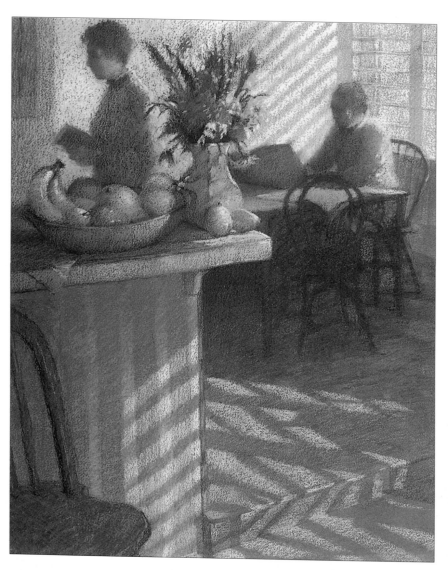

Interiors with figures

(Above) *If you are painting a portrait, the face or figure will be the main centre of attention, with other elements such as furniture playing a subsidiary role, but in Sally Strand's* Passing Quietly *the figures are fully integrated into the interior of the room. The real subject of the painting is light and colour, and the people have been treated almost as inanimate objects, echoing the still life on the counter and the chair in the corner.*

figure, standing or seated; other show half or three-quarters of the body including the hands, while many "crop" just below the neck to show only the head and shoulders.

FIGURES IN A SETTING

Figure painting and portrait painting are closely linked, but there is one essential difference. The dictionary definition of a portrait is a "likeness of an individual", while a figure painting, whether it be a nude study or a group of figures in an indoor or outdoor setting, need not necessarily perform this function. This is not to say that the figures should be unrecognizable as individuals. Just as you would want a tree in a landscape to look different from its neighbour, some characteristic of a person should be stressed, but this need not be features – it can be posture, general shape or even the colour of clothing. You might

SKETCHING

Although you can sharpen your technical skills and learn to analyse composition by copying, the best practice of all is gained by drawing – as much and as often as possible. If you are drawing people purely for practice, you can use any medium with which you feel comfortable; but sketching has another purpose too: a series of colour sketches made in pastel can give you a good basis for a finished portrait or figure study. Many portraits are carried out from sketches, sometimes with the aid of a photograph to provide more detailed visual information.

include a figure in a landscape, for example, simply because you want a bright accent of colour, or you might like the stark contrast of tone provided by a dark-clad figure in front of a sunlit whitewashed wall, in a Mediterranean town or village.

There are many reasons for drawing and painting figures other than portraiture, and the human element can be used, not as the whole subject of the painting, but as part of its visual "furniture". This is where the value of sketching really becomes apparent. People never remain in one place for long and you can seldom paint on the spot a landscape or townscape containing figures; such paintings are usually composed from sketches. Photographs are also a useful aid – don't become too reliant on them, but don't under-estimate their value either. Walter Sickert painted many urban scenes and figure compositions from photographs.

Composing the picture

(Right) *Even when you paint a head-and-shoulders portrait you need to consider how to place it on the paper and, in a full-length study, good composition is vitally important. In Maureen Jordan's* Amanda *the figure and sofa arm form a rough triangle, with the slope of the upper body balanced by the opposing line of the thigh. She has given only a hint of definition to the feet, allowing them to "bleed", out of the frame at the bottom so that the viewer's attention is focused on the face and body.*

Figure groups

(Below) *In landscape painting, a distant figure or group of figures is often introduced as a colour accent or an additional focus for the eye, but where figures form the whole subject, as in Sally Strand's charming* Crab Catch, *it is necessary to find ways of relating them to one another. Like many such compositions, this has an element of story-telling, with the boys sharing a common interest, but the artist has also used clever pictorial devices, notably the shapes and colours of the towel and bucket, to create a strong link between the two figures.*

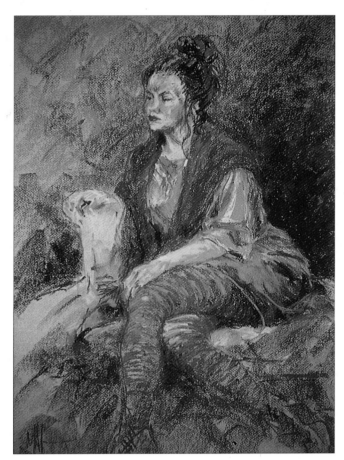

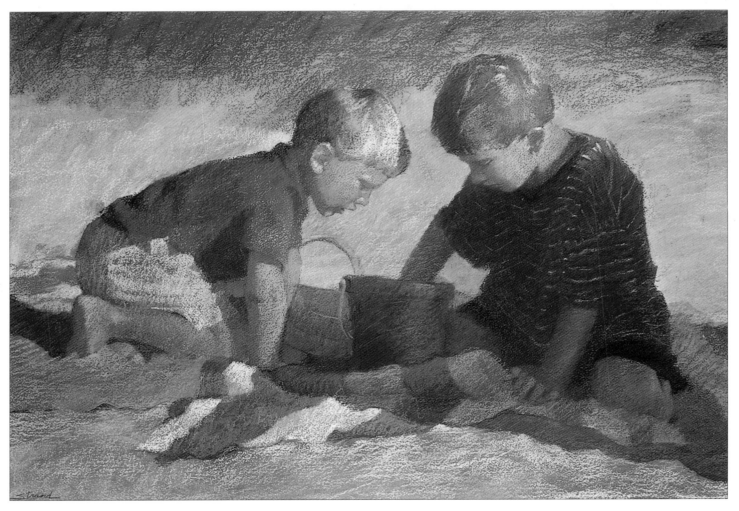

DEMONSTRATION

Ken Paine, a professional portrait painter, works occasionally in oils and acrylics, but principally in pastels, which he loves for their spontaneity and directness. He has a remarkable talent for achieving a likeness with no apparent effort, but his paintings also express character and atmosphere, which he sees as equally, if not more, important. By building up his colours thickly, in a highly painterly technique, he also achieves an almost sculptural feeling of weight and solidity. For this demonstration he has worked on grey Mi-Teintes paper, using the "right" side – that is, the more heavily textured one.

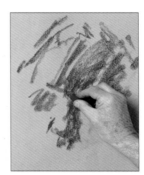

1 *The painting is begun in monochrome to provide a basis for the shadowed areas of the skin tones. The marks appear to be almost a random scribble, but already the forms of the face are beginning to emerge.*

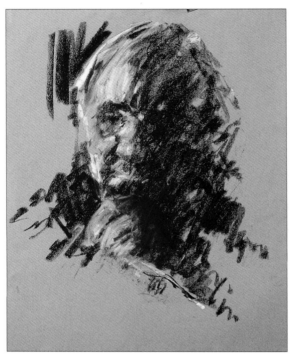

2 *The monochrome underpainting, which is now complete, provides a basic tonal structure on which to build up the colours. This method is only suitable for a painting which uses a limited palette of relatively sombre colours – a characteristic of this artist's work.*

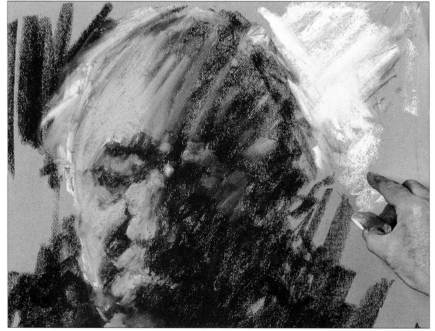

3 *The shadowed side of the head will be considerably darkened as the painting progresses, so the artist first lightens the background to enable him to judge the strength of colour needed. Tonal modelling is particularly important, and he continually assesses one tone against another.*

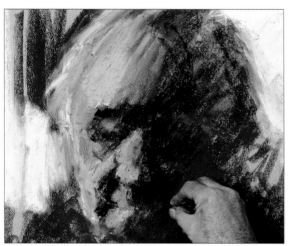

4 *Blacks and darker browns are now worked over and into the red-brown underpainting to build up the forms of the head. The artist uses short lengths of thick, soft-pastel sticks, which give the broad strokes he likes and enable him to push the edges of the colours together.*

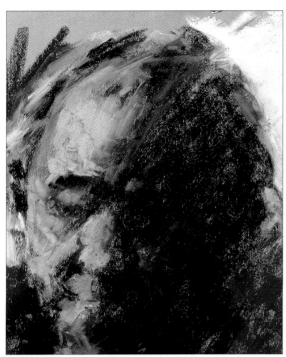

5 *With the darker tones established, further work has been done on the lit side of the face. Notice that the pastel is much thicker here; the artist's method is similar to that seen in many oil paintings, where the paint is thickest in the highlight areas, making them stand out from the shadows.*

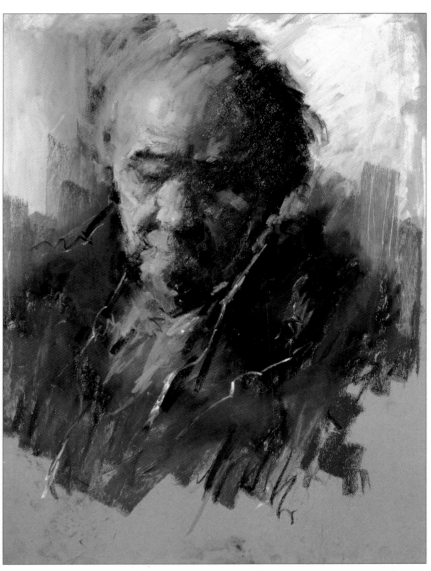

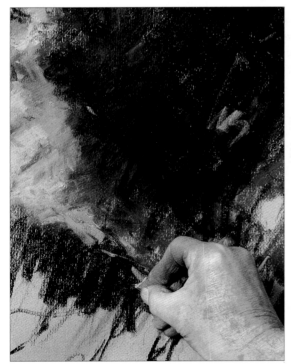

6 *The artist had originally planned a hand and wrist as part of the composition (see step 2), and now gives some additional definition to this area. However, he then decided to make a dramatic change, eradicating the hand completely, as you can see in the finished painting.*

7 *A complete transformation has now taken place – the hand has been painted out with heavy applications of dark green and red-brown, and suggestions of detail drawn in with an edge of white pastel (again, notice what fine lines can be produced in this way). The lighter colours below the chin, which suggest a shirt or cravat, balance the head much better than did the hand, and the composition is altogether more satisfactory.*

STOCKISTS & SUPPLIERS

**AUSTRALIA AND
NEW ZEALAND**

E & F Good
31 Lansdowne Terrace
Walkerville
SA 5081

Karori Art and Craft Centre
264 Karon Road
Karori
New Zealand

UK

Cornelissen & Son Ltd
105 Great Russell Street
London
WC1B 3RY
(020) 7838 1045

Daler-Rowney Ltd
PO Box 10
Southern Industrial Estate
Bracknell
Berkshire
RG12 8ST
(01344) 424621

Russell & Chapple Ltd
Canvas & Art Materials
23 Monmouth Street
London
WC2H 9DE
(020) 7836 7521

Winsor & Newton
Whitefriars Avenue
Wealdstone
Harrow
Middlesex
HA3 5RH
(020) 8427 4343

USA

Art Supply Warehouse
360 Main Avenue
Norwalk, CT 06851
Mail order

Daniel Smith Inc.
Fine Artists Materials
4130 First Avenue South
Seattle, WA 98134

NY Central Art Supply
62 Third Avenue
New York, NY 10003
Extensive catalogue, special papers
catalogue

Pearl Paint Corporation
308 Canal Street
New York, NY 10013

Utrecht Manufacturing Corporation
33 35th Street
Brooklyn, NY 11232

**ACRYLIC, OIL &
WATERCOLOUR PAINTS**

UK

Binney & Smith (Liquitex UK)
Ampthill Road
Bedford
MK42 9RS
(01234) 360201

John Mathieson & Co.
48 Frederick Street
Edinburgh
EH2 1HG
(0131) 225 6798

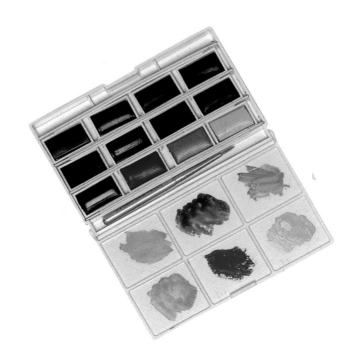

USA

Bocour Artists' Colors Inc.
Zipatone Inc.
150 Fence Lane
Hillside, IL 60162

Chromacryl (Australia)
US Distributor
Chrome Acrylics
40 Tanner Street
Haddonfield, NJ 08033

Liquitex
Binney & Smith Artists' Materials
1100 Church Lane
P.O. Box 431
Easton, PA 18042
Catalogue available

Standard Brands Paint Co.
4300 West 190th Street
Torrance, CA 90509–2956

Winsor & Newton, Inc.
US Office
11 Constitution Avenue
P.O. Box 1396
Piscataway, NJ 08855–1396
Catalogue available

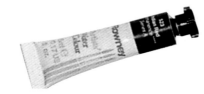

PAPER

AUSTRALIA

ACT Paper Pty Ltd
10 McGlore Street
Micham
Victoria 3132

UK

Falkiner Fine Papers Ltd
75 Southampton Row
London
WC1B 4AR
(020) 7831 1151

The Two Rivers Paper Company
Pitt Mill
Roadwater
Watchet
Somerset
TA23 OQ5
(01984) 41028

USA

Papersource Inc.
730 N Franklin Suite 111
Chicago, IL 60610

Strathmore Paper Company
Westfield, MA 01805

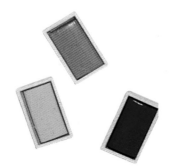

INDEX

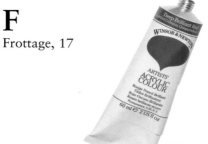
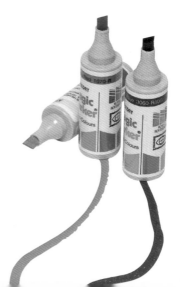

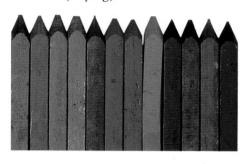

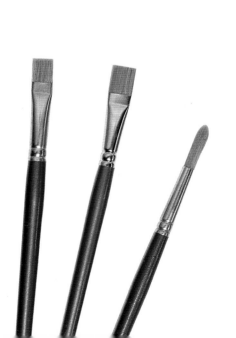

CREDITS

Cornelissen & Son Ltd
105 Great Russell Street
London WC1B 3RY
(020) 7838 1045

Daler-Rowney Ltd
PO Box 10
Southern Industrial
Estate
Bracknell
Berkshire
RG12 8ST
(01344) 424621

Russell & Chapple Ltd
Canvas & Art Materials
23 Monmouth Street
London WC2H 9DE
(020) 7836 7521

Winsor & Newton
Whitefriars Avenue
Wealdstone
Harrow
Middlesex
HA3 5RH
(020) 8427 4343

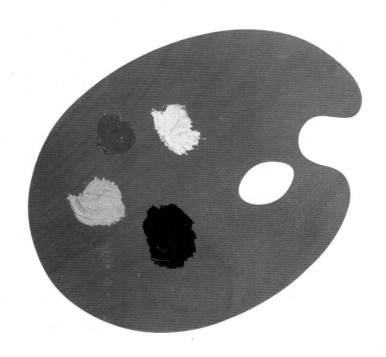

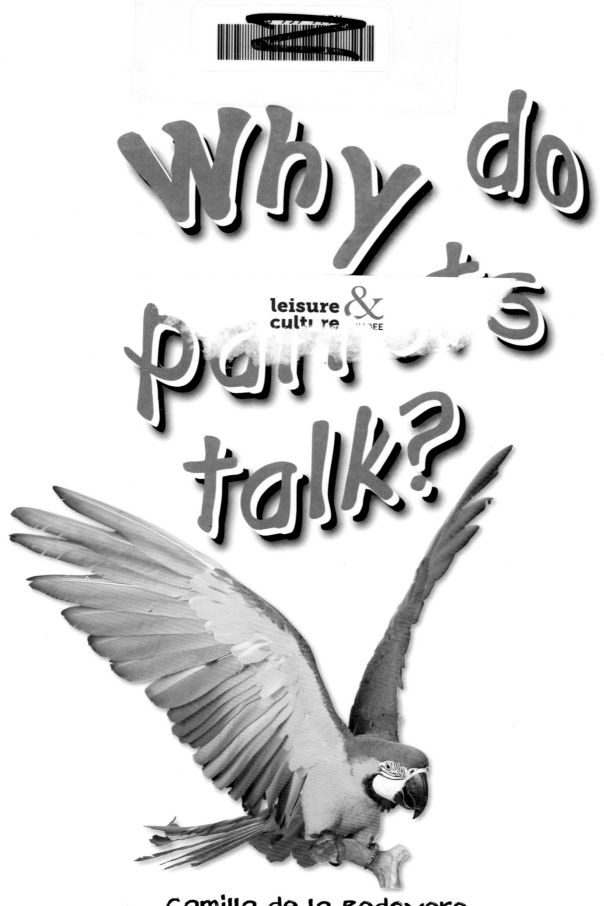

Why do parrots talk?

Camilla de la Bedoyere

Miles Kelly

First published in 2012 by Miles Kelly Publishing Ltd
Harding's Barn, Bardfield End Green, Thaxted,
Essex, CM6 3PX, UK

Copyright © Miles Kelly Publishing Ltd 2012

2 4 6 8 10 9 7 5 3 1

Publishing Director Belinda Gallagher
Creative Director Jo Cowan
Volume Design Redmoor Design
Cover Designer Kayleigh Allen
Image Manager Liberty Newton
Indexer Jane Parker
Production Manager Elizabeth Collins
Reprographics Stephan Davis, Thom Allaway

ISBN 978-1-84810-639-0

Printed in China

British Library Cataloguing-in-Publication Data

A catalogue record for this book is
available from the British Library

ACKNOWLEDGEMENTS
The publishers would like to thank the following
artists who have contributed to this book:
Mike Foster (character cartoons)
All other artwork from the Miles Kelly Artwork Bank

The publishers would like to thank the following
sources for the use of their photographs:

Fotolia.com 11 Jefery
Getty 24 Mitsuaki Iwago
Shutterstock.com 4 Juriah Mosin; 6 Eduardo Rivero;
9 Dr. Morley Read; 10 Ammit; 17 Eric Isselee;
21 Eric Isselee; 22 Sam Chadwick; 25 Eric Gevaert;
29 Uryadnikov Sergey

All other photographs are from:
Corel, digitalSTOCK, digitalvision, John Foxx, PhotoAlto,
PhotoDisc, PhotoEssentials, PhotoPro, Stockbyte

Every effort has been made to acknowledge the
source and copyright holder of each picture.
Miles Kelly Publishing apologises for any unintentional
errors or omissions.

Made with paper from a sustainable forest

www.mileskelly.net
info@mileskelly.net

www.factsforprojects.com

Contents

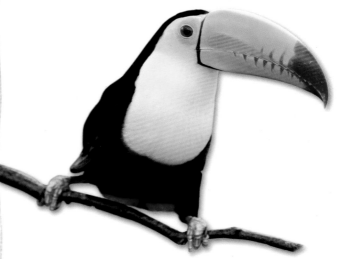